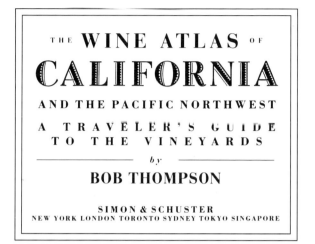

THE **WINE ATLAS** OF

CALIFORNIA

AND THE PACIFIC NORTHWEST

A TRAVELER'S GUIDE
TO THE VINEYARDS

by

BOB THOMPSON

SIMON & SCHUSTER
NEW YORK LONDON TORONTO SYDNEY TOKYO SINGAPORE

THE **WINE ATLAS** OF
CALIFORNIA
AND THE PACIFIC NORTHWEST

A TRAVELER'S GUIDE
TO THE VINEYARDS

by

BOB THOMPSON

SIMON & SCHUSTER
NEW YORK LONDON TORONTO SYDNEY TOKYO SINGAPORE

SIMON & SCHUSTER
Simon & Schuster Building
Rockefeller Center
1230 Avenue of the Americas
New York, NY 10020

Edited and designed by Mitchell Beazley,
part of Reed Consumer Books Limited
Michelin House, 81 Fulham Road,
London SW3 6RB

10 9 8 7 6 5 4 3 2 1

Thompson, Bob, 1934 -
     The wine atlas of California and the
Pacific Northwest: a traveler's guide to the
vineyards/Bob Thompson.
          p.   cm
     Includes bibliographical references and
index.
     ISBN 0-671-79663-1
     1. Wine and wine making - California.
     2. Wine and wine making - Pacific Coast
(U.S.) I. Title.
TP557.T5 1993
641.2' 2' 09794 - dc20   92 - 42938
                                                      CIP
ISBN 0-671-79663-1

The author and publishers will be grateful for
any information which will assist them in
keeping future editions up to date. Although
all reasonable care has been taken in the
preparation of this book, neither the publishers
nor the author can accept any liability for any
consequences arising from the uses thereof, or
from the information contained herein.

Editors Alexa Stace and Susan Keevil
Senior Art Editor Paul Drayson
Designer Paul Tilby
Map Editor Zoë Goodwin
Index Marie Lorimer
Commissioned photography Alan Williams
Picture Research Liz Fowler
Production Sarah Schuman
Executive Editor Anne Ryland
Art Director Tim Foster
Cartography Lovell Johns

Typeset in Century Old Style and Gill Sans
Reproduction by Mandarin Offset, Singapore
Produced by Mandarin Offset
Printed and bound in Singapore

The Wine Institute of California

The Wine Institute of California is a trade association of California wine-makers dedicated to creating a climate in which the industry can prosper and to expanding markets for wine. By tapping the collective talents of its members, the Institute makes it possible to do together, what would be impossible to do alone.

Today the Wine Institute's goals are much the same as when the organisation was formed in 1934: "To open new markets to California wines, to educate the consumer and the trade, to establish industry cooperation, and to fight the return of Prohibition". The Wine Institute is committed to preserving each individual's right to grow, produce, sell and enjoy wine without undue restriction or regulation.

From the beginning improving the quality of California wine has been a primary objective of the Wine Institute. One of the Institute's first priorities was the adoption of the California Definitions and Standards for Wine in 1934, which set the benchmark for American wine quality.

Today, California wine producers are recognized worldwide for their leadership in making and marketing wine. The Wine Institute is dedicated to ensuring that the industry continues to lead the way through a range of innovative programs and activities.

This book we believe will give people a taste of what makes our industry so special and what makes the California wine difference.

For more information contact:

Andrew Montague
Wine Institute of California
Regent Arcade House
19 - 25 Argyll Street
London
W1V 1AA
Tel: 071 - 287 3132

Steve Burns
Wine Institute of California
425 Market Street
Suite 1000
San Francisco
CA 94105
Tel: (415) 512 0151

Contents

Introduction

This book is the latest product of 80,000 tasting notes, give or take a few thousand, and 30-odd years of what seems like ceaseless wandering through the wineries and vineyards of California, Oregon, and Washington.

It comes at a chaotic time when wineries and growers are beset by recurrent phylloxera, resurgent antialcohol sentiments, and a dismal national economy. It also comes when the geography of wine is only beginning to be understood in regions where winegrowing and winemaking are young arts. Wineries come and go, winemakers come and go, home truths get lost in the traffic. And yet the common threads of flavor imparted by slope, soil, and sun have begun to reveal themselves at a quickening pace. For that reason the book is wholeheartedly about the associations of flavor and place.

In one stroke the task of tracing these common threads of flavor is made simple and impossible by the fact that almost every region is dominated by the same short list of grape varieties – Cabernet Sauvignon, Chardonnay, Pinot Noir, and Sauvignon Blanc.

Riesling, Gewürztraminer, and Zinfandel give a few regions some local color, but only in one or two places is any one of them allowed to define an area in the way one or more of the Big Four define the rest. Pinot Gris, Sangiovese, Syrah, and their neighbors are too new to have had a day in court.

And so it comes down to trying to decide just how the Santa Maria Valley affects Chardonnay differently from the Russian River Valley, the Russian River Valley from Yakima Valley, and so on through the roster, often working with skimpy evidence, always in the face of contradictory messages from the palate. Winemakers, unbound by tradition, seldom feel constrained by what their neighbors do, but may instead take their cues from more distant models. Critics wind up playing sun and soil against the human contributions of someone in Yakima aping the efforts of a Sonoma winemaker, who labors under a misapprehension of what once was done in Napa by an acolyte of a Burgundian, now deceased.

All of this flies in the face of European habits, where grape variety and appellation are always two reflections of a single climate, and where, in more cases than not, dominant grape varieties were born on the spot as successful adaptations of some ancestral muscat brought from distant lands by an invader or a returning traveler. Add two or four or ten centuries of refining the variety by selection, and the same long span of narrowing winemaking styles by trial and error, and European viniculture is a very different matter indeed from its American counterpart.

Similar lists of grape varieties have not made similar places out of all the Big Four's many homes in the American west. A practiced traveler in the Pacific states could no more mistake Prosser for Ashland or Ashland for Solvang than a seasoned voyager in Europe could be fooled into thinking Beaune was Castellina in Chianti.

If the same could be said about the wines, much of the fun would have gone. The ride is tricky, but exhilarating.

The original 1882 cellar of Inglenook now serves as a visitors' center and tasting room for the Napa Valley winery.

How to Use this Atlas

As with any atlas, the heart of the matter is in the maps. Poring over them in search of river courses, gaps in the hills and exposures to the sun tells much of the tale.

In this young part of the world, there must be one caveat. To locate a winery is not the same as locating an estate. In many cases winery and vineyard are separated by some miles, in some cases by appellation boundaries. Much of the text is thus an attempt to connect the two.

To the degree possible in a part of the winegrowing world not yet fully formed, each chapter follows a set pattern:
(1) overview of a district,
(2) description of the major wine types grown and made there,
(3) a more detailed description and maps of the AVA (American Viticultural Area) or AVAs within it,
(4) list of producers with notes on their wines, especially those of the home region, and
(5) brief travel information including hotels and restaurants.

The travel notes are personal, and not at all inclusive. Other guides should be consulted, especially for hotels.

The Pacific Coast of the United States is one of the most hospitable wine regions in the world. As an outgrowth of Prohibition, California invented the tasting room and cellar tour as a means of re-educating a populace that had lost all familiarity with fine wine. Both have become institutions in the years since, not just in California, but throughout the country. Travelers in all three states will find that nearly all wineries producing more than 10,000 cases per year operate public tasting rooms, sometimes for a fee, often at no charge. A majority of smaller ones are more restrictive; most require advance appointments; some permit no visitors at all (*see* the producers list in each chapter for information about cases).

The near-universal presence of tasting rooms at wineries in California, Oregon, and Washington does not mean that visitor facilities are homogeneous in every region. As a most obvious contrast, the Napa Valley is strong on luxury, and is not much of a place for bargains, while the Yakima Valley is the other way round. Predictably, the most famous regions with the greatest development of tourist facilities are the ones requiring advance reservations at both hotels and restaurants.

Happily for travelers from afar, most of the wine regions lie within easy reach of the four major population centers – Los Angeles, San Francisco, Portland and Seattle. When accommodation among the vineyards leaves something to be desired, winery visits can be made as day-trips from these cities.

A spectacular view in the Napa Valley.

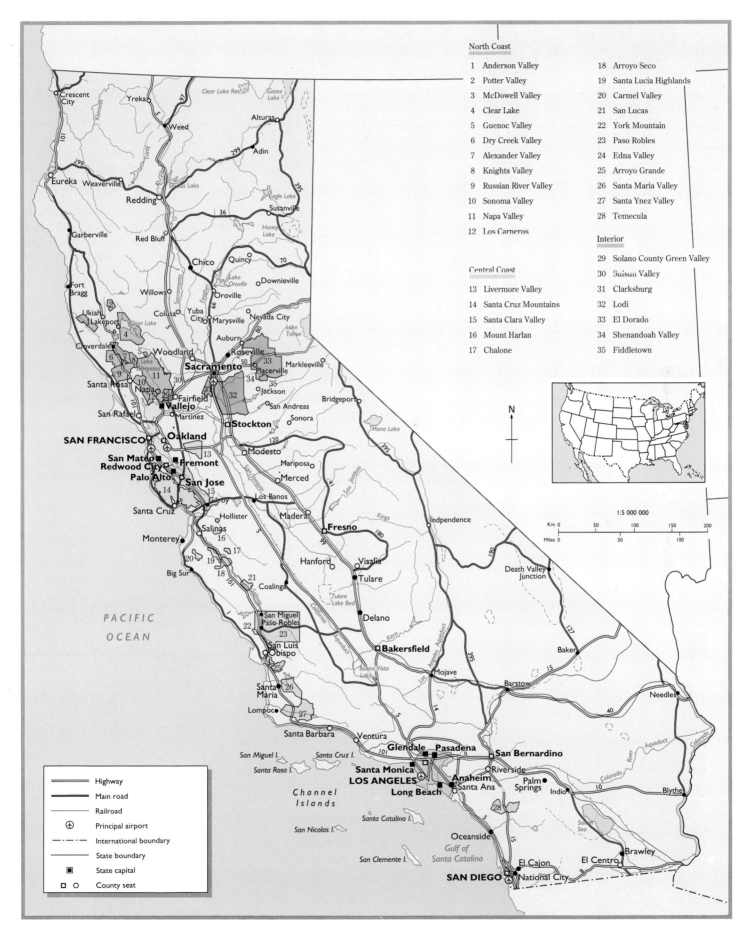

North Coast

1 Anderson Valley	18 Arroyo Seco
2 Potter Valley	19 Santa Lucia Highlands
3 McDowell Valley	20 Carmel Valley
4 Clear Lake	21 San Lucas
5 Guenoc Valley	22 York Mountain
6 Dry Creek Valley	23 Paso Robles
7 Alexander Valley	24 Edna Valley
8 Knights Valley	25 Arroyo Grande
9 Russian River Valley	26 Santa Maria Valley
10 Sonoma Valley	27 Santa Ynez Valley
11 Napa Valley	28 Temecula
12 Los Carneros	

Central Coast

Interior

13 Livermore Valley	29 Solano County Green Valley
14 Santa Cruz Mountains	30 Suisun Valley
15 Santa Clara Valley	31 Clarksburg
16 Mount Harlan	32 Lodi
17 Chalone	33 El Dorado
	34 Shenandoah Valley
	35 Fiddletown

N

1:5 000 000

| Km | 0 | 50 | 100 | 150 | 200 |
| Miles | 0 | | 50 | 100 | |

Highway
Main road
Railroad
Principal airport
International boundary
State boundary
State capital
County seat

9

Palms crop up in many Californian districts, clear evidence of the benign climate that rules over most of the state.

Maps

A California state map (*see* page 9) shows the relationships of its three main grapegrowing regions, the North Coast, Central Coast, and the great Central Valley. The first two are established as broadly inclusive American Viticultural Areas (appellations), which means their names may appear on labels as a statement of origin; the interior is not an AVA. A Pacific Northwest map (*see* page 194) establishes the relationships between decidedly different western Oregon and eastern Washington. Comparing these to the climate maps on page 14 is instructive.

Regional maps (*see* pages 26, 112 and 170) provide individual overviews of California's three major internal divisions. Color-coded outlines denote the major AVAs within each, a quick reference to what begins to be a complex mosaic of districts with some claim to distinctive growing conditions. The Pacific Northwest map serves this function for Washington and Oregon.

Appellation maps provide a close-up of vineyard and winery locations within the individual AVAs at their most detailed level. California's North Coast has more than 20 of these, its Central Coast more than a dozen. Some maps combine two or even three AVAs because of their relatively small size and

simplicity; the Napa Valley AVA, on the other hand, covers four maps because of its density of planting and wineries.

At this level, the fledgling AVA system begins to become double layered, developing what might be called subappellations in a mature system. The Stag's Leap District AVA, for example, is a small part of the Napa Valley AVA. In Sonoma, the Russian River Valley has within it subappellations called Sonoma-Green Valley and Chalk Hill, while the larger unit is, in its turn, one part of a more general AVA called Northern Sonoma (which is largely ignored in this atlas). As in the more broadly scaled maps, color-coded boundaries quickly distinguish the various appellations.

Some important grapegrowing regions, such as that around Ukiah in Mendocino County, do not have specific AVAs. That fact, too, emerges quickly on looking at the detailed maps. The much younger wine industry of the Pacific Northwest has only six appellations in the whole of Washington and Oregon.

Because AVAs vary enormously in size and density of planting, these maps are diverse in scale. For example, four maps were required to make clear the Napa Valley's concentration of 200 wineries and 33,000 acres of vineyard within a total area of 300,000 acres, while only two were needed to reveal the essen-

These almost startlingly bare hills are the southern end of the Sonoma Mountains, in the North Coast district called Carneros. Vineyards on the lower slopes are increasingly well regarded for Chardonnay and Pinot Noir in both still and sparkling wines.

tials of Willamette Valley, which has only 4,300 acres of vineyard and 70-odd wineries spread across 3.3 million acres. The appellation maps are scaled, as far as possible, to be immediately useful to travelers. Some will be usable alone, but others will need to be supplemented by detailed road maps for local routes.

Benchmark wines and other definitions

Descriptions of wines accompany each region, with listings by varietal type. For locally important types, general notes on regional characteristics are accompanied by lists of benchmark wines. These have been chosen specifically because they consistently reflect the core character of their region. While these wines are excellent, the lists are not in any sense intended as a selection of "bests;" indeed they ignore many highly praised but also highly stylized wines of all three winegrowing states along America's Pacific coast.

Assembled: Refers to wines produced from more than one vineyard, especially those from more than one district. This is common practice even at the highest price levels in both California and Washington, somewhat less so in Oregon. *See* blends.

Benchlands: Most of the Pacific coast is being lifted up by the action of tectonic plates. One result is that the rivers in coastal valleys are constantly carving deeper courses into ancient flood plains. The resulting benchlike landforms on either bank are favored locations for vineyards; there are frequent references in this book to this or that "bench."

Blends: Here taken to mean wines made from two or more grape varieties. The main examples are Cabernet Sauvignon-based reds called Meritage or some fantasy name. Sauvignon Blanc-Sémillon is a white counterpart. Blends of traditional Rhône varieties are also becoming common. This is distinct from "assembled" (*qv*).

Classic method: Heretofore *"méthode champenoise,"* which the EC has ruled off all non-Champagne sold in the community. Enough American producers have accepted the term "classic method" to give it currency in the home market.

Grower label: Many vineyard owners who do not have wineries have wine made from their grapes at other premises. The words are included in producer listings as an indication that there is no facility to visit.

Winemaker label: Like winemakers, enologists with an entrepreneurial bent may make wine for their own label in space leased from their main employer, or another. In producer lists this indicates that there are no premises to visit.

The United States' Appellation System

Grapegrowers and winemakers in the United States are at the very dawn of understanding the relationships of grape varieties to sun and soil. Even in the oldest and most densely planted districts, the choices of variety are undergoing constant revision as individual property owners learn, sometimes to their pleasure, sometimes to their horror, the results of their labors.

In full recognition of this situation, they caused the governing Bureau of Alcohol, Tobacco and Firearms (BATF) to institute a system of appellations of origin. That system of American Viticultural Areas is in every sense of the word rudimentary, and yet it has already begun to drive both producers and consumers to observe the boundaries it has established.

Officers of the regulatory agency require petitioners for appellations to show evidence of similar growing conditions throughout the region, and historic usage of the proposed name to describe the region. Historic evidence need not relate to grapegrowing or winemaking. There is an implicit understanding that AVA boundaries will not follow existing political boundaries, except where the political boundary itself follows a natural feature such as a river course, a ridge line, or the like.

Smith & Hook Cabernet Sauvignon vines in Monterey County.

These standards have been variably applied, sometimes with mildly comic effect.

In the description of each AVA, published upon its approval, BATF includes the following caveat: "BATF does not wish to give the impression that by approving the Place Name vicultural area that it is approving or endorsing the quality of the wines produced in this area. BATF is approving this area as being distinct from surrounding areas, not better than other areas... Any commercial advantage gained can only come from consumer acceptance of Place Name wines."

To use the name of an approved AVA on a label two requirements must be met:
(1) 85 percent of the wine must come from the region named.
(2) In the case of varietal wines, the federal law requires the minimum 75 percent of the named variety in a bottle to come from the named appellation.

No other restriction is imposed. Any AVA may grow any grape variety using any training method to produce any crop level.

Producers wishing to add information must follow some refinements of the basic rules.

If a vineyard is named on a label, 95 percent of the wine must come from that vineyard, which, in turn, must fall within an AVA named on the label.

To use the term "Estate Bottled," the winery and vineyard(s) must fall within the AVA named on the label, and the producing winery must "own or control" all vineyards used.

State laws add further requirements.

A California law requires that 100 percent of any wine bearing any California place-name must come from grapes grown in California. An Oregon law requires 100 percent of any wine bearing a geographical name to come from that place, be it AVA, county, or other unit.

Other labeling requirements
BRAND Mandatory. The single most important clue to style and quality is the brand name.

WINE TYPE Mandatory. Every wine must be named as a specific type. The broad categories are varietal wine (named after the dominant grape variety), generic (named for a place where a style originated or simply the color of the liquid), or proprietary (fanciful).

VARIETAL Under federal law, varietal wines must be made with a minimum 75 percent of the grape named on the label (51 percent for wines bottled before 1983). Most of the grapes named on pages 16 to 21 go into varietal wines. California and Washington operate under the federal law. Oregon state law requires a stricter 90 percent of the named variety on all but wines based on Cabernet Sauvignon, in which case it permits 75 percent because of the Bordeaux history of blending.

GENERIC California accepts the national law that permits certain European place-names to be used on generic wines. Burgundy, Chablis, Chianti, Champagne, Rhine, Port, and Sherry are foremost among them. Such wines observe no restrictions as to grape variety or any other characteristic. A "Burgundy" made in California might be made of Zinfandel, Alicante, Cabernet Sauvignon, or any blend. It might also be sweet. The usage is fading with all but huge-volume producers. Many modestly priced wines now call themselves Red Table Wine, White Table Wine, or Rosé. Some make a joke of it: Spaghetti Red, Pretty Good Red, &c.

Oregon state law prohibits all use of European place-names on generic and proprietary names.

PROPRIETARY Proprietary once meant the cheapest of wines. In recent years it has come to cover both extremes of price as producers seeking to improve on varietals have blended beyond the 75 percent limit, especially among varieties originating in Bordeaux and the Rhône.

At the bottom end are names that attempt to invoke Europe, i.e. Rhinecastle or the like. At the top end come such as Trilogy (to indicate a blend of Cabernet Sauvignon-Cabernet Franc-Merlot) and Le Cigare Volant (for a Rhône-inspired blend).

VINTAGE Optional. If used, 95 percent of the wine must have come from grapes grown in the year stated. The allowance permits practical topping-up of casks in the cellars.

BOTTLER Mandatory. Some wineries use a half-dozen labels for their wines. Somewhere on the label must appear the name and business location of the company that bottled the wine. Several variations of this statement are supposed to reveal the bottler's complete role in the production, but recent rulings have reduced these to gibberish.

ALCOHOL CONTENT Mandatory. Federal law requires table wines to note the alcohol content within a tolerance, plus or minus, of 1.5 percent, or to use the words Table Wine. The permitted range of alcohols in table wine, as a taxable product, is to 13.9 percent. Wines of 14 percent and more, but without added brandy, pay a higher tax and cannot substitute the words Table Wine for an enumerated alcohol content. Port-types, muscats, and other dessert-sweet wines with added brandy may have alcohols of 18 to 20 percent, with a permitted allowance of 1 percent from the actual content on the label. Sherry-types may have alcohols of 17 to 20 percent; again the label may differ from the actual content by 1 percent. Wines of 17 percent alcohol or more are categorized as dessert wines regardless of their sweetness, and taxed at a still higher rate than wines of 14 to 16.9 per cent. Only sparkling wines pay more.

CONTAINS SULFITES Mandatory in the U.S. on wines having 10 ppm or more of sulfites. For all reasonable purposes, a warning to certain severe asthmatics allergic to these compounds, usually sulfur based. The warning may not appear on U.S.-produced wines sold in Europe.

HEALTH WARNING Mandatory in the U.S. A caution to pregnant women that use of alcohol may cause birth defects, and to machine operators that its use may impair motor skills. The warning is not allowed on labels of U.S. wines sold in Europe.

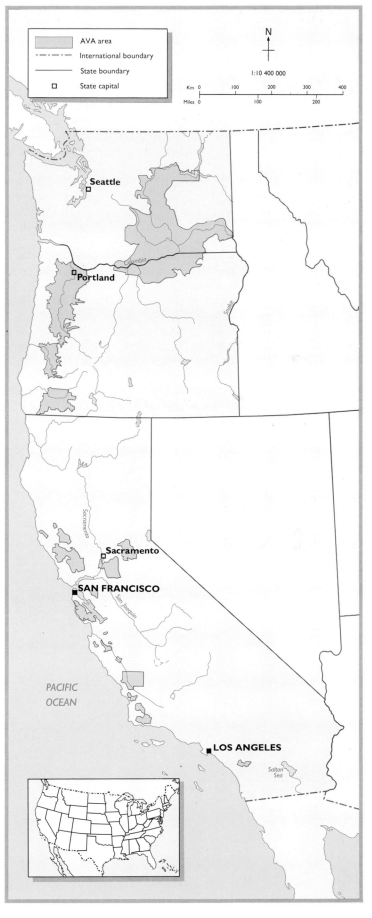

Climate

Throughout this Atlas, graphs show daily high and low temperatures in 30 grape-growing towns for the year 1990. The growing season was slightly warmer than average for most of the west, and a late December freeze was one of the most severe of the past 50 years for many areas. Still, for most growers, it was the kind of year they expect to see more often than not.

The graphs are a handy way to think about where different varieties of grapes might be expected to do well.

Researchers at the University of California at Davis categorize grape varieties as early, mid- and late-season ripeners depending on heat required to reach maturity. Others describe them as warm-region to cool-region varieties.

Warm-region/late-season varieties are represented by Cabernet Sauvignon and Sémillon. Both require substantial heat over a long growing season to ripen fully by late September to mid-October. St Helena in the Napa Valley and Healdsburg in the Alexander Valley typify the sort of summers in which late-season grapes prosper in vintage after vintage.

Cool-region/early-season varieties ripen (or overripen) as early as August in St Helena or Healdsburg; Pinot Noir is the classic example. To push such varieties back toward October harvest requires planting them in places with temperature profiles much more like Santa Maria in Santa Barbara County, Santa Rosa (as a stand-in for Sonoma's Russian River Valley), or Forest Grove in Oregon's Willamette Valley.

Most of the other familiar grape varieties find their optimum conditions between these extremes. Some, like Chardonnay, seem to do at least passably well in nearly all of the AVAs known for quality table wine, although Chardonnay most often excels in the cooler half of the range. Others, Merlot for example, do well only within an unpredictable range of tolerances having little to do with the daily marches of the thermometer.

Temperature alone is a perilously simple way to go hunting for regions suited to growing this grape variety or that. Not long after the repeal of Prohibition, the University of California devised a five-region system based on annual accumulations of heat, measured as degree days. These essentially reflected average temperatures. The system's divisions followed European models from the Rhine to Jerez. Thus, it was thought, Riesling would perform best in the coolest Region I, while Cabernet Sauvignon would reach its peak in Region III, and Palomino in Region V, the hottest zone in the scale. The school itself has long abandoned the measurement as inadequate. Varieties that should have fared well only in Region I made superior wines in Region III, sometimes even in IV, while others theoretically suited to III turned in their best performances in II, if not in I.

One of the problems with the scale was that identical average temperatures can disguise huge differences in growing conditions. For example, the hot days and cold nights of upland deserts can produce heat summations very close to those of shoreward areas, where highs and lows fall within a much narrower range. In California's foggy valleys, stations only five or six miles apart may reach the same maximum temperature and still be in quite different climates. That is, a mostly fog-free station can reach and hold a peak temperature for several hours, while one much more prone to fog may reach the same peak, but hold it for only a few minutes. The scale could not

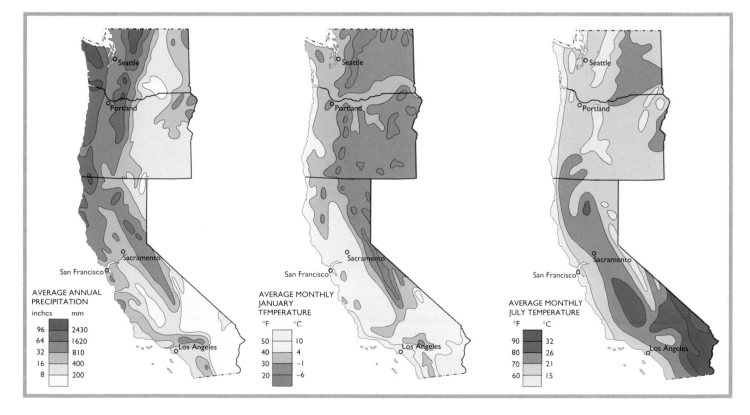

Like many higher peaks throughout the Coast Ranges, Napa's Mt St Helena is a major cause of intensified local precipitation, as snow reveals here.

accommodate these factors, let alone the variables of cloud cover, seasonal precipitation (not only how much, but when), wind, latitude (which affects the length of sunlight hours), or exposure to the sun (which also governs the length of the sun's day, but in a much more variable way within any one region).

None of this takes into account the other crucial variable, soil, important not only in itself but also in its interaction with all the factors of climate.

Still, as a means of quickly comparing different regions, temperatures have their uses. Extreme variations of high and low usually bespeak clear, sunny weather. Narrower ranges reveal clouds, fog, or at least humid sea air. With these generalities in mind, the charts at least begin to indicate where are the American west's closest counterparts to a Rhine on the one hand, a Jerez on the other. The color bands in this book's temperature charts (*see* for example page 31) help to make these variations as swiftly visible as possible.

Above 95°F At temperatures exceeding 95°F, grape leaves close the passageways that allow moisture to evaporate, and stop photosynthesis, which is to say the plant stops growing foliage or ripening fruit. (The exact fact is that the leaves shut down when the temperature on their underside reaches 95°F, usually requiring air temperatures somewhat above 100°F.)

70° to 95°F At temperatures between 70° and 95°F, grapevines work at maximum efficiency. For varieties that take a long, warm season to ripen, this is the ideal range.

50° to 70°F At temperatures between 50°F and 70°F, vines work along at a more deliberate pace, in conditions best suited to varieties that ripen too early in warm climates. Such temperatures require a long growing season with some warmer periods after the grapes have colored.

Below 50°F At temperatures below 50°F, little or no growth or ripening takes place. Abnormally cold years tend to be poor vintages because the storms come before ripeness can.

Below 32°F At temperatures below 32°F, foliage is subject to damage. In spring, especially, tender new leaves and buds can be killed and, with them, the unformed grapes. At various colder temperatures, individual varieties can be damaged even while dormant in winter. Most varieties can endure a short spell at 0°F while they are dormant, although at some possible loss of the next year's crop. Prolonged bitter cold of 0°F and below will damage the hardiest of them. Enough of it will kill them to the tips of their roots.

Grape Varieties

White

Aligoté

A Burgundian variety. There, it grows outside favored areas for use in low-priced quaffers bearing the varietal name. Statistical summaries do not include it, but one winery in Washington's Yakima Valley grows it and makes it into a varietal styled after Chardonnay.

Chardonnay (37,147 acres in California, 1,367 in Oregon and 2,658 in Washington)

The great white variety of Burgundy. Chablis, Meursault, Montrachet, and scores of other famous names make the rest of the world long to copy white Burgundy more than any other white wine in the world.

Chardonnay came to California in the 1870s or earlier. However, it made no impact before Prohibition and only a slight one for decades after repeal because it was so shy a yielder. Only after several memorable wines by tiny producers in the late 1950s and early 1960s did the variety turn into the irresistible force it has been since 1975, or thereabouts. Expansion of plantings remains startling; the 1990 figure cited will rise to more than 52,000 acres with the harvest of 1993. Careful selection has brought it to a typical 3.5 to 5 tons an acre, about the same as most other varieties. Cold regions and poor soils can drop the level to 1.5 to 2 tons; fertile soils and ample sunshine allow crops of 6 tons an acre.

It yields acceptable wines across an enormous range of conditions. By reputation, California Chardonnay comes to its peak in Carneros, much of the Napa Valley, the Russian River Valley, the Anderson Valley, and the Santa Maria Valley. Certainly these appellations have produced the greatest number of age-worthy wines. Style and place rarely coincide the way they do in Burgundy. No matter the district, some producers focus on the flavors of Chardonnay, fermenting cool in stainless steel and using oak only as a delicate seasoning. Others use every device winemakers know to add flavors: barrel fermentation, malolactic fermentation, aging on the lees in a high percentage of new oak. In recent years many have used small amounts of residual sugar to heighten whatever flavors they push to the forefront. Most take a position in the middle ground.

Oregon and Washington grow less generously flavorful Chardonnays than California. With that in common, other characteristics differ sharply from one state to the other. Style in both states leans more consistently to barrel and malolactic fermentation, and aging on the lees.

Chenin Blanc (32,666 acres in California, 673 in Washington)

A Loire variety most familiar in Vouvray. For the most part Chenin Blanc in both California and Washington is grown to satisfy a market for quickly accessible, off-dry, fruit-first sippers. California's plantings are heavily concentrated in the San Joaquin Valley, where the crop goes into both varietal and generic whites. The most distinctive flavors come from the small Clarksburg AVA in the Sacramento River delta.

Eastern Washington gives Chenin a greater delicacy of aroma and texture than does California. A handful of producers in both states pursues the techniques developed in Burgundy for Chardonnay. Now and then it is made into a botrytized or ice wine. The most memorable results have come from eastern Washington.

Oregon's plantings remain so small they do not appear in statistical summaries, but a half-dozen cellars were making varietal Chenin Blancs at the beginning of the 1990s, most of them in the no-oak, off-dry style.

Colombard (58,655 acres in California)

Like Barbera among reds, Colombard is a prized white in the San Joaquin Valley for its ability to deliver large crops (6 to 9 tons an acre) of crisply acidic wines in California's hottest growing regions. Some San Joaquin producers make Colombard as a varietal, but its primary role is as the spine in low-priced generics.

Acreage in the coastal counties is far more modest, the wines somewhat less so. Well used, Mendocino- and Sonoma-grown Colombard will yield varietal wine that serves much the same purpose as Müller-Thurgau in Washington or Oregon, or Liebfraumilch in Germany. That is, it makes a floral white better off-dry than dry and better young than older.

Gewürztraminer (1,838 acres in California, 246 in Oregon, 334 in Washington)

An Alsatian selection of a variety with origins in the Austro-Italian Alps. Gewürztraminer appears to be broadly adapted to all three Pacific states, yet is one of the most sensitive varieties to regional conditions.

It yields distinctive, long-lived wines in California's Anderson and Russian River valleys. Attractive but softer and apparently quicker-aging ones come from the Napa Valley, Santa Ynez Valley, and Monterey. These regions dominate plantings as much as critical response. Although the perfumes are milder than those of Alsatian Gewürztraminers, and a few dry wines persist, the vogue is for off-dry styles. All three of Oregon's AVAs coax different flavors out of Gewürztraminer than any part of California. Washington shares the flavors, but its Gewürztraminers are softer than Oregon's.

Gray Riesling (491 acres in California)

Apparently a descendant of Trousseau, a variety that has nearly disappeared in France. Once a popular off-dry, fruit-first sipper competing for the same market as Liebfraumilch or Colombard, it has almost dropped from view in California. Livermore wineries produce most of what remains available, although plantings are scattered throughout the North and Central coasts.

Melon (*see* Pinot Blanc)

Müller-Thurgau (155 acres in Oregon, 32 in Washington)

A back-cross of Riesling widely planted in the Rheingau and elsewhere in Germany. Yet another entry in the off-dry, fruit-first, immediately accessible derby of white wines, it is well adapted to the Willamette Valley and western Washington. In both regions it goes into varietal and generic wines of modest fame and modest price.

Most of Mendocino County's vineyards are in rolling hills.

Muscat Blanc (1,332 acres in California, 217 in Washington)
Widely grown in southern France and northern Italy, sometimes as Muscat de Frontignan, sometimes as Muscat Canelli. Varietal wines from this grape have appeared under all three synonyms; Muscat Blanc became the only permitted name under federal regulations adopted in 1993. Of several Muscats, this one is most used in wines of 10 to 13 percent alcohol, almost all of them sweet for casual sipping. Many regions in California and eastern Washington produce attractive varietal wines, Paso Robles perhaps foremost among them.

Pinot Blanc (1,839 acres in California)
One must plant an asterisk behind the California acreage, for it is partly the Pinot Blanc *vrai* of Alsace and Champagne, partly the Melon de Bourgogne used for Muscadet. Oregonians, new to the game and thus with certified stocks, sometimes get very sniffy about California's lack of genetic purity. Meanwhile, DNA testing has yet to make a clean separation of Pinot Blanc and Melon, so, going by feel more than fact, some producers call their wines Pinot Blanc, some Melon, and some Pinot Blanc-Melon clone. One even has ATF approval to call his Muscadet, an alternative varietal name for Melon de Bourgogne.

The wines are nearly impossible to separate by taste. Most are made in much the same range of styles as Chardonnays, to much the same effect.

Historically, California's finest Pinot Blancs, or Melons, or *mélanges* have come from Redwood Valley in Mendocino and hillsides of the Napa Valley. Some of these have lived in top form for a decade or more.

Oregon is still too new on the track to have shown what it can do.

Pinot Gris (292 acres in Oregon)
Most widely grown as Pinot Grigio in northern Italy (Veneto, Alto Adige, etc); also well planted and highly regarded as the Tokay d'Alsace.

The Willamette Valley of Oregon gave almost instant indications that it is well suited to Pinot Gris. Expanded plantings only confirmed the early impressions. California has tiny, experimental plantings.

Riesling (4,946 acres in California, 836 in Oregon, 2,118 in Washington)
The great variety of Germany's Mosel-Saar-Ruwer and Rheingau. Officially White Riesling in Oregon, sometimes Johannisberg Riesling in California and Washington.

The prevailing style is for freshly fruity, off-dry sippers throughout the Pacific states. A few producers push close to dry, a tiny minority to bone dry, but still cling to the varietal flavors. Mendocino's Anderson Valley produces many of California's proudest examples. Sonoma's Russian River Valley, the Napa Valley, Monterey, and Santa Barbara can compete.

The temptations of botrytis-sweetened wines attract a

The Rhine House at Beringer Vineyard in the Napa Valley.

considerable number of moths to the flame; Monterey, Santa Barbara, and the Anderson Valley produce them most consistently in California; Sonoma and the Napa Valley are more fitful but succeed often enough to command attention. The Willamette Valley and eastern Washington make fewer, but sometimes wonderfully effective, attempts.

Sauvignon Blanc (12,597 acres in California, 153 in Oregon, 806 in Washington)
A widely distributed French variety best known as the substantial partner in dry Graves, the junior contributor to Sauternes, the sole component in Pouilly Fumé and Sancerre.

Across the board, Sauvignon Blanc may well be California's best white grape variety. It has been a staple from Livermore north to Mendocino since the late 19th century. It grows well and yields good to excellent wine in all the coast counties, although not in every corner of each, and can be coaxed to do well in parts of the interior. That said, regional character produces pronounced differences in flavor and balance.

Some insist that more than one variety is grown as Sauvignon Blanc, adding confusion about the sources of a broad range of flavors. The argument was, in 1992, confined to the academy.

Washington State had to tame its Sauvignon Blanc to win commercial acceptance, but succeeded in doing so during the late 1980s. The variety remains something of a cipher in Oregon.

Sémillon (2,176 acres in California, 590 in Washington)
California has the acreage and history, but Washington has the edge. Sémillons from the Columbia Valley have a depth of flavor, a firmness of texture, and a readiness to meet oysters rarely found in any white other than Chablis. The best of them are among the most distinctive white wines in the world, in little need of oak aging or any of the other lipsticks and rouges winemakers often use to cover a plainness.

California Sémillon tends to lush textures and milder but hardly bland flavors. Livermore has the great history. Paso Robles shows promise. Assembled wines from ranging sources have shown the greatest character.

Oregon's plantings of Sémillon remain at the experimental level.

Viognier
A rarity in the Rhône, treasured there in the appellation of Condrieu. In 1992, plantings in California were just beginning to surpass the experimental level, the best known of them in San Benito (Calera) and the Napa Valley (Joseph Phelps). Both producers have achieved intensely floral perfumes in their first few vintages.

Red

Alicante Bouschet (2,042 acres in California)
A Mediterranean variety used mostly for everyday wines, it earned a foothold in California during Prohibition because it shipped well and had so much color that the skins could be sugared and washed enough times to yield 700 gallons a ton rather than a conventional 140 to 160 gallons. It is fading toward extinction, but still shows up rarely as a varietal from the San Joaquin Valley or Sonoma.

Barbera (10,646 acres in California)
The workhorse of Italy's Piedmont grows in huge acreages in the San Joaquin Valley of California, prized for its ability to hold acidity in hot climates. Most of that crop goes into generic reds, though varietals occasionally appear. It has shown a greater turn of speed than the nobler Nebbiolo in the coast counties, especially Sonoma and Mendocino, although plantings are minuscule and unlikely to increase.

Cabernet Franc (1,130 acres in California)
An important blend variety in Bordeaux is a recent arrival in all three Pacific states, originally brought in for the purpose of adding dimension to Cabernet Sauvignon. The first substantial California plantings began in the early 1980s. At the start of the 1990s, Washington and Oregon growers were just beginning to explore it. Like Merlot before it, Cabernet Franc has continued in the role of blend variety while also evolving into the source of a varietal wine, particularly in the Napa Valley and Sonoma County.

Cabernet Sauvignon (24,115 acres in California, 291 in Oregon, 1,419 in Washington)
The great grape of the Médoc has proved to be widely adaptable in all three Pacific states, though with marked regional variations of character.

Since 1880, the Napa Valley has written most of the historic definition of California Cabernet Sauvignon, thus all other regions are condemned to chase its models. Sonoma County Cabernet Sauvignons began during the 1930s, although sketchily, expanded their role during the 1960s, and became factors during the 1970s. Other regions planted their first Cabernet vines during the 1970s, so are only beginning to make their voices heard. Among the later bloomers, Mendocino and Santa Barbara's Santa Ynez Valley have shown particular promise.

Where once the reigning style was varietally pure unblended Cabernet, the current vogue is for blending it with others of the Bordeaux varieties, especially Merlot and Cabernet Franc. In part the idea is to achieve more complex flavors. In larger part it is to escape the sometimes brutish alcohols and tannins that California's suns and soils can impart.

Carignane (11,033 acres in California)

A workaday variety in southern France and Spain (as Cariñena) is workaday in California as well. Much of the acreage is in the interior valleys; some remains in Sonoma and Mendocino from the days when both concentrated their efforts on bulk wines. Now and again someone bottles it as a varietal, but most of the crop goes into generic blends.

Gamay (1,517 acres in California)

Old plantings of vines with gaps in their pedigrees cause viticultural confusion in many varieties in California, none grander than the bewilderment surrounding Gamay. Many older plantings widely known as Napa Gamay may be an obscure French variety, Valdiguié, or mutations of it. Some newer plantings are Gamay Noir à Jus Blanc, the dominant variety of contemporary Beaujolais. Still others, called Gamay Beaujolais, appear to be a clone of Pinot Noir (*see* page 21).

Within this framework, varietal wines are called Napa Gamay, Gamay, and Gamay Beaujolais with little or no regard to precise taxonomy, although the latter name has been ruled off the course by BATF as of 1993. Two or three producers call the wine from whatever they have Valdiguié.

The tempest has been moving, year by year, to a smaller teapot. Some successful wines in the style of Beaujolais began turning the market around at the turn to the 1990s. Most of them come from the North Coast, especially Napa and Sonoma counties.

Washington State made its first small plantings at the end of the 1980s, with attractive results.

Clos du Val, in the Stag's Leap District of the Napa Valley.

Gamay Beaujolais (1,424 acres in California)
In an enhancement of the confusion surrounding Gamay, the grape variety so-called in California has proven to be a pale, weak-flavored clone of Pinot Noir. Varietal wines named Gamay Beaujolais may be from it or any of the other varieties known as Gamay. In 1992, BATF was trying to rule "Gamay Beaujolais" off American wine labels. Simultaneously, growers were removing it from vineyards, or hanging onto small plots where it served a purpose in varietal Pinot Noir.

Grenache (12,418 acres in California, 45 in Washington)
The variety grows widely in the Rhône and in Spain (as Garnacha). For most of its career in California, Grenache has been concentrated in the warmer parts of the San Joaquin Valley, where it is a workhorse in sweet rosés and in port-types. With the advent of a vogue for Rhône-style blends, a few small plantings have returned to the coast counties, where it had been tried in the 1930s and 1940s and abandoned because of difficulties in ripening.

It has made superior wines in eastern Washington, but is almost impossible to sustain there because of susceptibility to harsh winter weather.

Lemberger
Washington's Columbia Valley has a practical monopoly in Lemberger in the American west. Wineries there make varietal wine from it, primarily in a fresh, fruity style, but sometimes with marked oak aging. Acreage is scant enough that it is not specified in statistical summaries, but ranges between 50 and 80 according to unofficial estimates. The variety is grown in Europe, mostly in Austria and farther east along the Danube.

Merlot (4,010 acres in California, 1,555 in Washington)
With Cabernet Sauvignon an important variety in Bordeaux, especially in St Emilion and Pomerol, where it dominates blends.

The Columbia and especially Yakima valleys in Washington State began producing rather memorable examples of Merlot as a varietal wine in the early 1980s.

The variety was tried and found wanting in much of California in the 1880s, disappearing from the arrival of Prohibition until a revival began in the late 1960s. Poor yields and overripeness were the main drawbacks; both problems have been mitigated.

The original idea behind the revival was to use it in blends that would soften the tannins of Cabernet Sauvignon. Much of the crop still goes to that end, but Merlot became popular as a varietal during the 1980s. Early styles soft-pedaled tannin; more recently many of the most popular Merlots have been every bit as hard or harder than typical Cabernet Sauvignon. Flavors of oak run a similar gamut from modest to bold. The Napa Valley, most of Sonoma's AVAs, and Santa Barbara's Santa Ynez Valley collect the most favorable critical notice.

Oregon has only begun to explore the variety. Growers in the Rogue Valley, especially, hold out high hopes.

Mourvèdre (210 acres in California)
An old variety in warmer parts of California acquired new virtues when it stopped being Mataro and became Mourvèdre at the instigation of an ad hoc group calling itself the Rhône Rangers. The tiny crop is divided between varietals and Rhône-inspired blends, most of them produced in the Santa Cruz

Sterling Vineyards perches on a volcanic knoll in Napa.

Mountains and in urban wineries on the east side of San Francisco Bay, from one old 140-acre vineyard in Contra Costa County. A number of new plantings, all small, went into Napa, Sonoma, and Mendocino during the late 1980s.

Nebbiolo
The grand grape of Barolo and Barbaresco from Italy's Piedmont region has never found its true home in California, but loyalists keep looking for a magic spot. Current candidates are Paso Robles in San Luis Obispo County and the Shenandoah Valley in the Sierra Foothills. Washington is also taking a whack in its Yakima Valley. Acreage, not reported in any Pacific state, approaches 40 in California, 6 in Washington.

Petite Sirah (3,023 acres in California)
Old grape variety, new mystery. France grows no grape by the name, but it has been in California and known by its current name since the 1880s. It was long thought to be a lesser Rhône variety, Duriff. Genetic tests have proved that it is not, without proving what it is.

A source of dark, tannic wines subtly flavored enough to blend well with many other varieties it has been a backbone in California generic reds since the 1880s, a modestly successful varietal since the 1960s. As a source of varietal wine, it has performed most consistently in Mendocino's interior valleys, and the Russian River and Alexander valleys in Sonoma County. The Napa Valley and Livermore valley also have done well with this variety.

Good as its record has been in generics, the Rhône Rangers have scorned it because the Rhône does. Some of them would do well to forget their francophilia and bring it into blends that cost a lot of money for not much form.

Pinot Meunier (160 acres in California)
Pinot Meunier is a useful blend variety in Champagne both for its yield and its readiness to ripen. Several sparkling-wine producers have established trial plantings in California. The Eyrie Vineyard in Oregon has made Pinot Meunier as a varietal wine from the winery's beginning. Plantings remained extremely limited in the early 1990s, varietal wines even rarer.

Pinot Noir (8,554 acres in California, 1,984 in Oregon, 250 in Washington)

The great black grape of Burgundy. Oregon laid strong claim to eminence as America's region for Pinot Noir during the 1980s, most especially in the lower Willamette Valley. By an enormous margin it dominates red wine production in the state. By an even larger margin it dominates critical approval of Oregon as a wine region.

California's long history with what may be the ficklest of all grape varieties is a tortured one, full of false starts and dashed dreams. However, it is beginning to be brighter with the emergence after 1970 of the Russian River Valley, the Santa Maria Valley, part of the Santa Ynez Valley, Carneros, and the Anderson Valley, all districts earlier ignored as too cool and damp for vineyards. Shorter times in oak barrels (a year rather than two) have coincided with its higher approval ratings.

Much of the California crop goes into classic-method sparkling wines, most of them from the same regions as the most favorably regarded still reds.

Ruby Cabernet (6,881 acres in California)

A University of California cross based on Cabernet Sauvignon and Carignane was bred to produce quality dry wines in warmer climates than Cabernet will tolerate. It enjoyed a brief vogue, but has nearly disappeared as a varietal wine. Deft blending could bring it back as part of a wine styled after other amalgams based on Cabernet Sauvignon. Lodi, in the lower San Joaquin Valley, grows it well. Some of the varietal wines from there during the 1970s were attractive on their own.

Sangiovese (39 acres in California)

The dominant grape of Tuscany came to California with Italian immigrants before Prohibition, but always lurked in obscurity. Much of it was planted in old-fashioned field blends in Sonoma County. Where it was not field-blended, it found its way into generic reds anyway. By the early 1980s, a Sonoma family named Seghesio may have had the only planting of it in the western U.S.; it had dropped out of all statistical summaries.

Only with the advent of the so-called Super Tuscans did Sangiovese begin to excite interest in California, where dozens of growers began planting it between 1985 and 1989, most

Vineyard and winery at Adelsheim in Oregon's Willamette Valley.

especially in Napa, Sonoma, and Amador counties, but also in Mendocino, San Luis Obispo, and others. Bearing acreage more than quadrupled in California between 1990, cited above, and 1993. The first varietal wines came from Napa in 1987.

Syrah (144 acres in California)

The great grape of Hermitage in the Rhône. Except for two or three old plantings, Syrah has emerged in California only since the 1980s. Its status as a varietal owes as much to Australian Shirazes and Hermitages as to Hermitage itself. It also plays a role in blends inspired by Châteauneuf-du-Pape and other Rhônes. If it has the capacity to become dominant in any region in California, that place has not yet emerged. The best hopes appear to be the Sierra Foothills, or in Santa Barbara County.

Washington State has shown promise from one experimental planting.

Zinfandel (27,989 acres in California)

Zinfandel is California's delicious mystery, indisputably a variety of *Vitis vinifera*, but one with no known antecedent in Europe. It is genetically linked to an Italian variety, Primitivo da Gaia, but appears to predate it.

Speculation about its origins turns again and again to eastern Europe, perhaps Hungary, more likely Croatia. The earliest sighting of Zinfandel as Zinfandel was in a New York State nursery in the 1830s. It arrived in California no later than 1856 or 1857, and has been a staple ever since as a varietal red in every style from fresh-fruity to aged oaky, as rosé, as the paler White Zinfandel, in generic blends, and, not infrequently, in port-types.

Its strength, versatility, is also its weakness. The consuming public recoiled from it during the 1970s and early 1980s when the range of red-wine styles became outright bewildering. Alcohols ranged down to 11 and up to 15 percent; tannins came at every level; oak played every role from dominant to none at all; even sweetness became a major variable. Zinfandel began to regain a footing late in the 1980s, with moderates putting its enticing, berrylike fruit flavors ahead of oak, keeping alcohol near 13 percent and moderating tannins.

As a source of reds, it has been at its finest in the North Coast, most especially the Dry Creek and Russian River valleys in Sonoma, and in Mendocino County. The Napa Valley and Lake County also yield excellent reds. Outside the North Coast, the Sierra Foothills and Paso Robles in San Luis Obispo County are Zinfandel's most admirable homes. Lodi can also offer a challenge.

White Zinfandel remains a major use of a large annual crop, most of the grapes for it coming from Lodi and nearby areas, although coast-counties grapes go to the purpose as well.

Tiny amounts of Zinfandel grow in Washington and Oregon, sometimes appearing as varietal wine, but too seldom to allow the vaguest generalities.

* All acreage figures are for the year 1990.

California

Californa drives non-Californians a little bit crazy. Everything is so easy. Stick the vines in the ground, wait two years, harvest big crops of ripe grapes, put the wine in automated cellars, winter in Hawaii, no problems.

It is a little bit like that, especially compared to Oregon and Washington, or the Rheingau and Champagne, even Chianti. The last truly damaging spring frost in California, in 1961, cut the North Coast crop to one-quarter of its normal size . In the past 30 years, only in 1976, and only in Alameda and Santa Clara counties, did the average ripeness of even one variety fall short of 11 percent of potential alcohol. In a run-of-the-mill year people celebrate Washington's birthday in February with picnics on ocean beaches, not just in southern California, but all the way north to Sonoma. On Thanksgiving weekend in the Napa Valley, as often as not, people in shirtsleeves read their newspapers under a gentle sun on the terraces of coffee

Vines at Trefethen Vineyard in the Napa Valley.

houses. In between, the weather is a good deal warmer and drier throughout the vineyards.

Outsiders often take the overarching image of perpetual sun shining down on endless white sand beaches as a sign that California must be homogeneous in matters of grapes and wine. But it is not quite so.

By the most generous definitions, a state that is 320 miles longer and 27,600 square miles larger than Italy, supports three, perhaps four distinct winegrowing regions with varied climates, dissimilar histories and contradictory ways of doing business. During the past decade, a market-driven wine trade has papered over some of those differences by making it almost imperative for everyone in every region to bottle Cabernet Sauvignon and Chardonnay as a matter of business survival. However, even the dictates of the marketplace have not erased regional identities rooted in nature. The distinct regions are North Coast, Central Coast, and interior valleys. The possible fourth, tiny though it is, is the Sierra Foothills.

European settlers dominated the first planting of vineyards and building of wineries in the North Coast between 1860 and 1880, and it remains the most familiar-looking region to those whose standards were shaped by France, Germany, and Italy. Except for a northern tip, the Central Coast emerged in its present form only with the 1970s, built, most of it, by ex-San Joaquin Valley farmers familiar with irrigation and the economies of scale. Their fathers and grandfathers made grapegrowing and winemaking what it is in the San Joaquin Valley, beginning in the 1930s. It had an earlier, largely forgotten history from the 1880s, before mass marketing and advertising and technical wizardry made high-volume winemaking what it now is. The Sierra Foothills are something of an anomaly, a small band of mostly local producers forced to be individualistic by mountain soils and weathers.

The North Coast, all told, has about 75,000 acres under vines, the Central Coast another 40,000. The San Joaquin Valley has 181,000 acres of wine grapes, another 265,300 of Thompson Seedless. These figures lie: San Joaquin expects 8 to 9 tons an acre from its vines, the coast counties 3 to 6.

By 1880, California wine already had much of this geographical outline. The coast, dominated at that time by Napa, Sonoma, Livermore, and Santa Clara, was for fine table wine. The interior was either for dessert wines or lesser table wines. Such recognition came with surprising swiftness, especially given the monochromatic start provided by the Franciscan missionaries who first brought European civilization to what is now California.

Diligent scholarship makes a convincing case that Fra Pablo de Mugartegui planted the first vines at Mission San Juan Capistrano, in what is now Orange County, in 1779. In succeeding years the priests established vineyards at each of their settlements until Fra Jose Altimira planted the last one at Sonoma in 1824, a decade before the Mexican government secularized all the missions. Every last vine was of a variety called Criolla, now known as Mission, which the priests brought with them from earlier missions in South and Central America.

Although it is *Vitis vinifera*, Criolla by any name has been unknown in Europe for more than a century. The supposition is that missionaries to South America carried seeds rather than vine cuttings, or at least that seeds survived the journey while cuttings did not, and that Criolla began as a mutation of an ancient, now forgotten, variety.

Whatever its ancestry, it is a warm-climate grape and not a noble one. It ripened at San Gabriel, Santa Ynez, and Sonoma, but not at Purissima Concepcion, Soledad or Santa Clara. It made less than admirable wine at all of them.

The first secular growers settled around the mission at what is now Los Angeles in the 1830s. Early grapegrowers in northern California also were at work by the late 1830s. Almost immediately, the pioneers of both north and south began throwing Mission grapes to the wolves. The most enterprising of the Los Angelenos, a Bordelais with the improbably apt name of Jean-Louis Vignes, imported cuttings of as many as 100 established French varieties in 1833. European varieties came later to Northern California, Pierre Pellier, Agoston Harazsthy, and others bringing major collections during the 1850s.

By 1881 the University of California could report on detailed studies of more than 300 varieties grown in test plots from the Napa Valley south to Paso Robles in San Luis Obispo County. At the same time, winemaking skills had reached a level that allowed participants to think of the era as a minor Golden Age of California wine.

Then came a long succession of disasters and dislocations. Phylloxera devastated vineyards on the North Coast between 1886 and 1900. National Prohibition closed down the fine wine business in 1913, and turned vineyardists to coarse, high-yielding, thick-skinned varieties that could be be shipped to home winemakers. Came repeal in 1933, and wine became legal at the nadir of the Great Depression, no propitious moment to restart fine wine as a business. Economic hard times carried into World War II. With the coming of war, the U.S. federal government commandeered all distilleries to produce fuel for torpedoes, among other uses of neutral spirits, leaving the populace to amuse itself with mediocre wines and worse. The bad taste left by that experience was both figurative and literal, and it carried over into peacetime.

In 1950, the Napa Valley's 150 or so acres of Cabernet Sauvignon amounted to 80 to 90 percent of the state total. Wente Bros. had a similar proportion of the Chardonnay, with fewer than 50 acres at Livermore. With such slender reeds, a handful of producers managed to rebuild a certain prestige for their regions, and then to attract a new generation of growers, winery owners and winemakers.

In the four decades since 1950, plantings of fine wine grapes have exploded in California. The Napa Valley has simultaneously gone from 150 to 9,000 acres of Cabernet Sauvignon, and dipped from 80 to 30 percent of total plantings. Chardonnay plantings stood at 57,000 acres in 1992 and showed no signs of having peaked. In comparison, Sauvignon Blanc, Pinot Noir, and other celebrated varieties tag along; in real terms, they too have expanded in startling fashion.

Because so much is new and unsettled, these grapes are traded and used in ways that confound Europeans. Wineries sell grapes from their own vineyards to rivals, then turn around and buy other grapes from independent growers. These growers are not always located in the buyer-winery's home region. Sometimes this type of trading is merely for commercial convenience. At other times it is very high-minded indeed, an effort to have better grapes than can be grown in winery-owned land. Whichever purpose, the upshot can be most confusing to people trying to sort out the differences among districts, not least because U.S. labeling laws permit 15 percent of a wine to come from outside the appellation named on the label.

Although it contributes to the confusion, the North Coast is by far the most fully explored and understood of all the larger regions. In its turn the Napa Valley is the most fully explored and understood district within the North Coast. It is still raw enough that the human element remains more important than some sensibly drawn interior divisions. Men and women are utterly paramount in regions of little or no history and yet are nearly absent from these pages in favor of lines drawn around the places where they work, because the long truth is, geography and climate will have their way.

North Coast

When Americans think of castles on steep hills, damp caves full of barrels, and old vintages resting in the cellar, their home-grown choices are the Napa Valley and Sonoma County, twin hearts of the North Coast.

This was the last of California's coastal regions to become involved in winemaking, for the simple reason that Sonoma proved to be the last leg of the Franciscan missionaries' long march north from San Diego between 1769 and 1825. On the other hand, the North Coast was the first to take wine seriously after the Gold Rush of 1849 brought wealth and booming populations to San Francisco while southern California languished.

The Franciscans established only one vineyard in what is now the North Coast, at what is now Sonoma, in 1825 or soon after. During the 1830s, their vines fell into secular hands after the Mexican government took for itself all the mission holdings. In 1857, Agoston Haraszthy became the first of many European emigrants to open a winery in Sonoma, and also the first to introduce a range of classic varieties where only the Mission grape had grown before. In 1859, one of his employees, Charles Krug, started commercial winemaking in the Napa Valley, where several ranchers had already established small vineyards.

Thereafter matters moved fast enough for the last two decades of the 19th century to be called the golden age of California wine by the people who lived through them. At some point in that short era wine caught hold in the North Coast in a way it did not anywhere else in the state. Proprietors and winemakers set about turning small advantage to large account with shrewdly planted vineyards and neat turns of style.

Between them, Napa and Sonoma have led fine winemaking in California ever since. A roll-call of great names from the Gay Nineties still has a familiar ring: Buena Vista, Gundlach-Bundschu, Korbel, Simi, Beringer, Inglenook, Charles Krug, and Schramsberg do well at summoning up some of the best days of both centuries. Almost as important as the leaders is the size of the supporting cast. Within the cozy confines of the Napa Valley more than 200 wineries jockey for position. Sonoma, slightly larger, has almost as many. Mendocino and Lake counties, if less populous and less heavily planted, still push for places in the front rows.

Gustave Niebaum built Inglenook's grand cellar in 1882.

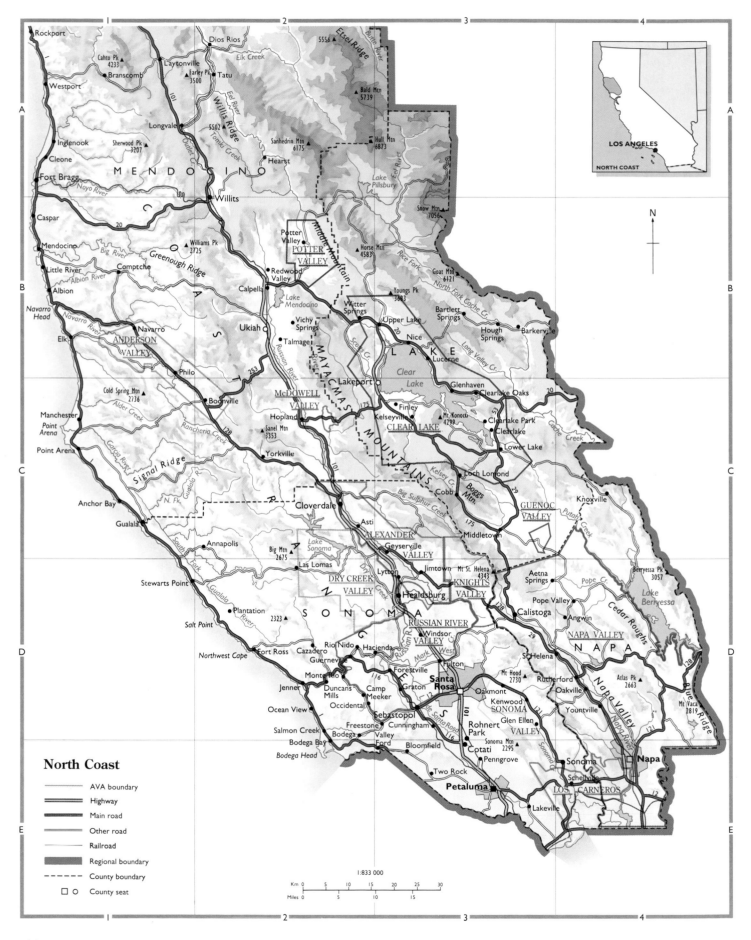

North Coast

————	AVA boundary
═══════	Highway
════	Main road
———	Other road
————	Railroad
▬▬▬	Regional boundary
─ ─ ─	County boundary
□ ○	County seat

1:833 000

Km 0 5 10 15 20 25 30
Miles 0 5 10 15

Mount Konocti looms over Kelseyville and algae-clouded Clear Lake.

Their playing field looks homogeneous compared to rivals in the south and east. San Franciscans named this the North Coast – even though California extends another 185 miles before it gets to the Oregon border – because it is north of them. Napa, Sonoma, Mendocino, and Lake counties form a slightly crooked rectangle, just over 100 miles long and not quite half that wide west to east. Adding in Marin County and its 15 or so acres of vineyard changes the basic outline but little.

Writ large, the climate is all of a piece: short, mild winters with enough rain for the region to be dry-farmed, and long, rainless, warm summers that nearly guarantee a ripe crop every year. If that sounds like the Mediterranean two-season climate, it is, but with one difference: the persistent summer fogs caused by warm water offshore in the Pacific Ocean and cold water alongshore.

Topography in these counties is restless but not dramatic. North-south ridges carve the whole into dozens if not scores of small to tiny, mostly shallow, valleys. At a modest 4,344 feet, Mt St Helena is high enough above the Coast Ranges to have been used as a navigation aid by 19th-century Russian fur traders, on their way to their base at Fort Ross on the Sonoma coast.

Still, the interplay between fog and hills delimits most of the AVAs within the North Coast. Pinot Noir defines Carneros, the Russian River Valley, and Anderson Valley because fog defines them first. Fog often fills these valleys because the hills provide little shelter. The remaining twenty or so appellations within the North Coast are better off thinking about varieties more suitable for relentless sun and more heat, because their hills are just high enough to keep the skies blue.

Just when climate and terrain promise some coherence, local geology complicates the choice of varieties to a bewildering degree. The San Andreas Fault, producer of California's most celebrated earthquakes, runs across the mouth of the Golden Gate at San Francisco, along the floor of Tomales Bay and through Bodega Bay before it goes out to sea. It is only the famous symptom of the on-going collision between the Pacific and North American plates. Almost every other feature in the landscape is a by-product of the same activity. Mt St Helena, although not a volcano, is of volcanic origin, as are most of the Napa Valley's eastern hills. Hills on the western side folded themselves upward out of an ancient seabed, and so, on the surface at least, are metamorphosed sediments. Scattered all through the North Coast are rock formations that appear to have been sledded in from far distant points by forces now disappeared. The lowlands are an incredibly fine mosaic of pieces quarried from all three sources.

For a while in the mid-1980s, Napa and Sonoma were the back-hoe capitals of the world, as viticulturalists dug a virtual infinity of deep holes between vine rows to map their soils and subsoils. They have quietly given up after endless variations on the theme of uncovering river rock 20 feet deep in one spot, and thick layers of clay not 20 feet away.

People who are used to the viticultural tidiness of France can become upset. Watch the fog and kick the dirt long enough, though, and growing Chardonnay alongside Cabernet Sauvignon alongside Gewürztraminer begins to seem middling normal.

Napa Valley

Other California coastal valleys are naturally handsomer than Napa. And many have carpets of vines every bit as thick. What the other valleys do not have, however, is a long, relentless, almost monomaniacal history of sorting out just where in the carpet are the special places. Only in this of all California valleys do residents remember 1935, 1946 and 1958 not so much because of wars or elections but because a wine was surpassingly good, and they remember exactly where it came from.

Contemporary Napa is full of the mystical messages initiates use to point toward superior vineyards, because certain blocks of vines, rather than mountains or waterways, began looming as Napa's foremost landmarks way back (the 1870s and 1880s being way back by California standards). Names like ToKalon, Inglenook, Glen Oaks, and Stanly echoed in wine collectors' minds then, the way Martha's Vineyard, Bosche, Eisele, and Fay have done in recent years.

It has been a narrow squeak. Napa started strong during the last quarter of the 19th century. Monumental old buildings at Krug, Inglenook, Greystone, and Chateau Chevalier attest to that. However, with an eerie foretaste of current times, economic depression drove many out of business in the 1880s, phylloxera killed scores of vineyards in the 1890s and Prohibition destroyed the American taste for wine between 1918 and 1933.

Of the more than 50 new starters at repeal, only Louis M. Martini, the Cesare Mondavi family at Charles Krug, and the extremely local Nichelini winery are still owned by the same families. Only Beaulieu, Beringer, the Christian Brothers, and Inglenook Vineyards join with them in having operated continuously since 1933, though with changes from family to corporate ownership. This handful of cellars produced the memorable Cabernet Sauvignons of the 1940s and 1950s, the wines upon which Napa's modern prestige rests.

At one point in 1960, the number of companies making wine in the valley was down to a dozen. Vineyard plantings eroded with them to a paltry 10,000 acres. Yet still the valley was making more fine wine than the national market would absorb. In 1962 and 1963 visitors to Beaulieu or Louis M. Martini could buy perfectly cellared Cabernet Sauvignon ranging back to the 1952 vintage at prices hardly greater than those of the current vintage. A good new wine cost $1.35 to 1.89 a bottle then, a fine older one $2.50. People who knew could go to Inglenook and get a gallon jug of pure Cabernet, cryptically labeled IVY, for $1.49. Nonetheless, the tiny cadre continued to rebuild Napa's reputation by making the finest wines it knew how.

Finally came the turnaround, hesitantly for a time, then in a rush. Heitz Cellars opened in 1962, the first new label in the Napa Valley in a decade. Robert Mondavi launched his winery in 1966, in the first new building of any size since the 1930s. By 1975 the valley had 45 wineries. By 1980 the number had passed 100, and by 1990 about 200 companies were making wine in the valley. Along with new wineries came an almost startling expansion in the vineyards. Local landowners uprooted walnut and plum orchards to plant large new vineyards, and ripped out back gardens to start small ones. From the ebb,

Napa wine-grape plantings grew to 22,000 acres in 1974, 28,000 by 1985, and 30,000 by 1990.

The valley in which all this has happened starts across the bay from San Francisco as a flat flood plain caught between a tumble of low, soft hills called Carneros, and a straighter ridge to the east. The Napa River's course reaches 25 miles north and west, its plain a long, narrow arc between steep hills that pinch together beyond the town of Calistoga, beneath the looming presence of Mt St Helena. The Sonoma Valley flanks it to the west. Lake Berryessa parallels it on the opposite side.

Exactly what makes it magnetic to people willing to spend fortunes on excelling with wine is not immediately apparent. Napa city is an ordinary American town. Ignore their restaurants and Yountville, St Helena, and Calistoga, together with the smaller villages up-valley, are distinguished almost entirely

by the more monumental of their wineries. And truth to tell, sun and soil are not so distinctive that no other district can compete. However, that magnet, whatever its force, appeared early.

A trapper named George Yount planted the valley's first grapes in the 1830s – the coarse Mission variety – wishing only to make wine for his own table. Still using Mission grapes in 1858, almost three decades later, a German named Charles Krug decided to put Napa wine onto a business footing. Two years in Krug's wake a doctor, George Belden Crane, decided that German grapes were a better idea than the gross Missions.

Crane swiftly proved right enough to bring an influx of Germans into Napa. They started late compared to Sonoma, Livermore and other districts in northern California, but, collectively, turned out to be the tortoise in a field of hares. By the mid-1880s Napa grapes commanded the highest prices in the state, as did the wines. Germans and Germanophiles ran the valley so thoroughly that old-timers remember their language being more common than English in many a home and cellar: Charles Krug, the brothers Frederick and Jacob Beringer, Groezinger, Thomann, Jacob Schram; the list ran on. It was even the daily language in W. W. Lyman's El Molino winery, according to his son. There were also French, English, and

plain old Yankees among the winery owners and winemakers, but they all played second fiddle to the efficient Germans. Napa winegrowing became both fashionable and lucrative. San Francisco socialites even bought summer homes to be near the vines. However, this first wine wave could not stave off a depression, phylloxera and Prohibition. When they had all run their courses, few of the people who had made the valley pre-eminent in California wine came back.

Italians, meanwhile, had begun settling in Napa during the late 19th century, more as stonemasons and cellarmen than winery proprietors. It was they who bought up much of the vineyard land during the national dry spell and the great depression which followed it. Italian families dominated Napa winemaking in their turn well into the 1970s. Cesare Mondavi and his sons Peter and Robert, and Louis M. and Louis P. Martini were and are the most visible names, but the valley was full of Strallas, Bartoluccis, del Bondios, and Fornis when the current, American-dominated but French, German, Swiss, Spanish, and Japanese-spiced cast of characters began to gather. The old Italian families are still around in vineyard and cellar alike; San Francisco socialites still flock to their weekend homes on side roads all over the valley; Napa is either still or again out in front of its rivals, thanks to a history that allows wineries to turn small advantage to large account, and allows niceties of style to mark out the differences between best and next.

Cabernet Sauvignon is the true heart of Napa wine, but not a universal success. It ripens easily on the Rutherford Bench, but less than a mile away, in heavy clays near the Napa River, it may not have quite enough sugar or color by Thanksgiving to make a good rosé. Sometimes Sauvignon Blanc does well where Cabernet cannot. Alternatively, Chardonnay answers the call. Other varieties fit narrower slots: Pinot Noir is retreating to its most suitable territory, Carneros; Riesling has faded from a prominence that lasted long after the German pioneers. The argument now is whether to play it down the middle, or chase after new challenges like Sangiovese, Syrah, or Viognier.

Climate and soil do not provide a ready answer. The range of temperatures between Napa city and St Helena can be greater than that between Pauillac and Beaune. Napa's geology is messy beyond description, a muddled slagheap of parent soils with and without explanation for being where they are. Terrain in this valley, like most of the other coastal wine valleys, is a product of the Pacific and North American plates grinding together. Some of the outcrops of rock appear to have been pushed so far that their source cannot be traced. Climate is a delicate result of sea air trying to push around or over the higher land.

Getting the right grape variety in the right place is a puzzle few Europeans understand until they see a bare rock wall on the east, a redwood-forested slope on the west, and feel the sea fog creeping up behind them. The real trouble, and it bothers Napa's wine producers every day, is that growers in the valley are continually under threat. More than six million Californians live within 90 miles of downtown St Helena, and pressures to suburbanize do not allow for many mistakes in managing vineyards. A local agricultural preserve that is a model for the nation protects the vineyards for now, but it will not last if Napa comes off its pinnacle. Hence the wary eye on Sangiovese and Syrah, just in case they are the new darlings.

Misty marine air turns the Napa Valley's hills as insubstantial as gauze by late afternoon on a typical summer's day.

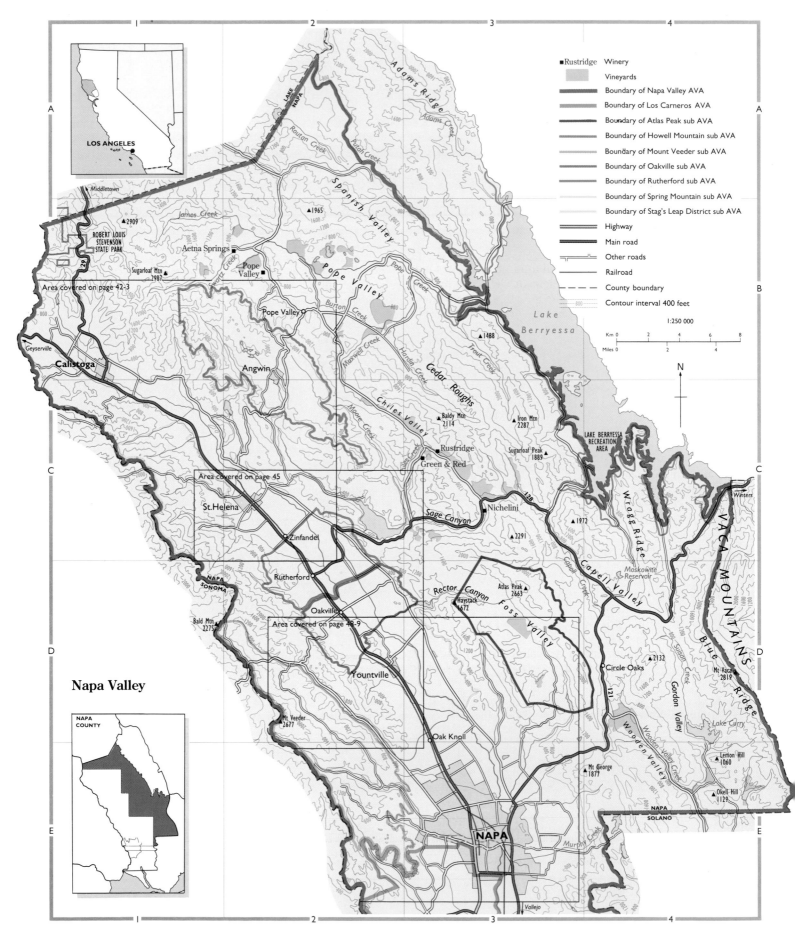

LOS ANGELES

■Rustridge   Winery

Vineyards

Boundary of Napa Valley AVA

Boundary of Los Carneros AVA

Boundary of Atlas Peak sub AVA

Boundary of Howell Mountain sub AVA

Boundary of Mount Veeder sub AVA

Boundary of Oakville sub AVA

Boundary of Rutherford sub AVA

Boundary of Spring Mountain sub AVA

Boundary of Stag's Leap District sub AVA

Highway

Main road

Other roads

Railway

County boundary

Contour interval 400 feet

1:250 000

Km 0   2   4   6   8

Miles 0   2   4

N

Adams Ridge

Adams Creek

LAKE NAPA

Routan Creek

Putah Creek

Middletown

▲2909

James Creek

▲1965

Spanish Valley

1600

ROBERT LOUIS STEVENSON STATE PARK

29

Aetna Springs

Sugarloaf Mtn 2987

Pope Valley

Pope Creek

& Pope Valley

Area covered on page 42-3

Swartz Creek

Pope Valley

Burton Creek

Lake Berryessa

Geyserville

Calistoga

Angwin

Maxwell Creek

Moore Creek

Chiles Valley

Hardin Creek

Cedar Roughs

Trout Creek

▲1488

LAKE BERRYESSA RECREATION AREA

Winters

Baldy Mtn 2114

▲Iron Mtn 2287

Sugarloaf Peak 1889 ▲

Rustridge

Green & Red

Chiles Creek

Area covered on page 45

St.Helena

Sage Canyon

Nichelini

128

▲1972

VACA MOUNTAINS

Wragg Ridge

Zinfandel

▲2291

Capell Valley

Capell Creek

Moskowite Reservoir

Rutherford

NAPA SONOMA

Rector Canyon

Atlas Peak 2663 ▲

Haystack 1672

Foss Valley

▲2132

Sunrise Creek

Blue Ridge

Oakville

Area covered on page 48-9

Circle Oaks

Mt Vaca 2819

Bald Mtn 2275

Gordon Valley

Yountville

1200

121

Wooden Valley

Wooden Valley Creek

Lake Curry

Mt Veeder 2677

Oak Knoll

Lemon Hill 1060

Napa Valley

NAPA COUNTY

Mt George 1877

Okell Hill 1129

NAPA SOLANO

NAPA

Murphy Creek

Vallejo

Climate

Typical of most of California's coastal wine valleys, Napa's daily temperature range, in the 25 miles that separate its cool southern foot from its warm northern head, on many days is greater than the difference between Burgundy and Bordeaux.

The Golden Gate lets marine air from the Pacific Ocean sweep across San Pablo Bay and onto the flats south of Napa city. From there it flows, ever more weakly, up the valley. Rising elevation affects the flow less than a topography dotted here and there with isolated hills that deflect cool air away from some spots, and toward others. To stand on a ridge for 90 straight days from June through August is to watch the resulting fog behave in 90 different ways, depending on exactly how much push is behind it. Overall, however, the process is one of the most orderly in the North Coast. Each passing mile from south to north brings warmer temperatures along the valley floor. Or almost. Because of a small dip in the Mayacamas Range, locals argue whether St Helena or Calistoga has the warmer average climate. Fog sometimes lingers over St Helena when Calistoga is sunny. At other times it drifts across the low spot to cover Calistoga when St Helena is already in sunshine.

The hills and eastern vales are a different story. Foggy marine air does not often reach them during the growing season, leaving elevation to produce the most important effects on both day and nighttime temperatures, especially the latter. Pope Valley, farthest to the interior, has notably warmer days and cooler nights than not only the main drainage basin of the Napa River but also lower valleys in the southeast corner of Napa County. Howell Mountain, which separates Pope from the upper Napa Valley, falls between their extremes. Its elevation keeps it slightly cooler during the day, slightly warmer at night than the lowlands on either side.

Hard freezes are rare in Napa. A string of six nights ranging between 11° and 17°F during the winter of 1990–91 was almost unprecedented. Frosty nights between 25° and 32°F are, on the other hand, rather common. A typical winter sees as many as 50 of them. Frosts in March and April, after bud-break in the vines, are seldom severe, but can be: three-quarters of the crop of 1961 was wiped out by 30 consecutive freezing nights, beginning in late March.

Because high hills squeeze water out of low clouds, the north end of the valley, under looming Mt St Helena, gets far more rain than the south end in typical years, although the lengthy drought of the late 1980s and early 1990s has disguised this fact for most of a decade. Still, Calistoga averages 38 inches of rain per year, St Helena 34, and Napa city only 25. Angwin, on Howell Mountain, has the highest officially recorded average, 40.5 inches a year.

The usual rainfall range in the upper valley is 25 to 45 inches, but the extremes are worth noticing. Calistoga bathed in 100 inches of rain in the wettest-ever winter of 1982–83, St Helena in 70 inches. St Helena received only 12.4 inches in droughty 1975–76, the driest year in its recorded history.

Typical of all the North Coast, the rainy season begins late in October or early in November, and extends into March. Both April and September can be soggy, to the discomfiture of grape growers, but this seldom happens.

* For the color code to the climate charts see pages 14-15.

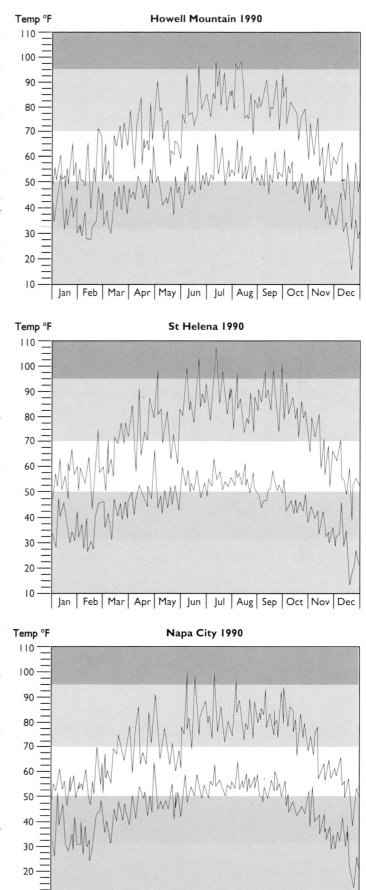

White Wine Varieties

In the years since 1970, Chardonnay has shot from middle of the pack to at least treble the acreage of its nearest rival, Sauvignon Blanc. In more than a minor degree, the increase was market-driven – in much of the valley Sauvignon Blanc performs nearer to its potential than Chardonnay does; recent replanting has begun to take that into account. One-time leader Chenin Blanc retains a substantial acreage; Riesling and Gewürztraminer have drifted down to niche roles; Pinot Blanc and Melon barely qualify at that level. Viognier is undergoing its first trials, most successfully at Joseph Phelps, also in plantings on Spring Mountain and Howell Mountain. Burger, Green Hungarian, Sauvignon Vert, and Sylvaner, once plentiful varieties for blending into generics, have all disappeared; Colombard and Gray Riesling tremble on the verge of extinction in a valley where land prices do not permit such ordinariness.

Chardonnay (430 acres in 1970, 8,144 in 1990)
White wines from different appellations in California are not separated by the same gulfs as reds often are. If Napa Valley Chardonnay is that much better than, say, its Russian River, Anderson Valley, or Santa Maria counterparts, then competitions, blind tastings and other dogged attempts at classification do not show it.

In somewhat the same vein, Chardonnay properties in the Napa Valley have not sorted themselves out to anywhere near the degree Cabernet plantings have. There are fewer estate bottlings, and many fewer single-vineyard examples. Somewhere in the valley, to be sure, Chardonnay comes to the margin where it stops being superior and becomes merely agreeable. Where that place might be has yet to be pinned down and marked with flags.

And yet where Chardonnay performs best in the Napa Valley, it performs well enough to get to the finals against all-comers, and to win a fair share of firsts. Almost always it gets toward the front of the pack with flavors of rich, ripe apples that linger in the memory, usually with a distinct touch of oak, often with a certain boldness of character.

Trefethen has held Chardonnay from its vineyard up to the light longer and with greater constancy than any other. What the light reveals tastes of perfectly spiced warm apple and has silken textures that hide a thoroughbred's bones. Very few Napa Valley Chardonnays age reliably beyond four or five years, perhaps more because of overvigorous winemaking than underendowed vineyards. Trefethen is a notable exception. Nearly every vintage that has aged a decade until now has done so in style. In its perfectly bred understatement the wine has been less a darling of critics than of diners.

What might be its exact opposite comes from Freemark Abbey. Its sturdily built Chardonnays shout out indelible grape variety flavors without being as clearly applelike or otherwise straightforwardly fruity as many Californians – the right tastes

Many of the Napa Valley's sharply sloping hillside vineyards are terraced against erosion from heavy winter rains.

for salmon and lobster rather than paler, leaner foods. Their individuality comes largely from the way Brad Webb has taught his winemakers to make the wine, although an adroit balancing of up- and down-valley vineyards must come into the equation as well. Freemark Abbeys from some vintages have made the 10-year mark in fine fettle, but one gambles less thinking of them as wines that should be drunk up within five or six years.

Stag's Leap Wine Cellars rivals the refined understatement of Trefethen's in both regular and Reserve bottlings, but has yet to show the same kind of durability in either. Silverado Vineyards also shows polish in its regular bottling, again without quite the capacity for long keeping. A Reserve, true to type, is much stronger in oak than Chardonnay flavors.

Crichton Hall makes an estate Chardonnay of greater intensity than Trefethen's but of no less elegant balance and harmony – not quite Freemark Abbey's, but tipped in that direction. Barrel fermentation and other tricks from the winemaker's bag are put to wise use to make the journey from excellent grapes to exceptional wine. Grgich Hills, drawing primarily from nearby vineyards, makes a wine in much the same stylistic vein, though the grapes make a stamp of their own. Mt Veeder, using mountain grapes, comes close to these in both style and substance.

St Andrews Vineyard, almost straight east across the valley from both Crichton and Trefethen, either goes one stride bolder with the oak, or grows grapes that show its effects sooner. Either way, these Chardonnays are pleasurable to drink year after year. More oak than this, though, begins to hamper any wine looking to be agreeable company at a dinner table.

Wines from the valley floor north of, say, Rutherford can be attractive in the bold, blowsy way that was popular in the 1970s. Their legacy, alas, has led to some of the same sort of bombast that marks some Cabernets. Winemakers with greatness on their minds rather than in their vineyards barrel-ferment their Chardonnays, push them through malolactic fermentations, flog them with new oak, and then announce that they do hands-off winemaking so the vineyard can express itself. Almost all of the evidence says that, whatever else, the vineyard is left with little or nothing to say.

Benchmarks:
Freemark Abbey (assembled; principally Carpy Ranch at Rutherford, Jaeger Vineyard on Big Ranch Road). **Grgich Hills** (assembled, from Oakville south). **Stag's Leap Wine Cellars** (assembled). **Silverado Vineyards** (from proprietor-owned vineyards at the winery and in Coombsville). **Crichton Hall** (estate). **Trefethen Vineyards** (estate). **St Andrews** (estate). **Mt Veeder** (from Mt Veeder AVA). **Stony Hill Vineyard** (estate).

Chenin Blanc (672 acres in 1970, 1,329 in 1990)

In the late 1950s Robert Mondavi coined Chenin Blanc as a varietal name, and developed the wine's now typical off-dry style. It was a successful bid to rescue the sagging fortunes of a dry wine called White Pinot. Ironically, Napa Valley Chenin Blancs are fading once again, because other districts seem better adapted to producing wines of this sort.

The grape can and does make better-than-everyday, drink-soon dry wine from vineyards where Chardonnay starts going over the top, as Folie à Deux and tiny Casa Nuestra have shown over and over again. But the variety does not respond well when pushed to be more than modestly charming. Its mile-wide, inch-deep fruit flavors are too slight to take more

than a tiny bit of oak. With or without oak, serious bottle age is not to be sought.

Napa Valley Chenin Blanc's greatest trouble comes from taking Vouvray as the model, which many wineries do. Where Vouvray and its neighbors have a sturdy core, Napa Chenin is soft by nature. A little bit of sugar makes the Napans pneumatic. At 1 percent, they can cloy. A majority of wineries bring them to bottle at 1.5 to 2 percent, at which point they are best suited to chicken swimming in pineapple and coconut, or one of those salads with lots of marshmallows.

Before other regions began planting it, Chenin was a staple in the valley. Its acreage reached 2,167 in 1983, dipped, picked up again to 2,182 in 1987, then dropped sharply, unable to fetch the same price as Sauvignon Blanc, let alone Chardonnay.

Gewürztraminer (120 acres in 1970, 152 in 1990)

California's finest Gewürztraminers have not come from the Napa Valley, where they are too soft and quick to age to match the best from the Anderson and Russian River Valleys. But there are some good ones, especially from vineyards that touch Big Ranch Road as it runs northward out of Napa city. Here vineyards catch lichee-like varietal flavors to perfection, and embody them in full, round wines with instant appeal. Therein is the limitation. The softness does allow them to be made dry, however, a virtue in the presence of many Cantonese dishes and smoked chicken or turkey.

Gewürztraminers from farther north exaggerate these tendencies: slightly as far up-valley as Oakville, more broadly beyond there. Few plantings of Gewürztraminer have gone into the higher hills, and then only with modest success.

Here, as in most of the rest of the coast, Gewürztraminer went through a boomlet, reaching 460 acres in 1982.
Benchmarks:
Beringer Vineyards (estate; from Gamble Ranch at Oakville). **Evensen Vineyards** (estate). **Rutherford Hill** (from the affiliated Jaeger Vineyard on Big Ranch Road).

Riesling *also* White Riesling, Johannisberg Riesling (486 acres in 1970, 436 in 1990)

Napa Valley Riesling is as purely Californian as the wine can be and still be of any account at all. The grand grape of the Rhine and Mosel sees far more sun and feels far more heat in Napa than it does in the climate that created it, resulting in wines of a ripe flavor and alcoholic heft unthinkable in the homeland.

That heft is not all bad when cold cracked crab and sourdough French bread, shrimp salad, or roast chicken is at hand. Dry, or just off, Napa Valley Riesling at its best balances exactly the way it should for these kinds of summery eating – all the better if outdoors in the kind of weather that made the wine.

Only a handful of properties deliver both balance and flavor in Riesling, and then only when the winemaker is especially careful to keep the residual sugar at 1 percent, give or take. Less is usually better. Slightly more may not do harm.

Trefethen, untouched by oak and driest of the lot, is as crisply refreshing as Napa Valley Riesling gets, more because of style than source.

Napa's genuinely memorable Rieslings, rare birds, have come from Spring Mountain. Vineyards on these woody slopes give the varietal wine tones of some tart, wild, unnameable berry when it is young, and allow it to keep this smack of fruit as it ages in bottle, rather than sliding off toward fern, or, worse, gasoline. Smith-Madrone is a letter-perfect example.

Trefethen Vineyards' main winery building dates from the 1880s.

Stony Hill Vineyard made estate Riesling every bit as fine until some of its vines were removed in 1991. The peerless property, though, is Draper. In 1968 it was the source of a nearly immortal Riesling for the long-ago Souverain Cellars of Lee Stewart – a wine that was almost as fresh and lively on its 20th birthday as it was coming out of the fermenting tank. That wine has had its nearest echoes in Smith-Madrones and Stony Hills of many a vintage, and surely will have clearer ones still in post-1990 Stony Hills made partly from Draper grapes.

Romantic memories aside, these Rieslings are more likely to hold their own in bottle than they are to grow greater: these are corks to pull before the next vintage rolls around.

Freemark Abbey's "Edelwein" is one of the last survivors of a vogue for botrytis-sweetened Rieslings that began in the mid-1970s and lasted for about a decade. Like many others from the North Coast it tastes of Riesling but feels more like a Sauternes. Grapes come from a small planting near the Napa River at Rutherford. The other ongoing player in that game is Joseph Phelps, using riverside vineyards east of St Helena. Both produce botyrized wines only in highly favorable vintages.

The roster of Riesling producers of all styles has dropped sharply in recent years, as have plantings. Riesling once commanded 1,378 acres in Napa (in 1979). Too much of it was mediocre and worse, an invitation to turn away rather than drink. Most of what is left belongs to growers who care about it.

Benchmarks:

Trefethen Vineyards (estate). **Joseph Phelps** (estate). **Freemark Abbey** (mostly Redbarn and Carpy). **Stony Hill Vineyard** (long estate, after 1990 partly from nearby Draper). **Smith-Madrone** (estate).

Sauvignon Blanc (412 acres in 1970, 2,941 in 1990)

Sauvignon Blanc takes on several shadings in the Napa Valley, starting in the cooler and especially the foggier areas with a flavor not unlike the juices of long-stalked spring meadow grasses, and progressing, as skies grow clearer and warmer, through tastes of sweet, fresh herbs to outright melon.

Everywhere in the valley, it does that neatest of all balancing acts: it tastes indelibly of what it is, yet is quiet about it. Depth, not breadth, carries the day. Yet even the most understated Sauvignon hangs onto the family features no matter how heavy the oak frame. Much of its subtlety is owed to revamped vine training begun in the mid-1980s and still in progress. As in other districts, the trick in Napa is to keep Sauvignon from tasting overgrassy by making it ripen grapes instead of growing new leaves all the way to harvest. The first line of defense is to keep the variety out of rich, slow-draining soils. The next is to use multiple arms so that the crop will be large enough to tax the leaves' capacities.

Silverado Vineyards achieves the perfect example of the juicy spring grasses flavor from its vineyards just at Yountville's south side. A deft seasoning from time in oak masks nothing of Sauvignon's character. Although Robert Mondavi's and Grgich Hills' Fumé Blancs both come from several sources, enough are at Yountville and farther south to give the wines flavors typical of the cooler end of the valley. Mondavi uses a much bolder approach to oak than the others do, but not to the detriment of varietal flavors which win out with ease.

Cakebread Cellars at Oakville and all to its north lean toward melon as the defining regional flavor. St Clement, taking grapes from Pope Valley, is as true to melon as Silverado Vineyards is to juicy grasses. Beaulieu Vineyard, using grapes from Rutherford and Pope Valley, states the case even more clearly because it uses no oak in a wine that positively lilts in youth, then goes silky but not shapeless with a few years in bottle.

Robert Pepi would seem to have planted his Sauvignon Blanc exactly at the boundary, halfway between Oakville and Yountville. In cool vintages the wine inclines gently in the direction of sweet grasses. In warm ones the tilt is to melon. Flora Springs gets its "Soliloquy" from particular blocks close to the river, flanking Oakville Cross Road; rather than leaning one way or the other it somehow manages to capture suggestions of both the herbaceous and fruity sides of the variety.

Frog's Leap with a delicately balanced wine and Spottswoode with a bigger, bolder one, manage to rouse thoughts of herb and melon all at once.

Part of Sauvignon Blanc's age-worthiness compared to Chardonnay's comes from winemaking style – it is subjected less to barrel fermentation, malolactic, and long turns in oak – but another part seems inherent. In any case, one gambles less leaving a sturdy, well-balanced Sauvignon in the cellar for five years than one does tucking away any Chardonnay that has a hint of toast or butter about it.

As many paragons of Sauvignon Blanc as the Napa Valley has, it should have more, and doubtless would had the dictatorship of Chardonnay in the marketplace not squeezed it out of several places where it makes the better wine of the two. The variety also must fight Cabernet Sauvignon and Merlot for well-drained soils all along the valley floor from Oakville north. The net effect is a drop in its plantings since 1988, when it peaked at 3,645 acres. Not one hillside planting of it comes to mind.

Silverado Vineyards (estate). **Flora Springs** "Floreal" (estate). **Flora Springs** "Soliloquy" (estate, from Crossroads Vineyard at Oakville). **Frog's Leap Winery** (assembled). **Grgich Hills** (assembled, mostly from south of Yountville). **Joseph Phelps** (assembled). **Robert Pepi** (estate). **Cakebread Cellars** (estate). **Beaulieu Vineyard** (assembled). **Robert Mondavi** (assembled). **St Clement** (mostly from Pope Valley).

Sémillon (207 acres in 1970, 301 in 1990)

Sémillon came to the Napa Valley well before Prohibition, but kept quiet about it. Varietal Sémillon did not surface until the 1980s, and then from a thin scattering of producers.

The probabilities are that this will always be a niche wine in Napa, one that flourishes in only a few spots. Though evidence is scant for lack of plantings, it appears to ripen too full and soft north of Oakville, and not ripen enough south of Yountville.

As elsewhere in California, most Napa Valley Sémillon has been made as dry table wine rather than botrytized and sweet, but there began to be a small vogue for the latter style in the mid-1980s. A substantial proportion of the tiny crop goes into varietal Sauvignon Blanc, or into Sauvignon-Sémillon proprietaries. These are most probably its long-term roles.

At the top of its form, dry Napa Valley Sémillon has a fullness that Sauvignon Blanc lacks, and flavors of greater depth and subtlety. Texture and taste alike call for monkfish and others of the richer fishes, most especially when cilantro or sweet peppers come into the preparation.

Bernard Portet of Clos du Val, Sémillon's relentless champion in the Napa Valley, marries the flavors of grape and barrel into a seamless whole rather than striking for pure varietal character. More to the point, flavor must follow impeccable balance. Only with 1989 was the winery able to produce an estate bottling of it from the Stag's Leap District. Before that vintage, Clos du Val had gathered grapes from as far afield as the Dunnigan Hills and Paso Robles to fill in the gaps left by the one available Napa source. The California-appellation Sémillon continues under the second, "Joli Val," label.

Gustave Niebaum Chevrier strikes more directly at varietal flavors. Leaner textures result too, perhaps because the grapes come from an especially gravelly vineyard, a literal island caught between two branches of the Napa River just where the Yountville Hills slope down to the valley floor south of town.

Monticello made a couple of estate Sémillons from its vineyards on Big Ranch Road. In a reversal of the usual practice in California, the winery had to use Sauvignon Blanc to fatten what would otherwise have been a blatantly lemony wine. They eventually gave up when they realized they could not get their Sémillon fully ripe even in the warmest years – hard evidence that the variety can flourish only in a narrow range of Napa conditions. Its best shot would seem to be on the higher hillsides, but it is rarely planted there.

For much of its career after Prohibition it went anonymously into the almost vanished, awkwardly named "Chateau" style: off-dry to sweet wines blended with Sauvignon as the majority and Sémillon as the minority. "Chateau Beaulieu" was a major player in that game throughout the 1950s and into the 1960s, before being finally abandoned.

Of the recent attempts to make botrytized sweet wine, most have been promising out of the gate, then quick to stumble. Oxidation has been the highest hurdle, vinegary notes the next. The particular exception, Beringer's Nightingale has aged beautifully, perhaps because botrytis is induced under laboratory conditions after the grapes have been harvested. The technique, developed by the late Myron Nightingale and his wife Alice, avoids both bogeys of late-harvest wines.

Stony Hill Vineyard for years has made a consistently fine, sometimes splendid estate-grown straw wine: "Sémillon du Soleil."

Benchmarks:
Gustave Niebaum Chevrier "Herrick Vineyard." **Clos du Val** (estate).

Sauvignon Blanc-Sémillon blends

Winemakers have tried scores of proportions in Sauvignon-Sémillon blends modeled on dry Graves, sometimes under a fanciful name, sometimes under one or other varietal name. Striking a satisfactory balance anywhere except fifty-fifty has been almost impossible. Most tries have denatured the majority variety rather than adding character to it. But fifty-fifty has, almost without exception, yielded wine clearly in the family yet personable on its own. In all three benchmarks, the flavors of Sauvignon dominate but the fullness of body is Sémillon. The Vichon, in particular, has aged well to five and six years. In the botyrized style, Beringer Vineyards' "Nightingale" (see above) comes as varietal Sémillon in most years, but sometimes is offered as a sixty-forty to fifty-fifty blend of Sémillon and Sauvignon Blanc.

Benchmarks:
Inglenook Gravion (assembled). **Vichon** Chevrignon (assembled). **Merlion** Sauvrier (assembled). **Beringer** Nightingale (estate).

Other varieties

Colombard (118 acres in 1990), Gray Riesling (55), Muscat Blanc (79), Melon and/or Pinot Blanc (131).

Sparkling Wines

In 1965 Schramsberg led the Napa Valley and the rest of California back toward a long-lost focus on Chardonnay and Pinot Noir as the major grape varieties for classic-method sparkling wine. Domaine Chandon joined the fray in 1973, Mumm Napa Valley in 1985.

Dry, sunny Napa seems an unlikely place for sparkling wines, but its best compete at the pinnacle, and do so in a remarkable range of styles. Schramsberg comes very close to opulent; Mumm Napa Valley takes the opposite approach with lean, crisp, cleansing wines; Chandon holds the middle ground.

All three big names look primarily to vineyards from Yountville south, especially ones on or near Big Ranch Road and in Carneros. However, they also use grapes from mountainous vineyards all the way north to Calistoga. Pinot Noir plays a slightly bigger part here than elsewhere on the North Coast, obviously in Blanc de Noirs, but in Bruts as well, because Napa Chardonnay makes sparkling wines that balk at developing the first hint of maturity.

Benchmarks:
Chandon n.v. Brut "Etoile." **Mumm** Brut "Vintage Reserve." **Schramsberg** vintage Brut "Reserve." **Schramsberg** vintage "Blanc de Noirs." **Chandon** n.v. Brut "Reserve." **Mumm** n.v. Brut "Cuvée de Prestige." **Chandon** n.v. "Blanc de Noirs."

Red Wine Varieties

Within its small compass, the Napa Valley is a diverse enough environment to do well with half a dozen black grape varieties from scattered origins, Gamay, Merlot, Petite Sirah, Pinot Noir and Zinfandel among them. However, in the years since 1972 Cabernet Sauvignon has begun to exert ever more pressure on all the rest, to the degree that it and its traditional cousins from Bordeaux now reign supreme among red wine grapes in all the valley above Napa city. Other established varieties hang on by the will of a few who battle the odds. Sangiovese and Syrah are the two greatest new hopes for those who wish to do something, anything, other than Cabernet.

Cabernet Sauvignon (1,568 acres in 1970, 7,385 in 1990)
A review of the longest list of benchmark wines in this atlas instantly suggests that it could be doubled at the least, probably trebled, and for one particular reason: Cabernet Sauvignon grows well in so many vineyards, making competition so severe, that growers and winemakers are forever working to raise the bar another notch before the next round of jumps. Tough as the wars may be, virtually no winery excuses itself from the fray.

The die was cast no later than the 1950s, when Beaulieu Vineyard, Inglenook Vineyards, and Charles Krug commanded the Napa stage with Cabernets that rang true to place and variety, yet managed to differ among themselves in all the details. (Louis M. Martini, the fourth player, was presaging Sonoma's eventual rise with Cabernets from Monte Rosso and Carneros.) Anyone who wished to challenge for a place in the front ranks had to show well against this quartet.

Though the winemaking was remarkably different among the four, every one of the Napa wines showed the essence of Cabernet in this valley: understated but unmistakable herbaceous notes married with a sunny ripeness, ending as old wines with hints of raisin flavors, a healthy level of alcohol, and firm tannins. As unblended Cabernets with little or no oak aging, the Krugs and Inglenooks still had enough depth to gain in bottle for five or six years, and to stay in mid-season form for 10 easily, 15 most of the time, and close to forever every now and again. Beaulieu Vineyards added American oak to the recipe without altering the basics.

With the 1960s came an explosion of styles: first French oak barrels were used, then French oak barrels by region of origin and toasting level, also mixtures of French and American oak. Time in barrel stretched here, shrank there. Extended postfermentation macerations joined the bag of tricks.

Merlot came to the party early in the 1970s, when "blending for complexity" began to replace medium toast Nevers oak as a buzz-phrase. It was followed by Cabernet Franc, and then by the Petit Verdot and Malbec varieties, which arrived with the end of the 1980s.

Add all of these effects together and they do not count for as much as the increase in combinations of exposure, drainage, fog, and soils that came with the tenfold increase in vineyards and the hugely broadened range in which they grow. Attentive tasters recognized subtle shadings among Cabernets from different parts of Napa early in the proliferation. One of the earliest comparisons contrasts firmly tannic Rutherford wines with softer Cabernets from the Stag's Leap District, Californian counterparts to Pauillac and Margaux. Other localisms exist. Vines to the east of Rutherford and Oakville usually taste more

of herbs than do those to the west. Calistoga gives every sign of a particular propensity for rock-hard tannins. More than a few of Napa's front-rank Cabernets are cogent reminders that land use is not yet mature anywhere in California, leaving some splendid vineyards to give their grapes to assembled wines.

The devil in the dance hall is the American willingness to overdo. If a little tannin makes a 10-year wine, a lot of it must make one good for 40. If oak adds depth, a lot of it must lead to still greater glories. All too many fine vineyards are still being rendered invisible in wines left too long in too much new oak. All too many modest vineyards are being forced to produce empty giants made of nothing but tannin for bones and oak sap for blood. The mind set is as if all were First Growth, nothing Bourgeois Supérieur.

If any one or two wines could serve as the benchmark of benchmarks, Raymond Vineyards' or Louis M. Martini's "Napa Valley Reserve" would most likely fit that bill. Both taste clearly of Cabernet as it grows in Napa; both have the sort of tannic structure that should, by logic, come from some point exactly halfway between Rutherford and the Stag's Leap District, but in fact can come from any point on the compass, or a collection of them. Robert Mondavi's regular bottling is much like them, except more forcefully tinted by the taste of French oak. Ditto Beaulieu Vineyard's "Rutherford," with the difference that American oak is the seasoning. The rest follow similarly cautious styles, but come from individual vineyards.
Benchmarks:
Raymond Napa Valley (assembled). **Robert Mondavi** Napa Valley (assembled). **Clos du Val** Napa Valley (assembled; added with '89).
From Calistoga-St Helena
Spottswoode Winery (estate bottled, at the foot of the hills west of town).

Grace Family Vineyard (estate, on a west-side slope at the north side of St Helena). **Tudal Winery** Napa Valley (near the Napa River on Big Tree Road). **Sterling Vineyards** "Diamond Mountain Ranch" (high in the western hills near Calistoga).
From Rutherford-Oakville
Beaulieu Vineyard "Georges de Latour Private Reserve" (estate grown from BV No. 1 and BV No. 2, both west of Highway 29). **Freemark Abbey** Napa Valley (from the closely clustered Wood, Carpy and Red Barn ranches between Rutherford and Conn Creek). **Freemark Abbey** "Cabernet Bosche" (Bosche vineyard adjoins BV No. 1). **Freemark Abbey** "Sycamore Vineyard" (at the foot of the western hills south of Rutherford). **Caymus Vineyard** (based in the estate and a St Helena neighbor to Spottswoode). **Caymus Vineyard** "Special Selection" (estate, east of Rutherford between Conn Creek and Silverado Trail).
From Yountville-Napa
Trefethen (estate). **Charles Krug** "Vintage Selection" (since '85 Slinsen ranch to the south of Yountville).
From Stag's Leap District
Clos du Val (estate). **Chimney Rock** (estate). **Shafer** Napa Valley (anchored in the estate). **Shafer** "Hillside Select" (estate). **Silverado Vineyards** (estate). **Stag's Leap Wine Cellars** "Stag's Leap Vineyard" (estate). **Pine Ridge** "Stag's Leap Cuvée" (estate, adjoining Stag's Leap Vineyard at its southwest corner).
From Mt Veeder
Mt Veeder Vineyards (estate). **Hess Collection** (estate). **Mayacamas** (estate or estate plus a neighbor).
From the eastern hills
Chappellet Vineyard (estate). **Louis M. Martini** Napa Valley "Reserve" (anchored in Glen Oaks in Chiles Valley).

Cabernet Franc (9 acres in 1970, 499 in 1990)
Fewer than a dozen producers have been trying in recent times to make Cabernet Franc into a star in its own right. Thus far, the grape variety seems more at home as a spice to Cabernet Sauvignon than as the basis of varietal wine. More plantings and further trials may change that.

Cabernet-based blends
The siren song of Bordeaux will not get out of the ears of Napa winery owners any more than it bypasses their rivals in newer districts. The idea that, somehow, oak-dotted slopes and olive groves bespeak a Bordelais climate has led, is leading, and will continue to lead growers and winemakers back to Merlot, Cabernet Franc, Petit Verdot and even Malbec as companions for Cabernet Sauvignon. The sincerest form of flattery . . .

Joseph Phelps' dark, emphatic "Insignia" launched the breed in 1974, although the original intention was that the best wine of the year would go into it, regardless of variety. Supple, polished Opus One, the joint venture of Robert Mondavi and Philippine de Rothschild, succeeds beautifully, in no small part because the proportion of Cabernet Sauvignon dwarfs the rest of the tribe. The partners are moving toward estate status for the wine; through the first decade it came from Mondavi vineyards neighboring Martha's Vineyard at Oakville. Franciscan "Meritage" from its estate at Oakville takes the same path of maximizing Cabernet Sauvignon. Flora Springs "Trilogy," a surprisingly sturdy, flavorful third-third-third marriage of Cabernet Sauvignon, Cabernet Franc, and Merlot, demonstrates the opposite approach to blending with more success than most. It comes from vines at the winery just south of St Helena. "Cain Five," true to its name, uses all five of the most familiar red

Left: Shafer Vineyards, in the foreground, are the hilliest plantings in the Stag's Leap District, which stretches away to the south beneath a looming wall of basaltic stone.

Above left: Kerosene or diesel-burning smudge pots are the oldest mechanical defense against spring frosts.

Above: Sterling Vineyards draws on monasteries in the Greek Isles for its architectural basis. It sits atop one of several plugs of volcanic rock in the Napa Valley.

varieties of Bordeaux. It follows no fixed proportions, but, like "Trilogy," achieves admirable depth of flavor in spite of giving Cabernet Sauvignon a less than dominant role.

Gamay (771 acres in 1970, 388 in 1990)
As elsewhere, Gamay, or Napa Gamay, is almost surely two things in Napa. Recent plantings are the Gamay Noir à Jus Blanc of Beaujolais. Older ones may be that or descendants of a variety known in France as Valdiguié. The differences are not vast. Gamay Noir's wines have a lighter, fresher quality. Valdiguié's look darker, feel more tannic, and taste more vinous than fruity.

The Charles F. Shaw winery practices a near monopoly on Napa appellation Gamay. Its wines do exactly what a good Beaujolais Villages does: balance a bit of substance with a good deal of lightheartedness. A steak, a summer's eve, and a bottle of this wine bring some rewards worth having at a price worth paying.

Merlot (63 acres in 1970, 1,454 in 1990)
Many scholars of the subject call Merlot the next most site-specific variety after Pinot Noir, usually in somewhat despairing tones. Experience to date in the Napa Valley would bear them out. A considerable acreage has yielded very few memorable wines over the past 15 years. All too often Merlot has been good for nothing more than weakening the character of those Cabernet Sauvignons and Meritages with which it is blended "to add complexity." The very best of them, however, beg to be noticed.

Though the final votes are decades from being cast, early evidence focuses sharply in the southeast quarter of the valley, in and above the Stag's Leap District. Quail Ridge Merlots wreathe themselves in such delicate perfumes of wood violets that their firmness on the palate almost escapes notice. Inglenook's "Reserve" comes closest to it. Clos du Val and Shafer hint at the same perfumes, but are softer and fuller. Watchers also have their eyes on nearby Carneros (*see* pages 60-65).

Calistoga, however odd it may seem, also merits further watching for wines of less delicate flavors and still greater austerity, if Sterling Vineyards and the "Three Palms" edition of Duckhorn Merlot are role models.
Benchmarks:
Quail Ridge Napa Valley (primarily or all Vandendriessche vineyard in Soda Canyon between Stag's Leap and Napa). **Inglenook** Napa Valley Reserve (assembled). **Sterling Vineyards** Napa Valley (assembled from winery-owned vineyards). **Clos du Val** (estate). **Shafer** Napa Valley (mostly estate plus a neighbor).

Petite Sirah (1,378 acres in 1970, 474 in 1990)
Of all the recent lost causes in Napa, Petite Sirah is the greatest. The wines need years in bottle to become truly inviting (although judicious blending hastens maturity at no cost to character). More difficult, they must compete with Cabernet Sauvignon which fetches two or three times the price with less trouble.

Varietal Petite Sirah is seen but rarely nowadays, although vineyards still linger because they can be used to salvage rain-diluted Cabernet Sauvignon or form a rock-solid base for red table wine.

Napa Valley Petite Sirahs taste faintly of black pepper, and are oak-sturdy with tannins, suited in youth to ribs and other barbecue foods. Even when they are made in a temperate style,

Clos Pegase, one of many architectural monuments in the Napa Valley, sits just to the south of a glider port reaching to downtown Calistoga. The view is from Sterling Vineyards.

five years barely suffices to give them enough grace notes and softness to be polite company to refined dishes. Some have not been over-aged at 20.

The comparatively gentle Louis M. Martini Napa Valley Reserve epitomizes the region these days. Gone are Freemark Abbey's dark, hauntingly cedary and earthy wonders from the York Creek Vineyard near Stony Hill, although lingering bottles of the 1975 make one wonder why the market is so heedless. Gone too the Stag's Leap Wine Cellars Petite Sirah, with its softening dollop of Pinot Noir, and Robert Mondavi's heady, well-oaked model.

Pinot Noir (603 acres in 1970, 2,475 in 1990)
Once as prominent around Oakville and Rutherford as Cabernet Sauvignon, Pinot Noir has been beating a steady

adjudge, it is foolhardy to attempt a characterization of Napa Sangiovese (Sangioveto Grosso), and yet, all available evidence points to probable success. Wines from young vines show consistent balance and engaging flavors despite coming from vintages as dissimilar as 1988 and 1989, and properties with such differing soils and exposures as Pepi at Yountville, Atlas Peak in the eastern hills above Stag's Leap, Rodeno in Chiles Valley. Much remains to be done, but Sangiovese is one to watch.

Zinfandel (857 acres in 1970, 1,885 in 1990)
At the start of the 1990s Napa Zinfandel found itself at a most peculiar crossroads. Acreage was going up, but the roster of producers was shrinking. Not only that, three major wineries were looking elsewhere for the grape: Sutter Home, especially to Amador County, Grgich Hills and Joseph Phelps to Sonoma.

One wonders where the crop goes with so little red-blooded Zinfandel available. Some gets swallowed into North Coast appellation wines, a good bit more is made into White Zinfandel, the real thing is left somewhere between rarity and endangered species. A shame, for Napa grows it well, especially at Oakville, in the eastern hills from Lake Hennessy to Howell Mountain, and in scattered spots from St Helena to Calistoga and beyond. At its best, it shows berrylike flavors just slightly tamer than those of the Alexander and Dry Creek valleys, and – odd though it may seem – rounder tannins too. On the other side of the coin, first-rate Napa Zinfandels taste more richly of berry and feel firmer than Mendocino County's from around Ukiah.

Frog's Leap consistently manages a certain delicacy of texture, almost an airiness, which makes the intensity of Zinfandel flavor a bit of a shock, welcome, but not predictable; oak figures as a grace note, never more. Franciscan has come to the game too recently to be a genuine benchmark, but the similarity of flavor and balance to Frog's Leap's leads straight to the conclusion that what it has done twice from its Oakville Estate it will be able to do again and again. The note from new French oak shouts at times, but not so much as to disturb the rest of the choir. Burgess makes a big wine all around. It has weight, alcohol, and plenty of oak flavors along with the taste of berries from its grapes. Caymus is rather in the same school, but slightly more restrained about it.

Most of the other producers come to rest between the poles of Frog's Leap and Burgess. A few let the grape get away. It will, here as much as anywhere else, overripen until its wine turns porty. Another consistent failing is too much oak. Zinfandel, for all the intensity its grapes bring to a wine, has a flavor that can disappear among the trees in a trice.
Benchmarks:
Frog's Leap Winery (from two vineyards north of St Helena plus one near Zinfandel Lane). **Franciscan Vineyards** (estate bottled from the winery's Oakville Estate). **Burgess Cellars** (from several vineyards in or near Howell Mountain sub-AVA). **Caymus Vineyards** (assembled, mostly from hill vineyards east of Rutherford). **Clos du Val** (estate from Stag's Leap District).

Other varieties
Pinot Meunier (130 acres in 1990) is mostly used in Carneros for sparkling wines; Syrah (25 acres in 1990) is an almost private project of Joseph Phelps; progress is slow. Alicante Bouschet, Carignane, Early Burgundy, Grand Noir, Mondeuse, and other lesser varieties all disappeared from acreage reports during the 1980s.

retreat into the Carneros region (*see* pages 60-65) since the mid-1980s at the latest. By 1990, the migration made it almost impossible to find a bottle of Napa Valley appellation Pinot Noir that was not half or more produced from Carneros-grown grapes. The one reliable exception is Monticello Vineyards' plummy, full-bodied softy from their estate on Big Ranch Road.

The old up-valley Pinots had their fascinations, although most resembled Rhônes more than burgundies if they resembled any other wine at all. That is, they had plenty of color and plenty of tannin to go with it, plus flavors that edged in the direction of dried fruits.

A substantial amount of the Pinot Noir still in the ground north of Carneros is harvested early for sparkling wines; most of that is along Big Ranch Road and north as far as Yountville Cross Road.

Sangiovese (0 in 1970, 130 acres in 1990)
With fewer than five vintages from fewer than four wineries to

Napa Valley AVA

Established: January 1, 1983
Total area: 300,000 acres
Area in vineyard: 33,200 acres
Wineries: approximately 220
Principal towns: Napa, Yountville, St Helena, Calistoga

In the not so distant past, Napa Valley meant to most wine buffs Cabernet Sauvignon from Rutherford, or very near. Any other grape from any other part of the county was tangential. As plantings expanded and Chardonnay caught on, people began to think more complicated thoughts.

History and reputation put Napa first in line in California for appellation status just when viticultural confusion reached its apogee. In 1980, a majority of the winemakers went into the BATF (Bureau of Alcohol, Tobacco, and Firearms) hearings with a proposal to draw the boundaries tight around the drainage basin of the Napa River. Independent growers with a major investment in Pope Valley, well to the east, took exception. The winemakers softened, and the expansionists carried the day. Only the arid, stony northeast corner of the county, where rattlesnakes have a hard time making a living, was excluded by the final boundaries.

A decade later, "Napa Valley" is taken as one of those blanket expressions that covers as much as it reveals, while ensuing sub-appellations called Howell Mountain, Spring Mountain, Rutherford, Oakville, Stag's Leap District, Mt Veeder, and Atlas Peak do not always conform to the way grape varieties are distributed, but do reflect geographical realities.

The immediate Napa River Valley, the floor and the lower elevations looking onto it from each side, has a coherence, a logic. North of Yountville, Cabernet reigns. South of that town Chardonnay has the strongest hand everywhere except in the Stag's Leap District, where Cabernet again rules. Cabernet intrudes into Chardonnay country and vice versa, but the broad picture holds well. Other varieties have their moments in both the upper and lower valley, Sauvignon Blanc and Zinfandel foremost among them. Riesling, Gewürztraminer and Petite Sirah could be less far behind than they are if the market would let them. Merlot is mainly an enigma. Sangiovese and Syrah are new prospects.

The western hills produce a less clear picture, partly because hilly terrain always does, but also because a long gap in their history leaves them less tested than the valley floor

On the lower slopes of Spring Mountain, the vines of Cain Cellars are a Napa rarity: an estate planted with the five major varieties of the Médoc, not just Cabernet Sauvignon.

around Rutherford. White grapes traditionally have held sway at the upper elevations of Mt Veeder and Spring Mountain – Riesling longest, Chardonnay more recently but also more vigorously. Cabernet becomes more prominent down lower.

If the western hills are less clear than the valley floor, the east side of the county approaches the opaque. In the first range of hills to the east, Howell Mountain has a long history of reds, especially Zinfandel. Cabernet Sauvignon and Merlot have been crowding in during the past decade. Increasingly, though, Chardonnay pushes against them all. In the far broader eastern vales, Pope Valley is a proven performer only with Sauvignon Blanc, but begins to be a bright hope with Sangiovese. It is at worst adequate with Chardonnay, Cabernet Sauvignon, and Merlot. Chiles Valley, separated from Pope Valley by a rise of 10 feet or so, has been harder yet to pin down. Zinfandel ripens with difficulty in several spots, yet is a ready ripener elsewhere. Cabernet Sauvignon sometimes seems more at home. Again, Chardonnay tends to be no worse than passable, but that is hardly news in a state where it does well enough to get by almost everywhere. Farther south and east, Wooden Valley's heavyweight Cabernets are signs that this is the warmest part of the appellation, though lack of official weather reporting stations makes this guesswork.

And so back to the main valleys and the hills that frame it. The simple theory of northern Cabernet and southern Chardonnay has a thousand and one holes in it. In this valley, alone in all of California, hard experience says that individual property boundaries might truly mean something, that next door neighbors are not equals in the growing of one variety or another because of exposure or drainage or the exact structure of the soil.

It is unlikely that anyone will ever troop through the Napa Valley making confident generalities about the soils as they do in the Médoc or along the Côte d'Or. It is a by-product of the on-going side-swipe collision between the Pacific and North American plates. Some of its steeper mountains used to be flat sea floor. Other, smaller hills are volcanic bubbles that stick up through the old seabed. Impressively large chunks are like flotsam on a beach, transported from so far away that no one knows where the rest of that part might be found. One of the most beautiful maps of the valley ever drawn shows more than 30 basic soil types. It dates from 1935; geologists have been elaborating on the picture ever since. On top of this, erosion. On top of that, just about 360 degrees of exposure. Still another layer, a near-whimsical pattern of marine air flowing in from the Pacific Ocean.

Calistoga to St Helena

If the Napa Valley were a Brobdingnagian hole of golf, with the tee at Napa and the green at Calistoga, it would be a miserably unfair par four, dog-leg left. To have any chance at all of making par, the tee shot would have to hug the right side and just reach St Helena, then the second would almost have to carry the green on the fly because the valley floor narrows until little is left that could be called fairway and a lot that could be called rough.

Vineyards thin out markedly and turn small in the eight miles between St Helena and Calistoga. Nearly as many acres are up in the hills on either side as are down on the valley floor, or the slants that break it into pieces.

The dog-leg is first formed by a long, bony ridge running

Old-time architecture flavors the main street of Calistoga, at the Napa Valley's northern end. The village is a favorite with tourists for its restaurants and spas.

right under Freemark Abbey's winery, then by a steep, wooded hill that crowds in against Frog's Leap. Beyond this point, the western hills are more southern hills, the exposures on them less east and more north. The upper slopes are known collectively as Spring Mountain, home most famously of Stony Hill Vineyard, but also of several other vineyards worth keeping in mind. The eastern hills turn right along with those on the west, but the vineyards in them do not. Howell Mountain strays eastward from the main valley, the planted parts of it on a near-level upland between the first and second steep rises of the Napa Valley's east hills.

All this tortured terrain produces exactly the kind of anomalies that you would expect. Somewhere between St Helena and Calistoga is the warmest part of the main valley, yet the vineyard which sparkling wine specialist Mumm Napa Valley picks last each year is hidden away in a box canyon northwest of Calistoga. It is little more than a stone's throw from Storybook Mountain, where Zinfandel can be overripened without going to a lot of extra trouble.

Among easily recognizable vineyards in the main valley, almost every one that stands out from the crowd is planted with Cabernet Sauvignon. Spottswoode, Grace Family, Tudal, and Chateau Montelena produce estate wines. Eisele yields a single-vineyard Cabernet for Joseph Phelps. They are scattered one from another, this quintet, in a district where Napa's terrain reaches its pinnacle of untidiness. Spottswoode, fairly flat, is ringed by residential St Helena. A mile or so north of town, tiny Grace Family tips fairly sharply to the east, part of the ridge that causes the valley to dog-leg left. Tudal, another and longer mile north, lies flat right along the riverbank, a miracle of drainage. Equally flat Chateau Montelena hugs the foot of Mt St Helena. Eisele sits on the floor of a little box canyon south of the palisades at Calistoga. Two hillside plantings of some note cling to Diamond Mountain, one of the best-defined hills west above Calistoga. Diamond Creek grows nothing but Cabernet, while Sterling Vineyards' Diamond Mountain Ranch is working on a reputation for Cabernet and Chardonnay.

Cabernet Sauvignon's cousins began gaining a foothold in northernmost Napa Valley in the mid-1980s, Merlot and

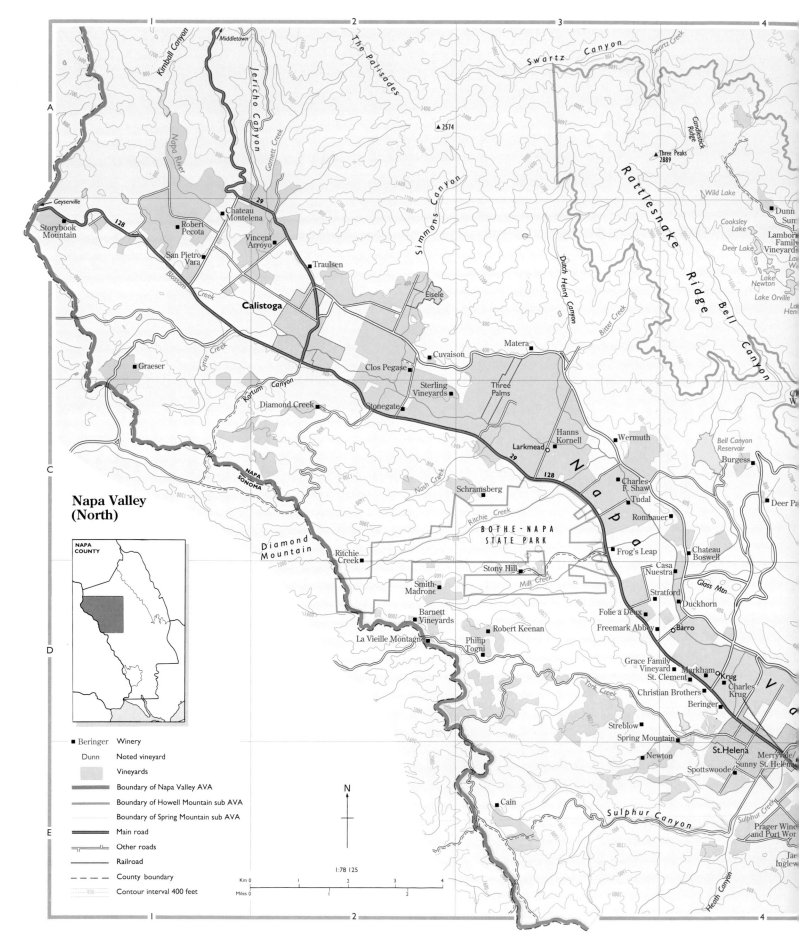

Napa Valley (North)

NAPA COUNTY

Legend

- ■ Beringer — Winery
- Dunn — Noted vineyard
- Vineyards
- Boundary of Napa Valley AVA
- Boundary of Howell Mountain sub AVA
- Boundary of Spring Mountain sub AVA
- Main road
- Other roads
- Railroad
- County boundary
- Contour interval 400 feet

1:78 125

Km 0 1 2 3 4
Miles 0 1 2

N

Map labels

Middletown · Kimball Canyon · Jericho Canyon · Garnett Creek · The Palisades · Simmons Canyon · Swartz Canyon · Swartz Creek · Napa River · ▲ 2574 · Candlestick Ridge · ▲ Three Peaks 2889 · Rattlesnake Ridge · Bell Canyon · Wild Lake · Cooksley Lake · Deer Lake · Lake Newton · Lake Orville · Geyserville · 128 · 29 · Storybook Mountain · Robert Pecota · Chateau Montelena · Vincent Arroyo · San Pietro Vara · Traulsen · Eisele · Dutch Henry Canyon · Bitter Creek · Calistoga · Dunn · Lambor Family Vineyards · Graeser · Cyrus Creek · Blossom Creek · Kortum Canyon · Matera · Cuvaison · Clos Pegase · Sterling Vineyards · Three Palms · Diamond Creek · Stonegate · NAPA SONOMA · Larkmead · Hanns Kornell · Wermuth · 29 · 128 · Bell Canyon Reservoir · Burgess · Deer Pa · Schramsberg · Ritchie Creek · Charles F. Shaw · Tudal · Rombauer · Nash Creek · BOTHE-NAPA STATE PARK · Diamond Mountain · Ritchie Creek · Stony Hill · Mill Creek · Frog's Leap · Chateau Boswell · Casa Nuestra · Glass Mtn · Stratford · Duckhorn · Smith-Madrone · Folie a Deux · Barro · Barnett Vineyards · Robert Keenan · Freemark Abbey · La Vieille Montagne · Philip Togni · Grace Family Vineyard · St. Clement · Markham · Krug · Charles Krug · York Creek · Christian Brothers · Beringer · Streblow · Spring Mountain · Newton · St. Helena · Merryvale / Sunny St. Helena · Spottswoode · Cain · Sulphur Canyon · Prager Wine and Port Wor · Heath Canyon · Sulphur Creek · Jac Inglew

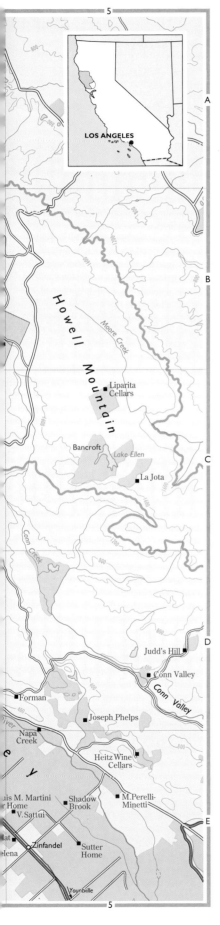

Cabernet Franc more than Petite Verdot or Malbec. Sterling Vineyards has been notably active on its own and as a collaborator with independent growers, the best known of them being Three Palms.

Three Palms is not a long way south of Eisele, but might as well be. It is more exposed, and almost as rocky as a river bed, in spite of which it is planted more with Merlot and Cabernet Franc than Cabernet Sauvignon, and has gained most of its fame for the first-named – thus running hard against the theory that Merlot belongs in heavier soils than Cabernet.

All of these borrowings from Bordeaux are relatively recent. Their forerunners, where they had any, were planted willy-nilly with Colombard, Petite Sirah, Charbono, even "mixed black," as old weigh tags used to read when nobody could figure out exactly what was what.

If the valley floor sticks mostly to Cabernet, it still makes one stop and think just a bit about Zinfandel and Gamay, and mourn just a little for Charbono. It would seem to offer good prospects for Sauvignon Blanc and Sémillon, but if it does they have gone largely unrealized.

Some of Napa's most characterful Zinfandels come from vineyards scattered at least as insensibly as the Cabernet properties. Storybook Mountain, being estate-grown, is most obvious. Also, two independent growers near Frog's Leap sell their grapes to that winery for its sterling Zinfandel.

Spring Mountain sub-AVA

Proposed: 1992
Total area: 8,600 acres
Area in vineyard: 800 acres
Wineries: 13
Principal town: None (St Helena adjoins)
The long slope up from St Helena to the ridge-pole of the Mayacamas has produced several Rieslings near enough to

Top: The product of an architectural competition, Clos Pegase is also nearly as much art gallery as winery, its owner having filled it with paintings and sculpture from his collection.
Above: Barrels of French oak fill several aging cellars at Sterling Vineyards.

43

celestial that, in the best of all possible worlds, quite a bit of it would be planted up where the redwoods have been cleared away. Some, arguably the best of it, actually is. The definitive vineyard is Draper, once a source for the oldest incarnation of Souverain Cellars, now a backbone for Stony Hill. Smith-Madrone comes very near matching its pace.

However, Chardonnay claims ever more of the available land, and not unreasonably. Fence-line neighbors Stony Hill and Smith-Madrone have been impressive, using completely different styles. Robert Keenan and others have also done well.

Cabernet Sauvignon and Merlot take over lower down, in Cain Cellars' vineyard, and Newton's, to name just two.

Howell Mountain sub-AVA

Established: January 30, 1984
Total area: 14,080 acres
Area in vineyard: 198 acres
Wineries: 6
Principal town: Angwin

History gives Zinfandel the palm on Howell Mountain. Reformers want Cabernet Sauvignon and/or Merlot in its place. Revolutionaries would dump both for Chardonnay.

For years, Ridge Vineyards reached into a vineyard long called Park-Muscatine for its Howell Mountain Zinfandel. The indigenous flag-bearer is Lamborn Family Vineyards. Both properties are toward the north end of the appellation.

Dunn Vineyards, once neighbor to Park-Muscatine, is now its owner. Owner-winemaker Randall Dunn was the first and remains the foremost advocate of Cabernet Sauvignon (and nothing but Cabernet Sauvignon) on these heights. La Jota, almost at the opposite end of the appellation, is Dunn's most visible ally in putting Cabernet first, although its owners have allowed a promising planting of Viognier to divide their loyalties.

Chardonnay has blossomed later than Cabernet, but, in numbers at least, more fully. Chateau Woltner brought instant attention to the idea by charging three times the going Chardonnay price for its first vintage, 1986, and widening the gap not long after when it asked $58 a bottle for its "Titus" and "Frederique" bottlings.

The rolling vineyards of Chateau Woltner are close to the western boundary of the appellation, at about the mid-point of the north-south axis. Near neighbors Bancroft and Liparita sit not far from La Jota, toward the southern end of Howell Mountain. Both were grower labels as the 1990s began, and both have taken more modest approaches to pricing their Chardonnay than the French-owned Woltner. Both also are growing substantial plantings of Merlot in the red earth common to most of the district.

Most of the appellation is, if not flat, fairly level at about 1,800 feet, table height more than bench. Where slopes give a particular orientation, it is most likely west or southwest. Unusually for the eastern hills, conifers rather than oak-dotted meadowlands prevail where man has not altered the landscape. On this evidence, in particular, have come the proponents of Chardonnay.

Rather ironically, the district is settled almost exclusively by teetotal Seventh Day Adventists, who have a college at Angwin and a hospital just downhill from there.

Rutherford to Oakville

As a state of mind, the Napa Valley began at Rutherford, probably around 1900 when Beaulieu Vineyard and Inglenook Vineyards first went head-to-head with Cabernet Sauvignon, and certainly no later than 1933, when the same two wineries resumed a rivalry interrupted by Prohibition.

Their original vineyards sit side by side on a wide, slowly sloping fan of gravel loam that drains quickly and slips into the shadow of Mt St John by mid-afternoon, both qualities benefiting Cabernet. Gustave Niebaum had both Cabernet and Merlot in his Inglenook vineyard by 1884 at the latest. Georges de Latour devoted much of "BV No. 1" to Cabernet as soon as he bought it in 1900. The two immediately began a King-of-the-Hill competition to see who could make the better wine.

John Daniel had inherited Inglenook by the time Prohibition ended, and installed George Deuer as winemaker. De Latour hired André Tchelistcheff soon after. Their approaches differed widely. Deuer made dark, tannic wines in 1,500-gallon oak ovals at Inglenook. Tchelistcheff made supple ones in 50-gallon American oak barrels at Beaulieu. Neither conceded an inch.

Within a fairly short time, Daniel acquired the vineyard he called Napanook, well south along the alluvial fan at Yountville, and De Latour bought what is now BV No. 2, at Oakville. The next years first saw a filling-in of Cabernet plantings along the west side, then a spilling out to other parts of the valley. The old King-of-the-Hill contest, likewise, gained participants and loosened its boundaries, but it still governs the way people feel about making wine in this valley.

Cabernet Sauvignon still rules the mid-section of the valley: other varieties are planted in Rutherford only after Cabernet fails to make the grade. Oakville, however, blessed or cursed by versatility, grows every grape for which Napa is famed.

Because Inglenook and Beaulieu were on the west side, there has been a long-standing tendency to think of it separately. The shorthand term is Rutherford Bench. Some would use it to re-divide Rutherford and Oakville into bench and not-bench. Others would have the heads of those who would have a bench.

One source of dissension is that this bench is not quite a bench – it lacks a little drop to mark its edge. There may be one

Caves at Beringer, hand-dug by Chinese laborers in the 1880s, hold bottles of Cabernet Sauvignon dating back to the 1930s.

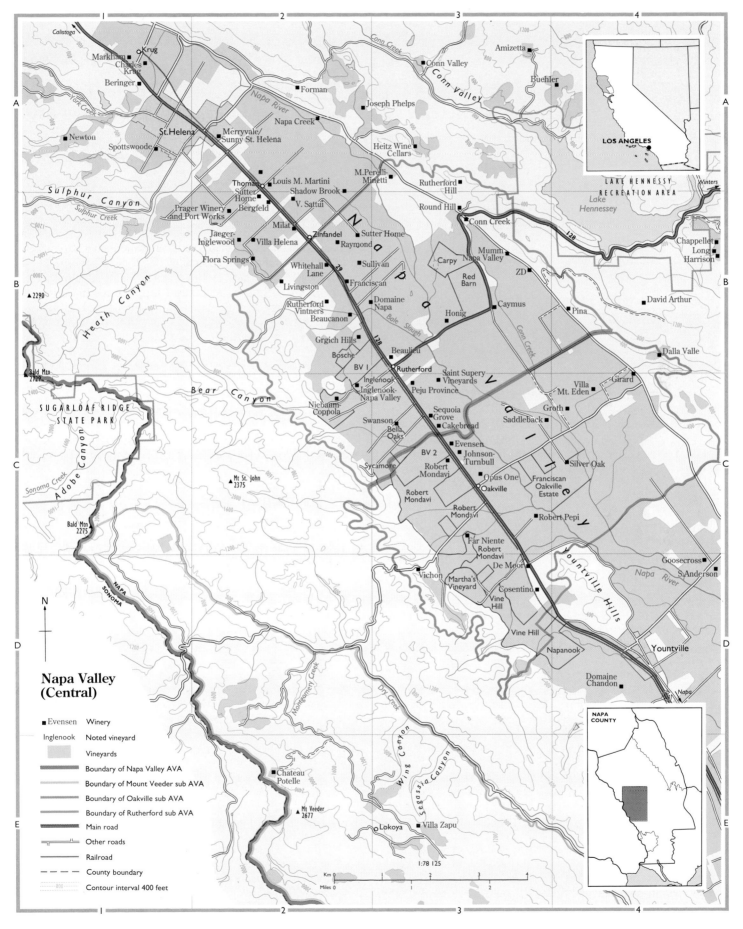

Napa Valley
(Central)

- ■ Evensen   Winery
- *Inglenook*   Noted vineyard
-    Vineyards
- ▬▬▬   Boundary of Napa Valley AVA
- ▬▬▬   Boundary of Mount Veeder sub AVA
- ▬▬▬   Boundary of Oakville sub AVA
- ▬▬▬   Boundary of Rutherford sub AVA
- ▬▬▬   Main road
-    Other roads
- ▬▬▬   Railroad
- – – –   County boundary
-    Contour interval 400 feet

1:78 125

Km 0   1   2   3   4

Miles 0   1   2

LOS ANGELES

LAKE HENNESSY
RECREATION AREA

NAPA COUNTY

45

Picnic tables for visitors are a common feature at many of Napa's wineries. This one flanks the aging cellars of the Vichon Winery in the hills directly east of Oakville.

buried under the alluvium; if so, no one has located it. Still, long-time growers and winemakers believe that exposure and especially soils change at a certain point. John Daniel, when he owned Inglenook, used to look for straggling prune orchards. André Tchelistcheff used Highway 29 as a ready marker. Louis P. Martini keeps in his mind a wavy line that stays a certain distance from the Napa River. The original Rutherford AVA petition sought sub-sub-appellation status for the benchlands, but the idea was dropped before final hearings began.

North and south raise less argument. At the south, proponents took the Yountville Hills as a boundary, on the grounds that they are a considerable dam to marine air flowing up-valley from San Pablo Bay. They leak, to be sure, but they also cause a measurable break from cooler to warmer afternoons, perhaps marked by Napanook, more surely by Bob Phillip's Vine Hill Ranch directly to the north.

The northern limit of Rutherford is both more and less abstract than the Yountville Hills. It follows Zinfandel Lane, concrete enough in itself, but not any kind of transition point in soil or climate. The lane does mark a gap in vineyards along the bench after Flora Springs home vineyard.

Rutherford sub-AVA

Proposed: 1991
Total area: 6,650 acres
Area in vineyard: 5,000 acres
Wineries: 30
Principal town: Rutherford (St Helena proximate)

Rutherford and Cabernet Sauvignon come within a hair's breadth of being synonymous in the Napa Valley. No other variety has managed to crowd into the highest ranks of wines from the vineyards surrounding this modest village.

Indeed, the proven vineyards of the region – Inglenook, Niebaum, BV No. 1, Bosche, Sycamore, Bella Oaks – owe all their fame to Cabernet Sauvignon. The list continues to grow. Most of these treasured properties run in a long, straight line along the base of the western hills, confirming the notion of a Rutherford Bench in the hearts of those who want one.

Cabernet's preeminence here is no new idea. Captain Gustave Niebaum's 19th-century Inglenook made Cabernets in 1887, 1888 and 1889 – these wines still survive. Georges de Latour (himself) began growing Cabernet in what is now BV No. 1 in 1900, and knew what he had. Other names, now gone, followed their suit around the time the century turned.

It is now impossible to know what might have happened in this township had Prohibition not reared its intemperate head from 1918 to 1933. But it is a sure fact that the Cabernets of Inglenook and Beaulieu reawakened the fame of the Napa Valley after Prohibition, and sustained it through hard economic times in the 1940s, 1950s, and 1960s.

Latterly, Caymus' estate-bottled Special Selection and Freemark Abbey's regular bottling have roused thoughts that Rutherford, not bench, is what counts.

Rutherford dust is the catchword for the particular character imparted to Cabernet by sun and soil here. An easier pair of qualities to grasp are decidedly herbaceous flavors and firmly tannic structures. These aspects are apparent in every winemaking style, every exposure, every soil type within the district, which is clearly demarcated by Zinfandel Lane on the north, the Silverado Trail on the east, the lower slopes of the Mayacamas Range on the west, and, only lately, by the proposed line separating Rutherford and Oakville on the south.

Oakville sub-AVA

Proposed: 1991
Total area: 5,800 acres
Area in vineyard: 4,200 acres
Wineries: 30
Principal towns: Yountville, Oakville

At Oakville, the valley begins to widen out to its broadest form. Marine air flows in a little more regularly. Soils become somewhat more diverse in character. Whether as a result or a coincidence, the curse (or blessing) of versatility that haunts the Napa Valley appears to center itself almost exactly within the proposed boundaries of this AVA. The epicenter is probably somewhere in Franciscan Vineyards' Oakville Estate, which appears equally adapted to growing grapes for Cabernet

Shelters for raised storage tanks of well water are a common architectural feature in the Napa Valley.

Sauvignon, Merlot, Chardonnay, and Late Harvest Riesling, not just of good quality, but of individual character.

For all of that, Cabernet Sauvignon and its kin rule here, too. BV No. 2, Stelling (for Far Niente), Martha's Vineyard (for Heitz Cellars), Robert Mondavi's best blocks, Vine Hill Ranch (for Robert Pepi) and Napanook (Dominus, among others) follow one another along what is or is not the Oakville Bench. Opus One faces Mondavi. Franciscan's Oakville Estate is out in the middle. So is the Groth Winery home vineyard. Toward the eastern edge of the valley floor is Beringer's excellent State Lane property. Several other vineyards contribute significantly to some of the valley's best assembled Cabernets.

Cabernet might rule, but it does have challengers. Robert Pepi and Jack Cakebread have estate plantings of Sauvignon Blanc behind two of the finest examples of that varietal wine in the valley. Robert Mondavi's Fumé Blanc gets its heart from plantings around the winery. Pepi also has two blocks of Sangiovese that have begun to turn heads.

As for the rest, Franciscan's Chardonnays and Zinfandels are lonely as examples from single vineyards, but both varieties are important in assembled wines.

Yountville to Napa

Chardonnay overshadows all other varieties from Yountville until builtup areas take over from vineyards at Napa, also dominating all the way to the hills on both sides. Crichton Hall carries the flag for several premier Chardonnay plantings along the west side from Yountville all the way down to the Carneros. Trefethen is the standard-bearer for the middle of the valley, with support from the Jaeger vineyard (for Rutherford Hill) and several of the most-prized blocks belonging to Beringer. East of the river, St Andrews sometimes produces benchmarks, sometimes milestones.

A long gentle slope east of Napa city, known locally as Coombsville, has still more fine Chardonnay vineyards, including Haynes, found under the vineyard owners' "Whitford" label.

In a way this part of the valley is about Chardonnay, Chardonnay and more Chardonnay, the way Rutherford concentrates on Cabernet Sauvignon. But in another way it is not. It does not dominate as Cabernet does farther north.

Two or three stone's throws north of St Andrews, is the Stag's Leap District, where Cabernet reigns supreme, with some assistance from Merlot. Clos du Val, Chimney Rock, Pine Ridge, Stag's Leap Wine Cellars, Steltzner, Silverado Vineyards, Stags' Leap Winery, and Shafer Vineyards is a lineup few places on earth could match for consistency or distinctiveness of character, Rutherford included among them.

The Bordelais grape varieties also do well in other quarters, notably White Rock (just off the valley floor in Soda Canyon), Trefethen, and Slinsen Ranch (for Charles Krug Vintage Selection). The last property is just south of Yountville. Sauvignon Blanc and Sémillon have some very good innings close to the river, most visibly in the "Herrick Ranch" wines from Inglenook and the Gustave Niebaum Collection. Gewürztraminer has done well in a vineyard or two, although it has virtually disappeared as a wine of identifiable origins.

As elsewhere, higher hills framing the main valley add complications, especially on Mt Veeder to the west in the Mayacamas range, and Atlas Peak to the east in the Vacas, both of them recently established sub-AVAs.

Stag's Leap District sub-AVA

Established: February 27, 1989
Total area: 2,700 acres
Area in vineyard: 1,300 acres
Wineries: 10
Principal town: None (Yountville, Napa proximate)

The Stag's Leap District is for Cabernet Sauvignon and its kin, both black and white, and forget the rest. A startling development given that the first Cabernet vines were planted as recently as the 1960s, and the majority of plantings only in the early 1970s.

An independent grower named Nathan Fay was first to plant Cabernet where there had been a good deal of hay and a few snippets of what Italians lovingly call "promiscuous agriculture" – which, in this particular instance, meant interplantings of prune trees, vines, and vegetables. On his heels came Richard Steltzner (first as a grower, later with a winery), Warren Winiarski of Stag's Leap Wine Cellars, and Bernard Portet of Clos du Val.

Both Winiarski and Portet saw their first vintage, 1972, show extremely well in much-publicized international blind tastings. Since then, there have been few or no second thoughts about what to plant in an alluvial apron that descends gently from the foot of a palisade down to the east bank of the Napa River. Shafer Vineyards, Pine Ridge Winery, Silverado Vineyards, and Chimney Rock Winery came along behind Clos du Val and Stag's Leap Wine Cellars as grower-producers. A handful of independent growers planted what the wineries did not. Compared to Rutherford, the filling-in of Cabernet vineyards came with blinding speed.

Except for Silverado Vineyards' home vineyard, almost all the Cabernet lies east of the Silverado Trail – originally a track for wagons hauling mercury-bearing ore from mines on Mt St Helena to smelters on San Pablo Bay. A fair acreage of Merlot is there too, some of it bottled as varietal wine, and as much or more blended into Cabernet Sauvignon or Cabernet-based blends. West of the roadway, on lower ground, Silverado Vineyards and Robert Mondavi Winery have some of the Napa Valley's most emphatically flavored Sauvignon Blanc.

The rule of thumb for planting here is the same one that works nearly everywhere in California's Cabernet country: Cabernet in the best-drained soils, Merlot where clays begin to add weight, Sauvignon Blanc or Sémillon in the heaviest stuff.

If there is any one surprise in the Stag's Leap District appellation, it is that Chardonnay does not rise much above passable. Going south, a matter of a few yards is enough to get into vineyards where Burgundy's great white grape approaches its finest quality in all California. Easy explanations do not exist.

Atlas Peak sub-AVA

Established: February 24, 1992
Total area: 11,400 acres
Area in vineyard: 565 acres
Wineries: 1
Principal town: None (Napa proximate)

Above the palisades of Stag's Leap, the Vacas dip into a shallow bowl called Foss Valley. The appellation's authors found more poetry in the name of the steep hill that looms over the north rim of the valley, so named their vineyard, winery and the

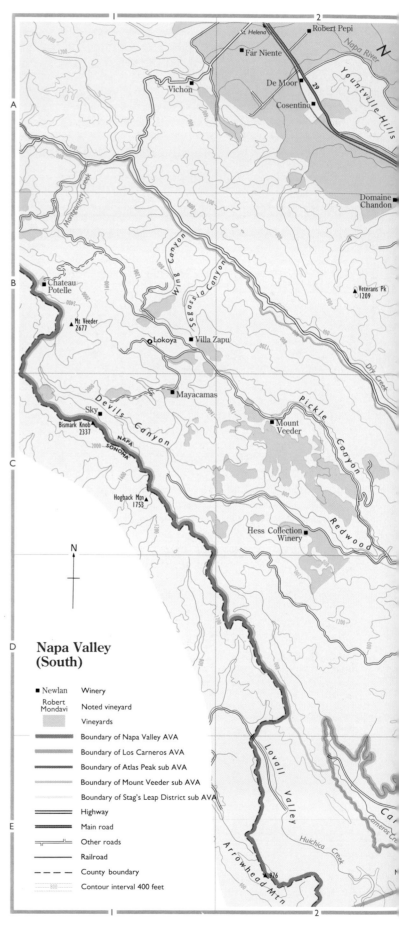

Napa Valley (South)

■ Newlan	Winery
Robert Mondavi	Noted vineyard
(shaded)	Vineyards
▬▬▬	Boundary of Napa Valley AVA
▬▬▬	Boundary of Los Carneros AVA
▬▬▬	Boundary of Atlas Peak sub AVA
▬▬▬	Boundary of Mount Veeder sub AVA
▬▬▬	Boundary of Stag's Leap District sub AVA
▬▬▬	Highway
▬▬▬	Main road
─┬─┬─	Other roads
▬ ▬ ▬	Railroad
─ ─ ─	County boundary
········	Contour interval 400 feet

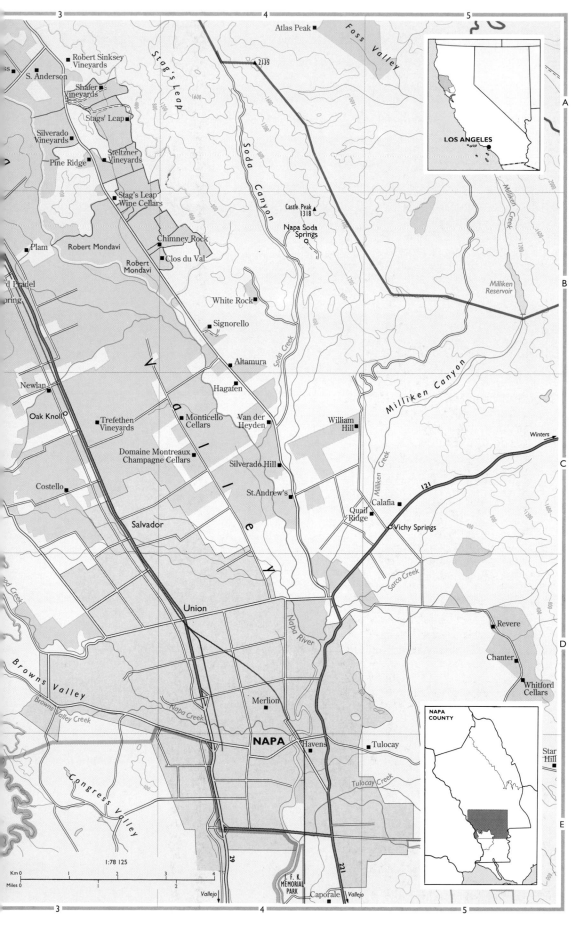

Top: The "25" on the central tower at Robert Mondavi Winery trumpeted the winery's 25th anniversary in 1992; it has since been removed. Above: Crossroads connect the north-south axes of Highway 29 and the Silverado Trail at a number of points between the towns of Napa and Calistoga.

appellation after the high point of the area, not the low.

Except for an old bit of Zinfandel on the craggy west rim, vineyards came late to Atlas Peak due to a lack of water. An ingenious engineering effort by Dr Richard Peterson turned rubble from the digging of winery caves into banks for three man-made lakes. Even in the droughty 1980s, winter rains filled these fast enough to transform a thin-soiled, sun-drenched semi-desert into the lush Atlas Peak Vineyard within five years.

The major planting is Sangiovese, 120 acres of it out of California's total 400. When it first went in, it more than doubled the state area devoted to Tuscany's great variety at the time. The first vintage, 1988, gave immediate hope; 1989 gave even more; 1990 promised much from the depths of the barrel.

Cabernet Sauvignon and Chardonnay are the other principal varieties in Atlas Peak Vineyard. Sauvignon Blanc, Sémillon, and Pinot Blanc are all planted in trial amounts. Five independent growers with small acreages complete the roster. Cabernet dominates all five properties.

Mt Veeder sub-AVA

Established: March 22, 1990
Total area: 15,000 acres
Area in vineyard: 1,000 acres
Wineries: 5
Principal town: None (Yountville, Napa proximate)

The Mayacamas Range begins to tail away about where it passes alongside Yountville. At the same point, two diverging ridges leave substantial plantable land in long swathes parallel to but well separated from the main valley floor. Those swathes, the watersheds of Redwood and Round creeks, hold most of the vineyards in the Mt Veeder sub-AVA.

All through the 1950s and 1960s, tiny Mayacamas Vineyards was up there all by itself, at the end of an unpaved road so long and pot-holed that the original owners of the winery put up a series of three roadside signs: "Don't despair / You're nearly there / Mayacamas." From the beginning, pilgrims trekked up that hard road for the Cabernet Sauvignon. The Chardonnay came later.

Mayacamas now has so much company that the signs are gone from an otherwise unchanged road. And still Cabernet Sauvignon and Chardonnay are the only two grape varieties that count for much, although the old Christian Brothers vineyard at Mont LaSalle grew some unfairly overlooked Chenin Blanc and Pinot St George, among other varieties.

Cabernet and Chardonnay from the hillier parts of Napa seldom separate themselves neatly by elevation, exposure or any other way that would make things easy for students. Here, they do less of it than in most places. Mt Veeder Vineyards grows only Cabernet Sauvignon and related varieties. However, its Chardonnay comes from a next-door neighbor. Mayacamas grows both, the Cabernet in a bowl around the winery, the Chardonnay up on a high ridge facing straight toward the Golden Gate Bridge. Hess Collection also grows both in situations not as dramatically different, but still different.

One other vineyard of considerable note in the district belongs to Domaine Chandon. Chardonnay from a round-backed hillock almost due west of the cellars gives square shoulders to all of Chandon's sparkling wines. Familiars of the winery will recognize its contribution most clearly from the original "Club Cuvée," released in 1990.

PRODUCERS

Acacia (See Carneros)

Aetna Springs Cellars (1990)
7227 Pope Valley Road, Pope Valley, CA 94567. Tel (707) 965-2675. 500 cases. Cabernet Sauvignon from the owning family's 21 acres at the winery and Chardonnay bought-in from near St Helena are the startup list.

Altamura Vineyards (1985)
4240 Silverado Trail, Napa, CA 94558. Tel (707) 253-2000. 2,000 cases. Grower-producer of ultra-toasty, heavyweight Chardonnay from 60 estate acres directly south of the Stag's Leap District.

Amizetta (1984)
1099 Greenfield Road, St Helena, CA 94574. Tel (707) 963-1460. 1,000 cases. Grower-producer in hills north of Lake Hennessy makes eccentrically minty Cabernet Sauvignon from 20 estate acres.

S. Anderson Vineyards (1979)
1473 Yountville Crossroad, Yountville, CA 94599. Tel (707) 944-8642. 10,000 cases. The Stanley Anderson family own a 32-acre vineyard at Yountville and a 70-acre one in Carneros, whence the core of assertive classic-method sparkling "Brut," "Blanc de Noirs," and "Tivoli" (*brut*). The properties also produce a thus far modest Chardonnay. A Stag's Leap District Cabernet Sauvignon from the neighbor's grapes was memorable in its 1989 debut.

Vincent Arroyo Winery (1984)
2361 Greenwood Avenue, Calistoga, CA 94515. Tel (707) 942-6995. 2,000 cases. Calistoga grower-producer of hearty, rustic wines from 60 acres seemingly well adapted to Cabernet and Petite Sirah.

David Arthur Vineyards (1985)
1519 Sage Canyon Road, St Helena, CA 94574. Tel (707) 963-5190. 4,000 cases. Grower-producer of only Chardonnay from a small estate vineyard near Chappellet on Pritchard Hill.

Atlas Peak Vineyards (1989)
PO Box 5660. Tel (707) 252-7971. 1,200 cases, to grow to 40,000. In its own sub-AVA high in hills above the Stag's Leap District, the 400-acre Antinori-Bollinger-Whitbread co-venture first released a promising estate Sangiovese in 1989, then a Cabernet Sauvignon-Sangiovese proprietary blend called "Consenso" from the following vintage. Chardonnay and, perhaps, Pinot Blanc too, were dancing in the wings.

Bancroft Vineyard (1986)
1000 Las Posadas Road, Angwin, CA 94508. Tel (707) 965-3080. 1,500 cases. Grower label for often outstanding Howell Mountain Chardonnay. The 90-acre property is also planted with Cabernet Sauvignon and Merlot, the latter taken by Beringer for a dark, tannic, vineyard-designated wine.

Barnett Vineyards (1989)
4070 Spring Mountain Road, St Helena, CA 94574. Tel (707) 963-0802. 1,000 cases. The initial roster is Cabernet Sauvignon, Merlot, Cabernet Franc, and Chardonnay.

Beaucannon Winery (1986)
1695 St Helena Highway South, St Helena, CA94574. Tel (707) 963-1886. 25,000 cases. Underrated winery belonging to the owners of France's Lebegue makes supple Cabernet Sauvignon and Merlot from its 117 acres north of St Helena, 65 at the Rutherford winery, and 73 near Napa. The white, also from winery-owned vineyards, is Chardonnay.

Beaulieu Vineyard (1900)
1960 St Helena Highway, Rutherford, CA 94573. Tel (707) 963-5200. 425,000 cases. Old-line firm now owned by Heublein is best-known for silky, American oak-aged, 100 percent Cabernet Sauvignon "Georges de Latour Private Reserve" from BV No. 1, BV No. 2, or both, and Cabernet Sauvignon "Rutherford" from those and other vineyards at Rutherford. Its dry Sauvignon Blanc is a model of melon-like flavors unsullied by oak. Carneros Pinot Noir and Chardonnay have merit. The winery draws upon 700 Heublein-owned acres, mostly at or near Rutherford and in Carneros, and has 700 more under contract in these and other parts of Napa.

The main elevation of Beaulieu Vineyard at Rutherford.

*Left: The original cellars of Beringer are now mainly ceremonial.
Below: Beringer winemaker Ed Sbragia.*

Bergfeld Winery (1934)
401 St Helena Highway S, St Helena, CA 94574. Tel (707) 963-7293. 60,000 cases. Originally Napa Valley Cooperative, renamed Bergfeld in 1988. 80 member growers provide grapes from every corner of the valley. In turning from bulk to bottled wines, the firm succeeded first with accessible Cabernet Sauvignon and Merlot under the "Bergfeld" and "J. Wile" labels.

Beringer Vineyards (1876)
PO Box 111, St Helena, CA 94574. Tel (707) 963-7115. 750,00 cases (plus 2 million Chenin Blanc and White Zinfandel). Nestlé-owned, major grower-producer best known for big, boldly oaked Private Reserve Cabernet Sauvignon and Chardonnay. Estate-bottled Chardonnay, mostly from vineyards along Big Ranch Road, sometimes surpasses its more celebrated sibling. Not to be overlooked for refined Napa Valley Fumé Blanc and Gewürztraminer from its 450-acre Gamble Ranch at Oakville, or deft Knights Valley Sonoma Cabernet Sauvignon. In all, owns 1,400 acres in Napa, 400 in Knights Valley.

Bouchaine (See Carneros)

Buehler Vineyards (1978)
820 Greenfield Road, St Helena, CA 94574. Tel (707) 963-2155. 25,000 cases. Steep vineyards looking south toward Lake Hennessey are the source of often estimable if tannically firm Cabernet Sauvignon.

Burgess Cellars (1972)
PO Box 282, St Helena, CA 94574. Tel (707) 963-4766. 30,000 cases. Solid Zinfandel from sources near the winery in hills east of St Helena; stolid Cabernet Sauvignon and thoroughly oaked Chardonnay come from the 50-acre, winery-owned Triere vineyard on the valley floor at Yountville.

Cafaro (1986)
591 Dean York Lane, St Helena, CA 94574. Tel (707) 963-7401. 800 cases. A winemaker label for intense Merlot and almost dense Cabernet Sauvignon assembled from a diversity of vineyards.

Cain Cellars (1981)
3800 Langtry Road, St Helena, CA 94574. Tel (707) 963-1616. 12,000 cases. All efforts focus on subtle, nuanced proprietary "Cain Five," from a 120-acre estate vineyard in the western hills above St Helena. The "five" refers to a blend of the premier five recommended red varieties of Bordeaux.

Cakebread Cellars (1973)
8300 St Helena Highway, Rutherford, CA 94573. Tel (707) 963-5221. 45,000 cases. All of the boldness in a bold group of wines comes from the grapes rather than oak or other winemaking. Sauvignon Blanc from a 30-acre vineyard at the winery is a model; a mostly bought-in Chardonnay also ranks high. A dark, sturdy Cabernet Sauvignon anchored in winery-owned grapes evolves slowly.

Calafia Cellars (1979)
4411 Redwood Road, Napa, CA 94558. Tel (707) 963-0114. 500 cases. Busman's holiday label of Hess Collection winemaker Randle Johnson, covering a consistently accessible, reasonably durable Cabernet Sauvignon.

Caporale (1982)
910-H Enterprise Way, Napa, CA 94558. Tel (707) 253-9230. 20,000 cases. Originally in Paso Robles, Napa since 1989. All bought-in Napa grapes for reliable Cabernet Sauvignon and Merlot.

Carneros Creek (See Carneros)

Casa Nuestra (1980)
3451 Silverado Trail, St Helena, CA 94574. Tel (707) 963-5783. 1,800 cases. Lawyer-owned small cellar with attention-grabbing dry Chenin Blanc from 10 estate acres north of St Helena.

Caymus Vineyard (1972)
8700 Conn Creek Road, Rutherford, CA 94573. Tel (707) 963-4204. 30,000 cases. Other wines are on the list, but dark, emphatic Cabernet Sauvignons are, properly, the source of Caymus's fame. "Napa Valley" is based on grapes from the 65-acre estate and a next-door neighbor to Spottswoode; "Special Selection" is an oakier wine entirely from the estate east of Rutherford. Liberty School is a second label, mostly for wines blended from bought-in lots.

Château Boswell (1979)
3468 Silverado Trail, St Helena, CA 94574. Tel (707) 963-5472. 1,000 cases. Middle-of-the-road Cabernet Sauvignon from bought-in grapes.

Chateau Chevre (1979)
2030 Hoffman Lane, Yountville, CA 94599. Tel (707) 944-2184. 3,000 cases. The centerpiece is dark, sturdy to rugged Merlot from 21 estate acres.

Chateau Montelena (1882, restarted 1972)
1429 Tubbs Lane, Calistoga, CA 94515. Tel (707) 942-5105. 30,000 cases. A sleek, polished Chardonnay from bought-in grapes somehow finds itself paired with an inky, tannic Cabernet from 72 estate acres that kiss the foot of Mt St Helena.

Chateau Potelle (1985)
3875 Mt Veeder Road, Napa, CA 94558. Tel (707) 255-9440. 20,000 cases. A young French couple steers away from pure California fruit in favor of subtle bouquets in well-honed, stylish Chardonnay and Cabernet Sauvignon, both recently from 45 estate acres in Mt Veeder sub-AVA.

Château Woltner (1985)
150 White Cottage Road S Angwin, CA 94508. Tel (707) 965-2445. 10,000 cases. One-time owners of Château Haut Brion believe they have found on Howell Mountain a perfect spot for Chardonnay. Made in a definitely but deftly oaky style, "Frederique," "St Thomas," and "Titus" are named after individual blocks in a 55-acre vineyard.

Chimney Rock (1986)
5350 Silverado Trail, Napa, CA 94558. Tel (707) 257-2641. 20,000 cases. From 75 estate acres in the Stag's Leap District, a pleasing, delicate Cabernet heads a short list. Sauvignon Blanc and Chardonnay are plainer.

Christian Brothers Winery
Once a major factor in Napa; recently a take-the-sweepings label for

Heublein, Inc.; may become part of a cacophony of brands from the corporate owner's San Joaquin Valley winery at Madera. (See Beaulieu Vineyard, Inglenook Vineyards and Gustave Niebaum Collection.)

Clos du Val Wine Co. (1972)
5330 Silverado Trail, Napa, CA 94558. Tel (707) 252-6711. 60,000 cases. Silky textures, seamless marriages of fruit and oak are the hallmarks of all the wines. Cabernet Sauvignon from 120 acres in the Stag's Leap District is the unchallenged star, though Merlot and Sémillon press the leader. The gem from a separate 102 acres in Carneros is Chardonnay.

Clos Pegase (1984)
1060 Dunaweal Lane, Calistoga, CA 94515. Tel (707) 942-4981. 40,000 cases. Balanced, refined Chardonnay is consistently worth seeking, and still improving as winery-owned 70-acre vineyard in Carneros comes more into play. The winery is always worth watching to see what has come of the latest explorations of offbeat varieties.

Codorniu Napa (See Carneros)

Conn Creek (1974)
8711 Silverado Trail, St Helena, CA 94574. Tel (707) 963-5133. 30,000 cases. Sound, rather than spectacular, before and after acquisition by Washington State's Stimson Lane. Cabernet Sauvignon is especially steady. Chardonnay can be considerably better than average.

Conn Valley Vineyards (1987)
680 Rossi Road, St Helena, CA 94574. Tel (707) 963-8600. 4,000 cases. The first wines from 26 acres in hills east of St Helena were rustic, but the vineyard shows some promise.

Corison (1987)
1427 Kearney Street, St Helena, CA 94574. Tel (707) 963-0826. 1,800 cases. A winemaker label for a mannerly Cabernet Sauvignon. Cathy Corison spent 10 years at Chappellet before launching out on her own.

Cosentino Wine Co. (1980 in Modesto, to Napa in 1989)
PO Box 2818, Yountville, CA 94599. Tel (707) 944-1220. 8,000 cases. Shout-it-out style in all the wines, but especially well-oaked, broad-shouldered reds; all from bought-in North Coast grapes.

Costello Vineyards (1981)
1200 Orchard Avenue, Napa, CA 94558. Tel (707) 252-8483. 10,000 cases. Estate-grown Chardonnay from vines on Napa's northwest corner.

Top: Bernard Portet left Bordeaux in 1971 to make wine at Clos du Val, in the Stag's Leap District.
Above: Dawnine Dyer is the champagne master of Domaine Chandon, one of several women filling that role in California sparkling wine houses.

Crichton Hall (1985)
PO Box 187, Rutherford, CA 94573. Tel (707) 224-4200. 4,000 cases. Grower-producer of polished, restrained, yet deep-flavored, epitome-of-Napa Chardonnays from 17 sloping acres on the first slopes of Napa's western hills just south of Yountville.

Cuvaison, Inc. (1970)
PO Box 384, Calistoga, CA 94515. Tel (707) 942-6266. 55,000 cases. Accidents put the winery in Calistoga, but 425 acres of estate grapes are in Carneros, whence a crisp, cleansing, understatedly delicious Chardonnay and a more assertive Merlot. A Reserve Chardonnay offers richer flavors of oak for those who prefer it.

Dalla Valle Vineyard (1984)
7776 Silverado Trail, Napa, CA 94558. Tel (707) 944-2676. 4,000 cases. Cabernet-based "Maya," assembled

from a ridge-cresting property east of Rutherford and another down on the valley floor, is the dark, tannic, rather heady leader of the list.

Deer Park Winery (1979)
1000 Deer Park Road, Deer Park, CA 94576. Tel (707) 963-5411. 3,000 cases. Steady, straightforward varietals, mostly from purchased grapes, though the winery has small holdings in Napa and, of all places, San Diego.

DeMoor (1973 as Napa Cellars, name changed in 1983)
PO Box 348, Oakville, CA 94562. Tel (707) 944-2565. 20,000 cases. Producer of middling varietals from bought-in grapes.

Diamond Creek Vineyards (1972)
1500 Diamond Mountain Road, Calistoga, CA 94515. Tel (707) 942-6926. 3,000 cases. Tiny, unabashed producer of 3 burly, big-bucks

Cabernets called "Red Rock Terrace," "Volcanic Hill," and "Gravelley Meadow" after separate blocks of 20-acre estate vineyards above Calistoga.

Domaine Carneros (See Carneros)

Domaine Chandon (1973)
1 California Drive, Yountville, CA 94599. Tel (707) 944-2280. 500,000 cases. Major producer of classic-method sparkling wines, reliable for Brut and Blanc de Noirs, memorable for Reserve and Etoile. Mostly from 500 acres in Carneros, but also western hill and valley-floor vineyards.

Domaine Montreaux (1987)
4101 Big Ranch Road, Napa, CA 94558. Tel (707) 252-9380. 1,000 cases. Affiliate of Monticello Vineyard is trying to get the handle on big, barrel-fermented style classic-method sparkling wines.

Domaine Napa (1985)
1155 Mee Lane, St Helena, CA 94574. Tel (707) 963-1666. 20,000 cases. French owner Michel Perret and New Zealand winemaker Grant Taylor have met as minds over quietly firm, age-worthy Cabernet Sauvignon, Sauvignon Blanc and Chardonnay, all from mid-valley vineyards owned or managed by Perret.

Dominus (1983)
PO Box 3275, Yountville, CA 94599. Tel (707) 944-8954. 4,000 cases. Christian Moeuix, of Château Pétrus fame, has designed and put a high price to an austerely tannic, resolutely farmyardy Cabernet-based blend grown in the old, 124-acre Napanook vineyard at Yountville. The first vintage, 1983, was still hard enough to scar a diamond in its ninth year.

Duckhorn Vineyards (1976)
3027 Silverado Trail, St Helena, CA 94574. Tel (707) 963-7108. 30,000 cases. Headline acts are dark, weighty, fully-oaked single-vineyard Merlots from Three Palms and Vine Hill Ranch.

Dunn Vineyards (1982)
PO Box 886, Angwin, CA 94508. Tel (707) 965-3642. 5,000 cases. Signature wine is dark, hard Howell Mountain Cabernet Sauvignon from owner-winemaker Randall Dunn's 5 acres and a neighbor's 5. A slightly softer Cabernet comes from purchased valley-floor grapes.

Etude (1985)
PO Box 344, Oakville, CA 94562. Tel (707) 963-7357. 3,000 cases. Winemaker label of skillful Tony Soter for intriguing Carneros Pinot Noir, savoury mid-valley Cabernet Sauvignon, both from bought-in grapes.

Far Niente (1979)
1 Acacia Drive, Oakville, CA 94562.
Tel (707) 944-2861. 24,000 cases. A
high-end producer with grand visions
for thus far heavily-oaked, round-
shouldered Cabernet Sauvignon from
affiliated Stelling Vineyard at Oakville,
and tub-of-butter Chardonnay mostly
from same source.

Flora Springs Wine Co. (1981)
1978 W Zinfandel Lane, St Helena,
CA 94574. Tel (707) 963-5711.
30,000 cases. Beautifully understated
Sauvignon Blanc "Soliloquy" and bolder
Cabernet-based "Trilogy" are the flag-
ships of a winery that draws only upon
300 acres of its owners' vines.
Chardonnay, Sauvignon Blanc and
Cabernet Sauvignon offered under the
"Floreal" label are often good value.

Folie à Deux Winery (1981)
3070 St Helena Highway, St Helena,
CA 94574. Tel (707) 963-1160.
18,000 cases. True-to-the-grapes
Chardonnay from vineyards at the
winery and in Oakville has been the
staple. A similarly styled Chenin Blanc
advances the breed.

Forman Vineyards (1983)
1501 Big Rock Road, St Helena, CA
94574. Tel (707) 963-0234. 3,000
cases. Longtime Napa winemaker
(Sterling, Newton, Charles F. Shaw)
now has his own cellars for well-
balanced, distinctively styled Cabernet
from his vineyard in hills east of St
Helena, and Chardonnay from a co-
owned property at Rutherford Cross.

Franciscan Vineyards (1972)
PO Box 407, Rutherford, CA 94573.
Tel (707) 963-7111. 40,000 cases.
The mid-1980s advent of co-
owner/manager Agustin Huneeus and
winemaker Greg Upton revitalized a
long-unsteady label. Its 204-acre
Oakville Estate yields reliably fine-
value Chardonnay, Cabernet
Sauvignon, Meritage and Zinfandel. A
separate Chardonnay, "Cuvée
Sauvage," pushes the limits of the
toasty style. The company also owns
the excellent "Estancia" (Alexander
Valley and Monterey) and "Pinnacles"
(Monterey) labels.

Freemark Abbey (1967)
PO Box 410, St Helena, CA 94574.
Tel (707) 963-9694. 40,000 cases.
Often underrated producer of 3
Rutherford Cabernet Sauvignons
(Bosche and Sycamore from those
vineyards) and 2 Chardonnays (Carpy
Vineyard bottling being barrel-tement-
ed, the Napa Valley not). All grapes
come from partner-owned vines.

Frisinger Cellars (1988)
2277 Dry Creek Road, Napa, CA
94558. Tel (707) 255-3749. 2,500
cases.

Frog's Leap Winery (1981)
3358 Highway 29, St Helena, CA
94574. Tel (707) 963-4704. 20,000
cases. Crackerjack Zinfandel and textbook Sauvignon Blanc have been the
great strengths of the winery. A
Cabernet Sauvignon based in vineyards at Rutherford has pulled even.
Carneros Chardonnay is ultra-toasty.

Girard Winery (1980)
7717 Silverado Trail, Oakville, CA
94562. Tel (707) 944-8577. 20,000
cases. Oak is obvious in all the wines.
Owned vineyards at the winery and in
the western hills above Yountville provide most or all of the grapes.

Goosecross Cellars (1985)
1119 State Lane, Yountville, CA
94599. Tel (707) 944-1986. 8,000
cases. Year by year the winery's 2
Chardonnays (one from 10 estate
acres east of Yountville, one from
bought-in local grapes) grow more
polished and complete.

Grace Family Vineyards (1978)
1210 Rockland Road, St Helena, CA
94574. Tel (707) 963-0808. 200 cases.
Two sloping acres north of St
Helena regularly produce a dark, age-
worthy Cabernet Sauvignon that
tastes exactly as Napa Valley
Cabernet should.

Graeser Winery (1985)
255 Petrified Forest Road, Calistoga,
CA 94515. Tel (707) 942-4437. 2,000
cases. The emphasis is on Bordeaux
varieties, blended and solo, from the
winery's own vineyard.

Green and Red Vineyard (1977)
32008 Chiles-Pope Valley Road, St
Helena, CA 94574. Tel (707)
965-2346. 2,500 cases. From 17
sloping acres in Chiles Valley comes a
lean, understated Zinfandel with the
balance of a Tuscan red.

Grgich Hills Cellar (1977)
PO Box 450, Rutherford, CA 94573.
Tel (707) 963-2784. 50,000 cases.
Mike Grgich stubbornly insists on
firm, slow-to-develop Chardonnay
and Cabernet Sauvignon of
distinctive character. Both come
primarily from Napa Valley vineyards
owned by Grgich at Yountville,
and partner Austin Hills at
Rutherford and Napa. An estimably
subtle Sauvignon Blanc is ready
quicker.

Groth Vineyards & Winery
(1982)
PO Box 390, Oakville, CA 94562. Tel
(707) 944-0290. 40,000 cases.
Polished, agreeable Cabernet
Sauvignon and Chardonnay are fine
reflections of 2 vineyards, 100 acres
on the flats east of Oakville and 43
south of Yountville.

Hagafen Cellars (1980)
PO Box 3035, Napa, CA 94558. Tel
(707) 252-0781. 6,000 cases. The pioneer producer of kosher *vinifera* wines
continues to show the way to the rest
with steady, sometimes stylish
Cabernet Sauvignon, Chardonnay and
Riesling.

Harrison Vineyards (1991)
1527 Sage Canyon Road, St Helena,
CA 94574. Tel (707) 963-8726. 2,000
cases.

Havens Wine Cellars (1984)
775 8th Street, Napa, CA 94558. Tel
(707) 255-7337. 5,000 cases.
Amateur-turned-professional winemaker Michael Havens has a talent for
Merlot from Truchard Vineyard in
Carneros.

Heitz Wine Cellars (1961)
500 Taplin Road, St Helena, CA
94574. Tel (707) 963-3542. 40,000
cases. The first reputation was for
Chardonnay but the enduring one
is for boldly flavorful, long-aging
single-vineyard Cabernet Sauvignons
from Martha's Vineyard and Bella
Oaks Vineyard, the former in
Oakville, the latter in Rutherford.

Hess Collection Winery (1982)
4411 Redwood Road, Napa, CA
94558. Tel (707) 255-1144. 60,000
cases. From vineyards well up on Mt
Veeder, polished, stylish Chardonnay
and Cabernet Sauvignon. A second
label, Hess Selection, covers
California-appellation Chardonnay
and Cabernet from diverse regions.

William Hill Winery (1976)
1761 Atlas Peak Road, Napa, CA
94558. Tel (707) 224-4477. 100,000
cases. The winery draws on vineyards
near Napa City and up on Mt Veeder
for solid Cabernet Sauvignon and
thoroughly oaked Chardonnay.

Honig Cellars (1980)
850 Rutherford Road, Rutherford, CA
94573. Tel (707) 963-5618. 12,000
cases. Founded upon estate-grown
Sauvignon Blanc, the winery has since

Three Palms Vineyard (the third palm, lost to winter cold, has been replanted) is most famous for Merlot.

Charles Krug Winery uses the original 1870s coach house as an aging cellar for wines in barrel.

added a Cabernet Sauvignon (also estate) and Chardonnay. All are steady.

Inglenook-Napa Valley (1879)
1991 St Helena Highway, Rutherford, CA 94573. Tel (415) 967-3300. 120,000 cases. Indecision at Heublein, Inc., has kept the historic winery off-balance since the 1970s, yet its vineyards are fine enough to produce excellent Cabernet Sauvignon, Merlot and Gravion (proprietary Sauvignon Blanc-Sémillon blend) more often than not.

Jade Mountain (1984)
520 Edgemont Lane, Angwin, CA 94508. Tel (707) 965-3084. 5,000 cases. From the original 34 acres near Cloverdale (Sonoma), 25 newer acres on Mt Veeder and bought-in grapes, come varietals and blends based in varieties from the Rhône, especially Syrah.

Jaeger Inglewood Cellars (1979)
PO Box 322, St Helena, CA 94574. Tel (707) 963-1875. 5,000 cases. A partner in Freemark Abbey and Rutherford Hill reserves this label for a dark, well-wooded Merlot from 20 acres just south of St Helena.

Johnson Turnbull (1979)
PO Box 410, Oakville, CA 94562. Tel (707) 963-5839. 5,000 cases. Minty-ripe Cabernet Sauvignon from the winery's 20-acre vineyard at Oakville is the main event. There is also a Knights Valley Chardonnay from a William Turnbull-owned vineyard.

Judd's Hill (1989)
PO Box 415, St Helena, CA 94574. Tel (707) 963-9093. 1,400 cases. Now on his own, the long-time winemaker at Whitehall Lane is making fairly stylish Cabernet Sauvignon from bought-in grapes.

Robert Keenan Winery (1977)
3660 Spring Mountain Road, St Helena, CA 94574. Tel (707) 963-9177. 10,000 cases. Styles have shifted through a series of winemakers; the proprietor's 47-acre vineyard on Spring Mountain appears adapted to Chardonnay and Merlot in particular.

Hanns Kornell Champagne Cellars (1952)
Bank foreclosure in 1992 appears to have ended the run of a small, family-owned specialist in classic method sparkling wines.

Charles Krug Winery (1861)
PO Box 191, St Helena, CA 94574. Tel (707) 963-2761. 600,000 cases. Old-line firm with excellent vineyard holdings in St Helena, Yountville and Carneros appears to be getting back on the rails after a wobbly time. Carneros Chardonnay and Pinot Noir are agreeable, but the attention-getter is an intense, long-aging Special Selection Cabernet Sauvignon from the winery's Slinsen vineyard, on the west bench immediately south of Yountville.

La Jota Vineyard (1985)
1102 Las Posadas Road, Angwin, CA 94508. Tel (707) 965-3020. 4,000 cases. Dark, tannic, well-wooded Cabernet from a 28-acre Howell Mountain vineyard. Also a pioneer with worthy Viognier from the same property.

La Vieille Montagne (1981)
3851 Spring Mountain Road, St Helena, CA 94574. Tel (707) 963-9059. 1,000 cases. The headliner is Cabernet Sauvignon from 7 estate acres high on Spring Mountain.

Lakespring Winery (1980)
2055 Hoffman Lane, Napa, CA 94558. Tel (707) 944-2475. 22,000 cases. Polished, understated Cabernet Sauvignon and Merlot can rise up to challenge the leaders. Chardonnay and Sauvignon Blanc are steady middle-of-the-roaders.

Lamborn Family Vineyards (1982)
2075 Summit Lake Drive, Angwin, CA 94508. Tel (415) 547-4643. 2,000 cases. A defender of the faith sticks with exuberant, likable Zinfandel from 30 acres on Howell Mountain.

Liparita Cellars (1987)
1,500 cases. Originally a grower's label for an attractive Chardonnay. Work on a 5,000-case winery began in 1992. Chardonnay dominates 42 acres of vines toward the southern tip of Howell Mountain; Cabernet Sauvignon and Merlot are minorities.

Livingston Wines (1984)
1895 Cabernet Lane, St Helena, CA 94574. Tel (707) 963-2120. 3,000 cases. Dark, tannic, thoroughly oaked Cabernet Sauvignon from the same-owner, 10-acre Moffett Vineyard south of St Helena.

Long Vineyards (1977)
PO Box 50, St Helena, CA 94574. Tel (707) 963-2496. 3,000 cases. The star turn is rich, flavorful Chardonnay from a 20-acre estate winery near Chappellet on Pritchard Hill.

Macauley Vineyard (1984)
3291 St Helena Highway N St Helena, CA 94574. Tel (707) 963-1123. 1,000 cases. Sauvignon Blanc from 2 acres on Spring Mountain, Cabernet from 5 in St Helena.

Markham Vineyards (1978)
2812 St Helena Highway N St Helena, CA 94574. Tel (707) 963-5292. 20,000 cases. Three vineyards (two south of Yountville, one in Calistoga) totaling 250 acres are the sources for reliably attractive wines,

especially Cabernet Sauvignon (estate, from Yountville), Chardonnay, and Merlot.

Louis M. Martini Winery (1933)
PO Box 112, St Helena, CA 94574. Tel (707) 963-2736. 300,000 cases. An established family firm turns its widely flung, 900-acre empire of important vineyards to good account, increasingly with single-vineyard wines. Historic Glen Oaks Vineyard (200 acres in Chiles Valley), grows the basis for a defines-the-variety Napa Valley Reserve Cabernet Sauvignon. Las Amigas and La Loma vineyards in Carneros, 350 acres between them, are devoted to Pinot Noir and Chardonnay, the latter extra-toasty. A lean, fruit-first Carneros-Russian River Valley Chardonnay from the family-owned vineyards is impeccable. And tart, juicy Russian River Valley Merlot and Gewürztraminer come from 172-acre Los Vinedos del Rio; round, rich Sonoma Valley Cabernet Sauvignon from 240-acre Monte Rosso.

Matera Wine Cellars (1990)
4300 Silverado Trail, Calistoga, CA 94515. Tel (707) 942-6283. 1,500 cases. An estate Chardonnay is the main wine.

Mayacamas Vineyards (1944)
1155 Lokoya Road, Napa, CA 94558. Tel (707) 224-4030. 5,000 cases. In both Cabernet Sauvignon and Chardonnay – the two regulars on the Mayacamas list – the monster style long in evidence began giving way with the '85s to more temperate balances.

Merlion Winery (1985)
880 Vallejo Street, Napa, CA 94558. Tel (707) 226-5568. 12,000 cases. The two winemakers who launched Vichon's 50-50 Sauvignon Blanc-Sémillon blend are repeating that success in their own winery with a wine called Sauvrier. Also of interest: an intriguing Melon de Bourgogne named "Coeur de Melon," All the grapes are bought-in.

Merryvale Vineyards (1983)
1000 Main Street, St Helena, CA 94574. Tel (707) 963-2225. 12,000 cases. Winery partners provide most of the grapes for reliable, conservatively styled Chardonnay "Starmont," "White Meritage" (Sauvignon Blanc-Sémillon blend), Cabernet Sauvignon, and "Profile" (Cabernet-based blend). "Sunny St Helena" is a second name for lower-priced Napa Valley varietal wines.

Milat Vineyards (1986)
1091 S St Helena Highway, St Helena, CA 94574. Tel (707) 963-0758. 3,000 cases. Quietly building a reputation for solid, attractive Cabernet Sauvignon, Sauvignon Blanc, and a dry Chenin Blanc from a 22-acre family vineyard and winery just south of St Helena.

Robert Mondavi Winery (1966)
PO Box 106, Oakville, CA 94562. Tel (707) 963-9611. 650,000 cases. At Robert Mondavi's constant prodding, the winery is relentlessly experimental in technique yet unshakably traditional in style. All of the wines are anchored in but not limited to the family's 1,500 acres of vineyard, which includes 700

acres flanking the winery at Oakville, 300 acres at the southwest corner of the Stag's Leap District, and 450 acres in Carneros, the latter acquired only in 1988. Fine Cabernet Sauvignon and definitive Fumé Blanc put varietal character foremost; Pinot Noir and Chardonnay have a stronger dash of oak. The Reserve bottlings of all of these are decidedly bigger wines with much more prominent doses of oak. A second label, Robert Mondavi-Woodbridge (see p 189), is operated separately out of a winery in Lodi. The winery and/or family members also own all or part of Opus One, Vichon, Byron (see p 123), and Montpellier (see p 191).

Mont St John Cellars (See Carneros)

Monticello Cellars (1981)
4242 Big Ranch Road, Napa, CA 94558. Tel (707) 253-2802. 30,000 cases. From 225 acres at the north end of Big Ranch Road, estate-grown Chardonnay "Jefferson Cuvée" is relentlessly austere with tannins and oak, the pricier "Corley Reserve" even more so. Bought-in Cabernet Sauvignon "Corley Reserve" echoes the Chardonnays, but "Jefferson Cuvée" is polished, accessible, specific to Cabernet.

Mt Veeder Winery (1973)
1999 Mt Veeder Road, Napa, CA 94558. Tel (707) 224-4039. 7,500 cases. From an established 26-acre vineyard, Cabernet Sauvignon and Cabernet-based Meritage rank among the most refined advertisements for

mountain-grown wines. The neighbor's vineyard is just as good for well-oaked Chardonnay.

Mumm Napa Valley (1985)
8445 Silverado Trail, Rutherford, CA 94573. Tel (707) 942-3400. 105,000 cases. Canadian (Seagram)-French (G. H. Mumm) joint venture is consistently stylish with classic-method sparkling wines. Most individualistic: single-vineyard "Winery Lake" *cuvée*. The foundation stone: non-vintage "Brut Prestige." A vintage Reserve and Blanc de Noirs are the others.

Napa Creek Winery (1980)
1001 Silverado Trail, St Helena, CA 94574. Tel (707) 963-9456. 12,000 cases. Middle-of-the-road, reliable Chardonnay, Cabernet Sauvignon, and Merlot, all from bought-in grapes.

Newlan Vineyards and Winery (1977)
5225 Solano Avenue, Napa, CA 94558. Tel (707) 257-2399. 6,000 cases. In good years Newlan achieves a distinctively perfumey, almost floral Pinot Noir from one of 2 winery-owned vineyards near Napa city. Cabernet Sauvignon is soft and agreeable.

Newton Vineyard (1978)
2555 Madrona Avenue, St Helena, CA 94574. Tel (707) 963-9000. 35,000 cases. On an especially steep part of Spring Mountain, 62 acres of terraced vineyards anchor ripe, full, fully-wooded Cabernet Sauvignons and Merlots. A buttery-toasty Chardonnay depends more on bought-in grapes.

Neyers Winery (1980)
PO Box 1028, St Helena, CA 94574. Tel (707) 963-8293. 3,000 cases. Supple estate Merlot comes from the first 7 of 21 acres. Solid Chardonnay from bought-in grapes is the white.

Nichelini Winery (1890)
2950 Sage Canyon Road, St Helena, CA 94574. Tel (707) 963-0717. 2,000 cases. An extended family uses a cousin's El Dorado County winery (Boeger) to make wine from its Chiles Valley vines; includes possibly the last varietal Sauvignon Vert (beautifully made). More conventionally, they offer Cabernet Sauvignon and Zinfandel.

Gustave Niebaum Collection (1985)
25,000 cases. A Heublein-owned label capitalizes on some of the finest vineyards under contract to its wineries for single-vineyard wines. An impeccable Chevrier (Sémillon) "Herrick Vineyard" may be the prize, but 2 Carneros Chardonnays ("Laird," "Bayview") and two mid-valley Cabernet Sauvignons ("Mast," "Tench") are worthies. Production is at Inglenook.

Niebaum-Coppola Estate (1979)
PO Box 208, Rutherford, CA 94573. Tel (707) 963-9099. 2,500 cases. The enterprise of filmmaker Francis Ford Coppola wavered through its early years, but is steadying with Cabernet-based "Rubicon" from Rutherford vineyards, originally a part of Inglenook.

Opus One (1979)
7900 St Helena Highway, Oakville, CA 94562. Tel (707) 944-9442. 15,000 cases. Thoughtful, refined, Cabernet-based red: expensive, but worth the money as a demonstration of French (Mouton Rothschild) and American (Robert Mondavi) winemaking sensibilities brought to harmonious resolution. Increasingly from the close-planted 110-acre estate vineyard at Oakville after a decade based on selected blocks at Mondavi's nearby ToKalon Vineyard.

Pahlmeyer Winery (1986)
PO Box 2410, Napa, CA 94558. Tel (707) 255-2321. 1,400 cases. The bombast of an inky Cabernet-based red is overshadowed only by that of the same winery's oaky Chardonnay. Both come from a single vineyard near Rutherford.

Robert Pecota Winery (1978)
PO Box 303, Calistoga, CA 94515.
Tel (707) 942-6625. 20,000 cases.
The winery has settled in as a steady
producer. A rich, ripe Sauvignon Blanc
and sturdy Cabernet Sauvignon from
40 acres at the winery north of
Calistoga head the list.

Peju Province Winery (1982)
8466 St Helena Highway, Rutherford,
CA 94573. Tel (707) 963-3600.
20,000 cases. The long, skinny, 30-acre
"HB" estate vineyard at Rutherford
yields distinctively flavored, naturally
balanced Cabernets for which the
winery is increasingly well known.

Robert Pepi Winery (1981)
7585 Highway 29, Oakville, CA
94562. Tel (707) 944-2807. 30,000
cases. The winery was founded to
specialize in Sauvignon Blanc from a
70-acre estate vineyard south of
Oakville, and it still makes that wine
well, but Cabernet Sauvignon "Vine
Hill Ranch" and an estate Sangiovese
sub-titled "Colline dei Sassi" have
become the showcase wines.
Chardonnay from bought-in grapes
often is among Napa's leaders.

Mario Perelli-Minetti Winery
(1988)
PO Box 368, Rutherford, CA 94573.
Tel (707) 963-8762. 5,000 cases.
Chardonnay and Cabernet Sauvignon
come from bought-in Napa grapes.

Joseph Phelps Vineyards (1973)
PO Box 1031, St Helena, CA 94574.
Tel (707) 963-2745. 80,000 cases.
After winning its first fame for
Johannisberg Rieslings, dry and Late-
Harvest, the winery has refocused
twice, first on Cabernet Sauvignon and
Cabernet-based "Insignia," then on
Rhône-inspired wines. Under the "Vin
du Mistral" label: increasingly stylish
dry Grenache rosé, Syrah, and, above
all, a blend called just "Mistral" which
manages to offer most of the charms
of good Côte du Rhônes. Cabernet
and "Insignia" are still wines to watch
on a long, steady list, much of it based
on winery-owned vineyards at St
Helena, Rutherford, and the Stag's Leap
District.

Piña Cellars (1979)
8060 Silverado Trail, Rutherford, CA
94573. Tel (707) 944-2229. 400 cases.
Sturdy, straightforward Chardonnay
from the owning family's vineyards.

Pine Ridge Winery (1978)
5901 Silverado Trail, Napa, CA 94558.
Tel (707) 253-7500. 65,000 cases. The
proprietors have assembled a group
of small vineyards to take advantage of
Napa's variables of sun and soil in
really solid Cabernet Sauvignons sub-

titled "Stag's Leap Cuvée," "Rutherford
Cuvée" and "Diamond Mountain
Cuvée," and solidly oaky Chardonnays
"Knollside Cuvée" and "Stag's Leap
Cuvée." Merlot is worth watching too.
Favored years see Cabernet-based
"Andrus Reserve" named after the
managing partner.

Plam Vineyards (1984)
6200 Washington Street, Yountville,
CA 94599. Tel (707) 944-1102. 9,000
cases. Chardonnay and a recently
impressive Cabernet Sauvignon are
the mainstays from a 26-acre vineyard
south of Yountville.

Bernard Pradel Cellars (1983)
2100 Hoffman Lane, Yountville, CA
94599. Tel (707) 944-8720. 2,500
cases. French sensibilities govern the
understated style of Cabernet from 20
acres at the winery south of Yountville.

Prager Winery and Port Works
(1980)
1281 Lewelling Lane, St Helena, CA
94574. Tel (707) 963-3720. 1,000
cases. The quixotic quest is port-types
from, especially, Napa Cabernet
Sauvignon and Petite Sirah.

Quail Ridge Winery (1978)
1055 Atlas Peak Road, Napa, CA
94558. Tel (707) 257-1712. 30,000
cases. The winery was founded to
make Chardonnay, which remains the
main item, but a splendid Merlot
(from the Vandendriessche family's
White Rock vineyard) and an excellent Sauvignon Blanc (assembled) have
attracted greater praise.

Kent Rasmussen Winery
(See Carneros)

Raymond Vineyard & Cellar
(1974)
849 Zinfandel Lane, St Helena, CA
94574. Tel (707) 963-3141. 120,000
cases. This family has been making wine
in Napa since the end of Prohibition.
Its knowledge of local vineyards
reveals itself in fine Cabernet
Sauvignon and solidly varietal
Sauvignon Blanc. Chardonnay is the
other mainstay.

Revere Vineyard and Winery
(1985)
2456 Third Avenue, Napa, CA 94558.
Tel (707) 224-7620. 2,500 cases.
Rather hulking Chardonnays from a
winery-owned vineyard in the
Coombsville area.

Ritchie Creek Vineyard (1974)
4024 Spring Mountain Road, St
Helena, CA 94574. Tel (707) 963-
4661. 1,200 cases. Eight shy-bearing
acres high on Spring Mountain yield
lean Chardonnay, austere Cabernet

Sauvignon and a surprisingly floral
Viognier, one of Napa's first such.

Rombauer Vineyards (1982)
3522 Silverado Trail, St Helena, CA
94574. Tel (707) 963-5170. 15,000
cases. Firm, flavorful Cabernet, Merlot,
and a blend of the two called
"Meilleur du Chai" all come from
bought-in grapes. Also: Chardonnay.

Round Hill Winery (1977)
1680 Silverado Trail, Rutherford, CA
94573. Tel (707) 963-5251. 300,000
cases. Early-on the emphasis was all
on cent-saver negociant wines.
Latterly, steady Napa Valley Cabernet
Sauvignon and Merlot from bought-in
grapes have led a fairly priced basic list
while darker, oakier Cabernet and
Merlot from partner-owned vines
have competed at higher prices under
the Rutherford Ranch label.

Rustridge Vineyards and Winery
(1984)
2910 Lower Chiles Valley Road, St
Helena, CA 94574. Tel (707) 965-
2871. 3,000 cases. From 54 acres in
lower Chiles Valley, sturdy to rustic

Riesling, Chardonnay, Cabernet
Sauvignon and Zinfandel.

Rutherford Hill Winery (1976)
200 Rutherford Hill Road, Rutherford,
CA 94573. Tel (707) 963-1871.
120,000 cases. Merlot commands 80
percent of production, but slow-
developing, built-to-age Chardonnay
"Jaeger Vineyard" and "XVS" and
Cabernet Sauvignon "XVS" are worthy of note. A dry Gewürztraminer
from Jaeger Vineyard on Big Ranch
Road is among Napa's finest.

Rutherford Ranch (See Round Hill)

Rutherford Vintners (1974)
1673 St Helena Highway, Rutherford,
CA 94573. Tel (707) 963-4117.
15,000 cases. One of Louis M.
Martini's longtime employees struck
out on his own, having learned that
balance is the key to likable, agable
Cabernet Sauvignon. Bernard Skoda
grows his own grapes near
Rutherford.

Saddleback Cellars (1983)
7802 Money Road, Oakville, CA

Profits from a delicatessen-and-tasting room built V. Sattui's fine cellars.

94562. Tel (707) 963-4982. 2,400 cases. The busman's holiday winery of Groth Vineyards winemaker Nils Venge is most notable for a firm, fresh Pinot Blanc. The rest of the list is solid.

St Andrew's Winery (1981)
2921 Silverado Trail, Napa, CA 94558. Tel (707) 252-6748. 21,000 cases. Firm-textured, deftly toasty Chardonnay from an impressively consistent 34 acres near the river just north of Napa City is the reason-for-being of a winery owned since 1989 by Clos du Val (see p 52).

St Clement Vineyards (1975)
PO Box 261, St Helena, CA 94574. Tel (707) 963-7221. 10,000 cases. Age-worthy, flavorful Sauvignon Blanc (based on Pope Valley grapes) and deftly oaked Chardonnay (mostly Carneros) put the winery in Napa's front ranks. An estate Carneros Chardonnay "Abbott's Vineyard" is more austere and oakier to taste. The reds are dense.

St Supery Vineyards & Winery (1988)
PO Box 38, Rutherford, CA 94573. Tel (707) 963-4507. 30,000 cases. Sound, attractively accessible Chardonnay, Merlot, and Cabernet Sauvignon from the winery's 450-acre Dollarhide Ranch all speak well of Pope Valley's suitability for these varieties. A Sauvignon Blanc, meanwhile, is curiously subdued.

Saintsbury (See Carneros)

San Pietro Vara Vineyards and Winery (1983)
1171 Tubbs Lane, Calistoga, CA 94515. Tel (707) 963-0937. 3,500 cases. The producers of Charbono, Cabernet Sauvignon, and other reds from this organic vineyard north of Calistoga seem more concerned that their wines be organic than delicious.

V. Sattui Winery (1975)
1111 White Lane, St Helena, CA 94574. Tel (707) 963-7774. 32,000 cases. Fine, flavor-rich Dry Johannisberg Riesling and well-defined, husky Cabernet Sauvignon "Preston Vineyard" are the cream of a list, mostly from bought-in Napa Valley grapes. All wines are available only direct from the winery.

Schramsberg Vineyards (1965)
1400 Schramsberg Road, Calistoga, CA 94515. Tel (707) 942-4558. 40,000 cases. Jack and Jamie Davies revivified classic-method sparkling wine in California by starting the winery. They have patiently built a house style since, using grapes from most of Napa. Pinot Noir-rich Reserve has

been the capstone; new-in-1992 luxury *cuvée* called J. Schram, four years or more on *tirage*, is richer yet.

Sequoia Grove Vineyards (1979)
8338 St Helena Highway, Rutherford, CA 94573. Tel (707) 944-2945. 20,000 cases. Estate Chardonnay and Cabernet Sauvignon from 22 acres at Rutherford and a Chardonnay from an affiliated Carneros vineyard are bold in every way.

Shadow Brook Winery (1984)
360 Zinfandel Lane, St Helena, CA 94574. Tel (707) 963-2000. 7,000 cases. Chardonnay from three winery-owned properties (one at Rutherford, two near Napa) is the mainstay. Sales are principally to restaurants.

Shafer Vineyards (1978)
6154 Silverado Trail, Napa, CA 94558. Tel (707) 944-2877. 20,000 cases. Long-aged, unblended, stylishly understated Cabernet Sauvignon "Hillside Select" is the showpiece from 65 acres in the Stag's Leap District. From the same source: polished, accessible Cabernet Sauvignon and Merlot, each blended with a touch of the other. A soft, often forward Chardonnay based in 17 Shafer-owned acres nearby may evolve as grapes from the winery's 70 acres in Carneros come into play beginning in the early 1990s.

Charles F. Shaw Vineyard & Winery (1979)
1010 Big Tree Road, St Helena, CA 94574. Tel (707) 963-5459. 10,000 cases. In the midst of all the Cabernet, Shaw opted to challenge Beaujolais Villages with estate-grown Gamay "Domaine Elucia" from 50 acres between St Helena and Calistoga. The winery has done well with that, and a crisp, melony Sauvignon Blanc, also from the estate vineyard.

Signorello Vineyards (1985)
4500 Silverado Trail, Napa, CA 94558. Tel (707) 255-5990. 5,000 cases. Take-no-prisoners, ultra-buttery Chardonnay from 30 acres on slopes just south of the Stag's Leap District has won a cult following. An estate Sauvignon Blanc follows the same style. Pinot Noir and Cabernet Sauvignon promise to be boomers as well.

Silver Oak Cellars (1973)
915 Oakville Crossroad, Oakville, CA 94562. Tel (707) 944-8808. 25,000 cases. The proprietor uses a lavish hand with American oak for ultra-ripe, fleshy Cabernet Sauvignons from Alexander Valley and Napa Valley. Bonnie's Vineyard, a 4-acre parcel near the winery in Oakville, goes into a separate, single-vineyard bottling.

Silverado Hill Cellars (1979 as Pannonia, renamed Louis K. Mihaly in 1981; current name since 1989)
PO Box 2640, Napa, CA 94558. Tel (707) 253-9306. 32,000 cases. Intense aromas of heavily-toasted oak outweigh those of Chardonnay from a well-situated 34-acre vineyard on the Silverado Trail directly north of St Andrews and east of Monticello.

Silverado Vineyards (1981)
6121 Silverado Trail, Napa, CA 94558. Tel (707) 257-1770. 100,000 cases. Polished, indelible Sauvignon Blanc and supple Cabernet Sauvignon from estate vineyards in the Stag's Leap District have earned the winery a lofty reputation. From winery-owned vineyards there and in Coombsville comes a deftly oaked, well-balanced Chardonnay (a Reserve bottling, true to type, is much oakier).

Robert Sinskey Vineyards (1986)
6320 Silverado Trail, Napa, CA 94558. Tel (707) 944-9090. 10,000 cases. In

Grower John Shafer and his winemaker son, Doug.

spite of the winery location, all 105 acres of vineyard are in Carneros. Chardonnay and Pinot Noir both reveal a proprietary fondness for plenty of oak. A dark, firmly tannic "Claret" is based on Merlot blended with Cabernet Franc and Cabernet Sauvignon.

Sky Vineyards (1979)
1500 Lokoya Drive, Napa, CA 94558. Tel (707) 935-1391. 1,500 cases. Intense, austerely tannic, rustic Zinfandel from vineyards high on Mt Veeder.

Smith-Madrone Vineyards (1977)
4022 Spring Mountain Road, St Helena, CA 94574. Tel (707) 963-2283. 5,000 cases. 40-acre vineyard almost on Sonoma County line is one of Spring Mountain's great sources for ripe, round Riesling and heady, boldly oaked, sometimes age-worthy Chardonnays.

Soda Canyon Winery (1985)
4130 Silverado Trail, Napa, CA 94558. Tel (707) 226-8789. 3,000 cases. Dark gold, fully oaked Chardonnay from 10 estate acres was the whole list until a red came along in 1990.

Spottswoode Winery (1982)
1902 Madrona Avenue, St Helena, CA 94574. Tel (707) 963-0134. 6,500 cases. Deep, almost somber tones from aging in oak distinguish an estate Cabernet Sauvignon that moves from subtly varietal to fully bouqueted over a 10-year span. The 40-acre vineyard in residential St Helena has lost its Sauvignon Blanc, but the winery continues to make a superior one with bought-in grapes.

Stag's Leap Wine Cellars (1972)
5766 Silverado Trail, Napa, CA 94558. Tel (707) 944-2020. 30,000 cases. Professorial Warren Winiarski does not make any wine without a lot of thought The results: polished, often forward Cabernet Sauvignon (a Napa Valley from bought-in grapes, SLV from the estate), and wondrously subtle Chardonnays (regular and Reserve, both from bought-in grapes). "Cask 23," no longer identified as a Cabernet Sauvignon, is the luxury red. A Riesling "Birkmyer Vineyard" can head the parade of that variety.

Stags' Leap Winery (1972)
6150 Silverado Trail, Napa, CA 94558. Tel (707) 944-1303. 25,000 cases. The original emphasis was on Petite Sirah and Chenin Blanc, but Cabernet Sauvignon has taken over as the headliner. From 88 acres at the heart of Stag's Leap, the latter is pushed one

step further toward tannic austerity than most from the region.

Star Hill Winery (1988)
1075 Shadybrook Lane, Napa, CA 94558. Tel (707) 255-1957. 1,000 cases. Chardonnay and Pinot Noir of the hearty school, mostly from bought-in grapes.

Steltzner Vineyards (1977)
5998 Silverado Trail, Napa, CA 94558. Tel (707) 252-7272. 1,500 cases. From 54 estate acres a wine that makes every effort to build bold flavors and firm textures into Stag's Leap District Cabernet Sauvignon.

Sterling Vineyards (1969)
1111 Dunaweal Lane, Calistoga, CA 94515. Tel (707) 942-3344. 250,000 cases. Under Seagram's ownership, the winery has turned increasingly toward single-vineyard wines from its widely scattered 1,140 acres. Pinot Noir "Winery Lake," Cabernet Sauvignon "Diamond Mountain," Chardonnay "Diamond Mountain," and the Merlot-based proprietary "Three Palms" are the leading examples. Regular bottlings of Cabernet Sauvignon, Sauvignon Blanc, and Chardonnay assembled from these and other properties are often as or more attractive.

Stonegate Winery (1973)
1183 Dunaweal Lane, Calistoga, CA 94515. Tel (707) 942-6500. 15,000 cases. Sturdy, straightforward Chardonnay and Cabernet Sauvignon, principally from a winery-owned vineyard on Diamond Mountain.

Stony Hill Vineyard (1952)
PO Box 308, St Helena, CA 94574. Tel (707) 963-2636. 4,000 cases. Ever more the emphasis is on estate Chardonnay from a candidate for the most beautifully set vineyard in the valley. Recent vintages have been slightly fuller and quicker to mature than earlier ones, which took forever but were worth it. A round, berrylike Riesling (now partially bought in from the nearby Draper Vineyard) is wonderful with cracked crab.

Storybook Mountain (1980)
3835 Highway 128, Calistoga, CA 94515. Tel (707) 942-5310. 9,000 cases. Heartily oaked, fully ripened Zinfandels from 36 acres in an east-facing amphitheater north of Calistoga.

Stratford Winery (1982)
3222 Ehlers Lane, St Helena, CA 94574. Tel (707) 963-3200. 40,000 cases. The firm has wavered back and forth between buying in wines and buying in grapes, but skillful enologists

keep the Napa appellation reds and especially the California-appellation Chardonnay not only price-worthy but outright attractive.

Strauss Vineyards (1985)
498 Petrified Forest Road, Calistoga, CA 94515. Tel (707) 942-9525. 4,000 cases. Dark, tannic Merlot from bought-in grapes.

Streblow Vineyards (1985)
PO Box 233, St Helena, CA 94574. Tel (707) 963-5892. 3,000 cases. Fleshy, heartily oaked Cabernet Sauvignon from 8 acres on lower Spring Mountain. Also: Chardonnay.

Sullivan Vineyards (1985)
1090 Galleron Lane, Rutherford, CA 94573. Tel (707) 963-9646. 7,000 cases. Rustic Cabernet Sauvignon and Merlot from 8 acres near Rutherford.

Summit Lake Vineyards (1986)
2000 Summit Lake Drive, Angwin, CA 94508. Tel (707) 965-2488. 1,200 cases. A family-owned winery and vineyard makes stout, intensely flavored Zinfandel in the grand tradition of Howell Mountain.

Sutter Home Winery (1947)
277 St Helena Highway S St Helena, CA 94574. Tel (707) 963-3104. 4.5 million cases. Far the largest part of the awesome total is a fat, frankly sweet White Zinfandel from widespread sources. By far the most characterful wine is a prototypical Amador Zinfandel. Most of the winery-owned vineyards are in Sacramento, Yolo, and Lake Counties; Sutter Home has one small vineyard at Calistoga. Proprietors also own Montevina (see p181).

Swanson Vineyards and Winery (1987)
1271 Manley Lane, Rutherford, CA 94573. Tel (707) 944-1642. 10,000 cases. Deftly toasty Chardonnay from one of the winery's three vineyards made the first great impression (the Reserve is much oakier). Cabernet is still finding a footing; Sangiovese and Syrah are in R&D.

Philip Togni Vineyard (1983)
PO Box 81, St Helena, CA 94574. Tel (707) 963-3731. 1,500 cases. Proprietor-winemaker willfully sticks to making slow-developing Cabernet Sauvignon and Sauvignon Blanc in a drink-now society. They come from his vineyard on Spring Mountain.

Traulsen Vineyards (1980)
2250 Highway 29, Calistoga, CA 94515. Tel (707) 942-0283. 500 cases. Heady, tannic Zinfandel from a garden-sized property.

Trefethen Vineyards (1973)
1160 Oak Knoll Avenue, Napa, CA 94558. Tel (707) 255-7700. 75,000 cases. Important 625-acre vineyard just north of Napa city shines most especially for understated but unmistakable Chardonnay capable of long life. Cabernet Sauvignon, more berry-like than herbaceous, increasingly bids for the limelight. Crisply dry White Riesling and Chardonnay-like "Eshcol White" are good and good value.

Truchard Vineyards (See Carneros)

Tudal Winery (1979)
1015 Big Tree Road, St Helena, CA 94574. Tel (707) 963-3947. 2,000 cases. The only wine is distinctively spicy Cabernet from 10 miraculously well-drained acres right next to the Napa River south of Calistoga.

Tulocay Winery (1975)
1426 Coombsville Road, Napa, CA 94558. Tel (707) 255-4064. 2,400 cases. Individualist often rings the bell with balanced, polished, and well-oaked Pinot Noir and Cabernet Sauvignon. Source vineyards are in the Coombsville district.

Van der Heyden Vineyard (1987)
4057 Silverado Trail, Napa, CA 94558. Tel (707) 257-0130. 1,000 cases. Thus far standard Napa Chardonnay.

Viader Vineyards (1989)
PO Box 280, Deer Park, CA 94576. Tel (707) 963-3816. 1,500 cases. Aims to do well with estate-grown Cabernet Sauvignon-Cabernet Franc blend from 18 rocky acres in hills east of St Helena.

Vichon Winery (1980)
1595 Oakville Grade, Oakville, CA 94576. Tel (707) 944-2811. 45,000 cases. Robert Mondavi-owned cellar is a leader with deftly herbeceous Napa Valley Chevrignon (50-50 Sauvignon Blanc-Sémillon). Also: sturdy Napa Valley Cabernet Sauvignon "SLD" (for Stag's Leap District), toasty Napa Valley Chardonnay. Lower-priced California-appellation "Coastal Selection" line leans on Central Coast vineyards. All grapes bought-in.

Villa Helena Winery (1984)
1455 Inglewood Avenue, St Helena, CA 94574. Tel (707) 963-4334. 500 cases. Weekend winemaker turns out a broad range of mini-lots.

Villa Mt Eden (1974)
PO Box 147, Oakville, CA 94562. Tel (707) 944-2414. 24,000 cases. Contrasting supple, stylish '86 and later Cabernet Sauvignon with earlier vintages amply demonstrates that assem-

bled can be better than estate. Firm, noticeably oaked Chardonnay also has improved since the sources expanded beyond 80 acres at the winery. These Napa Valley wines are subtitled "Grand Reserve" to further distinguish them from lesser-priced California appellation "Cellar Select" line introduced by VME's second owner, Washington State's Stimson Lane Company.

Villa Zapu (1986)
3090 Mt Veeder Road, Napa, CA 94558. Tel (707) 226-2501. 7,000 cases. Through its first 6 years, variable Chardonnay and Cabernet Sauvignon made in leased space with bought-in grapes. The vineyard has been planted; winery construction began in 1993.

Wermuth Winery (1982)
3942 Silverado Trail, Calistoga, CA 94515. Tel (707) 942-5924. 3,000 cases. Colombard and Gamay from small vineyards near Calistoga separate it from the pack.

Whitehall Lane Winery (1980)
1563 St Helena Highway, St Helena, CA 94574. Tel (707) 963-9454. 30,000 cases. A 1990 change in winemakers and shifting vineyard sources leave much up in the air. Chardonnay and Cabernet are the mainstays.

Whitford Cellars (1987)
4047 E Third Avenue, Napa, CA 94558. Tel (707) 257-7065. 2,000 cases. Erratic, sometimes fine Chardonnay comes under a grower label for the owners of Haynes Vineyard in Coombsville district, a property that has done well for Stag's Leap Wine Cellars and others.

Z D Wines (1969)
8383 Silverado Trail, Napa, CA 94558. Tel (707) 963-5188. 18,000 cases. American-oaked Carneros Pinot Noir often makes an impressive case for that approach. Brazenly oaky California-appellation Chardonnay (from Carneros and Santa Barbara) is the popular favorite.

Travel Information

The quote on the cask head comes from Robert Louis Stevenson, who honeymooned in Napa in 1881-82.

PLACES OF INTEREST

Calistoga The valley's most vivacious and down-to-earth town built itself on hot springs, mineral waters, mud baths, and other staples of the spa which caused pioneer Samuel Brannan to name it by a slip of the tongue-when he said it would become the "Calistoga of Sarafornia" when he meant the Saratoga of California. A glider port at one end of the main street, Lincoln Avenue, offers rentals and excursion flights. A long-time Walt Disney illustrator designed an agreeable museum of local history (1311 Washington Street). In hills west of town a private attraction, Petrified Forest, has some of the largest intact petrified trees in the world.

Napa The county seat and the valley's largest town has never quite tied itself to the wineries and vineyards, but rather stayed largely a blue-collar community for workers in industries farther south. It does have some worthy restaurants and several hotels and motels.

St Helena What was a sleepy, farm town main street in the 1960s has turned into a trendy shopping street for yuppies, many of them resident, most just visiting. They coincidentally have turned the town into a minor mecca for serious eaters, so serious, in fact, that local sidewalks roll up right after the dining hour. Within the municipal library (1400 Library Lane) is the Napa Valley Wine Library, a substantial collection of both popular and scholarly literature on vines and wines. Also in that building is the Silverado Museum, a major collection of Robert Louis Stevenson materials.

Yountville Two or three lively bars and several informal restaurants have turned Yountville into the preferred haunt of the valley's party animals. One of the valley's largest pre-Prohibition wineries now houses specialty shops known collectively as Vintage 1870.

HOTELS AND RESTAURANTS

Auberge du Soleil 180 Rutherford Hill Road, St Helena. Tel (707) 963-1211. Casually chic restaurant with sweeping views of the valley is part of a luxury inn. Largely traditional French menu and a long wine list.

Bosko's Ristorante 1362 Lincoln Avenue, Calistoga. Tel (707) 942-9088. Sawdust-on-the-floor informal. Ample, inexpensive pastas and salads; modest wine list.

La Boucane 1178 2nd Street, Napa. Tel (707) 253-1177. In a cozy, revamped Victorian home, a highly traditional French chef keeps to a short, highly traditional, skillfully executed menu. Good wine list.

Brava Terrace 3010 St Helena Highway, St Helena. Tel (707) 963-9300. Heaped plates of cassoulet, risotto, and other hearty Mediterranean fare by owner-chef Fred Halpert; modestly long but thoughtful wine list. An airy interior and a peaceful terrace in summer.

Domaine Chandon California Drive, Yountville. Tel (707) 944-2892. Glass walls give views of a parklike setting around the winery. Expensive, catering for a modestly dressy clientele. Intriguing Italian and Asian touches spark a menu built upon the French foundations of chef Phillipe Jeanty. Skilled staff. An excellent wine list.

Four Seasons Café 1400 Lincoln Avenue, Calistoga. Tel (707) 942-9111. Eclectic light and luncheon fare; staggering selection of American wines from a connected wine store.

The French Laundry 6640 Washington Street, Yountville. Tel (707) 944-2380. Home cooking carried to its zenith in a quiet restaurant where each table is reserved for the whole evening. Reservations are hard to come by.

Mustard's Grill 7399 St Helena Highway, Yountville. Tel (707) 944-2424. Ever-abuzz casual room. Ever-changing casual food by owner-chef Cindy Pawlcyn, much but not all of it grilled. Mostly Napa wine list. The same group owns Tra Vigne.

Napa Valley Lodge PO Box L (Madison at Washington), Yountville. Tel (707) 944-2468. Later arrivals are fancier but for comfort and price this is still the leader.

Piatti 6480 Washington Street, Yountville. Tel (707) 944-2070. A noisy, happy restaurant where the walls are mostly windows. Solid kitchen, mainly inspired by northern Italy. Good wine list.

Starmont Grill at Meadowood 90 Meadowood Lane, St Helena. Tel (707) 963-3646. The Starmont Grill is part of of a small golf (9 holes) and tennis (8 courts) resort secluded in hills east of St Helena. French management. Bright country French decor everywhere. Classical French accents inform a California menu; exceptional Napa wine list.

Terra 1345 Railroad Avenue, St Helena. Tel (707) 963-8931. Wolfgang Puck protégé Hiro Sone offers a deliciously eccentric Japanese-tinged French and Italian menu in two handsome, stone-walled rooms. The wine list is short but well chosen.

Tra Vigne 1050 Charter Oak Avenue, St Helena. Tel (707) 963-4444. Under founding chef Michael Chiarello, the restaurant has developed a style rather as if northern Italians had invented a new province full of ingredients and combinations close to but not exactly like any known to restaurateurs in the old ones. Jolly atmosphere. A fairly long California section anchors an international wine list.

Trilogy 1234 Main Street, St Helena. Tel (707) 963-5507. Quiet, small. A classical French-oriented menu manages to surprise with highly original details in ingredients and preparation by resourceful owner-chef Diane Pariseau. Rich California wine list.

Napa's volcanic origins are regularly evoked by a small, regular-as-clockwork geyser north of the town of Calistoga. It is visitable for a small entry fee.

WINE ROUTE

With some 200 wineries open to visitors in a valley 18 miles long and 2 miles wide, wine routes are mainly a matter of editing the list of cellars to be visited. One useful note: when SR 29 is bumper-to-bumper from Yountville to St Helena on a summer weekend, the Silverado Trail may be almost empty of cars.

USEFUL ADDRESSES

Calistoga Chamber of Commerce 1458 Lincoln Avenue, Calistoga, CA 94515.

Napa Chamber of Commerce 1556 1st Street, Napa, CA 94558.

Napa Valley Vintners Association PO Box 141, St Helena, CA 94574.

St Helena Chamber of Commerce 1080 Main Street, St Helena, CA 94574.

Yountville Chamber of Commerce 6795 Washington Street, Yountville, CA 94599.

Carneros

Already, with the United States' system of appellations still in its infancy, Carneros (sometimes known as Los Carneros) has made a solid argument in its favor by escaping from the tall shadows of the Napa and Sonoma valleys in less than a decade.

Abandoning a name with as much cachet as Napa Valley takes courage, especially when regulations permit its use alongside or in place of a relative unknown. However, the trend is strong because Carneros's vineyard and winery owners alike have a firm and growing belief that their relentlessly windy, foggy, meager-soiled district is not the Napa Valley at all, nor Sonoma either, but rather Carneros through and through. They reached their conclusion quite sensibly. During the first discussions about establishing a Carneros appellation, owners of the district's major wineries assembled a panel of seasoned palates and asked them to try to differentiate between Carneros and non-Carneros wines in a blind tasting. The tasters succeeded to near perfection.

Out of that effort came both the appellation boundaries (what tasted like Carneros is in, what did not is not) and an organization called Carneros Quality Alliance. CQA is a promotional arm. It also is a clearing house of technical information

The soft but relentless rolling hills of Carneros – coupled with its winds – make thoughtful site selection imperative for each variety.

for winemakers and growers, and has already had important effects in focusing style and character in the wines.

Despite all this Carneros insiders do not have a clear track toward becoming a breakaway province. Prominent Napa Valley names are among the major vineyard owners: Beaulieu Vineyard, Clos du Val, Cuvaison, Domaine Chandon, Charles Krug, Louis M. Martini, and Robert Mondavi lead them, and none is anxious to give up on Napa Valley as part or all of the identity of the wines they make from Carneros grapes. Sonoma Valley has fewer divided loyalties. Buena Vista might have been one prime example for historic reasons, but instead it is a spearhead in the CQA, its 1,100 acres of vineyard making it the largest grower in the appellation.

If specific identity is a recent development, Carneros still has a worthy, surprisingly long, and remarkably consistent history. It had at least one vineyard by 1830. Its first winery came during the 1870s. And by the end of the 1880s at the latest, wines from the Stanly Ranch, Debret et Priet, and the Talcoa estate brought respectful nods from sharp palates of the day.

First phylloxera then Prohibition built long gaps into the record. Tough growing conditions kept vineyards rare in the landscape throughout the Great Depression, and for years after it, as wine was a tough sell. The boom that turned Carneros from dairy pasture to vineyard did not come until the 1970s.

Louis M. Martini kept the district going when he bought part of the Stanly Ranch and another property in the 1940s, planting Pinot Noir in both. André Tchelistcheff of Beaulieu bought grapes in Carneros until 1961, when he coaxed his proprietors into buying land next to Martini for Pinot Noir and Chardonnay. One other current planting upholds the old judgments. What was originally Talcoa and later Debret et Priet was revived in the 1960s by independent grower Rene di Rosa as Winery Lake Vineyard. It now belongs to Seagram, which uses it primarily as the source of a vineyard-designated sparkling wine from Mumm Napa Valley and a vineyard-designated Pinot Noir from Sterling Vineyards.

White Wine Varieties*

In 1992 Chardonnay accounted for nearly half of Carneros's 6,200 acres of vines, most of it devoted to table wine, a fair amount to classic-method sparkling wine. Riesling, Gewürztraminer and a tiny amount of Pinot Blanc added less than 100 acres to the total.

Chardonnay
If any other variety is to challenge Chardonnay in Carneros it has yet to raise its flag. By all the standards – depth of flavor, balance, age-worthiness – the great white grape of Burgundy is the great grape here.

Young, a typical Carneros Chardonnay, can bring to mind an apple baked with honey, most particularly a sage honey. Apple is Chardonnay's specific contribution. Honey and herb seem to spring straight from Carneros' sun and soil. As the wines mature – most will age four to six years in top form – apple, honey, and herb slowly become one without quite losing their initial identities. In 1992, to choose one of the most memorable examples, a 1981 Saintsbury could only be counted a marvel of all the things a white wine should be: silken, bouqueted, and still with a vitality and a richness of Chardonnay flavor that put it nowhere near the end of its tether.

Not every bottling has quite so much character, but the average on all counts is impressively high, so much so that it can be very difficult to tear oneself away from Chardonnay in order to taste the Pinot Noirs of those who put Pinot Noir first. At any comprehensive tasting of the appellation's wines, the Chardonnays almost surely will be the classiest field overall, one of them almost certain to come away with the cup for best in show.

Winemakers have the luxury of being able to use malolactic fermentations, aging on lees, and other sources of swift maturity in the wines, or to skip them. Their wines have enough flavor on their own to shine through definite efforts to impose style – sufficiently naturally endowed to need no such makeup and perfume. Buena Vista is the model. MacRostie and Saintsbury are deft paragons of toastiness. In style, others in the list of benchmarks fall between these examples.

Benchmarks:
Acacia "Marina Vineyard" (estate). **Buena Vista** (estate). **Carneros Creek** (assembled). **Clos du Val** (estate). **Cuvaison** (estate). **MacRostie** (Sangiacomo). **Roche** (estate). **Saintsbury** (assembled). **Saintsbury** "Reserve" (assembled).

Gewürztraminer
Gewürztraminer has virtually disappeared from Carneros except for 35 acres at Buena Vista, which does well enough with the variety to make one wonder why its star has fallen so low. Winery Lake once had a planting which yielded excellent wines in the early 1970s for a fledgling Z D, but abandoned it in favor of Pinot Noir. Before that Louis M. Martini produced some fine examples from vines in its La Loma vineyard. At least Martini replanted its Gewürztraminer, first at Monte Rosso, then later, to outstanding effect, in its Los Vinedos del Rio vineyard in the Russian River Valley.

Riesling
A glum Louis P. Martini once grumbled that Carneros Riesling would rot before it ripened every time. The claim was almost true. Riesling demands uncommon care in these fog-shrouded, wind-blown vineyards to ripen in full health. Given that care, it will yield wine worth drinking in all the summery contexts in which California's round, berrylike Rieslings shine best, especially when young and fresh, and most especially with heaped plates of cold cracked crab, mounded bowls of steamed clams, or a little pâté, all with plenty of French bread.

"Wind machines" – the colloquial term for propellers that can raise the chilly night air enough to avert spring frost damage.

* California grape acreages are recorded by county and therefore Carneros's totals are included with those given in the Napa and Sonoma chapters.

61

Others have grown Riesling in Carneros in the past, but, as with Gewürztraminer, it is Buena Vista that survives as the guardian of the old order. Its 38 acres have only 10 in Mont St John's Madonna vineyard for company.

Sparkling Wines

Carneros has secured a place toward the head of the list of California AVAs where sparkling wine does well. It might be at the top. Certainly it has an impressive roster of grower-producers in Domaine Carneros (Taittinger-directed), Codorniu Napa (owned by the Spanish house of the same name), and Gloria Ferrer (owned by the proprietors of Spain's Freixenet). Domaine Chandon also has 700 acres of vines in Carneros, enough to permit a Carneros appellation for the domain's Blanc de Noirs.

Among them, these wineries produce almost a fifth of all Carneros's wine, the range of styles reflecting what California can do with techniques developed in Champagne. Gloria Ferrer, in both its "Carneros Cuvée" and "Royal Cuvée," consistently produces vintage bottlings with Pinot Noir at about 60 percent of each cuvée, Chardonnay at 40 per cent. (The firm's nonvintage Brut, which incorporates some Sonoma grapes from outside Carneros, uses closer to 90 percent Pinot Noir).

The creamy "Carneros Cuvée" spends nearly four years on its yeasts, one of the longer aging times in all of California. Chandon, in its Blanc de Noirs, uses reserve wine to give the picture its tints of age. As the name promises, it is nearly all Pinot Noir and Pinot Meunier. It is marketed fairly young, then develops impressively under cork (*see* page 35).

Domaine Carneros makes a lean, firm Blanc de Blancs, mainly from Chardonnay, and a nonvintage Brut usually from 60 per cent Chardonnay, 40 percent Pinot Noir (the Pinot Noir percentage tending to creep up). Last, not least, Mumm Napa Valley "Winery Lake," another 60 Pinot Noir, 40 Chardonnay, became California's first avowed single-vineyard sparkling wine with its first vintage, 1985.

Benchmarks:

Domaine Carneros Blanc de Blancs (nonvintage). **Domaine Carneros** Brut (nonvintage). **Domaine Chandon** Blanc de Noirs (nonvintage). **Codorniu Napa** Brut (nonvintage). **Gloria Ferrer** Carneros Cuvée (vintage). **Mumm** Napa Valley "Winery Lake" (vintage).

Red Wine Varieties*

Pinot Noir tops plantings with 1,400 acres, but does not dominate as Chardonnay does in whites. Cabernet trails with 360 acres, Merlot with 300.

Cabernet Sauvignon

Louis M. Martini's 1979 "La Loma" and Buena Vista's 1985 "Private Reserve" make one wonder why Cabernet Sauvignon has not found a greater home in Carneros. Other vintages point out why. In the best years Cabernet makes a tart wine as well as a flavorful one, a balance that usually makes it better suited to blending with blander fruit than standing on its own. It does pay to keep an eye out for the treasures.

---

* California grape acreages are recorded by county and therefore Carneros's totals are included with those given in the Napa and Sonoma chapters.

Merlot

Though acreage remains at a scant 300, one Napa Valley producer, Jan Shrem of Clos Pegase, has gone on record as believing Merlot will at least equal, perhaps surpass, Pinot Noir in Carneros. He planted some of his own vineyard to Merlot based on that belief. The evidence that tipped him comes from three vineyards, Buena Vista, Cuvaison, and Truchard. Buena Vista, characteristically, puts grape flavors foremost. Cuvaison leans rather more on oak and, with it, tannin. Truchard Vineyard, after growing the grapes for several impressive bottlings under the Havens label, bonded its own winery with Michael Havens as winemaker.

Benchmarks:

Buena Vista (estate). **Cuvaison** (estate). **Havens** (Truchard).

Pinot Noir

Carneros Pinot Noirs, rather curiously, manage to fall between those of the Russian River Valley and Santa Barbara County in both flavor and texture. A typical one is not quite as rich or ripe or fat as the Russian River's best, nor quite as pungent with herb or mint as the Santa Barbarans. But it will have more herb or mint than a Russian River, and more flesh than a Santa Barbaran.

These wines come in two distinct styles. One, epitomized by Buena Vista's estate bottling, Carneros Creek's "Fleur de Carneros" and Saintsbury's "Garnet," emphasizes fresh fruit flavors and delicacy of texture. The other strikes for bolder flavors and greater richness of texture. In the latter style, in vintages since 1984, Saintsbury has caught the brass ring more often than any other cellar in the appellation, partly, it would seem, by building a wine out of numerous blocks, as many as a dozen different vineyards in most years.

At Carneros Creek, Francis Mahoney prefers to use many strains of Pinot Noir from its own vineyard in making both regular and "Reserve" bottlings. The division is simple: the regular bottling is run of the vineyard, while the Reserve comes from a long, narrow but steep slope where crops naturally restrict themselves to 7 lbs per vine, about half the normal yield. The "Reserve" gets enough time in new oak to partially cloud the contributions of the vines, but instructive differences remain.

Acacia, also working with single vineyards, circles around and around Saintsbury. The "St Clair" is leaner, firmer and fuller of minty tones, the "Madonna" a little fleshier and inclined ever so slightly more toward cherry as its main fruit flavor. (Mont St John's own version of Pinot Noir from its Madonna vineyard proves to be an instructive comparison to the Acacia.)

All of these are wines of some substance and considerable charm, but they seldom measure up to the Chardonnays. Old memories of a 1957 Louis M. Martini and new ones of a Domaine Chandon trial lot of Pinot Meunier suggest that Carneros could do more than break away from Napa and Sonoma, it could also turn away from Burgundy – or at least turn to two unheralded cousins of Pinot Noir for qualities Pinot Noir often lacks. The Martini, which still has more than mere echoes of a long period of greatness, has Pinot St George in it. The uncommercialized Chandon has depths and facets that surely deserve a place in the sun.

Benchmarks:

Saintsbury Carneros (assembled). **Saintsbury** Carneros "Garnet" (assembled). **Carneros Creek** Carneros (estate). **Carneros Creek** Carneros "Fleur de Carneros" (assembled). **Buena Vista** Carneros (estate). **Acacia** Carneros (assembled). **Acacia** Carneros "St Clair," **Acacia** Carneros "Madonna." **Roche** Carneros (estate).

Carneros AVA

Established: September 19, 1983
Total area: 36,900 acres
Area in vineyard: 6,200 acres
Wineries: 17
Principal town: None (Napa, Sonoma nearby)

Three wines preoccupy Carneros: Pinot Noir, classic-method sparkling wines, and Chardonnay, probably in that order. Merlot, somehow, was beginning to establish itself as a dark horse in the early 1990s.

Saintsbury and Carneros Creek beat the drum most fervently for Pinot Noir. Domaine Carneros, Codorniu Napa, and Gloria Ferrer make sparkling wine and nothing but, and have no intentions of clouding the issue. But no Carneros-based producer promotes Chardonnay with the same kind of fervor. That task falls to the Sangiacomo family, growers whose several hundred acres of it go into as many as a score of wines in every vintage.

The environment in which all of this takes place has a particular look and feel about it. Carneros slopes up from the top-most loop of San Pablo Bay, part of it onto the Sonoma Mountains, part onto the Mayacamas Mountains. For most of the year, the soft, near-treeless hills rising toward the Sonoma ranges to the north look like old lion hides casually tossed aside. Farther east, the rump of the Mayacamas is not quite so bare, but could hardly be called heavily forested. Grapes do not grow any more easily than trees. In four or five years the trunks of vines around Oakville will grow as thick as a fighter's forearm. In the same span, their peers in Carneros will not get much thicker than a pencil. During any one growing season the story is about the same. Grape leaves in Oakville get as big as dinner plates, just the thing for giant servings of dolmades, but in Carneros leaves of the same variety will be not only tiny, but tough.

Lean soils bear some of the responsibility. Although there are several named types of clay loam in the appellation, winemakers and growers divide them into dark and light to account for the amount of heat reflection, and let it go at that. ´

A fog-cooled growing season does its bit. Carneros does not have an official weather station of its own, but Napa temperatures (*see* page 31) are actually very similar (if perhaps a degree or two warmer because the station at Napa State Hospital is much more wind-sheltered than most of Carneros).

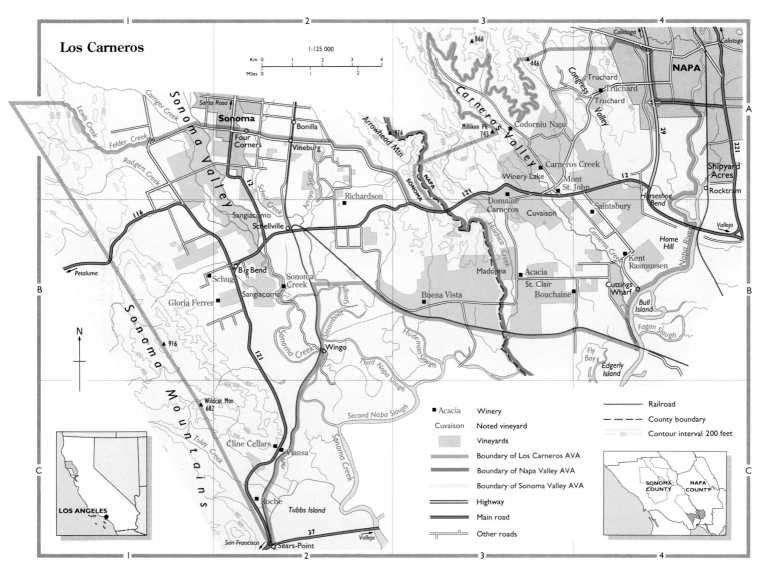

San Francisco lurks in the mists across San Pablo – San Francisco Bay. The white building on the extreme left is Domaine Carneros, a sparkling-wine specialist.

It is, in fact, the nearly eternal, usually howling, wind that distinguishes Carneros from the more sheltered parts of Napa and Sonoma. The same gales that lay sailing boats almost flat in the Raccoon Straits keep on blowing right across Carneros; they are strongest on the western half of Buena Vista's long, skinny vineyard, but not weak anywhere. Velocities are such that they cause vines to protect themselves against dehydration by shutting down their whole metabolic process for some part of almost every day between June and September.

Pinot Noir may be scrawny to look at, but it ripens well in most of Carneros. Most growers keep it on the windy sides of hills where harvest season molds occur less frequently. These molds can be particularly troublesome in gullies and on northern exposures because of wind shelter and lack of drying sunshine. The St Clair, Lee, Madonna, Winery Lake, Carneros Creek, and most other highly regarded vineyards follow the rules. Pinot Meunier, meanwhile, is beginning to creep in alongside Pinot Noir in several vineyards owned by sparkling-wine specialists, most notably in those belonging to Domaine Chandon.

Chardonnay, unlike Pinot Noir, ripens less well in windy spots than more sheltered ones. It is also harvested earlier in the season – to the relief of owners of north-facing slopes. Resulting small crops make independent growers reluctant to plant the variety on hillsides, but are an added incentive for wineries to do so. For Chardonnay, Sangiacomo is the famous name in an appellation much more apportioned to assembled wines than single-vineyard ones among its own producers. Producers with vineyards in Carneros but wineries elsewhere in Napa are by far the most likely to stick with a single property: Beaulieu Vineyard, Clos du Val, Cuvaison, Charles Krug, and several smaller cellars all demonstrate.

Although thinking about growing it gives Pinot Noir fanciers headaches, Merlot may turn out to be the most widely adapted of all the varieties planted in the Carneros appellation. Some see it as being better suited to the darker, warmer soils lying away from bay-facing exposures. The long-established Truchard is a proven case in point. However, it also ripens well in Buena Vista's coolest soils and its windiest exposures. Carneros, incidentally, is one of only two cool appellations where Pinot Noir and Merlot vines may actually begin to compete with each other for space – the Russian River Valley being the other.

Cabernet Sauvignon, although little planted, serves as an index variety for some growers. It ripens only in dark, relatively rich soils in warm spots. Sometimes it does so to splendid effect. Louis M. Martini's La Loma vineyard and Buena Vista have all the plantings.

PRODUCERS

Acacia (1981)
2750 Las Amigas Road, Napa, CA 94559. Tel (707) 226-9991. 50,000 cases. Much focused on single-vineyard wines from the district, Acacia has rattled off a string of fine, firm Chardonnays from its own 40-acre Marina Vineyard, and quite good Pinot Noirs from St Clair and Madonna. No other variety clouds the issue.

Bouchaine (1981)
1075 Buchli Station Road, Napa, CA 94559. Tel (707) 252-9065. 15,000 cases. After struggling early, Bouchaine begins to do well with a well-oaked Chardonnay. Pinot Noir is still in question. A Russian River Valley Gewürztraminer entices.

Buena Vista (1857)
PO Box 182, Sonoma, CA 95476. Tel (707) 252-7117. 120,000 cases. The Titan, with 950 –1,100 acres of vineyard, provides a wonderfully accurate index to the rest, especially with perfectly varietal Chardonnay, zesty Pinot Noir (1989 and later), and rich Merlot. Tartly berryish Cabernet Sauvignon can be an eye-opener. Riesling and Gewürztraminer also appeal. The Private Reserves, miracle of miracles, are not overdone.

Carneros Creek (1972)
1285 Dealy Lane, Napa, CA 94559. Tel (707) 253-9463. 22,000 cases. All the emphasis is on Pinot Noir in three grades (drink-quick "Fleur de Carneros" from bought-in grapes, solid "Blue Label" from 20 estate acres, well-oaked "Reserve" from a sharp slope within the estate), but the bought-in Chardonnay is occasionally the wine of the vintage.

Francis Mahoney of Carneros Creek at the top of the "Reserve" slope.

Cline Cellars (1982 in Contra Costa County; to Carneros in 1990)
24737 Arnold Drive, Sonoma, CA 95476. Tel (707) 935-4310. 10,000 cases. This history is a Rhône range of Mourvèdre-based blends (Côtes d'Oakley, Oakley Cuvée) from 180 acres near the town of Oakley. The first plantings on the Carneros property were of Viognier and Syrah.

Codorniu Napa (1990)
1345 Henry Road, Napa, CA 94559. Tel (707) 224-1668. 25,000 cases. Early *cuvées of* Brut showed technical skill; style is still evolving.

Domaine Carneros (1987)
PO Box 5420, Napa, CA 94581. Tel (707) 257-0101. 30,000 cases. Source of the leanest, most austere, of all the Carneros sparkling wines, perhaps all of California's. A year or two in bottle brings depth and richness to the style.

Gloria Ferrer (1982)
PO Box 1427, Sonoma, CA 95476. Tel (707) 996-7256. 65,000 cases. Subtle, balanced, harmonious sparkling wines: "Carneros Cuvée" most completely reflects the region, and "Brut" and "Royal Cuvée" are also among those most consistently attractive in California.

MacRostie (1987)
17246 Woodland Avenue, Sonoma, CA 95476. Tel (707) 996-4480. 7,700 cases. Steven MacRostie's winemaker label began with a deftly toasty Chardonnay from Sangiacomo grapes. That remains the headliner, joined later by Carneros Merlot and Pinot Noir.

Mont St John (1979)
5400 Old Sonoma Road, Napa, CA 94559. Tel (707) 255-8864. 15,000 cases. Without ever rousing the critics, the winery has plugged away at making

reliably drinkable wines at fair prices – all but the Cabernet is from its owner's Madonna Vineyard. Pinot Noir is the linchpin.

Kent Rasmussen (1986)
2145 Cuttings Wharf Road, Napa, CA 94559. Tel (707) 252-4224. 3,000 cases. Pinot Noir from 10 estate acres is the mainstay, but Rasmussen experiments relentlessly with other, often off-beat varieties such as Dolcetto.

Richardson (1980)
2711 Knob Hill Road, Sonoma, CA 95476. Tel (707) 938-2610. 2,000 cases. Proprietor Dennis Richardson is burly. So are his Cabernet Sauvignon, Merlot and Pinot Noir, all from bought-in Carneros grapes.

Roche Winery (1988)
28700 Arnold Drive, Sonoma, CA 95476. Tel (707) 936-7115. 3,000 cases. Supple, subtle Chardonnay and Pinot Noir from the westernmost vineyard in Carneros.

Saintsbury (1981)
1500 Los Carneros Avenue, Napa, CA 94559. Tel (707) 252-0592. 30,000 cases. In blind tastings, the Pinot Noir shows every time as the very essence of Carneros. The winery's Chardonnay is a model of restraint in the toasty style.

Schug Carneros Estate (1980 in the Napa Valley, to Carneros in 1991)
602 Bonneau Road, Sonoma, CA 95476. Tel (707) 939-9365. 8,000 cases. Both Chardonnay and Pinot Noir "Beckstoffer" are designed lean and firm, with long bottle-aging in mind.

Sonoma Creek (1987)
23355 Millerick Road, Sonoma, CA 95476. Tel (707) 938-3031. 5,000 cases. From a 40-acre vineyard at Schellville, vigorously oaked estate Chardonnay. Reds are from bought-in Sonoma Valley grapes.

Truchard Vineyards (1990)
3234 Old Sonoma Road, Napa, CA 94559. Tel (707) 252-7153. 800 cases. A 168-acre vineyard in the northeast quarter of Carneros has begun taking small lots of its own crop after carving out a particular reputation for Merlot.

Viansa (1983)
25200 Arnold Drive, Sonoma, CA 95476. Tel (707) 935-4700. 12,000 cases. Sam J. Sebastiani founded the winery on the premise that blending Napa and Sonoma Chardonnay and Cabernet Sauvignon produces more than the sum of the parts. The focus has switched to Sangiovese and other Italian varieties since 1988.

Top: Winemaker Jill Davis has done much to earn Buena Vista its current high reputation.
Above: Saintsbury is one of Carneros's leaders in Pinot Noir.

Sonoma County

One of the stereotypes cultivated by Sonomans is that they bounce around in pickup trucks while Napans glide along in BMWs. The implication is that Sonomans make honest little country wines which they sell at their farmhouse doors for the equivalent of egg money, while Napans build castles and set their prices to impress the jet set. In 1970 that might have approached the truth. Ten years later it had the earmarks of a fib, and by 1990 it was mostly a lingering myth.

In 1970 Sonoma's vineyards were just beginning to pick themselves up from their lowest state in history, the first few plots of Cabernet Sauvignon and Chardonnay slipping in among the still-dominant fields of Carignane and Colombard. The first wave of new wineries since the 1930s had not yet come. Most of the firms then in business sold their wines in bulk to people who, if they did not blend them into faceless commodities, hid their Sonoma origins behind the gross appellation of California.

By 1990 Cabernet, Pinot Noir, and Chardonnay dominated plantings, with Riesling having already fired and fallen back. Not one but two new waves of wineries had joined the field, some of them in castles that could rival anything in Napa.

The interplay of sea-fogs and elevation is a major factor in what is planted where, and when the harvest begins in Sonoma.

BMWs were abundant. Single-vineyard bottlings were all the rage with the upmarket newcomers, and most of the old bulk wineries were producing under their own names, sometimes for prices way out of the egg money class.

And yet something of the old air also remains. In Sonoma, much more than Napa, winery owners prune their own vines, haul their own hoses, wash their own barrels, drive ratty pickup trucks, and thus keep a certain earthiness about them that is lacking among the many gentleman farmers in both counties. This renewed Sonoma resists definition or comparison with any other region. When appellations became a fact early in the 1980s, no other county leapt so quickly to establish so many. Though the Russian River, Dry Creek, and Alexander valleys radiate from a common hub at Healdsburg, they differ enough in terrain and climate to reach their pinnacles with different grape varieties. Within Russian River, the sub-AVAs of Chalk Hill and Sonoma-Green Valley are surprisingly different in climate and terrain, and thus in plantings. Sonoma Valley stands apart from them all, tipped toward San Francisco Bay rather than the Pacific Ocean. It shares size, but not much else, with Dry Creek. Like Russian River it has a pair of disparate sub-sections in Sonoma Mountain and Carneros. Sonoma Valley's identity, unlike that of Russian River Valley, is being complicated by Carneros trying to live entirely by its own name (*see* page 60).

Sheer size is always a centrifugal force in Sonoma, distance making it much easier to get from downtown Sonoma to Yountville than it does to get from Sonoma's plaza to Healdsburg's. Even getting across the mountains from Healdsburg to Calistoga takes less trouble than the trek to Sonoma town.

Terrain contributes at least as heartily as distance to the divisions. Geological maps and soil surveys of the county look like visuals of the chaos theory, or maybe early Jackson Pollocks. Evidence of volcanic activity is abundant, as are relics of much of the county's long career as a Miocene seabed. Sometimes the two come mixed together, though less flagrantly than in Napa. Sonoma's more recent, calmer episodes of soil formation have added alluvium from Mendocino to the catalog of source materials.

The county's climate is more orderly than its geology, but not much, depending as it does on a complicated interplay of sea-fogs and low mountains. The basic North Coast weather pattern prevails over most of Sonoma: wet, cool winters and dry, warm to hot summers. Only the coast is truly steeped in California's persistent summer fog, so much so that vines are rare out there.

Interior Sonoma differs from neighboring Napa and Mendocino in having more deep channels through its coastal hills, and a few stretches where even the highest ridges do not rise to the heights that keep fog from rolling right over their tops. The upshot is an uncommonly wide range of summer temperatures between the coast and the interior, and uncommonly unpredictable swings from growing season to growing season at points where fog depends on larger climatic forces. Some vineyards in the Russian River Valley, in particular, may be swathed in fog almost daily one year, then will hardly see it the next.

Where fogs are common, redwoods cluster thickly. Where the sun shines every day, oaks dot grassy hills. Where things are less certain, the two pictures come together along sinuous lines that, more than any other natural sight, symbolize this place. These patterns are so complex that even the fondest proponents of Sonoma's AVAs admit that these areas define geographical places, not homogeneous conditions suited to some specific grape variety in the way that the Côte d'Or and Médoc are, not to mention such fine shadings as Beaune and Pauillac.

Sonoma is large and widely suited to viticulture, but its vineyard holdings and wineries still tend to be small, 50 acres and 15,000 cases coming close to the norm. Its biggest growers have only 1,200 to 1,500 acres when all of their properties are added up – modest in comparison with Monterey and Santa Barbara. The two largest individual vineyards in Sonoma, Gallo's 600 acres in Dry Creek Valley and Clos du Bois's 540 in Alexander Valley, seem tiny by the standards of the Central Coast. Upstart Glen Ellen, at more than three million cases, is the largest winery based in Sonoma County, though much of its volume comes from grapes grown elsewhere. Only Sebastiani and Korbel can rival it in size.

Sonoma's history

That Sonoma reached 1970 in such a dim condition is difficult to believe, because it had a substantial headstart on all its peers in northern California. Franciscan priests planted the first vineyard in the 1820s, at what would become the town of Sonoma. Within a decade their vines had been taken over by the Mexican governor of Alta California, General Mariano Vallejo. What ensued had overtones of comic opera, soap opera, or both. To summarize: the Gold Rush caused California to become an American state and brought a wave of new settlers, among them a Hungarian émigré, Agoston Haraszthy. He arrived in Sonoma town in 1857, started what would become Buena Vista, planted as many as 100 varieties of grapes, and launched a competition with the deposed but still prominent Vallejo to see which man could make the better wine. Haraszthy took the State Fair grand prize in 1858 and again in 1859. On the heels of that success he revisited Europe in 1861 to collect vine cuttings from all the important districts in his native land, Germany, France, and Italy. The state reneged on its agreement to pay for his travels, compounding financial difficulties caused by his impetuous management of Buena Vista. Haraszthy's partners in the winery threw him out and he then went to Nicaragua, where he is thought to have been eaten by a crocodile while attempting a river crossing.

Agoston left two sons, married to two Vallejo daughters, in the wine business in San Francisco and Sonoma. By the time he left California, several German wine merchants based in San Francisco had invested heavily in the Sonoma Valley. The sum of all their efforts had made it the premier wine district in the state by 1860, and kept it in the front ranks through 1890, when California's first bout of phylloxera began draining its energies.

The Russian River was, by and large, being settled by small farmers, many of them immigrants from Italy. Their winemaking was more casual than the Germans', their wine

The top line is a genuine invitation at many wineries.

marketing far more so. Though there came to be scores of wineries in the Alexander and Dry Creek valleys in the era between the Gold Rush and national Prohibition, most made wine in bulk for sale to merchants elsewhere. Few of their old buildings survive, fewer of the names that went with them. Foppiano, Korbel, Seghesio, and Simi are virtually the entire alumni association. What phylloxera did not close down during the 1890s, national Prohibition did after 1913. After a first burst of optimism in the 1930s, Sonoma went right back to sleep as a wine region, and it stayed asleep for three decades.

When a bold man named Russell Green bought Simi in 1970, that winery was barely alive. Foppiano, Pedroncelli, Fredson, and Martini & Prati were mainly or purely small-scale bulk producers. Geyser Peak was a vinegar works. Nervo, Cambiaso, and a couple of others were, like Simi, selling the odd bottle at the cellar door. Cooperative-owned Italian Swiss Colony was the big name with cent-saver stuff that, at its pinnacle, was identified as "Napa-Sonoma-Mendocino." Gallo-owned Frei Brothers was the big producer, but not for the glory of Sonoma. Korbel gave what luster there was to northern Sonoma.

Matters were not much different in the Sonoma Valley in 1970. Sebastiani and Val-Moon made bulk wine. A journalist had bought long-idle Buena Vista during World War II and opened its doors a crack, but had not made the kind of headway that would encourage others. Tiny Hanzell had fired an impressive shot when a 1957 Chardonnay came remarkably close to the goal of James D. Zellerbach of equalling first-rate white Burgundy. However, Zellerbach had died before any gain could be consolidated, and the winery he founded was just getting into its second life.

The real problem for all of Sonoma was not inferior vineyards. No rival district had much acreage devoted to fine varieties, either. Rather it was its willingness to settle for bulk winemaking, its failure to see itself in a leading role. Once Zellerbach died, another decade drifted by before Green struck the match that lit the fire that brought Sonoma back.

Climate

It is uncertain fog, more than Sonoma County's notoriously fractious geology, that keeps its growers extra cautious when they choose varieties to plant. A local agricultural adviser divides the county into two essential zones, coastal cool and coastal warm, with sea-fogs making coastal cool, and their absence producing coastal warm. In the simplest terms, coastal cool is the territory of Chardonnay and Pinot Noir, while coastal warm is the province of Sauvignon Blanc and Cabernet Sauvignon.

It is a nifty set of definitions, one that works almost perfectly in any one year. The difficulty with it shows up in longer spans of time, with the simple fact that Sonoma's fogs wax and wane enough to move large acreages back and forth between coastal cool and coastal warm, sometimes with stunning force.

In more or less ideal 1990, the city of Santa Rosa was wrapped in fog day after day. At a low spot on a plain where cool air currents pouring through two gaps in the Coast Ranges can converge, its high temperatures throughout the growing season stayed 4 to 10 degrees cooler than those of Healdsburg, 14 miles north, cooler still than those of Cloverdale. All in all a fairly typical picture of cool coastal Russian River Valley and

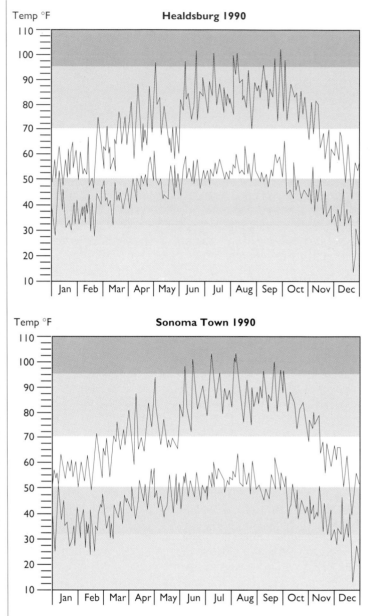

warm coastal Alexander Valley.

The weather at Graton, west of Santa Rosa in the Russian River Valley, was not so typical. All summer long its temperatures very nearly equalled the daytime highs at Healdsburg because fogs rolling north from Petaluma were too thin to cover it much past sunrise. When those fogs are thin, there is no chance at all of cold, gray air pouring straight across the hilltops from the Pacific Ocean. However, in years when the fog bank rolls like combers across the ridgetops, Graton shivers with Santa Rosa.

The Sonoma Valley and Carneros can be, and usually are, even more striking examples of cool and warm because Carneros looks obliquely across the bay to the Golden Gate while steep hills draw Sonoma town tight against their skirts. Within the three miles separating bay-facing vines from those on the slopes above Sonoma, temperatures climb at a dizzying pace. Still, 1990 was an exaggeration. The weather was cooler in Carneros (best represented by Napa city, *see* page 31) than in Santa Rosa, while Sonoma broiled along, 2 to 4 degrees warmer than Healdsburg.

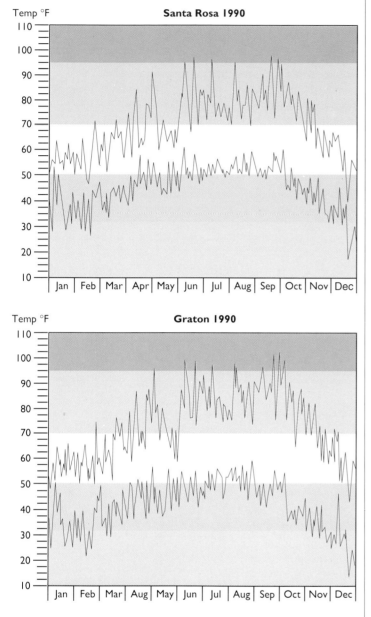

Temp °F

Santa Rosa 1990

Jan | Feb | Mar | Apr | May | Jun | Jul | Aug | Sep | Oct | Nov | Dec

Temp °F

Graton 1990

Jan | Feb | Mar | Aug | May | Jun | Jul | Aug | Sep | Oct | Nov | Dec

White Wine Varieties

Sonoma came to the Chardonnay party much later than the Napa Valley but, in acreage, caught and passed its neighbor and old rival in a hurry once it got going. It prospers in reputation as well. The only other variety claiming much attention is Sauvignon Blanc. Gewürztraminer surely should have a greater place of honor, and Riesling and Pinot Blanc may also deserve better fates. Other familiar and near-familiar varieties – Chenin Blanc, Colombard, and the assorted Muscats – struggle for recognition because a good deal is known; Arneis, Marsanne, and Viognier, on the other hand, struggle because almost nothing is.

Chardonnay (130 acres in 1970, 8,701 in 1990)
The long list of benchmarks (*see* page 70) and soaring acreages tell the story: Chardonnay is ubiquitous, adaptable and reliable in nearly all the county. Only the floor of Knights Valley seems ill-suited: this is an early-budding variety in California and Knights Valley can see frost well into spring. Curiously, given Sonoma's giddy range of climates and diversity of soils, most of the county's Chardonnay has a homogeneous flavor, sticking closely to the traditional University of California flavor association of apples. Flavors and textures are, or can be, so close among widespread sources that dividing these wines by style comes more easily than sorting them out by appellation.

Alderbrook and Handley, almost side-by-side where the Dry Creek and Russian River Valleys meet, have turned out notably lean, crisp wines tasting so clearly of Chardonnay that they ought to be regarded as textbook examples. Alexander Valley's de Lorimier came closer to them than any other wine until the style shifted toward fuller body and woodier flavors with the 1990. Gundlach-Bundschu's Sonoma Valley "Rhinefarm" replaced it by moving away from oak and toward clearer fruit flavors and crisper textures with its 1990.

From the evidence presented by Jordan, Clos du Bois "Calcaire," and others, it would seem that Alexander Valley Chardonnays naturally lean in the direction of weighty textures and toasty-buttery to outright butterscotchy flavors. However, the de Lorimier demonstrates that it ain't necessarily so, while Kistler and others have coaxed butterscotch from other zones.

For those who would try to find the core characteristics of Sonoma's appellations, Chateau St Jean and Kistler provide the most elaborate lessons, each making Chardonnays from several districts using constant styles. Landmark and Sonoma-Cutrer also test the contributions of nature versus nurture, though less broadly. Still, it may be that the latter's round, almost lush "Cutrer" and firm to austere, long-lived "Les Pierres" together make the most forcible argument that every place is not the same in Sonoma. If any one appellation stands apart from the rest it is Russian River. In Chardonnay as in other varieties, this region seems to give a rich, almost juicy texture not found elsewhere, and nowhere on better display than in De Loach "OFS," Fritz Cellars, and Sonoma-Cutrer's "RRR" and "Cutrer."

With Chardonnay, the simple appellation of Sonoma County is to be sought after, not scorned. Matanzas Creek, in particular, has rounded up sources that could stand alone in older regions, where what is left after the grand properties have had their turn is only leftovers.

Sparkling wine specialists take a healthy cut of the crop every year, mostly from Russian River Valley and Carneros.

Just how persistent is this pattern is hard to know, but it characterized several years in the 1980s. Growers whose careers go back to the 1960s remember that decade as being rainier, foggier, and far more prone to spring frosts than the 1980s. Even the 1970s were, in the same recollections, markedly cooler than the 1980s.

Rainfall in Sonoma varies almost as widely as temperature, in an oddly inverted way. In northern Sonoma, districts with the warmest summers tend to get the wettest winters because hills high enough to squeeze summer air dry are also high enough to squeeze extra rain out of winter storms. Sonoma town, on the other hand, sits in a rain shadow. However, even during the long drought of the 1980s, nowhere were annual totals scant enough to require irrigation of any but newly planted vines. For all practical purposes the whole county is dry-farmed.

Damaging spring frosts have been rare since the mid-1970s in all of Sonoma. When they do come, upland Knights Valley has been most susceptible, followed by the lowest spots in the Russian River Valley.

* For the colour code to the climate charts see pages 14–15.

Spraying helps to fight frost in spring, and water stress in summer.

Benchmarks:

Fritz Cellars Sonoma County (from two affiliated vineyards in Russian River plus estate in Dry Creek). **William Wheeler** Sonoma County (broadly assembled). **Matanzas Creek** Sonoma County (broadly assembled). **Château Souverain** Russian River Valley "Allen." **De Loach** Russian River Valley "OFS" (estate). **Dehlinger** Russian River Valley (estate). **Fritz Cellars** Russian River Valley (winery-affiliated vineyards). **Kistler** Russian River Valley "Vine Hill Road" (winery-owned). **Sonoma-Cutrer** Russian River Valley "RRR" (from three winery-owned ranches). **Sonoma-Cutrer** Russian River Valley "Cutrer" (estate). **Taft Street** Russian River Valley (assembled). **Alderbrook** Dry Creek Valley (estate). **Dry Creek Vineyard** Dry Creek Valley "Reserve." **Handley** Dry Creek Valley (affiliated vineyard; *see page 107*). **J. Pedroncelli** Dry Creek Valley (assembled). **Gundlach-Bundschu** Sonoma Valley "Rhinefarm" (estate). **Kistler** Sonoma Valley "Kistler Estate" (estate). **Landmark** Sonoma Valley "Two Williams" (estate). **St Francis** Sonoma Valley (estate). **Sonoma-Cutrer** Sonoma Valley "Les Pierres" (winery-owned). **Chateau St Jean** Alexander Valley "Robert Young." **Chateau St Jean** Alexander Valley "Belle Terre." **Clos du Bois** Alexander Valley "Calcaire" (estate). **Landmark** Alexander Valley "Damaris" (winery-owned). **White Oak** Alexander Valley "Myers Limited Reserve" (assembled).

Chenin Blanc (214 acres in 1970, 466 in 1990)

The relatively sparse acreage is firm evidence that Sonoma is anything but synonymous with Chenin Blanc. A more telling indicator is that the four Sonoma wineries (Grand Cru, Hacienda, Kenwood, and Dry Creek Vineyards) with the greatest reputations for the variety all use grapes from elsewhere, mostly the Delta. When the variety does well, it is most often in the warmer parts of Dry Creek and Alexander Valleys. Both the benchmark wines are fairly dry, with little or no emphasis on oak.

Benchmarks:

Preston Dry Creek Valley (estate). **Seghesio** Sonoma County.

Gewürztraminer (40 acres in 1970, 433 in 1990)

The apparent 10-fold increase in Gewürztraminer hides a boom that went bust. In 1984 it peaked at 1,172 acres. A slow decline in the mid-1980s quickened in 1989 and the downward plunge continues. Had quality, not a single-minded market, been the governor, the decline would not have happened.

Russian River Valley dominates the field. It is California's only really close rival to Anderson Valley, farther north in Mendocino County. Not only do wines from here achieve lichee as a flavor, they have almost as great a firmness of texture as their more northerly rivals: "almost" because they have a juiciness characteristic of almost every varietal from Russian River Valley grapes. Hop Kiln is much the firmest. De Loach is juicier, also slightly sweeter. Russian River juiciness helps keep the favored style dry, or barely off-dry. Several important producers give their wines at least a brief turn in oak to add depth and complexity, but even in these the variety's floral to spicy aromas stay well out in front. Within the county, Russian River Valley's nearest competitor is Sonoma Valley, particularly the southerly end, and most especially Gundlach-Bundschu's "Rhinefarm" Vineyard. Flavors here come closer to sweet-pea blossoms than lychee, and the wines have a lighter feel about them. Again, the style is dry and focused on grape flavors. That the most impressive assembled Gewürztraminer, a dry one from Adler-Fels, should marry Russian River with Sonoma Valley grapes cannot be a surprise.

The odd vineyard in Alexander Valley can cough up satisfactorily aromatic if soft and short-lived Gewürztraminer. James Miller's Garden Ranch is the heart and soul of a noticeably sweet, richly flavorful bottling from Grand Cru. However, few vines of Alexander Valley Gewürztraminer survived the purges of the 1980s.

Benchmarks:

Davis Bynum Russian River Valley (assembled). **De Loach** Russian River Valley (estate). **Hop Kiln** Russian River Valley (assembled). **Louis M. Martini** Russian River Valley (estate). **Gundlach-Bundschu** Sonoma Valley "Rhinefarm" (estate). **Adler-Fels** Sonoma County (assembled from one Russian River and one Sonoma Valley vineyard).

Riesling, *also* White Riesling, Johannisberg Riesling (81 acres in 1970, 342 in 1990)

Sonoma Riesling has not escaped the near-universal fate of the variety. The market for it began to decline in the late 1970s to early 1980s. Failure to reverse the trend soon led to diminishing acreage. Its future now rests with a few stubborn souls who are battling not only the market but a long string of modest wines. To judge by the premier examples from other regions, Sonomans did not plant high enough in the hills .

Late Harvest Rieslings rather than drier ones have given Sonoma most of its reputation. A majority of the plantings subject to botrytis stretch along the banks of the Russian River from Robert Young Vineyard down to Mark West Vineyard. This breed is dwindling along with the drier styles, sadly, for it is an intriguing original that opposes the airy flavors of Riesling with a dense texture almost like Sauternes.

Richard Arrowood is the most persistent and skillful maker of these nectars, first for Chateau St Jean, and in more recent vintages under his own label. Not every vintage succeeds: 1982 and 1985 soared above the others; 1989 shows prospects of joining them.

Benchmarks:

Arrowood Sonoma County "Late Harvest." **Chateau St Jean** Alexander

Valley "Late Harvest" (Robert Young Vineyard). **Clos du Bois** Alexander Valley "Late Harvest."

Sauvignon Blanc and Fumé Blanc (304 acres in 1970, 1,563 in 1990)

Good as Sonoma Chardonnay is, adaptable as it is, Sauvignon Blanc may well be the county's finest white grape over the widest range of soil and climate. And it is as distinctive by appellation as Chardonnay is not. Sauvignon has a core flavor in Sonoma. Years' worth of notes from blind tastings are full of the remark "Sonoma grassy." Far oftener than not it has fallen correctly on Sonoma wines (and, when not, almost always on Sauvignon from southern Napa Valley). Grassy may be a bit unfair, since many use the adjective disparagingly. However, Sauvignon from Sonoma does not bring a herb to mind, and certainly not a vegetable, while it does summon up thoughts of the sweet-sapped meadow grasses that are as common as, well, grass in the rainy lowlands of western Washington State.

Within Sonoma, there is grassy and grassy, or maybe there are just bunches of different grasses. Dry Creek Valley Sauvignons are the epitome of Sonoma grassy when they do not suggest one of the muskier melons. Alexander Valley bottlings are, curiously, a little less sweet as grass goes, but a little riper when they suggest melon. Russian River Valley Sauvignons carry that district's juiciness and an abundance of the sweetest kind of grassiness. Sonoma Valley understates the flavors, whatever they are.

During the 1980s, growers rethought earlier planting and vine-training schemes with an eye to diminishing the grassy notes in favor of melons. They began to succeed in the latter half of the decade, and were still gaining momentum in 1992.

Not many Sonomans approach the variety as an estate or other single-vineyard wine. Many think of it as being better if assembled, a choice which blurs the distinctions among appellations on the one hand, but often heightens Sauvignon's character on the other. One of the most characterful of all Sonoma Sauvignons comes from Kenwood Vineyards, where winemaker Marty Lee varies the basic proportions of 45 percent Sonoma Valley, 27 percent Alexander Valley, 23 percent Russian River Valley and 5 percent Chalk Hill according to the vintage. Its close rivals include Dry Creek Vineyards Sonoma County and Matanzas Creek Sonoma County, both assembled using quite different percentages.

Simi, as if to point out that the flavor differences within Sonoma fall within a narrow band, uses only the Alexander Valley in satisfactory vintages, but dips into Mendocino or Napa for riper fruit in the cool years.

Thus far, Sonoma's winemakers have not responded much to the vogue for the barrel-fermented, on-the-lees, malolactic style known widely, and with light scorn, as Poor Man's Chardonnay. Notes of oak do crop up in many, though far from all of them, but only as a subtle spice. Blending Sémillon with Sauvignon is not widely practiced, either. Fresh as the typical Sonoma Sauvignon is going to bottle, it almost surely will reward a year or two of cellaring, sometimes even a decade.
Benchmarks:

Alderbrook Dry Creek Valley (anchored in the estate). **Dry Creek Vineyards** Dry Creek Valley "Reserve" (estate). **J. Pedroncelli** Dry Creek Valley (assembled). **Preston** Dry Creek Valley (estate). **Quivira** Dry Creek Valley (estate). **Benziger of Glen Ellen** Sonoma Mountain (estate). **Chateau St Jean** Russian River Valley "La Petite Etoile" (winery-owned vineyard). **De Loach** Russian River Valley (estate). **Rochioli** Russian

Pickers dump freshly harvested grapes from plastic lug boxes into 3- to 5-ton gondolas for the trip from vineyard to winery.

River Valley (estate). **Château Souverain** Alexander Valley "Barrel Fermented." **Rodney Strong** Alexander Valley "Charlotte's Home." **White Oak** Alexander Valley (estate). **Dry Creek Vineyards** Sonoma County (assembled from broad sources). **Ferrari-Carano** Sonoma County (from winery-owned properties in Dry Creek and Alexander valleys). **Kenwood** Sonoma County (assembled from broad sources). **Matanzas Creek** Sonoma County (assembled from several sources). **Seghesio** Sonoma County (from estate properties in Alexander Valley and Dry Creek Valley). **Simi** Sonoma County.

Sémillon (186 acres in 1970, 192 in 1990)

Sparse though the plantings are, already they have given notice that Sémillon will do in much of Sonoma what it does in several other coastal counties: give a fatter, riper-tasting wine than its cousin, Sauvignon Blanc. A considerable proportion of the annual crop joins Sauvignon Blanc in proprietary blends to achieve just those effects. A small amount is allowed to be itself. Alderbrook has the track record. Its Dry Creek Valley wine has a lightness rare in the variety; good flavors and solid balance have allowed several vintages to age well, always a useful mark of inherent quality. The rest of the field is too new to judge, but the young wines show real promise.
Benchmarks:

Alderbrook Dry Creek Valley (from two properties at mid-valley). **Benziger of Glen Ellen** Sonoma Valley (estate). **Simi** Sonoma County (mostly Alexander Valley).

Sauvignon-Sémillon blends

The breed is newer in Sonoma than several other regions, thus still unsettled. Of the early efforts, de Lorimier Alexander Valley "Spectrum" and Benziger Sonoma Valley "A Tribute," both estate wines, were the most telling signposts in the late 1980s and early 1990s.

71

Sparkling Wines

Sonoma County has developed swiftly as a source of classic-method sparkling wines since Chateau St Jean and Iron Horse began making them in the 1970s. They now have Piper-Sonoma, "J" and Van der Kamp as fellow specialists as well as several others who produce these wines as a sideline.

All of them use the Russian River as a geographic base; some blend in grapes from other appellations in the county to complicate the end product. The traditionalists limit themselves to Chardonnay and Pinot Noir, with perhaps a small amount of Pinot Blanc or Pinot Meunier. The best of these are wines of considerable individuality. Iron Horse has found a crisp, clear style in which all is subtlety. Van der Kamp essays a richness readily found in its old-fashioned dry rosé. Piper-Sonoma leans to the austere, even in its long-on-tirage Tête de Cuvée, making some further bottle age a rewarding idea. "J" (from Jordan) in just two vintages began emerging as the most polished and complex of them all.

Venerable F. Korbel & Bros. goes back to the early days, but it marches to a different tune, especially in its Brut, which has not been a Sonoma wine for years, and which employs varieties other than the traditional ones of Champagne. The wine makes an instructive comparison with the others.
Benchmarks:
"J" Brut (assembled with an estate vineyard in the Russian River Valley as base). **Iron Horse** "Blanc de Noirs" (estate from Sonoma-Green Valley). **Piper-Sonoma** "Tête de Cuvée" (assembled, almost entirely from Russian River Valley grapes). **Van der Kamp** "Midnight Cuvée" (assembled, substantially from Sonoma Valley-Carneros).

Other varieties

Burger (55 acres and dropping) mostly grown by producers of non-classic sparklers for its acidity; Colombard or French Colombard (690 acres and dropping, alas) cold-fermented, off-dry Colombards were appealing sippers until the last producer gave up on them; Gray Riesling (42 acres); Muscat Blanc (53 acres) attractive in some of the warmer spots; Pinot Blanc (204 acres) some proportion of it probably Melon, all of it looking for a footing against Chardonnay; Symphony (39 acres) an off-shoot of Muscat with loyal followings at Chateau De Baun and Sebastiani.

Simi's estate vineyard in Alexander Valley is planted mostly with Cabernet Sauvignon. Vine spacing is closer than normal, but the sprawling canes are typical of California.

Red Wine Varieties

While Cabernet Sauvignon has come from nowhere to dominate the acreage of black grape varieties in Sonoma County, its place at the head of the list in quality is less certain because Zinfandel and Pinot Noir do so well. In the grand marketplace, Merlot seems to be blossoming both as a varietal and an element in luxury blends; among the more hard-nosed critics its status is more modest. Petite Sirah and Gamay scrap for roles in the niche market. As in most of California, Sangiovese, Syrah, Cinsaut, and other Italian and Rhône varieties were being explored with increasing intensity as the 1990s opened.

Cabernet Sauvignon (569 acres in 1970, 5,431 in 1990)
The longish list of benchmarks (see below) suggests that Sonoma is widely adapted to the great variety of the Médoc: yes and no. The county has a number of fine Cabernet vineyards, but they tend to crop up here and there, without much competition elsewhere in the immediate neighborhood. As the acreage figures point out, Cabernet is largely a newcomer here, still being tested in the vineyard as much as the cellar. In trying to assess what is personal style and what is regional substance, tasters must go cautiously, because any Alexander Valley Cabernet has every chance of resembling a rival from the Sonoma Valley more than its next-door neighbor. If it is easy to make a mistake identifying regions, the consolation is that you cannot go far wrong, for Sonoma, indeed the whole North Coast, gives Cabernet a fairly solid identity, nowhere better displayed than in any assembled wine on the list of benchmarks.

Among districts, Alexander Valley had the upper hand in 1990 for sheer number of good Cabernets, but Sonoma Valley has produced the four or five most memorable bottles in vintages from 1970 onward. Gundlach-Bundschu "Rhinefarm," Louis M. Martini "Monte Rosso" and Laurel Glen have earned the honors.

Californian Cabernets rarely summon up the University of California's most surprising flavor association for the variety: olivaceous; but "Rhinefarm" does with some consistency and an admirable subtlety. Though its tannins give it the lean, firm feel that make people think, "Aha, an ager," it is the depth of flavor that should encourage waiting at least a few years.

Louis M. Martini "Monte Rosso" comes from nearby, Laurel Glen from near the other end of Sonoma Valley, yet they resemble each other more than either brings "Rhinefarm" to mind. The Monte Rosso leans slightly more to herb than berry, hides its tannic bones with a comforting amount of flesh, and lasts forever. Laurel Glen sits on the flavor fence between berries on the one side and herbs on the other, leaving a taster to waver between the two thoughts. This wine and its neighbors on Sonoma Mountain also have a healthy layer of flesh from the beginning. Its similarities to Kenwood Vineyards' "Jack London" and Benziger's estate bottling are mildly obscured by varying tastes for oak, but not disguised.

Taken as a whole, the Alexander Valley is a complete enigma. Limit it to the benchlands at the southern end, which many Cabernet growers on those benches would love to do, and the wine takes on more shape. Alexander Valley Vineyards has had the pioneer's luxury of writing the definition: abundant berry flavor, tannins just firm enough to keep the wines lean and dry, and middling alcohols. The reserves of both Simi and Château Souverain exaggerate it, partly by using new oak with a more lavish hand; Rodney Strong's "Alexander's Crown" goes one step better in both tannins and alcohol.

Alexander Valley Cabernets from richer soils closer to the river level are a slightly different breed. Jordan Winery epitomizes the story with definite herbaceous flavors, modest acidities, and tannins less drying than most. Riper, oakier Clos du Bois "Briarcrest" is a perfect demonstration of how winemaking can put leagues between two vineyards with a shared boundary. Estancia has captured the middle ground among those with vines not far above river level.

Dry Creek Valley Cabernet is only beginning to emerge. Its most promising plantings – A. Rafanelli, Lambert Bridge, Dry Creek Vineyard, and Quivira notably included – offer balanced wines with depths of flavor not often found anywhere else in Sonoma. It is a development to be mourned as much as celebrated, for these are also places whence flow incomparable Zinfandels. Here, as in most of Sonoma, the herbaceous side of Cabernet has the greater role, based on performance so far. In size, the wines are middleweights with just enough tannins to be firm and dry.

Sonoma Cabernets can age well. Simi's 1935, from a plot now buried under freeway US101, was a splendid guest at its own 50th birthday party. Martini's Monte Rosso from 1951 is still quite lively. But the payback is too small and too seldom to encourage keeping recent vintages beyond 15 years. Most climb on to the plateau at eight and stay there until 15 or 16.
Benchmarks:
Alexander Valley Vineyards Alexander Valley (estate). **Château Souverain** Alexander Valley (assembled). **Château Souverain** Alexander Valley "Reserve" (usually from the southernmost vineyard on the river's right bank). **Clos du Bois** Alexander Valley "Briarcrest" (estate). **Estancia** Alexander Valley (from two winery-owned ranches east of Jimtown). **Jordan** Alexander Valley (estate); **Rodney Strong** Alexander Valley "Alexander's Crown" (estate). **Lambert Bridge** Sonoma County (Dry Creek Valley). **Beringer Vineyards** Knights Valley (from a winery-owned vineyard).

Cabernet-based blends

Sonoma County has a large community of winemakers working away at blends using only the classic varieties of Bordeaux. Through the 1980s and into the 1990s, most of them leaned heavily on Merlot, as that was the only variety with substantial bearing acreage. Cabernet Franc, in particular, began coming into stronger play with the vintage of 1990. As elsewhere, the early results repeatedly proved that blending is not an easy art. Half a dozen wineries offer both a varietal Cabernet and a blend; five of six Cabernets came first in statistically significant blind trials, with the sixth inconclusive. Blends, on the other hand, almost always beat back the challenges of varietal Merlots, which suggests where the root of the problem may be.

The two most successful bottlings to date are Estancia Alexander Valley "Meritage" 1987 (a Cabernet Sauvignon in disguise) and de Lorimier Alexander Valley "Mosaic" 1987. Others that may be instructive: Clos du Bois "Marlstone," Dry Creek Vineyards "David Stare Reserve," Geyser Peak Alexander Valley "Reserve Alexandre" and Hacienda Sonoma County "Antares."

Merlot (36 acres in 1970, 1,052 in 1990)

Here, as in the rest of California, Merlot promised more than it achieved in the 1980s and early 1990s, its tolerance of growing conditions so narrow that only a handful of distinctive vineyards have emerged, and these in so spotty a pattern as to defy one good generalization. Even the best assembled bottlings have plenty to be modest about. The typical shortcomings of Sonoma Merlot are the typical shortcomings of all Californian Merlot: pallid flavors, weak textures, or both, frailties that show up in its readiness to slip past its prime, even more in its inability to outshout the taste of oak.

Sonoma Valley Merlots hit a balance often enough to make current vintages of that appellation the safest blind bet in the county. However, even at Gundlach-Bundschu's Rhinefarm, one of the coolest vineyards in its district, the picking must be done all in a rush to avoid pruney flavors and high alcohols. Scattered plantings in the Russian River Valley hint that that appellation may be Sonoma's best hope for Merlot because the variety ripens slower and steadier there, giving winemakers a more comfortable target. I would hesitate to trade a middling good Cabernet for any of the Merlots offered as benchmarks, with the Louis M. Martini "Los Vinedos del Rio" a probable exception. It offers indelible tart berry flavors and a bracing acidity, a sort of better Barbera. Gundlach-Bundschu's boldly styled "Rhinefarm" and St Francis's American-oaked estate bottling bear closer scrutiny than most. After these, assembled wines do better than single vineyards because winemakers can finesse overripeness and other problems. In almost every case wines containing a fair bit of Cabernet Sauvignon, Cabernet Franc, or both, do better than pure varietals.

Benchmarks:

Clos du Bois Sonoma County (assembled). **Matanzas Creek** Sonoma County (assembled). **Louis M. Martini** Russian River Valley "Los Vinedos del Rio" (estate). **Gundlach-Bundschu** Sonoma Valley "Rhinefarm" (estate). **St Francis Sonoma Valley** (estate). **Alexander Valley Vineyard** Alexander Valley (estate). **Château Souverain** Alexander Valley (assembled).

Petite Sirah (1,278 acres in 1970, 308 in 1990)

The acreage figures are enough to depress a saint. In spite of appearances, Sonoma grows Petite Sirah as well or better than anywhere else in California. The Russian River seems to grow it better than anywhere else in Sonoma. From there, it almost surely will have the telltale taste of black pepper about it, and need not have the drying tannins that can make it hard going for its first 30 years in bottle. In reaching its peak in the Russian River Valley, Petite Sirah does not seem fussy about where, but begs to be made from ancient vines. Graybeard plots in Dry Creek and Alexander valleys can yield wines to challenge the best from younger plantings in the Russian River Valley, but the ancient plantings were going fast as the 1990s began. Hop Kiln gave up on its 1880 plot after the harvest of 1990, while the owners of Field Stone cannot hold out much longer with a block planted in 1895.

Christopher Creek, though a young label, draws on deep-rooted vines to make a deeply flavored Petite Sirah that is not as hard as its color promises. Hop Kiln makes the firmest model, with stiff challenge from Field Stone. Foppiano, ever polite, turned even more so with an almost lilting 1990 that the owners hold up as a model of what they want to do in future.

Benchmarks:

Christopher Creek Russian River Valley (estate). **Foppiano** Russian River Valley (estate). **Hop Kiln** Russian River Valley (estate). **Field Stone** Alexander Valley (estate).

Pinot Noir (312 acres in 1970, 2,632 in 1990)

Carneros excepted (as it is in this book), the Russian River Valley lays almost all the claim Sonoma County has on Pinot

A one-time hop kiln has become the Hop Kiln Winery.

Noir. Only the Sonoma Valley adds a dimension. Two adjacent Russian River vineyards get most of the attention, Rochioli and Allen, which deliver Pinot Noirs tasting closer to an original from Burgundy than any other Californian region can produce. Each regularly yields such wines for at least two wineries. Williams & Selyem (located on Allen) makes single-vineyard wines from each property, lavishing smoky new-oak flavors upon both without extinguishing the meaty taste of ripe, black cherries. The "Rochioli" is the firmer of the two. The Rochiolis themselves make an estate wine less oaky and a shade riper to the taste than the Williams & Selyem. Gary Farrell "Allen" also takes a more cautious approach with new wood than the Williams & Selyem counterpart, with Farrell underplaying the taste of Pinot as well.

Much the same flavor comes from a Seghesio vineyard not far north. The Seghesios approach their wine more modestly, downplaying oak in particular, yet the echoes of flavor among the three vineyards are haunting. All five wines develop quickly in bottle, the bouquets of age beginning to appear within a year or two. In most vintages, they are at their best in the first four to seven years, unless one dotes on balances that owe everything to time, nothing to fresh grapes.

Elsewhere in the valley, Pinot Noir may flourish, but it takes on a different coloration, its flavors not quite as indelible, not quite as forcibly reminiscent of burgundy. Not far south of the river and east of Rochioli, De Loach Vineyards, Dehlinger Vineyards, and Joseph Swan are near-neighbors whose Pinot Noirs share not only a similarity of flavor, but a certain tannic firmness. Dehlinger and Swan use new oak fearlessly, with grapes that taste more like red cherries, less like black ones than Rochioli or Allen. Oddly, oak flavors show less early, but more later than in the wines from Williams & Selyem. De Loach Vineyards somehow produces still brighter fruit flavors, as if from redder cherries. Through the 1980s, the winery tried insistently to amplify the particular taste of its Pinot Noir by using less and less toasty oak, and also to soften the wine's textures by curbing every source of tannin.

In the Sonoma Valley, Gundlach-Bundschu's "Rhinefarm," just on the edge of Carneros, yields a Pinot Noir that could be mistaken for one from there, having a persistent note of something leafy rather than fruity. It is, in most years at least, the only Sonoma Valley wine that clings to most of the hallmarks of Pinot Noir as Burgundy has defined its varietal character.

The Sonoma Valley may be of further interest for its clear lessons on how important foggy skies are to keeping that character rather than moving on toward the sun-baked flavors and firm tannins more readily associated with varieties from the southern Rhône. An old block at Hacienda, about a mile north, turns out Pinot Noirs of just such character. Hanzell, up the hill from Hacienda, does the same only more so.

The shadings in what makes a superior Pinot Noir appear to be so fine that in this, and only this, variety, no assembled wine comes to mind as a benchmark: not one assembled from two districts, not even one assembled from within an appellation. There are some good such Pinot Noirs, but they do not come to the shoulders of the most intriguing examples from individual properties. It is to be remembered that perhaps half, perhaps more of all Sonoma Pinot Noir goes into sparkling wines, and that another, less specific amount goes into rosés and their paler cousins.

Benchmarks:

Williams & Selyem Russian River Valley "Rochioli." **Williams & Selyem** Russian River Valley "Allen." **Gary Farrell** Russian River Valley "Allen." **Rochioli** Russian River Valley (estate). **Seghesio** Russian River Valley (estate). **Dehlinger** Russian River Valley (estate). **Gundlach-Bundschu** Sonoma Valley "Rhinefarm."

Zinfandel (3,664 acres in 1970, 3,924 in 1990)

Zinfandel has found congenial homes in most of Sonoma County. Dry Creek Valley is the nonpareil, and the Alexander and Sonoma valleys do not lag far behind. If the Russian River Valley grows precious little, what it grows is precious.

Better than anywhere else Dry Creek's benchlands coax out of Zinfandel the arrestingly tart, untamed flavors of wild blackberries that make the wine exactly right with spicy sauces, especially ones that start with tomatoes. The only trouble is that winemakers do not have to overshoot by much before they get dry port for their trouble, because fully ripe grapes and damn-the-torpedoes uncontrolled fermentations are at the root of success. Dave Rafanelli learned at his father's knee, and his father learned at an even older knee, just how to walk that wire. A good vintage of Rafanelli is not only incomparable with a bowl of cioppino, it is a throwback to an earlier, bolder, brasher approach to all the pleasures of the table. No one else makes it with the same boldness, but Ridge Geyserville and Lytton Springs come close.

The new generation of Dry Creekers, who have come from

outside, pick a little sooner and use vanillin-rich French oak to sweeten the berries. Doug Nalle of Nalle Vineyards has shown the way under his own label and also in setting the style for Quivira when he was there. Château Souverain leans not quite as far in the same direction. Preston Vineyards & Winery leads the quest for understatement in a zone where that may be the hardest trick of all.

If it is as easy to coax high sugars and ripe flavors out of Russian River Zinfandels, it is not so easy to cross the line into raisins, or port. During the 1980s Cecil de Loach just about cornered the market on Olivet Lane "old vines" Zinfandel by buying up the 10- to 20-acre plots Ralo Barberi, Carlo Paperi, and Alcide Pelletti planted between 1885 and 1905. The grapes from them go into the world as single-vineyard bottlings or in the De Loach estate blend. Either way, the wines taste and feel fresher, brighter, brisker than their rivals from Dry Creek Valley. They do not, alas, have many peers. Only Williams & Selyem make Zinfandels under the appellation. Their style leans more on oak than De Loach.

Sonoma Valley Zinfandel, tamer in flavor than either Dry Creek or Russian River Valley, plays the quiet, well-mannered cousin who lives in the shadow of extrovert redheads. Few contemporary examples exist to test the theory, the most consistent and agreeable of them coming from Kenwood Vineyards. That winery makes both an assembled Sonoma Valley bottling and a single-vineyard "Jack London" one. The Sonoma Valley tastes more ringingly of fresh berries. The London has greater depths of flavor, and is given rather more new oak from which to pick up grace notes.

Alexander Valley falls between Dry Creek and the Sonoma Valley, but its Zinfandel comes much closer to Dry Creek in both flavor and habits of growth. Sausal shows how closely the two compare in echoing Rafanelli in more ways than not. However, the single most striking wine under the appellation in vintages from 1987 to 1990 has been the "Scherrer" made by outsider Greenwood Ridge, of Mendocino's Anderson Valley. Critics have taken to it for its impeccable balance, clear taste of Zinfandel, and delicate seasoning from new oak. Though made for immediate pleasure, it shows signs of keeping well for at least a few years. As in the case of Pinot Noir, the gross acreage and the amount of red wine cannot be compared: a huge amount of Sonoma Zinfandel goes into White Zinfandels and Zinfandel rosés. Some should, but not as much as does.

Benchmarks:

Château Souverain Dry Creek Valley (from two properties). **Nalle** Dry Creek Valley (assembled from three tiny patches). **Quivira** Dry Creek Valley (estate); **J. Pedroncelli** Dry Creek Valley (estate-based). **De Loach** Russian River Valley (estate). **Greenwood Ridge** Alexander Valley "Scherrer" (*see* pages 86 and 107). **Kenwood** Sonoma Valley (assembled). **Kenwood** Sonoma Mountain "Jack London" (estate). **Seghesio** Sonoma County (assembled from family vineyards in Dry Creek and Alexander valleys)

Other varieties (1990 plantings)

Alicante Bouschet (55 acres); Barbera (25 acres); Cabernet Franc (336 acres) all planted after 1984; Carignane (359 acres) falling, as against 1,774 in 1970; Gamay (220 acres); Grenache (10 acres) down 75 percent from 1970; Sangiovese (130 acres) Seghesio's long-standing monopoly ended with the 1980s; Syrah (11 acres) most going into Christopher Creek's trailblazer, first made in 1989.

Sonoma Valley AVA

Established: January 24, 1982
Total area: 103,200 acres
Area in vineyard: 5,950 acres
Wineries: 30
Principal towns: Sonoma, Boyes Hot Springs

Strangely enough, this relatively homogeneous, oldest, most-tested of Sonoma wine districts is the one that has yet to find its signature wine. Physically, the valley is only one ridge away from Cabernet-dominated Napa, exactly parallel to it and a good deal senior in vineyards. Part of the old Franciscan mission vineyard now grows Cabernet Sauvignon vines for Sebastiani's "Cherryblock." Almost next door, part of Agoston Haraszthy's original Buena Vista vineyard produces the Pinot Noir of Hacienda as its most identifiable wine. A few hundred yards farther on, the Bundschu family has harvested its "Rhinefarm" in every vintage since 1858, to include, in recent years, Gewürztraminer every bit as good as its Cabernet and Pinot Noir. A dozen other threads run deep into the past, in still other directions.

Part of the problem is that this valley, along with the rest of Sonoma, faltered for a long time. From the worst depredations of phylloxera until long after Prohibition, it had few wineries. As late as 1965, Sebastiani, Pagani Brothers, and Val-Moon dealt more in bulk than in bottled wines, leaving a minuscule Buena Vista to carry the flag. Only with the 1970s did such as Chateau St Jean, Gundlach-Bundschu, and Kenwood Vineyards come to typify it with wines grown and made within its boundaries – too short a history for any grower to know what might be the best choice for his particular plot.

Greater blame for the viticultural confusion in Sonoma Valley vineyards belongs to the mysterious behavior of local fogs. The valley, wide open at its bay end, narrows quickly, but fails to seal itself against sea air ebbing southward from Santa Rosa. When a 600-foot-deep bay fog rushes up from the south, a thin remnant of ocean fog drifts down from Santa Rosa at the north, the two meeting at Kenwood somewhere around 5 a.m. Lesser fogs do not come together. For all that the south tip of the valley gets thicker fog more often, the hills there set up air currents that cause temperature variations down on lowlands that seem better suited to cool-climate varieties than they are.

The current rule of thumb in a valley without much floor is Chardonnay and Pinot Noir at the south end, especially where Sonoma Valley and Carneros offer dual citizenship to vines, Cabernet Sauvignon in the east-facing hills, and Zinfandel in the west-facing hills. Sauvignon Blanc and scraps of Gewürztraminer fit in where they can. It is a rule that makes every winemaker in the valley talk first of the exceptions.

The rule of thumb starts out well with Chardonnay. Landmark's "Two Williams" vineyard almost butts up against Carneros on the east side of the valley. So does Gundlach-Bundschu's "Rhinefarm." The glorious "Les Pierres" of Sonoma-Cutrer sits on a flat almost at the western edge of the valley, due west of the other two. Also in the neighborhood is Fallenleaf, which physically straddles the Carneros boundary. The serious challengers to these properties all belong in the realm of exceptions to the rule. After a long gap to accommodate the towns of Boyes Hot Springs and Agua Caliente, and a

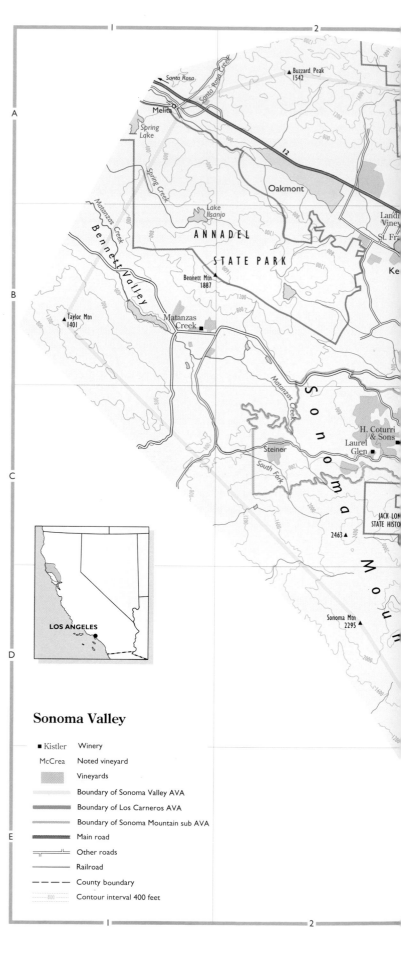

Sonoma Valley

■ Kistler	Winery
McCrea	Noted vineyard
▨	Vineyards
	Boundary of Sonoma Valley AVA
	Boundary of Los Carneros AVA
	Boundary of Sonoma Mountain sub AVA
	Main road
	Other roads
	Railroad
- - -	County boundary
800	Contour interval 400 feet

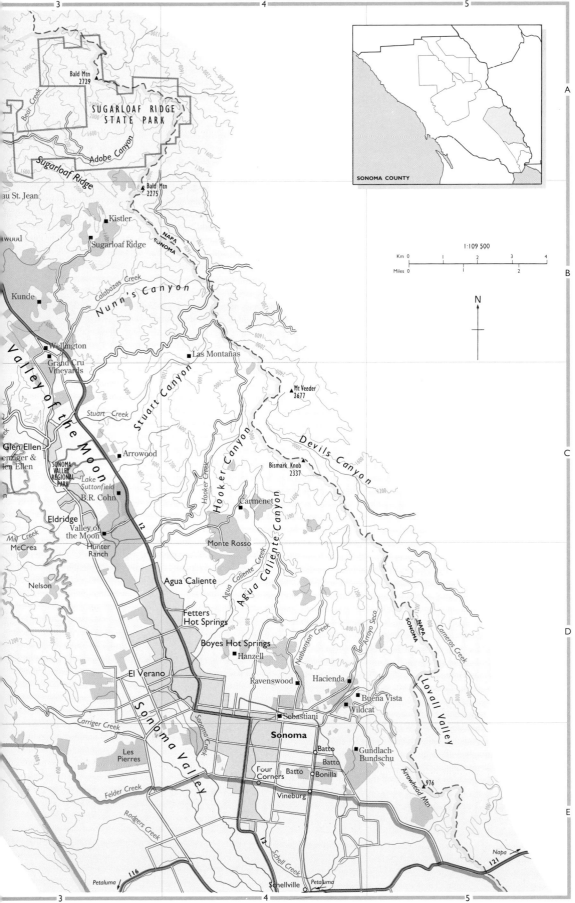

WINE ROUTE

Electing a wine route in sprawling Sonoma is difficult only for the embarrassment of riches. Santa Rosa is a natural hub for looking into Sonoma Valley and any or all of the northerly districts. Healdsburg is the logical choice for exploring the Russian River, Dry Creek, and Alexander Valleys, even interior Mendocino or the upper Napa Valley. Sonoma town is best positioned for visiting the Sonoma Valley and Carneros. The lower Napa Valley is also well within reach of the old mission town.

For a first-time visitor, the classic grand tour begins west of Santa Rosa at the point where River Road intersects West Side Road. From there, drive north on West Side Road and narrow, bucolic West Dry Creek Road. Exit Dry Creek Valley on Canyon Road (it passes J. Pedroncelli). Cross US101 and drive the length of Alexander Valley on SR128 to Chalk Hill Road, a twisting country lane that rejoins US101 not far north of Santa Rosa. If vineyards are the main event, redwood groves and oak-dotted meadows are the bonuses. Healdsburg should come just in time for lunch, given a 9 a.m. start.

Sonoma Valley vines.

longer gap apparently better suited to other grapes, Chardonnay has a brief resurgence right around Kenwood, not for any coherent reason. Kistler is high in the east hills, Kunde Estate down lower. St Francis Vineyards occupies bottomlands. McCrea Vineyard is up on Sonoma Mountain.

Pinot Noir behaves less predictably than Chardonnay right from the beginning, probably because no other variety shows fog's presence or absence more clearly. One can quite literally taste a lightning-swift accumulation of heat, sunlight, or both, from Gundlach-Bundschu "Rhinefarm" to Hacienda to Hanzell. A "Rhinefarm" Pinot Noir can be very hard to separate from a Carneros bottling of the same variety, while Pinot Noir from Hanzell is more likely to be confused with something from the Rhône. Save for a plot in Kenwood's "Jack London Ranch," the variety hardly exists north of Hanzell.

Cabernet Sauvignon echoes Chardonnay in range but stops shorter in numbers. As advertised, it finds its most consistently impressive sites on Sonoma Mountain, but the challengers are far removed. The greatest of Sonoma Valley's Cabernet plantings, in Louis M. Martini's superb "Monte Rosso," look obliquely across the valley to Sonoma Mountain from even greater heights at the ridgepole of the Mayacamas range. The curiously versatile Rhinefarm is down on the flats. If any other vineyard is to deliver topflight Cabernet, it has yet to declare itself.

Many other varieties do well here, but none quite reaches the front ranks all on its own. Zinfandel comes closest, or would if more growers would take it to heart. Sauvignon Blanc and Gewurztraminer do well, but . . . The list goes on.

The Sonoma valley is but one of many framed by the sharp, close-packed ridges of the Coast Ranges.

Sonoma Mountain sub-AVA

Established: February 22, 1985
Total area: 5,000 acres
Area in vineyard: 633 acres
Wineries: 3
Principal town: None (Glen Ellen, Kenwood adjoin)

While Sonoma Mountain has a fair amount of Chardonnay and bits of Pinot Noir and Zinfandel scattered through it, its reason for being is Cabernet Sauvignon. Its slopes look east to the morning sun, and find it early because the appellation's founders drew its lower boundary to stay above the Sonoma Valley's overnight fogs. The top boundary, on the other hand, was defined so as to avoid losing reradiated evening heat from the valley floor. What they sought was the valley's warmest-summer climate, not for enduring extreme heat in the day but for avoiding deep chill at night. Growers on these sparsely settled slopes believe with some passion that this is exactly what is wanted to ripen Cabernet Sauvignon to perfection. Sonoma Mountain's three best-known Cabernet vineyards, Laurel Glen, Jack London, and Benziger estate, all hug the midline of elevation. They also share thin, well-drained soils. Among Cabernet properties regularly identified on labels only Steiner is a bit of a freak: higher on the ridge, tipped more to the west, most of it in heavier clay than the other three, and, as a result, more prone to herbaceous flavors.

Most of what is not Cabernet shares its need for heat. Jack London Ranch is rightly treasured for its Zinfandel almost as much as for its Cabernet. Sauvignon Blanc and Sémillon at Benziger are worth a hunt as well. One Chardonnay vineyard does stand out: McCrea, often used in vineyard-designated wines by Chateau St Jean, sometimes by others.

Russian River Valley AVA

Established: November 21, 1983
Total area: 96,000 acres
Area in vineyard: 8,375 acres
Wineries: 35
Principal towns: Forestville, Sebastopol

Conventional wisdom has it that grapes came to the Russian River Valley late because the Italians who dominated viticulture in northern Sonoma from the 1870s until Prohibition were not crazy enough to plant anywhere so chilly and damp. The theory says it took WASPs with serious tax incentives to see the possibilities for Chardonnay and Pinot Noir, with and without fizz. This does not take into account the long presence of Rochioli and Prati and Barberi on vineyards west of Santa Rosa, but it is true that the place did not blossom viticulturally until the 1970s, when the two great varieties of Burgundy came to dominate it, one by volume, the other more by pure excellence.

By acreage, by sheer popularity in the marketplace, Chardonnay had become this valley's king by the early 1980s. Hardly a winery in the AVA does not keep it at the head of its list of whites, as De Loach, Dehlinger, Iron Horse, and Merry Vintners all attest. Sonoma-Cutrer makes nothing else. Classic-method sparkling-wine producers Chateau St Jean, Jordan, Iron Horse, and Piper-Sonoma use copious volumes of Russian River Valley Chardonnay as well. Consistently good as it is, Chardonnay has somehow failed to find a place within the AVA where it evokes poetic rhapsodies the way Montrachet does within the Côte d'Or. Perhaps Russian River has not found its local answer to Montrachet because Chardonnay is so new to the area, or because it is fated to be steady rather than spectacular. Certainly the list of vineyards where it does well is long, scattered, and so far not marked by any incomparables.

The task of making legends may belong to Pinot Noir, as the variety tests its limits in more and more vineyards. Already, Pinot Noir has found one of its most rewarding homes in all California, out toward the northeastern boundary of this AVA, on east-facing bumps and knolls that hem the Russian River, from Davis Bynum up to the Belvedere winery. In these precincts are the lustrous Rochioli and Allen vineyards. A small plot of Seghesio's upstream near the mouth of Felta Creek shares much of their character. The opposite bank shows similar flavors in Rodney Strong's River East vineyard.

A fair consensus has sprung up among growers that Pinot Noir needs to stay very close to the river banks to shine. The farther upstream, the firmer the belief, for it is based on long hours of fog and short hours of sunshine, as well as a high proportion of gravel in the soils. It takes less and less elevation to rise above both mists and gravels as one goes inland. Even with these strictures, the vision of several score acres more of Pinot between Rochioli and Seghesio is a dream to relish.

Growers elsewhere on this broad, undulating plain argue that the river bank is not the only place for Pinot Noir. Some of their wines are eloquent on their behalf. The most notable come from two low rises facing each other across one of many low, boggy spots in this old seabed. Williams Selyem is beginning to pay close attention to the grapes from Olivet Lane Vineyard, in the angle formed by Olivet and River roads and tipped slightly toward the setting sun. De Loach Vineyards, a little more than a mile south along Olivet Road, has a similarly oriented plot with grapes of commanding flavor. Dehlinger Vineyards and Joseph Swan Winery have staked out claims for a low ridge facing east toward Olivet Road.

Although Pinot Noir and Chardonnay dominate, this is not some little Burgundy, not by half.

The district grows excellent Gewürztraminer in a wide range of locales, fine Sauvignon Blanc and Zinfandel in a narrower range. Botrytized Riesling from these precincts hovers near the top of California's lists. Here, where fogs are fairly universal and grapes tend to cluster atop gentle rolls, drainage more than gray skies may be the key to successful planting, but generalizers live as dangerously in the Russian River Valley as anywhere else in Sonoma. That said, the finest haunts for Gewürztraminer stay close to those for Pinot Noir. Hop Kiln and Louis M. Martini each has a patch next door to Rochioli, while De Loach Vineyards has a memorable block farther downstream.

Sauvignon Blanc succeeds in a surprising number of sites, though it cannot be planted willy-nilly. Of recognized sources, Rochioli, Chateau St Jean's Petite Etoile, and De Loach carry the flag highest. Most of Chalk Hill needs watching (*see* page 81).

Zinfandel is striking not only for what it is, but for where it grows. All along Olivet Road it yields intensely aromatic wines from sites as close to top-drawer Pinot Noir as adjoining rows, no farther from it than the width of a 20-foot county road. This is not to be explained by mortals. It does not happen anywhere else in California.

Petite Sirah comes very close to its peak in this valley, based on three plantings at Foppiano, Hop Kiln and Christopher Creek. Its successes have not inspired many imitators. One other grape lurks, too rarely planted to categorize, but impressive in at least one instance: Merlot from Louis M. Martini's Los Vinedos del Rio has flavors that bear imitating.

Sonoma-Green Valley sub-AVA

Established: December 21, 1983
Total area: 32,000 acres
Area in vineyard: 1,000 acres
Wineries: 2
Principal town: Forestville

Out among the firs and redwoods at the far western edge of the Russian River Valley, some of Sonoma-Green Valley is cooler than much of the rest of the larger AVA because sea-fogs settle into its low spots with uncommon persistence throughout the growing season. It was this that led growers to carve themselves a particular niche, blithely ignoring warmer temperatures than average on the ridges around Graton and elsewhere. The main drainage of Green Valley slips just west of Forestville as it descends northward toward the Russian River. Its vineyards thus look either west or east from low, rolling ridges. Those of Iron Horse, much the best-known of its wineries, look mostly to the east. Marimar Torres Estate, source of impressive Chardonnay in a short career, looks more to the south. Among independent vineyards, Dutton Ranch is often the source of vineyard-designated Chardonnays. Most of Sonoma-Green Valley's vineyards grow Chardonnay and Pinot Noir, no little of it for sparkling wines. It is officially Sonoma-Green Valley to distinguish it from Solano-Green Valley.

Russian River Valley

■ Hanna   Winery

Olivet Lane   Noted vineyard

   Vineyards

Boundary of Russian River Valley AVA

Boundary of Alexander Valley AVA

Boundary of Green Valley sub AVA

Boundary of Chalk Hill sub AVA

Highway

Main road

Other roads

Railroad

800   Contour interval 400 feet

LOS ANGELES

Cloverdale

Chiquita

Digger Bend

Fitch Mtn
991

Healdsburg

Optima

Campe Rose

White Oak Vineyards

Black Peak

Bailhache

Russian River

Wild Hog Hill

Domaine St. George

Black Mountain/
J.W. Morris

Grant

Foppiano
Vineyards

Christopher Creek

Dry Creek

Mill Creek

Felta Creek

Rabbit
Ridge
Vineyards

Rodney Strong
Vineyards

Piper-Sonoma Cellars

Belvedere

De Natale
Vineyards

Wild Hog Hill
1150

Windsor

East Windsor

Mt Jackson
1652

Gilder Ridge

Hop Kiln

Williams - Selyem

Rochioli

Rio Nido

Porter Creek

Black Mtn
1435

Porter Creek
Vineyards

Davis Bynum

Shiloh

Fife Creek

El Bonita

Russian River

Hulbert Creek

Pool Ridge

1095

Rolands

Korbel
Champagne
Cellars

Hacienda

Mark West

Chateau
DeBaun

Guerneville

Korbel

Hilton

Forest
Hills

Mark West
Vineyards

Fulton

Gabes Rock
942

Highcroft

Rio Dell

Monte
Rosa

Summerhome

Green Valley Creek

Sonoma-Cutrer
Vineyards

Windsor Creek

Mark West Creek

Guernewood
Park

Vacation
Beach

Noel Heights

Mirabel
Heights

River Road
Vineyards

Trenton

Rose Family Wines

Duncans
Mills

Russian River

Mays Canyon

Pocket Canyon

Joseph Swan
Vineyards

Z-Moore/
Martinelli

Northwood
Heights

Vine Hill

The Merry
Vintners

116

Villa Grande

Smith Creek

Taft Street

Forestville

Olivet
Lane

Topolos at
Russian River
Vineyards

Martini &
Prati Winery

De Loach
Vineyards

Monte Rio

Bohemian
Grove

1011

La Crema

Sellards

Tyrone

Iron Horse Vineyards

Gan Eden

Dehlinger

Laguna de Santa Rosa

Dutch Bill Creek

Manzana

Marimar
Torres Estates

Mt. Pisgah
425

Graton

Hanna

116

Chateau
St. Jean

Santa

Camp
Meeker

Barlow

Molino

Purrington Creek

Caswell
Vineyards

ATASCADERO REGIONAL PARK

12

Occidental

Salmon Creek

Atascadero Creek

Sebastopol

Petaluma

Chalk Hill sub-AVA

Established: November 21, 1983
Total area: 21,120 acres
Area in vineyard: 1,000 acres
Wineries: 1

The warmest part of the Russian River Valley begins on flats south of Healdsburg, and climbs onto hills, mostly west-facing, bordering the Alexander Valley. The sub-AVA takes its name from the misnamed principal peak, which has chalk-white soils that are actually coarse, quick-draining volcanic ash. The ash is everywhere, and there are only scattered small patches of alluvial soil, even on the flats at Windsor.

To an overwhelming degree these white soils grow white grapes. Of the 1,000 acres of vineyard, 900 grow mostly Chardonnay and Sauvignon Blanc, with bits of Sémillon. The reds are Cabernet Sauvignon and its near relatives.

Overall, Chardonnay appears to have an edge. Of all the Chardonnay in Rodney Strong Vineyards' 1,200 acres, Rodney Strong himself chose a 145-acre piece on the Windsor flats for the winery's flagship Chardonnay, vineyard-designated as "Chalk Hill." One of three properties used in Sonoma-Cutrer's Russian River Ranches, Chardonnay is on the same flats. Chalk Hill Vineyards, the biggest grower with 278 acres, has had Sauvignon Blanc as its brightest star in nearly every vintage, but its Chardonnay appears to be gaining.

Chalk Hill Vineyards persists with Cabernet Sauvignon, though the grand variety of the Médoc has performed so marginally on its own here that the proprietor has steadily increased proportions of other varieties from Bordeaux from the beginning (1980). In 1992 he was planning to take another, longer, step in that direction. The only definitive result in reds was the failure of Zinfandel to ripen more often than one year in 10 for the now-defunct Balverne. Sonoma-Cutrer bought the 200-acre property in 1992.

Chateau St Jean took the chance to acquire a splendid old country house in the Sonoma Valley for its head-quarters. More and more Sonoma wineries enjoy this kind of luxury after a long era when it scarcely existed.

N

1:125 000

Km 0 | 1 | 2 | 3 | 4
Miles 0 | 1 | 2

ONOMA COUNTY

Dry Creek Valley AVA

Established: September 6, 1983
Total area: 80,000 acres
Area in vineyard: 5,500 acres
Wineries: 21
Principal town: Healdsburg

It is not true (by a few yards) to say that Healdsburg is the principal town in the AVA. Strictly speaking, Dry Creek has no town, and therein lies one of its charms. The valley was settled in the late 1800s, mostly by Italian farmers, and it has kept much of the character they brought to it: smallholdings, fertile kitchen gardens, noisy dogs, and wayward roads. West Dry Creek Road is still better suited to a horse than a car. Mixed orchard and vineyard, the other gift of the early settlers, remains only in a few tiny patches.

As far as vines are concerned, the real AVA is much smaller than the official one. Upstream of Warm Springs Dam, more than half the valley is a trackless tumult of steep hills and deep gullies, though a few once-prized vineyards drowned when the reservoir filled after 1985. Existing vineyards stick close to the creek below the dam. They cannot grow far away, for the valley is never more than two miles between ridges. Two hills right at the mouth of the creek powerfully affect its climate by shutting out most of the fog creeping up the Russian River.

On the sunny side of those hills, Zinfandel is *the* grape in this warm valley, and has been since Italian immigrants began planting it in the 1870s. Real Zinfandel drinkers are apt to take their caps off when they pass Rafanelli, Quivira, Bradford Mountain, Pedroncelli, Nalle, and half a dozen other plots. The general rule is to keep it on the benchlands on both sides of the creek, which slants northwest to southeast from the headwaters in Mendocino County to its junction with the Russian River at Healdsburg. Though both benches are dominated by red soils, local winemakers believe they taste a difference, with the westerly bench delivering slightly the leaner, more

The cellars of Preston Vineyards & Winery in Dry Creek Valley.

restrained wine of the two because it offers morning sun and afternoon shade. Quivira and Rafanelli epitomize that side of the valley. Hambrecht's Bradford Mountain (in Château Souverain Reserve) shows what higher elevation does. Pedroncelli, Lytton Springs, and Nalle show the easterly bench to its best advantage.

Most contemporary Dry Creek Zinfandel comes from varietally pure vines planted since the 1970s. A small proportion still comes from gnarled ancients, concealing some Petite Sirah, Gamay or Early Burgundy vines among their numbers, and with them a useful lesson. The interlopers are there because the Italians who first planted the valley wanted something Zinfandel lacked, or had a spot where Zinfandel didn't grow well. The old fellows had their eyes open. Water does not always stick to the gullies here. Where it comes sheeting down tipped bedrock, Zinfandel will grow endless leaves but will not ripen a crop. In those spots the brightest of the modern growers abandon Zinfandel for Syrah, Petite Sirah, or another less vigorous variety. Some keep the resulting wines separate, while others make blends not unlike those made by the pioneers.

The Rhône-born varieties have been enticing local growers since the mid-1980s. Some think Syrah will do well from Warm Springs Dam down, especially in the cooler downstream half. Others would avoid it in favor of Grenache, Cinsaut and other varieties of the southern Rhône, on the grounds that the whole of Dry Creek is too warm for Syrah. Preston Vineyards leads in exploring not only the red varieties of the Rhône, but the whites as well. Other growers would skip the Rhône altogether in favor of Italian varieties, particularly Sangiovese, though the first practical results had yet to come in 1992.

Cabernet Sauvignon, meanwhile, is having better luck at getting into the club than any of them, partly for market considerations, partly because it shows promise. Admirers of Zinfandel rather rue the discovery, feeling, sometimes strongly, that a trendy market for Cabernet threatens the valley's highest calling as a producer of Zinfandel. Their feelings are heightened by the fact that Cabernet has looked thus far to be at its best in exactly the spots where Zinfandel is regarded as close to holy.

By acreage and reputation, Sauvignon Blanc is Dry Creek's white. It is almost a no-fail choice on much of the well-watered valley floor, producing herbaceous wines in the gravels, more melony ones in heavier soils and warmer spots. It might do even better on the benches, but is not going to push reds off while the current growers have anything to say about it.

On the foggy side of the valley-mouth hills, enough cool air from the Russian River pools to make Chardonnay grow well. The rough boundary is Lambert Bridge Road. The farther down-valley from there the better, if Alderbrook, the adjacent Handley vineyard, and Clos du Bois's "Flintwood" are any indication. Pinot Noir has performed decently in one property at the very tip, but Dry Creek is not a place for early ripeners.

Ignoring E. & J. Gallo's overwhelming Frei Bros. operation, small is the byword among wineries in this small appellation. Domaine Michel, Nalle Vineyards, Preston Vineyards & Winery, and Rafanelli stay entirely within it. J. Pedroncelli focuses its efforts within the appellation. Rather more typical of Sonoma County, Dry Creek Vineyards, Ferrari-Carano and Fritz Cellars take as many or more grapes from elsewhere as they do from their home territory. Curiously, Gallo is the old-timer. David Stare started the new era when he launched Dry Creek Vineyards in 1972. J. Pedroncelli dates from 1927, but its focus on its home valley is a recent decision.

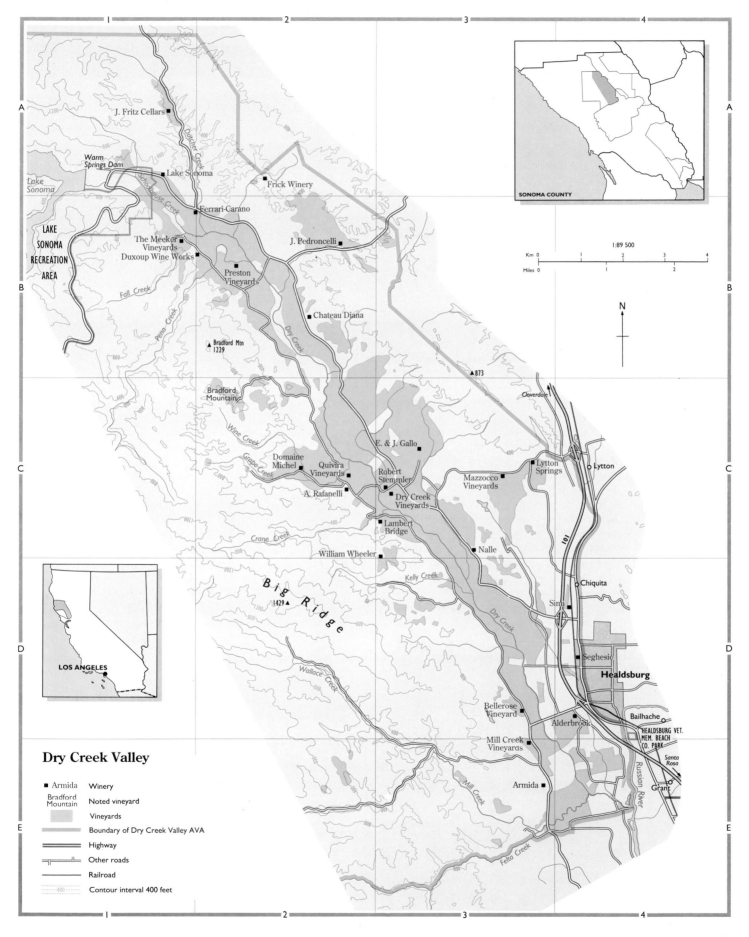

SONOMA COUNTY

1:89 500

Km 0 1 2 3 4
Miles 0 1 2

N

LAKE
SONOMA
RECREATION
AREA

J. Fritz Cellars

Warm
Springs Dam

Lake Sonoma

Lake
Sonoma

Frick Winery

Ferrari-Carano

The Meeker
Vineyards
Duxoup Wine Works

J. Pedroncelli

Preston
Vineyards

Fall Creek

Chateau Diana

Bradford Mtn
1229

Bradford
Mountain

▲873

Cloverdale

Wine Creek

E. & J. Gallo

Lytton
Springs

Lytton

Domaine
Michel

Quivira
Vineyards

Robert
Stemmler

Mazzocco
Vineyards

Grape Creek

A. Rafanelli

Dry Creek
Vineyards

101

Crane Creek

Lambert
Bridge

Nalle

William Wheeler

Chiquita

Kelly Creek

Simi

Big Ridge

1429▲

Dry Creek

Wallace Creek

Seghesio

Healdsburg

LOS ANGELES

Bellerose
Vineyard

Alderbrook

Bailhache

HEALDSBURG VET.
MEM. BEACH
CO. PARK

Mill Creek
Vineyards

Mill Creek

Santa
Rosa

Armida

Russian River

Grant

Felta Creek

Dry Creek Valley

■ Armida — Winery

Bradford
Mountain — Noted vineyard

▨ — Vineyards

▬ — Boundary of Dry Creek Valley AVA

══ — Highway

═╤═ — Other roads

── — Railroad

‑‑‑400‑‑‑ — Contour interval 400 feet

Alexander Valley AVA

Established: November 23, 1984
Total area: 66,000 acres
Area in vineyard: 6,500 acres
Wineries: 20
Principal towns: Geyserville, Cloverdale

This longest of AVAs in Sonoma is either the most versatile or the most ambiguous. Those who dislike ambiguity believe the Alexander Valley needs to be subdivided to make real sense. Admirers of versatility like it the way it is. Ironically, when the AVA was first proposed, one group wanted a north boundary at Geyserville, but lost to a rival with larger designs when ATF officials could find no natural dividing point there. The winners still had all the edge in the early 1990s because opponents had yet to find any new way to carve the pie.

A greater problem is that this was long the heart of bulk wine production, and thus the home of Alicante and Colombard rather than Cabernet and Chardonnay. Only since the mid-1970s has a significantly large roster of winemakers been testing the climates and soils with dedication. Alexander Valley Vineyards, Clos du Bois, Jordan, and Simi were early. Behind them came de Lorimier, Field Stone, Murphy-Goode, White Oak and others. Their experience is still sometimes disquieting in its inconsistency.

Yet there is a certain coherence to what grape varieties are being grown where in Alexander Valley. Beginning at the southern end, on the ridge that forced the Russian River to make its sharp turn westward, this is Cabernet country. For as long as State Highway 128 goes downhill on its way upstream, the prized ranches grow Cabernet on both sides of the stream. Here the valley is so narrow that most of the vineyards crowd onto bench-lands. The Alexander Valley Vineyards estate first showed the way on the east side of the stream. The Stuhlmuller vineyard (in Château Souverain "Reserves") has the most solid reputation on the other bank. The Alexander's Crown vineyard (Rodney Strong) has led many to suspect that west-bank properties

The Jimtown Store sells a cup of coffee alongside antiques.

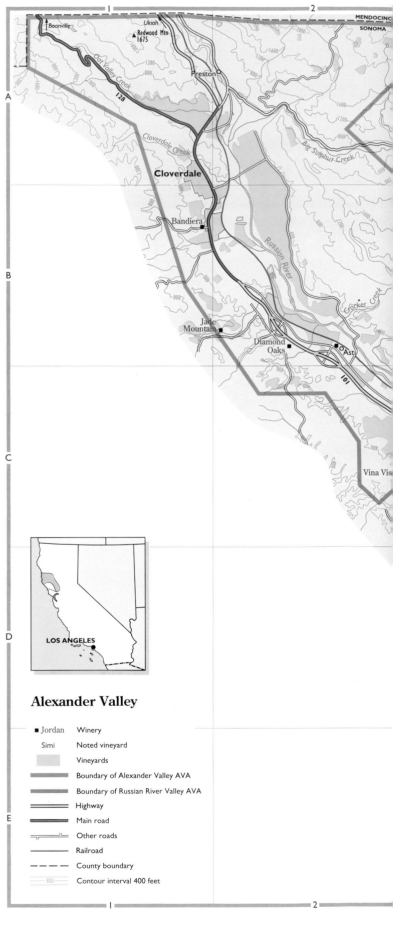

Alexander Valley

■ Jordan	Winery
Simi	Noted vineyard
	Vineyards
	Boundary of Alexander Valley AVA
	Boundary of Russian River Valley AVA
	Highway
	Main road
	Other roads
	Railroad
	County boundary
	Contour interval 400 feet

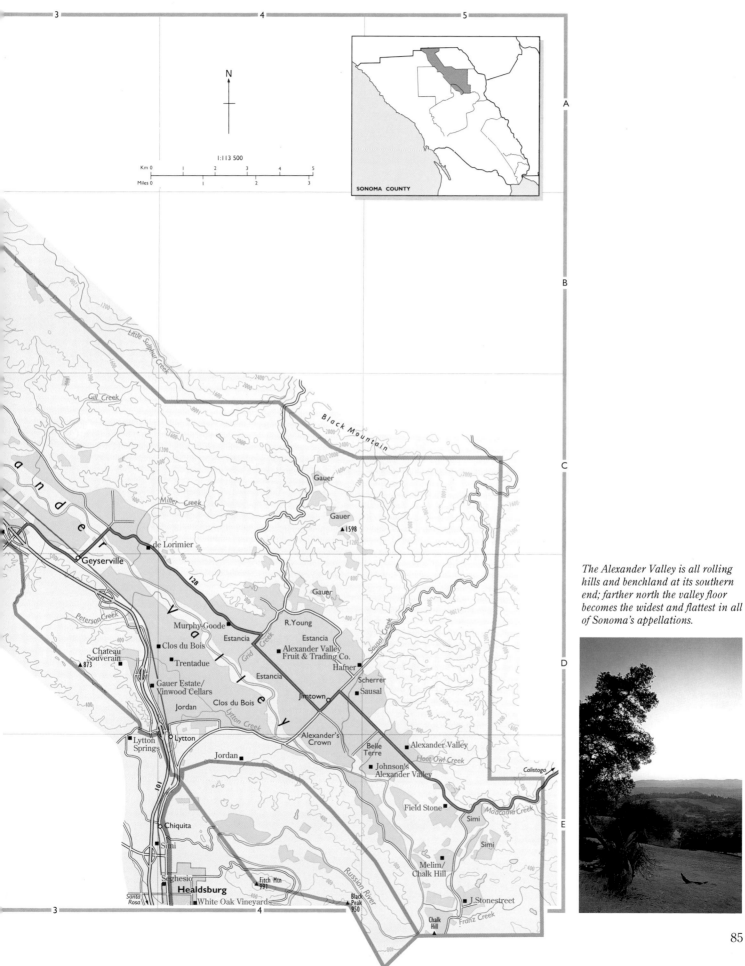

N

1:113 500

Km 0   1   2   3   4   5
Miles 0   1   2   3

SONOMA COUNTY

3   4   5

A

B

C

D

E

Little Sulphur Creek

Gill Creek

Black Mountain

Miller Creek

Gauer

Gauer
▲1598

de Lorimier

Geyserville

128

Gauer

Peterson Creek

Murphy-Goode

R.Young

Estancia

Estancia

Grid Creek

Sausal Creek

Clos du Bois

Alexander Valley
Fruit & Trading Co.

Chateau
Souverain
▲873

Trentadue

Estancia

Hafner

Scherrer

Gauer Estate/
Vinwood Cellars

Sausal

Jordan

Clos du Bois

Jimtown

Lytton Creek

Lytton
Springs

Lytton

Alexander's
Crown

Belle
Terre

Alexander Valley

Jordan

Hoot Owl Creek

Johnson's
Alexander Valley

Calistoga

Field Stone

Simi

Maacama Creek

Chiquita

Simi

Simi

Melim/
Chalk Hill

101

Seghesio

Santa
Rosa

Healdsburg

Fitch Mtn
▲991

White Oak Vineyards

Black
Peak
▲950

Russian River

J.Stonestreet

Chalk
Hill
▲

Franz Creek

3   4

The Alexander Valley is all rolling hills and benchland at its southern end; farther north the valley floor becomes the widest and flattest in all of Sonoma's appellations.

85

A luxurious manor house fronts the Jordan winery.

naturally give firmer tannins to their wines, but the evidence is ambiguous for lack of numbers. Here and there deep, swift-draining gravels nearly at river level imitate the benches, as Hoot Owl Creek has done repeatedly since it first appeared in Simi Cabernets in the early 1970s. The difference between well- and less well-drained is the difference between berries and herbs.

Where the highway makes its abrupt right turn into Jimtown, the Alexander Valley more than doubles in width, and the focus changes markedly toward white wines, especially on the broad, flat floor. Chardonnay and Sauvignon Blanc have a curious symbiosis in the stretch from Jimtown north to Geyserville. Chardonnay finds its most congenial situations in heavier soils on the valley floor. Belle Terre, Calcaire and Robert Young are the familiar sources for single-vineyard Chardonnays. All three sit close to river level not far from Jimtown. Calcaire is part of the Clos du Bois vineyard just west of the river. Belle Terre and Robert Young sit just east of it. These properties are further linked in having the loamy but not especially fertile soils that keep Chardonnay suitably moist but not overlush in vegetative growth. Hafner and Jordan make estate Chardonnays from vineyards in much the same area, with much the same soils.

In the view of some, Chardonnay is at its limit here. Simi looked to the Russian River Valley in buying 100 acres for Chardonnay. Château Souverain turned away from Alexander Valley in the late 1980s in favor of the Russian River and Carneros. Estancia removed Chardonnay from its Jimtown vineyards in favor of Cabernet. Those who have stayed believe that it is crazy to abandon the promised land.

The finest of the Sauvignon Blanc vineyards start in the midst of the Chardonnays and range farther north to Geyserville. But they are not in the same soils: to avoid excess foliage and ultra-grassy flavors, single-vineyard Sauvignon sources of Wasson (several wineries over time), Charlotte's Home (Rodney Strong) and de Lorimier are in patches where fast-moving runoff water keeps soils gravelly and spare.

Although these whites do rather take over, Cabernet Sauvignon does not disappear from the picture here. Among several well-regarded vineyards, Jordan and Clos du Bois' Briarcrest sit side-by-side on flats very near the Russian River's right bank, their wines unified by the herbaceous flavors that tend to come from such spots. Even plots higher above river level lean more to herbs than berries at this latitude. High hills on the east side may give Cabernets more like those from the benches farther south. At least Gauer Ranch managed to suggest such an outcome with its first two vintages, 1987 and 1988. Almost inevitably, one vineyard stands out for its versatility. In this region, it is de Lorimier's ranch due east of Geyserville. Within the tiny compass of 64 acres, the property grows excellent Chardonnay, Sauvignon Blanc, Cabernet Sauvignon, and Merlot.

The less densely planted northern half of the AVA, from Geyserville up to Cloverdale, has few vineyards that might be taken as beacons. An ancient planting of Sangiovese at the Seghesio vineyard at Chianti Station suggests that Tuscany's premier grape might do well here. New plots of Rhône varieties belonging to Jade Mountain at Cloverdale, the first certified Rhônist in the region, also hint at being well adapted. Petite Sirah has an honorable history in the vineyards, but seems forever doomed to disappear into blends.

Zinfandel should not be overlooked, though few wines bore the appellation in the late 1980s and early 1990s. Much of it becomes boldly ripe and a bit heady, as Sausals often show. Degree of ripeness may be a matter of choice more than necessity, judging by Greenwood Ridge's efforts from the adjoining Scherrer vineyard in the disparate vintages of 1987, 1988 and 1989. Pinot Noir has seemed miscast in the Alexander Valley. Gewürztraminer and Riesling crop up here and there: neither variety seems perfectly at home, except when botrytis-affected grapes turn in a superior performance.

Knights Valley AVA

Established: November 21, 1983
Total area: 36,240 acres
Area in vineyard: 1,000 acres
Wineries: 1
Principal town: None (Calistoga is nearest)

Knights Valley lingers closer than any other to the pure coastal ecosystem of northern California: ragged rocks toward the tops of volcanically formed higher hills, rounded knolls down lower, grass everywhere, a few pines, and oaks, oaks, and more oaks, many of them spindly and bearded with gray club mosses. A handful of houses and a spidery network of roads and vineyards intrude but lightly. Even the vineyards fill the eye from one or two vantages, no more.

The AVA is not mapped in the same detail as others in Sonoma County for the simple fact that one winery – the Napa Valley's Beringer – dominates plantings with more than 400 acres. A tiny firm called Peter Michael has the only winery in the AVA; its vineyard began to bear in 1990. Part of a Ferrari-Carano property laps across the boundary from Alexander Valley, where it follows a ridgetop at Knights Valley's northern tip; development of it began in 1991. A handful of small, anonymous patches round out the field.

And so Cabernet Sauvignon and Sauvignon Blanc from Beringer's Knights Valley Estate define it as much as it has been defined in recent times. Cabernet has all the signs of being a good red to grow here. As Beringer makes it, it keeps a distinctive flavor through extended wood aging, and lasts fairly well in bottle. Sauvignon Blanc has repeatedly shown a softness, a fragility in face of age, although Beringer's oaky style doubtless contributes to its swift course from youth to senescence. Peter Michael offered the first chance to compare two Knights Valley Sauvignon Blancs with its 1990.

Knights Valley's single greatest wine up to 1991, curiously, was a 1972 Riesling Late Harvest, again from Beringer. However, botrytis comes rarely, and not always in years that favor Riesling. The 1972 has had only one successor vintage of any note at all.

Other AVAs

The Northern Sonoma AVA gathers Russian River Valley, Dry Creek Valley, Alexander Valley and Knights Valley into a mixed bag. The appellation was drawn by E. & J. Gallo to encompass all of that company's Sonoma vineyard holdings. Its boundaries deviate insignificantly from the more particular ones.

Somona Coast is an outlandish confection drawn to the same end, but by Somona-Cutrer. Its boundaries take in most of the coast west and south of the existing Russian River Valley and Sonoma-Green Valley appellations, some of the Russian River Valley and a chunk of southern Sonoma Valley designed to include "Les Pierres." Labeling regulations are the underlying motive: winery and vineyard must fall within the same AVA for the wine to be entitled to "estate bottled" status. Neither is mapped.

Château Souverain is modeled on the hop barns once common in the locality.

PRODUCERS

Adler Fels Winery (1981)
5325 Corrick Lane, Santa Rosa, CA 95405. Tel (707) 539-3123. 12,000 cases. Gewürztraminer (Russian River plus Sonoma Valley) and Sauvignon Blanc are gems. All from bought-in grapes.

Alderbrook Winery (1982)
2306 Magnolia Drive, Healdsburg, CA 95448. Tel (707) 433-9154. 30,000 cases. Sought out for superior Dry Creek Valley Sémillon, consistently attractive Dry Creek Valley Chardonnay (mostly or all from 55 affiliated acres at the winery). Sauvignon Blanc also estimable.

Alexander Valley Fruit & Trading Company (1982)
5110 Highway 128, Geyserville, CA 95441. Tel (707) 433-1944. 10,000 cases. Rustic Cabernet Sauvignon and Zinfandel from 40 estate acres northeast of Healdsburg in Alexander Valley.

Alexander Valley Vineyards (1975)
8644 Highway 128, Healdsburg, CA 95448. Tel (707) 433-7209. 50,000 cases. The old hand in Alexander Valley is one of its strongest producers of Cabernet Sauvignon with Merlot close behind. Both come from the Wetzel family's 250-acre vineyard near the southeast tip of its AVA.

Armida (1990)
2201 Westside Road, Healdsburg, CA 95448. Tel (707) 433-2222. 4,000 cases. Estate Russian River Valley Merlot, Chardonnay, and Pinot Noir from 14 acres at the winery south of Healdsburg, 20 acres near Windsor.

Arrowood Vineyards & Winery (1985)
14347 Sonoma Highway, Glen Ellen, CA 95442. Tel (707) 938-5170. 20,000 cases. Long-time Chateau St Jean winemaker Richard Arrowood, now on his own, devotes most of his production to thoughtfully assembled Chardonnay and Cabernet Sauvignon, and also makes tiny lots of Late Harvest Riesling. All from bought-in Sonoma County grapes.

Bandiera Winery (1937)
155 Cherry Creek Road, Cloverdale, CA 95425. Tel (707) 894-4295. 150,000 cases. Though in Alexander Valley, it is steadiest with Cabernet Sauvignon from an affiliated vineyard in Napa's Chiles Valley.

Bellerose Vineyard (1978)
435 W Dry Creek Road, Healdsburg, CA 95448. Tel (707) 433-1637. 6,000 cases. Rustic Cabernet Sauvignon, Merlot and a blend of the two from 35 organically farmed acres at the downstream tip of Dry Creek Valley.

Belvedere Winery (1979)
4035 Westside Road, Healdsburg, CA 95448. Tel (707) 433-8236. 70,000 cases. Winery in Russian River revamped in 1991 to focus on Dry Creek Valley Zinfandel from the then-new owner's 190 acres there (two properties). Alexander Valley Chardonnay anchored in his 210 acres near Jimtown, and Russian River Valley Chardonnay from the vineyards of others. A second, 250,000-case negociant line, "Belvedere Discovery," is made in a separate facility at Healdsburg.

Benziger of Glen Ellen (1981)
1883 London Ranch Road, Glen Ellen, CA 95442. Tel (707) 935-3000. 80,000 cases. Proud brand name of an aggressive family firm also selling over 3 million cases under Glen Ellen and M.G. Vallejo labels. The 85-acre estate vineyard in Sonoma Mountain AVA is noteworthy for Cabernet Sauvignon, Merlot, Sauvignon Blanc, and Sémillon. Bought-in Sonoma grapes provide other bottlings of these, plus good Carneros Chardonnay.

Black Mountain (See Morris, J.W.)

Braren-Pauli (1979)
1611 Spring Hill Road, Petaluma, CA 94952. Tel (707) 778-0721 [outside mapped areas] 9,000 cases. From an isolated location almost in Marin County, reaches to affiliated vineyards in Mendocino's Potter Valley for Chardonnay, Dry Creek Valley for Cabernet Sauvignon and Merlot.

Buena Vista Winery (See Carneros)

Davis Bynum Winery (1975)
8075 Westside Road, Healdsburg, CA 95448. Tel (707) 433-5852. 28,000 cases. Steadily attractive Russian River Valley Chardonnay, Pinot Noir, and Gewürztraminer from bought-in grapes.

Carmenet Vineyard (1982)
1700 Moon Mountain Drive, Sonoma, CA 95476. Tel (707) 996-5870. 30,000 cases. Part of the Chalone empire, it makes a Cabernet-based red blend and Sauvignon Blanc-based white one from a 60-acre Sonoma Valley estate high in the hills east of Boyes Hot Springs.

Caswell Vineyards (1981)
13207 Dupont Rd, Sebastopol, CA 95472. Tel (707) 874-2517. 2,000 cases. Old-vines Zinfandel is the pride of a winery operated as a sideline by a family that grows 20 acres of grapes along with fruit for cider, jellies etc.

Chalk Hill Winery (1980)
10300 Chalk Hill Road, Healdsburg, CA 95448. Tel (707) 838-4306. 55,000 cases. Sprawling estate with 278 acres of vines in the Chalk Hill appellation. Shines brightest with Sauvignon Blanc.

Chandelle of Sonoma (1987)
14301 Arnold Drive, Glen Ellen, CA 95442. Tel (707) 938-5862. 2,000 cases. Small negociant firm catering for specialist aviator market with art-labeled Sonoma County Chardonnay and Cabernet Sauvignon.

Château De Baun (1986)
1160 Hopper Avenue, Santa Rosa,

A typical modern crushing operation at Ferrari-Carano.

CA 95403. Tel (707) 544-1600. 25,000 cases. Russian River winery with 100 acres at Fulton. Founded to show off Symphony but is finding its real footing with estate Chardonnay and Pinot Noir.

Château Diana (1979)
PO Box 1013, Healdsburg, CA 95448. Tel (707) 433-6992
Essentially a negociant label with a fluctuating roster of wines.

Chateau St Jean (1973)
PO Box 293, Kenwood, CA 95452. Tel (707) 833-4134. 175,000 cases. Has done much to define Chardonnay in Sonoma County with many single-vineyard bottlings, most notably Robert Young and Belle Terre in Alexander Valley, McCrea in Sonoma Valley. Once almost as prolific with Sauvignon Blanc but now largely settled on winery-owned Petite Etoile in Russian River Valley. A major player in the late-harvest game with Riesling, Gewürztraminer, Sauvignon Blanc-Sémillon. Separate facility is devoted to classic-method sparkling wines, mostly from Russian River Valley Chardonnay and Pinot Noir.

Château Souverain (1973)
PO Box 528, Geyserville, CA 95441. Tel (707) 433-8281. 125,000 cases. With Beringer (see p 51) and Meridian (see p 135), one of Nestlé Inc.'s Wine World holdings. Skillful winemaker

with modern winery in Alexander Valley canvasses all Sonoma for best-of-appellation grapes: Dry Creek Valley Zinfandel, Alexander Valley Cabernet Sauvignon and Sauvignon Blanc, Carneros and Russian River Valley Chardonnays. In 1990 began production of single-vineyard Chardonnays "Sangiacomo" (Carneros) and "Allen" (Russian River).

Christopher Creek (1972 as Sotoyome, renamed 1988)
641 Limerick Lane, Healdsburg, CA 95448. Tel (707) 433-2001. 2,500 cases. Varietals and blends from long-planted Syrah and Petite Sirah, plus a later patch of Cinsaut on 10 rolling acres south of Healdsburg.

Cline Cellars (See Carneros)

Clos du Bois (1974)
PO Box 940, Geyserville, CA 95441. Tel (707) 857-1651. 350,000 cases. Named blocks within a 540-acre river-bank vineyard west of Jimtown yield prototypical Alexander Valley Chardonnay "Calcaire," Cabernet Sauvignon "Briarcrest," and Cab-based "Marlstone." Dry Creek Valley Ultra-toasty Chardonnay "Flintwood" and assembled Pinot Noir and Sauvignon Blanc also can be worthy of note.

B.R. Cohn Winery (1984)
15140 Sonoma Highway, Glen Ellen,

CA 95442. Tel (707) 938-4064. 8,000 cases. Produces heavily oaked estate Cabernet Sauvignon from 65 acres between Glen Ellen and Boyes Hot Springs in Sonoma Valley. Chardonnay was grafted out in 1992 to allow the better-suited red plantings to expand.

H. Coturri & Sons (1979)
PO Box 396, Glen Ellen, CA 95442. Tel (707) 525-9126. 2,500 cases. Rustic organic varietals.

Dehlinger (1976)
6300 Guerneville Road, Sebastopol, CA 95472. Tel (707) 823-2378. 8,000 cases. Graceful Chardonnay and dark, musing Pinot Noir from 50 estate acres near Forestville in the Russian River Valley.

De Loach Vineyards (1975)
1791 Olivet Road, Santa Rosa CA 95401. Tel (707) 526-9111. 85,000 cases. Chardonnay, Sauvignon Blanc, Gewürztraminer, Pinot Noir, and Zinfandel – highly popular all-American originals every one – from not so much an estate as a 278-acre, 12-ranch domain spread across the Russian River Valley.

de Lorimier Vineyards & Winery (1985)
2001 Highway 128, Geyserville, CA 95441. Tel (707) 433-7718. 8,000 cases. From 64 estate acres in Alexander Valley east of Geyserville: Cabernet-based blend of depth, and Chardonnay of grace. Also a Sauvignon Blanc-based white.

De Natale (1985)
11020 Eastside Rd, Healdsburg, CA (94558). Tel (707) 433-8381. 1,000 cases. Chardonnay from a 7-acre vineyard has won praise.

Domaine Laurier
Once a producing winery in the Russian River Valley; now a merchant label shortened to just Laurier.

Domaine Michel (1984)
4155 Wine Creek Road, Healdsburg, CA 95448. Tel (707) 433-7427. 22,000 cases. Of greatest interest for an estate Cabernet Sauvignon from 53 acres at mid-Dry Creek Valley.

Domaine St George (1934 as Cambiaso, renamed 1986)
PO Box 548, Healdsburg, CA 95448. Tel (707) 433-5508. 300,000 cases. Bargain-priced Chardonnay, Cabernet and White Zinfandel from diverse sources.

Dry Creek Vineyards (1972)
PO Box T, Healdsburg, CA 95448. Tel (707) 433-1000. 110,000 cases. Estate Reserve Chardonnay and Cabernet-

based red blend have the high profiles, but assembled Sonoma Fumé Blanc, Chardonnay, and Cabernet Sauvignon are as or more noteworthy. The winery has 100 acres of vineyard divided among 7 parcels in Dry Creek and Alexander valleys.

Duxoup Wine Works (1981)
9611 W Dry Creek road, Healdsburg, CA 95448. Tel (707) 433-5195. 1,200 cases. Dark-hued, firm, assertively flavored Dry Creek Valley reds from Gamay and Syrah are the main story; a similarly styled Napa Valley Charbono pushes into even less usual territory.

Eagle Ridge Winery (1982)
111 Goodwin Avenue, Penngrove, CA 94951. Tel (707) 664-9463. [not mapped] 3,000 cases. Cheerfully eccentric producer cares most about having the first and still only US Ehrenfelser from his 5-acre vineyard at Penngrove.

Estancia (1986)
100,000 cases. Memorable estate Cabernet Sauvignon from 240 acres in 2 properties at Jimtown. Wines made at Franciscan, the owner of both label and vineyards (see p. 53).

Fallenleaf Vineyards (1986)
3,000 cases. A grower label for 15 acres straddling the Carneros-Sonoma Valley boundary. Good Chardonnay, superior Sauvignon Blanc.

Gary Farrell Wines (1982)
PO Box 342, Forestville, CA 95436. Tel (707) 433-6616. 3,500 cases. An eponymous winemaker's label offering excellent Pinot Noir and Chardonnay from bought-in Russian River Valley grapes.

Ferrari-Carano (1981)
8761 Dry Creek Road, Healdsburg, CA 95448. Tel (707) 433-6700. 50,000 cases. From 500 acres scattered through 11 domaine vineyards in Dry Creek and Alexander Valleys come Cabernet Sauvignon, Merlot, Chardonnay and much-praised Fumé Blanc; a 12th property in Carneros grows the grapes for a highly wooded Reserve Chardonnay.

Gloria Ferrer (See Carneros)

Field Stone Winery (1977)
10075 Highway 128, Healdsburg, CA 95448. Tel (707) 433-7266. 12,000 cases. Several vineyards totalling 140 acres spread across the owners' 800-acre Redwood Ranch in southernmost Alexander Valley. From them comes frequently impressive Petite Sirah, often fine Cabernet Sauvignon. Rosés of both varieties lead the field.

Fisher Vineyards (1979)
6200 St Helena Road, Santa Rosa, CA 95404. Tel (707) 539-7511 [not mapped]. 15,000 cases. The owner has 10 acres of Chardonnay, 9 of Cabernet at the winery high on a ridge between Santa Rosa and St Helena, plus 8 of Chardonnay and 19 of Cabernet in the Napa Valley near Calistoga.

Foppiano Vineyards (1896) 12707 Old Redwood Highway, Healdsburg, CA 95448. Tel (707) 433-7272. 25,000 cases. Old-line family coaxes wonderful Petite Sirah and intriguing Cabernet Sauvignon (latter under Fox Mountain Reserve label) from 200 gravelly acres on Russian River bank just south of Healdsburg. The 150,000-case Riverside Farms label belongs to the Foppianos.

Frick Winery (1977 in Santa Cruz County; moved to Sonoma 1988) 23072 Walling Road, Geyserville, CA 95441. Tel (415) 362-1911. 2,000 cases. 10-acre Dry Creek Valley vineyard planted with Syrah and Viognier is supplemented by more Viognier and Cinsaut from a neighbor.

J. Fritz Cellars (1979)
24691 Dutcher Creek Road, Cloverdale, CA 95425. Tel (707) 894-3389 or (415) 771-1900. 20,000 cases. Chardonnays from two excellent Chardonnay vineyards in Russian River Valley and a good one in Dry Creek Valley are sometimes offered separately, sometimes blended together as "Sonoma County." Also to look out for: estate Sauvignon Blanc from the 90-acre Dry Creek property.

Gan Eden (1985)
4950 Ross Road, Sebastopol, CA 95472. Tel (707) 829-5686. 40,000 cases. Strictly kosher wines from several sources; Chardonnay and Cabernet Sauvignon the mainstays.

Gauer Estate Winery (1987)
PO Box 1431, Healdsburg, CA 95448. Tel (707) 857-3175. 10,000 cases. From highly selected blocks in 350 acres of vineyards high in east hills of Alexander Valley comes promising Cabernet Sauvignon.

Geyser Peak (1880, revived 1972)
PO Box 25, Geyserville, CA 95441. Tel (707) 957-9463. 500,000 cases plus. A bright Aussie winemaker has swiftly boosted the stock of a flagging winery, mostly with grapes from its owner's 1,150 acres of vines in Alexander and Russian River valleys. Especially to look out for: Cabernet Sauvignon and Cabernet-based "Reserve Alexandre."

Golden Creek Vineyards (1983)
4480 Wallace Road, Santa Rosa, CA 95404. Tel (707) 538-2350. 1,000 cases. A 15-acre estate vineyard all by itself in the hills behind Santa Rosa has produced some of Sonoma's most flavorful Merlot.

Grand Cru Vineyards (1971)
Until 1992 a producing winery in Glen Ellen, now a negociant label for J F J Bronco (see p 190). Cabernet Sauvignons from 1985 through 1989 are worth seeking out.

Gundlach-Bundschu Winery (1858, revived 1973)
PO Box 1, Vineburg, CA 95487. Tel (707) 938-5277. 50,000 cases. Estate "Rhinefarm" vineyard has been in Bundschu family hands since 1855. From 140 acres in lower Sonoma Valley come impressive Gewürztraminer, Cabernet Sauvignon, Merlot, and, sometimes, Pinot Noir. Two other family properties nearby bring vineyard holdings to 360 acres.

Hacienda Winery (1973)
As an independent, known for Alexander Valley Cabernet Sauvignon and Gewürztraminer, and Clarksburg Chenin Blanc. In 1922 became a negociant label for J F J Bronco (see p 190).

Hafner Winery (1982)
PO Box 1038, Healdsburg, CA 95448. Tel (707) 433-4675. 12,000 cases. From the owning family's 95 acres east of Jimtown in Alexander Valley comes reliable, regionally typical Chardonnay and Cabernet Sauvignon.

Hanna Winery (1985)
5345 Occidental Road, Santa Rosa, CA 95401. Tel (707) 575-3330. 12,000 cases. Ambitious grower-producer was developing 600 acres of vines in the early 1990s. Steady Chardonnay from 10 acres at the winery in Russian River Valley. Cabernet Sauvignon and Sauvignon Blanc were just beginning to come from 100 acres in southern Alexander Valley.

Hanzell Vineyards (1956)
18596 Lomita Avenur, Sonoma, CA 95476. Tel (707) 996-3860. 3,000 cases. The winery launched French oak barrels as the aging vessel of choice in California with a memorable 1957 Chardonnay from Napa grapes. Since 1965 it has produced ripe, bold Chardonnay, Pinot Noir, and Cabernet Sauvignon from 33 mostly west-facing acres on hills just up-valley from Sonoma town.

Haywood Winery (1980)
15,000 cases. Originally an estate winery at Sonoma town; since 1991 a label owned by Buena Vista, which

uses the original owner's 100-acre "Los Chamizal" vineyard for Chardonnay, Cabernet and Zinfandel, bought-in grapes for lower-priced California-appellation "Haywood Selection" (see Buena Vista, p 65).

Hop Kiln Winery (1975)
6050 Westside Road, Healdsburg, CA 95448. Tel (707) 433-6491. 10,000 cases. Best known for Petite Sirah from ancient vines next to the winery in the Russian River Valley – pulled out after the 1988 harvest. Also fine dry Gewürztraminer from nearby growers.

Iron Horse Vineyards (1978)
9786 Ross Station Road, Sebastopol, CA 95472. Tel (707) 887-1507. 32,500 cases. Three-part operation primarily focused on estate classic-method sparkling wines from a 110-acre property in Sonoma-Green Valley, the leaders being Brut and Blanc de Noirs "Wedding Cuvée." Same property yields still Chardonnay and Pinot Noir. Affiliated 24-acre Alexander Valley property is source of Cabernet-based red and Sauvignon Blanc.

Johnson's Alexander Valley (1975)
8333 Highway 128, Healdsburg, CA 95448. Tel (707) 433-2319. 8,000 cases. From 70 acres, rustic Cabernet Sauvignon and Zinfandel are steadiest.

Jordan Sparkling Wine Company (1987)
PO Box 1919, Healdsburg, CA 95448. Tel (707) 431-5200. 11,000 cases. Flossy, classic-method sparkling wine called "J." Originally from bought-in grapes; after 1990 anchored in 85 estate acres in Russian River Valley.

Jordan Vineyard & Winery (1976)
PO Box 878, Healdsburg, CA 95448.

Jordan's Rob Davis.

Tel (707) 433-5250. 70,000 cases. Estate-grown Cabernet from 275 acres along the Russian River bank due east of Lytton epitomizes the character of Alexander Valley floor. Winery also offers toasty Chardonnay from the same property.

Kenwood Vineyards (1972)
PO Box 447, Kenwood, CA 95452. Tel (707) 833-5891. 175,000 cases. Prides of the house are single-vineyard Cabernet Sauvignon and Zinfandel "Jack London" from leased property in the hills above Glen Ellen. Assembled Sonoma Valley Zinfandel and Sonoma County Sauvignon Blanc are fine.

Kistler Vineyards (1978)
997 Madrone Road, Glen Ellen, CA 95442. Tel (707) 996-5117. 11,000 cases. Superior toasty-school Chardonnays from several sources: "Estate" from 15 hilly acres in Sonoma Valley, "Vine Hill Road" from 15 owned acres in Russian River Valley, "Durrell" from bought-in Sonoma Valley grapes, and "Dutton" from bought-in Russian River Valley grapes.

Korbel Champagne Cellars (1882)
13250 River Road, Guerneville, CA 95466. Tel (707) 887-2294. 1.3 million cases. Old-line specialist in bottle-fermented sparkling wines, sometimes with classic grape varieties, sometimes with others. Most fruit is bought-in.

Kunde Estate Winery (1990)
10155 Sonoma Highway, Kenwood, CA 95452. Tel (707) 833-5501. 60,000 cases. Long-time Sonoma Valley growers with more than 650 acres made an impressive debut with Chardonnay and Sauvignon Blanc.

La Crema (1979)
4940 Ross Road, Sebastopol, CA 95472. Tel (707) 829-2609. 60,000 cases. Through a complicated history has blended Russian River Valley and Central Coast Chardonnay and Pinot Noir into characterful wines at fair prices. Intelligent Chardonnay/Chenin Blanc/Sémillon blend called Crème de Tête gives consistent pleasure at a still lower price.

Lake Sonoma Winery (1982)
9990 Dry Creek Road. Geyserville CA 95441. Tel (707) 431-1550. 3,500 cases. From 10 acres in upper Dry Creek Valley, rather countrified Zinfandel, Cabernet Sauvignon and others.

Lambert Bridge (1975)
4085 West Dry Creek Road, Healdsburg, CA 95448. Tel (707) 433-5855. 25,000 cases. Admirable Cabernet Sauvignon, Chardonnay mostly from 115 estate acres in lower

Stainless steel fermenting tanks at Kenwood.

Dry Creek Valley. The firm went out of business in 1993.

Landmark Vineyards (1974)
101 Adobe Canyon Road, Kenwood, CA 95452. Tel (707) 833-0053. 25,000 cases. Chardonnay specialist has 3 with good track records as agers: "Damaris" from 56 acres in Alexander Valley, "Two Williams" from 17 acres in Sonoma Valley near Carneros, and Sonoma County from those and other Sonoma sources.

Las Montanas (1982)
4400 Cavedale Rd, Glen Ellen, CA 95442. Tel (707) 996-2448. 1,500 cases. Producer of hearty, organic Cabernet Sauvignon and Zinfandel from bought-in mountain grapes.

Laurel Glen Vineyard (1981)
PO Box 548, Glen Ellen, CA 95442. Tel (707) 526-3914. 3,500 cases. Produces a distinguished estate Cabernet Sauvignon from 35 east-sloping acres at the heart of Sonoma Mountain.

Lyeth
One-time estate producer in upper Alexander Valley; now merchant label of Nuit-St-Georges-based Jean-Claude Boisset for Cabernet-based red, Sauvignon-based white, and Chardonnay.

Lytton Springs Winery (1975)
650 Lytton Springs Road, Healdsburg, CA 95448. Tel (707) 433-7721. 7,000 cases. Mostly hearty to heady estate Zinfandel from turn-of-the-century vines in 50-acre vineyard on the ridge separating Dry Creek from Alexander Valley north of Healdsburg. Bought from founder in 1991 by Ridge Vineyards (see p 158).

MacRostie Winery (See Carneros).

Mark West Vineyards (1974)
7000 Trenton-Healdsburg Road,

Forestville, CA 95436. Tel (707) 544-4813. 15,000 cases. Originally an estate; since 1992 part of the Marion Group. Brightest star: Gewürztraminer from the founder's 65-acre vineyard in the Russian River Valley.

Martinelli Winery (1987)
3360 River Road, Windsor, CA 95492. Tel (707) 525-0570. 2,000 cases. A Russian River Valley grower's label with some excellent Gewürztraminer and good Pinot Noir on its record.

Martini & Prati Winery (1951)
2191 Laguna Road, Santa Rosa, CA 95401. Tel (707) 823-2404. Old-line bulk producer offers small bottlings of Fountaingrove Cabernet Sauvignon from its own vineyards.

Matanzas Creek Winery (1977)
6097 Bennett Valley Road, Santa Rosa, CA 95404. Tel (707) 528-6464. 25,000 cases. Chardonnay (partly from 40 estate acres midway between Santa Rosa and Kenwood) shines consistently; Sauvignon Blanc and Merlot can do.

Mazzocco Vineyards (1984)
1400 Lytton Springs Road, Healdsburg, CA 95448. Tel (707) 433-9035. 25,000 cases. Chardonnay from 14 acres in Alexander Valley and Cabernet Sauvignon from 13 acres in Dry Creek are the mainstays.

The Meeker Vineyards (1984)
9711 West Dry Creek Road, Healdsburg, CA 95448. Tel (707) 431-2148. 5,000 cases. Heavyweight Zinfandel and Chardonnay from a mostly steep, east-facing 60-acre vineyard, just below Warm Springs Dam in Dry Creek Valley.

Melim Vineyards (1986)
15001 Chalk Hill Road, Healdsburg CA 95448. Tel (707) 433-4774. 8,000 cases. Estate-grown Chardonnay and

Cabernet Sauvignon from 80 acres on the Alexander Valley side of Chalk Hill Road.

The Merry Vintners (1984)
3339 Hartman Road, Santa Rosa, CA 95401. Tel (707) 526-4441. 7,500 cases. Burgundy-fancier pursues lofty goals with bought-in Chardonnay in toasty reserve edition, and also a more fruit-focused regular one.

Peter Michael Winery (1988)
12400 Ida Clayton Road, Calistoga CA 94515. Tel (707) 942-4459. 3,000 cases. From 50 acres well up in Knights Valley's hills, Chardonnay.

Mill Creek Vineyards (1974)
PO Box 758, Healdsburg, CA 95448. Tel (707) 433-5098. 12,000 cases. Family-owned 75-acre estate in Dry Creek Valley just yards from its boundary with Russian River Valley has been most notable for growing Merlot.

J.W. Morris (1975 in Alameda, moved to Sonoma in 1983)
PO Box 988, Healdsburg, CA 95448. Tel (707) 431-7015. 120,000 cases. A one-time Alameda-based specialist in port-type wine gave its name to its major grower. J.W. Morris goes on port-types and cent-saver table wines; prestige label for estate Chardonnay, Cabernet, and others is "Black Mountain," after the 275-acre vineyard on the slopes at Healdsburg's south side.

Murphy-Goode Estate Winery (1985)
4001 Highway 128, Geyserville, CA 95441. Tel (707) 431-7644. 40,000 cases. Sauvignon Blanc is the flagship from the winery's own 150 plus 165 affiliated acres at the eastern side of the Alexander Valley.

Nalle Winery (1984)
PO Box 454, Healdsburg, CA 95448. Tel (707) 433-1040. 3,000 cases. Zinfandel to the nth from Doug Nalle's own and an affiliated Dry Creek Vineyard. Cabernet Sauvignon is up-and-coming.

Nelson Estate Vineyards (1987)
1,500 cases. Grower label for Cabernet Franc from the family's 15 acres in Sonoma Valley.

Olivet Lane (See Pellegrini Bros)

Optima (1984)
PO Box 1691, Healdsburg, CA 95448. Tel (707) 431-8222. 3,000 cases. Cabernet Sauvignon or a Cabernet-based blend from bought-in grapes is consistently well made.

J. Pedroncelli Winery (1927)
1220 Canyon Road, Geyserville

95441. Tel (707) 857-3531. 125,000 cases. Topflight Sauvignon Blanc, more-than-priceworthy Cabernet Sauvignon and Zinfandel come mostly from the family's 120 acres on the Dry Creek side of a ridge separating that valley from Alexander Valley. A fine Chardonnay from vines where Dry Creek joins the Russian River.

Pellegrini Bros. (1986)
PO Box 2386, South San Francisco, CA 94083. Tel (415) 589-1313. 10,000 cases. The best known of three grower labels of Pellegrini Bros. of San Francisco is "Olivet Lane," which goes on Russian River Valley Chardonnay and Pinot Noir from their Olivet Road vineyard. Cloverdale Ranch goes on Cabernet Sauvignons from a second vineyard near Cloverdale. "Cotes de Sonoma" is a lower-priced label.

Piper-Sonoma Cellars (1980)
11447 Old Redwood Highway, Healdsburg, CA 95448. Tel (707) 433-8843. 140,000 cases. Russian River-based subsidiary of Piper Heidsieck buys in most of its grapes from the home region for classic-method Brut, Blanc de Noirs, and Tête de Cuvée. Always polished, beginning to be distinctive.

Porter Creek Vineyards (1982)
8735 Westside Road, Healdsburg, CA 95448. Tel (707) 433-6321. 2,000 cases. Pinot Noir and Chardonnay from 20 acres at the winery.

Preston Vineyards (1975)
9282 West Dry Creek Road, Healdsburg, CA 95448. Tel (707) 433-3372. 30,000 cases. Important Dry Creek Valley grower looks ever more to Rhône (Marsanne, Viognier, Syrah) and Italy (Barbera) for grape varieties for his 125-acre estate not far below Warm Springs Dam. Its finest pre-Mediterranean hours have been with a Sauvignon Blanc called Cuvée de Fumé and Zinfandel.

Quivira Vineyards (1983)
4900 West Dry Creek Road, Healdsburg 95448. Tel (707) 431-8333. 15,000 cases. Stellar Sauvignon Blanc from the bottom and Zinfandel from the bench of 90 estate acres on the west side of Dry Creek Valley. Cabernet coming along well.

Rabbit Ridge Vineyards Winery (1981)
3291 Westside Road, Healdsburg, CA 95448. Tel (707) 431-7128. 4,000 cases. Busman's holiday winery of Belvedere winemaker Erich Russell gets top marks for Chardonnay from his 45 acres in Russian River Valley.

A. Rafanelli Winery (1979)
4685 Westside Road, Healdsburg, CA 95448. Tel (707) 433-1385. 6,000 cases. Lusty Zinfandel and Cabernet Sauvignon from 60 estate acres on the west bench of Dry Creek Valley.

Ravenswood (1976)
18701 Gehricke Road, Sonoma, CA 95476. Tel (707) 938-1960. 15,000 cases. Test-your-mettle Sonoma Valley "Old Hill Vineyard" Zinfandel is its pride ; Dry Creek Valley-based Sonoma County Zinfandel is rather more mortal in scale.

Richardson Vineyards (See Carneros)

Roche Vineyards (See Carneros)

Rochioli Vineyards (1985)
6192 Westside Road, Healdsburg, CA 95448. Tel (707) 433-2305. 5,000 cases. One of California's grand vineyards for Pinot Noir, also makes Sauvignon Blanc of swiftly increasing stature. The 130-acre vineyard, also a source for several other wineries, flanks the Russian River several miles downstream from Healdsburg.

St Francis Winery (1979)
8450 Sonoma Highway, Kenwood, CA 95452. Tel (707) 833-4666. 35,000 cases. Sonoma Valley estate of 100 acres has done notably well with Merlot and Chardonnay.

Sausal Winery (1973)
7370 Highway 128, Healdsburg, CA 95448. Tel (707) 433-2285. 12,000 cases. Long-time growers in Alexander Valley focus on Zinfandel from 100 acres (plus 50 affiliated) on east side near Jimtown.

Sea Ridge Winery (1980)
13404 Dupont Road, Occidental, CA 95465. Tel (707) 875-3329 [not mapped]. 2,500 cases. Former marine biologist with vineyards as close to the Pacific shore as he can find them, especially for Pinot Noir and Chardonnay.

Sebastiani Vineyards (1900)
PO Box AA, Sonoma, CA 95476. Tel (707) 938-5532. Over 3 million cases. The titan of Sonoma Valley and for years virtually its only protector against extinction. Is of greatest interest for Cabernet Sauvignon Sonoma Valley "Cherryblock," Merlot Sonoma Valley, and Zinfandel Sonoma Valley.

Seghesio Winery (1905)
14730 Grove Street, Healdsburg, CA 95448. Tel (707) 433-3579. 120,000 cases. Long-established family has 400 acres scattered across Sonoma, including the Russian River Valley, from

where a lovable Pinot Noir, Alexander Valley, source of a superior Zinfandel Reserve, and Dry Creek Valley. Favorite is Sangiovese (alone and blended) from ranch between Geyserville and Asti. Whites are good, too, especially Sauvignon Blanc.

Sellards Winery (1980)
6400 Sequoia Circle, Sebastopol, CA 95472. Tel (707) 823-8293. 1,200 cases. Mostly Cabernet Sauvignon and Chardonnay from bought-in Alexander Valley grapes.

Simi Winery (1867)
PO Box 698, Healdsburg, CA 95448. Tel (707) 433-6981. 140,000 cases. Cabernet-Chardonnay dominated winery keeps homing in on preferred sources. Once Sonoma County, Cabernet Sauvignon is now Alexander Valley, largely from 100 estate acres at south tip of AVA. Chardonnay still a Mendocino-Sonoma-Napa blend while 100 acres in Russian River Valley come into bearing. Sonoma County Sauvignon Blanc (mostly Alexander Valley) is a keeper. Dandy Mendocino Chenin Blanc is worth a look.

Sonoma Creek Winery (See Carneros)

Sonoma-Cutrer Vineyards (1981)
4401 Slusser Road, Windsor, CA 95492. Tel (707) 528-1181. 80,000 cases. Chardonnay specialist offers 3: "Russian River Ranches" from 3 estate properties in that AVA is a quick-developing bargain; "Les Pierres" from Sonoma Valley is an age-worthy legend; "Cutrer Vineyard" from Russian River is in-between. The winery bought 200-acre Balverne in Chalk Hill in 1992.

Robert Stemmler Vineyards (1977)
10,000 cases. The Pinot Noir-only label was bought in 1988 by Buena Vista (see p 65); Stemmler still makes the wine from bought-in Sonoma County grapes. Stemmler makes other wines in his own winery in Dry Creek Valley under the Bel Canto label.

J. Stonestreet (1990)
25,000 cases. In the Kendall-Jackson family (see p 108). Based in 54 acres at southern tip of Alexander Valley, from whence Cabernet and Merlot. Buys Sonoma County grapes for Pinot Noir and Chardonnay.

Rodney Strong Vineyards (1961 as Sonoma Vineyards, renamed 1984)
11455 Old Redwood Highway, Healdsburg, CA 95448. Tel (707) 433-6511. 225,000 cases. Informative

Below and bottom: Zelma Long has brilliantly rebuilt Simi into a major force in Sonoma County.

for Chalk Hill Chardonnay "Chalk Hill Vineyard," Russian River Valley Pinot Noir "River East," and at its best with Alexander Valley Cabernet Sauvignon "Alexander's Crown" and Alexander Valley Sauvignon Blanc "Charlotte's Home."

Joseph Swan Vineyards (1969) 2916 Laguna Road, Forestville, CA 95436. Tel (707) 573-3747. 1,500 cases. Individualistic Pinot Noir and Chardonnay from 10 estate acres near Forestville in Russian River Valley.

Taft Street Winery (1982). 2030 Barlow Lane, Sebastopol, CA 95472. Tel (707) 823-2049. 20,000 cases. Russian River Valley Chardonnay from bought-in grapes, could be the prototype for its appellation. Sonoma County bottling also good.

Topolos at Russian River Vineyards (1978) PO Box 358, Forestville, CA 95436. Tel (707) 887-1575. 7,000 cases. Rustic Zinfandel, similar (and rare) Alicante Bouschet. Mostly from owned or leased vineyards.

Marimar Torres Estates (1990) 11400 Graton Road, Sebastopol, CA 95472. Tel (707) 823-4365. 12,000 cases. From 60 estate acres in Sonoma-Green Valley, polished, stylish Chardonnay by the daughter of Spain's famous Torres winemaking family in Penedès.

Trentadue Winery (1969) 19170 Redwood Highway, Geyserville, CA 95441. Tel (707) 433-3104. 12,000 cases. Classic old-vines Alexander Valley Zinfandel from 200 acres between Healdsburg and Geyserville.

Valley of the Moon (1943) 777 Madrone Road, Glen Ellen, CA 95442. Tel (707) 996-6941. 50,000 cases. Zinfandel is the best bet from 200 family-owned acres in mid-Sonoma Valley.

Van der Kamp Wine Cellars (1981) PO Box 609, Kenwood, CA 95452. Tel (707) 833-1883. 5,000 cases. Small sparkling-wine specialist producing a range; every member bold in style.

Viansa Winery (See Carneros)

Viña Vista (1971) PO Box 47, Geyserville, CA 95441. Tel (707) 857-3722. 2,000 cases. The founding name is now a second label for Sonoma Cabernet Sauvignon and Merlot. "Chauffe-Eau" is the top-of-

the-line name for Carneros Chardonnay, Alexander Valley Cabernet Sauvignon, and Sonoma Valley Merlot.

Weinstock Cellars (1984) 638 Healdsburg Avenue, Healdsburg, CA 95448. Tel (707) 433-3186. 30,000 cases. Kosher wines, Chardonnay the most satisfactory, from 90 family-owned acres in upper Dry Creek Valley.

Wellington Vineyards (1990) PO Box 568, Glen Ellen, CA 95442. Tel (707) 935-6671. 5,000 cases. A range of varietals from local grapes; still seeking a style.

William Wheeler Winery (1981) PO Box 881, Healdsburg, CA 95448. Tel (707) 433-8786. 22,000 cases. Dry Creek Valley Cabernet Sauvignon "Norse Vineyard" from a 30-acre estate is the flagship, Sonoma County Sauvignon Blanc the steadiest wine.

White Oak Vineyards & Winery (1981) 208 Haydon Street, Healdsburg, CA 95448. Tel (707) 433-8429. 10,000 cases. "Myers Limited Reserve" Chardonnay and Cabernet Sauvignon from the proprietor's 6 acres in Alexander Valley are the flagships of a reliably attractive list otherwise made with bought-in Sonoma grapes.

Wild Hog Hill Winery (1988) PO Box 189, Cazadero, CA 95421. Tel (707) 847-3642. 1,500 cases. Broad range of small lots from bought-in, mostly Dry Creek Valley grapes.

Wildcat Wines (1985) 19100 Old Winery Road, Sonoma CA 95476. Tel (707) 996-8955. 3,000 cases. Owner-grown Sonoma Valley Merlot is the centerpiece.

Williams & Selyem (1981) 6575 Westside Road, Healdsburg, CA 95448. Tel (707) 433-6425. 2,000 cases. Staked a claim as producers of California's most memorably individual Pinot Noirs, especially single-vineyard bottlings from Rochioli and Allen vineyards (where the winery is located). Zinfandel is secondary.

Z Moore Winery (1985) 3364 River Road, Windsor, CA 95492. Tel (707) 544-3555. 6,000 cases. To be sought out for a remarkable dry, barrel-fermented Russian River Valley Gewürztraminer from the adjoining Martinelli Vineyard.

Steven Zellerbach Once a winery where J. Stonestreet now is. A merchant label since 1988. Chardonnay and Cabernet Sauvignon.

Travel Information

PLACES OF INTEREST

Cloverdale (pop 3,000) On US 101, a town caught between forest products and winemaking. Of interest to visitors mostly for having several modest, modestly priced motels.

Geyserville (pop 1,000) Aerville village, now bypassed by US101, harbors at its heart the regional clubhouse for old-school local winemakers.

Glen Ellen (pop 1,000) To this secluded Sonoma Valley village Jack London repaired during his last years. In the hills above a five-store main street, a museum in hikeable Jack London State Park celebrates the author's wanders and works.

Healdsburg (pop 9,500) Sits exactly at the hub of Alexander Valley, Dry Creek and the Russian River appellations – a perfect headquarters for wine-touring. The Currier & Ives town square is home to an on-going series of festivals from spring to early autumn. A recent wave of upmarket residents has made this a town of superior bakeries as well as good restaurants. Two comfortable motels on Dry Creek Road, at Healdsburg's north side, help make it a useful headquarters. Lake Sonoma Recreation Area, above Warm Springs Dam at the head of Dry Creek Valley, offers a change of pace from wine touring.

Kenwood (pop 1,000) Near the head of Sonoma Valley, Kenwood is

The rugged coast offers glorious respite from the winery-packed Sonoma Valley.

HOTELS AND RESTAURANTS

Bonito 133 East Napa Street, Sonoma, CA 95476. Tel (707) 939-1266. Seafood restaurant, with Italian touches.

Café Citti 9049 Highway 12, Kenwood, CA 95452. Tel (707) 833-2690. Informal Italian leaning toward Tuscany; deli good for takeout picnic foods.

Catelli's The Rex Geyserville Avenue, Geyserville, CA 95441. Tel (707) 857-9904. Catelli's is the clubhouse for local winemakers. The decor is plain, the prices fair, the food richly flavorful country Italian.

Doubletree Hotel 3555 Round Barn Boulevard, Santa Rosa, CA 95403. Tel (707) 523-7555. This hotel is just far enough east and uphill from US 101 to be quiet; spacious, well-appointed rooms.

l'Esperance 464 First Street West; Sonoma, CA 95476. Tel (707) 996-2757. Hidden toward the rear of a short close branching off the plaza, an almost-casual restaurant serving traditional French menu. Good local wine list.

La Gare 208 Wilson Street, Santa Rosa, CA 95403. Tel (707) 528-4355. On an out-of-the-way street, a quiet, comfortable restaurant with a quiet, comfortable French menu and a good local wine list.

Kenwood Restaurant and Bar 9900 Highway 12, Kenwood, CA 95452. Tel (707) 833-6326. For lack of a better word, California cuisine. Good wine list and handy location draw many local winemakers for working lunches and dinners.

Madrona Manor 1001 Westside Road, Healdsburg, CA 95448. Tel (707) 433-3231. On a quiet hill at the mouth of Dry Creek Valley, in what

began as the mansion of a local magnate, is a quaint hotel and often excellent restaurant serving fresh, country foods.

Mixx 135 4th Street, Santa Rosa, CA 95403. Tel (707) 573-1344. A restaurant eclectic enough for the kitchen to borrow about equally from Japan and Italy, the decor from Victorian wherever. Many local wines by the glass.

Piatti 405 First Street West, Sonoma, CA 95476. Tel (707) 996-2351. Bright, bustling, voluble enough to be in Italy. Consensus rather than any regional cookery.

Samba Java 109A Plaza Street, Healdsburg, CA 95448. Tel (707) 433-5282. Eclectic sandwiches and spicy grilled dishes anchor the menu of a lively local lunchtime hangout on the town square.

Sonoma Cheese Factory 2 Spain Street, Sonoma, CA 95476. Tel (707) 996-1931. Browser's selection of local wines plus deli for picnic-style luncheon fare.

Sonoma Mission Inn PO Box 1447, Sonoma, CA 95476. Tel (707) 938-9000. The Spanish colonial-style buildings are mostly a spa, but the grill offers well-prepared fresh food and a long list of Sonoma wines. Comfortable rooms, a great pool, good tennis courts. Northwest of the plaza by several miles, in the old resort community of Boyes Hot Springs, this is the site of the annual Sonoma County Showcase and Wine Auction.

Traverso's 3d at B Street, Santa Rosa, CA 95401. Tel (707) 542-2530. Superior selection of local and other wines. Also a source of fine take-out picnic fare and mostly Italian specialty foods.

Tre Scalini 241 Healdsburg Avenue, Healdsburg, CA 95448. Tel (707) 433-1772. Perhaps the most refined Italian cookery anywhere in the Russian River Valley. The style is Tuscan, with California overtones. Ranging local wine list. Just off the town square.

USEFUL ADDRESSES

Healdsburg Chamber of Commerce, 217 Healdsburg Avenue, Healdsburg, CA 95448. Tel (707) 433-6935.

Sonoma County Wineries Association, 5000 Roberts Lake Road, Robert Park, CA 94928. Tel (707) 586-3795.

Sonoma Valley Visitors Bureau, 453 First Street East, Sonoma, CA 95476. Tel (707) 996-1090.

very modest as a town, save for the concentration of wineries in and near it, and two good restaurants they have helped to spawn.

Santa Rosa (pop 113,300) Long-time commercial center for the whole North Bay, now supports Sonoma County's only guaranteed daily traffic jam – a result of rapid growth caused by the arrival of several high-tech industrial firms. One link with quieter times remains: the garden at the intersection of Santa Rosa and Sonoma avenues in which Luther Burbank did some of his greatest botanizing. The town is not closely tied to the wine industry, but its central location between the Sonoma and Russian River Valleys usefully positions its hotels (abundant) and restaurants (less plentiful) for wine touring.

Sonoma (pop 8,100). Here Sonoma was born, here the cradle remains in

place. The Franciscan mission San Francisco Solano (1835) sits at one corner of a plaza begun and largely finished while the town was still a Mexican pueblo. It and several other standing buildings dating to that era are the core of a state historical park. General Mariano Vallejo's restored home just four blocks west along Spain Street is also part of that park. However, the contemporary atmosphere is anything but sleepy Mexican pueblo. Rather, the old plaza is a hub for busy townsfolk and tourists who have come to eat at any of a dozen restaurants, drink at whichever of about that many bars, buy books in the only such store, or tour the mission and other remnants of the origins. Close to the plaza at 315 Second Street East is Vella Cheese Company, last producer on earth of hard, nuttily delicious Dry Sonoma Jack.

Mendocino and Lake Counties

In all of Lake and the most heavily planted regions of Mendocino, the climate is similar enough that both share not only pear orchards but also vineyards full of Sauvignon Blanc, Cabernet Sauvignon and Zinfandel. Share is the operative word. Wineries casually and continually reach back and forth across the county line for grapes.

But it is odd that the two wine communities are joined at the hip. Put aside grapes and pears, and the climate that begets them, and these side-by-side counties are not alike at all. At the heart of Lake County, sun-baked, false-fronted, farm-oriented main street Kelseyville feels like a movie set for one of those gritty yarns about an impoverished ranch family hanging on against a thin-lipped land baron with foreclosure on his mind. Listening to the conversation in local bars and cafés does not always spoil the illusion.

Lakeport, only five miles away, looks as although it belongs to a different country. It sits on sharp slopes leading right down to the water's edge. Charmingly old in some spots, scruffily old in others, it is everywhere far from the little Ascona or Como it might have become had it succeeded in drawing an upper-crust summer crowd. Summer crowds there are – boaters on Clear Lake are the town's lifeblood – it is just that many of them face the morning in road-worn Winnebagos, while almost none wake up in fully-staffed pink villas.

In and near these two towns are most of Lake County's vineyards, many of them hidden behind walls of pears. The Clear Lake AVA circles Clear Lake, but agricultural land is scarce on the steep hills that crowd in against most of its long shoreline. Only around Kelseyville is there a sizable flat area with soils of some depth: this 5 by 5-mile district calls itself Big Valley, and accounts for a quarter of all the county's farmland.

Deeper into the landscape, a lack of wineries means that wine production peters out more quickly than vineyards do. As late as 1992, only three wineries were operating in the Clear Lake AVA proper. Guenoc is away by itself between Middletown and the Napa County line, in an upland valley that more or less extends Napa's Pope Valley north into Lake County. A fourth, tiny, lies in the countryside between.

Mendocino's major vineyards grow along the Russian River, border country to Lake County by location and climate. However, Ukiah is neither Kelseyville nor Lakeport, nor anything close. In a county that still wears a substantial if tattered blanket of redwoods a century and a half after the first loggers came, the town is wedded closer to the timber industry than to pears or grapes, and has the gauziest of Victorian airs in its older residential quarters because of that.

For many visitors to the Mendocino Coast, the sun seems to be coming up and going down in the wrong points of the compass, so much do its weathered towns and rocky shore look like New England. The loggers who pioneered Mendocino came from America's northeast, and built so closely in the style of their original homes that the region not only looks like a

Although well distant from the nearest vineyards, Mendocino town is the County's premier destination for visiting wine buffs.

movie set of Maine, it is one. In fact it has portrayed Maine so often it should have honorary citizenship. But it does not take a motion picture director to be spellbound by the haunting light along this coast. A very different kind of tourist mecca from Clear Lake, it is a place for quiet and contemplative readers and walkers rather than noisy admirers of thundering boats.

Between Ukiah and the coast, between sun and fog, sits the Anderson Valley. Psychologically, it does not fit into any recognizable slot. In 1990 its newspaper publisher spent a few days in jail for fist-fighting with an elected official with whom he disagreed. Locals do not hike willy-nilly in the woods because the patience of well-armed marijuana guests dwindled from a low start after too many turned out to be various kinds of police. (The county agricultural commissioner listed marijuana as Mendocino's top money crop in one of the annual reports required by the state. His taste was questioned but his estimates were not.) Curious as it might seem, here and only here in these two counties does wine dominate, although it came

late, and although apples and sheep still have important roles in the local economy. Anderson Valley wines are as distinctive as everything else local. Where sun-roasted interior growers focus their attention on Sauvignon Blanc, Cabernet and Zinfandel, their fog-chilled counterparts in Anderson Valley concentrate on Chardonnay, Gewürztraminer, and, above all, sparkling wines.

Historically, Lake County came out of the starting gate a little sooner and much fancier than Mendocino. Its first vine-grower arrived in 1857. Its first famous winemaker was Lillie Langtry, the English actress who raised a lot of eyebrows before she raised her first grape. When the Jersey Lily bought the Guenoc Ranch in southern Lake county, in 1877, the better to shed an unwanted husband, she found grapes on the property. She immediately hired a French winemaker, who apparently did a creditable job, although Langtry Farms wines never did make it to the commercial market under their own name. By the time Lillie sold Guenoc in 1903, Lake County winemaking had peaked at 5,000 acres and 36 wine cellars.

Mendocino's pioneer grower and winemakers were later, less newsworthy, and less numerous than Lake's. The first of them probably came in 1880. Records are not easy to find, but nothing suggests either acreages or numbers of cellars to equal Lake County at its peak. It was not until late in the 19th century that Lake County was carved out of Napa, and

Mendocino out of Sonoma. The remoteness of both from the main markets caused their wines to stay at home, or be shipped in bulk, Lake's to Napa wineries, Mendocino's to Sonoma's.

Because the wine industries in these two counties had little or no identity of their own, Prohibition did them catastrophic harm. Vineyards shrank in Mendocino and disappeared from Lake County. Through the exertions of the Parducci family in Ukiah, Mendocino developed and kept a modest presence in the difficult years from 1933 until the beginnings of the wine boom in the mid-1960s. Vines and wines did not come back to Lake County until the 1970s.

Even now, both counties remain comparatively small as wine regions. Mendocino has 12,000 acres of vines and 40 wineries. Lake County has but 3,500 acres and half a dozen cellars. In spite of limited resources, each county has spawned a comparative giant. Between 1968 and 1988 Fetzer Vineyards made a dizzying 20-year run from a 15,000-case beginning to a 2 million-case power in coastal winemaking, assembling a 2,000-acre empire of its own vines in Mendocino County on the way. Kendall-Jackson, a later starter, was still growing toward a million cases in 1990, and had nearly all of its vineyard base outside Lake County.

The 19th-century Presbyterian church in Mendocino town.

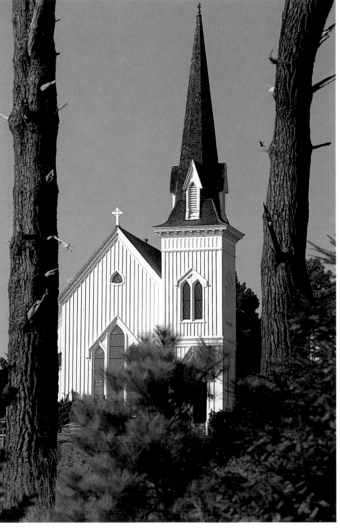

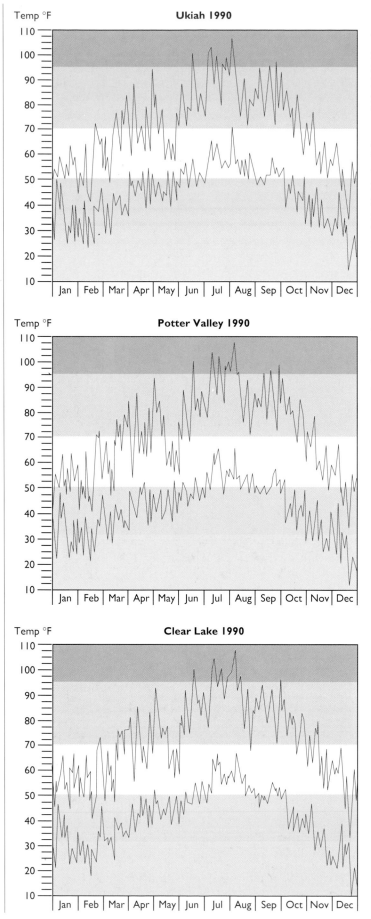

Temp °F — **Ukiah 1990**

Temp °F — **Potter Valley 1990**

Temp °F — **Clear Lake 1990**

Climate

With the singular exception of Anderson Valley, the marine fogs that govern so much of what grows where in Napa and Sonoma fade from the picture completely in these counties. High coastal hills and sheer distance from the sea do away with fog in all Mendocino's share of the Russian River drainage basin, and every corner of Lake County.

As important, or more so, is the fact that these two counties are just at the southern edge of the Aleutian winter storm track, with several important consequences. Spring frosts and hailstorms imperil the beginning of the growing season, and autumn rains shorten the other end. Also, they get more winter rain than regions farther south. Ukiah's average, for example, is nearly 12 inches more than St Helena's. Less predictably, Clear Lake and the interior districts of Mendocino have periods of higher summer temperatures than either Napa or Sonoma; these are interspersed with sudden, unpredictable dips, especially at night.

Mendocino's Potter Valley lives with the extremes because of its elevation and lack of a tempering body of water. Residents there are not at all surprised to go from 95°F on a summer's afternoon to 37° or 38°F that same night. The differences between it and Ukiah are not huge, but are persistent enough to give the two districts harvest dates for the same grape varieties that differ by as much as 10 days.

The Clear Lake AVA, at still higher elevation than Potter Valley, endures the same sort of summer heat, but is somewhat less subject to deep night chills because of the lake. Vineyards close to the shore also escape frosts that attack points farther from it, or higher in the hills. Stations all around the lake report almost identical daily weather.

Anderson Valley lacks a reporting station, so hard evidence is difficult to come by. Still, the pattern is, by observation, not greatly different from the Carneros to Yountville section of the Napa Valley. That is, the seaward end is similarly foggy and cool, the interior end almost as reliably sunny but far from fog-free. It differs from southern Napa in being slower to warm in spring, quicker to cool in autumn, and in having substantially greater winter rainfall.

* For the color code to the climate charts see pages 14–15.

White Wine Varieties

Chardonnay (70 acres in Mendocino, 0 in Lake in 1970; 2,668 in Mendocino, 268 in Lake in 1990)

Out of the cool, foggy Anderson Valley come Chardonnays of strikingly firm texture and taste and a certain unwillingness to grow old. Navarro epitomized the breed for years, sometimes all alone. Handley joined the chorus in 1980, and Greenwood Ridge became a factor from 1988 onward. Husch and Lazy Creek have not been perfectly consistent, but are admirable at their peaks. These wines do not come to full flower a week after they are bottled. Far from it. The best of them need three, four, even five years for their flavors to deepen and make the mysterious shift from fresh apple to baked, spiced apple. More than most California wines, Anderson Valley Chardonnays from good vintages will put up with a long time in new oak barrels and still hold their grape flavors. Neither does malolactic fermentation automatically turn them buttery.

Chardonnays from the interior of Mendocino County are, predictably, fuller, riper wines. This does not prevent some of

Right: The first autumnal colors have crept into Pinot Noir vines in Anderson Valley.
Below: The estate vineyard of Handley Cellars.

them from being keepers, as Simi's splendid 1980 from a vineyard at Talmage proved a few months after its 11th birthday. As with most types from the interior, wines from identifiable properties or even well-defined regions can be hard to find. The ones that do turn up have yet to give a clear advantage to anywhere specific within the region. Redwood Valley consistently produces Chardonnays of early charm for Lolonis and Konrad (originally Olson).

Blends of the two regions can surpass wines of narrower origin when the goal is balance, not quantity. Husch is one demonstration, blending from its vineyards at Philo and Talmage. Navarro supplements Anderson Valley with a portion of Potter Valley Chardonnay in most years.

Benchmarks:

Handley Anderson Valley (assembled, based in estate). **Navarro** Anderson Valley "Premier Reserve" (estate). **Greenwood Ridge** Anderson Valley (assembled). **Konrad** Mendocino (from Redwood Valley). **Lolonis** Mendocino (estate from Redwood Valley). **Husch** Mendocino (assembled from owned Talmage, Anderson Valley properties). **Navarro** Mendocino (assembled, mostly from Anderson Valley, some from Potter Valley).

Chenin Blanc (139 acres in Mendocino, 0 in Lake in 1970; 551 in Mendocino, 55 in Lake in 1990)

Off-dry, resolutely uncomplicated sippers have been the rule, are the rule, and most likely will continue to be the rule. Husch would appear to be a model of what the grape can do in the Ukiah Valley.

Colombard (869 acres in Mendocino in 1970, 0 in Lake; 470 in Mendocino, 0 in Lake in 1990)

Mendocino is the last stronghold of Colombard in all the coastal counties, Parducci the last of its champions.

Gewürztraminer (8 acres in Mendocino, 0 in Lake in 1970; 269 in Mendocino, 0 in Lake in 1990)

Gewürztraminer grows in other parts of Mendocino County, and even gives wines of a certain sweet, easy virtue here and there, but the racy stuff comes from Deep End Anderson Valley. Nowhere else in California does the variety achieve

such memorable depths of flavor and firmness of texture.

Quality and character show early, then last for four or five years, sometimes more. More than once, a bottle from a good vintage has lost itself somewhere in a cellar only to pop up 10 years later in the best of health, but this does not happen often enough to make 10-year waits a sound basic plan. Varietal flavor here easily achieves lichee character year after year. In the finest seasons, it can be almost spicy, as Alsatians think of the word.

For years Navarro stood alone at the head of the class. Now, Lazy Creek, Handley and Husch can all challenge in any one vintage; no surprise given the cosy confines within which all their vineyards are found, and the vigorous rivalry they all enjoy. To keep the playing field level, all four compete within a narrow range of style: dry or barely off-dry, uncompromising varietal flavor, and no more than the faintest touch of oak.

Benchmarks:

Handley Anderson Valley (estate). **Husch** Anderson Valley (estate). **Lazy Creek** Anderson Valley (estate). **Navarro** Anderson Valley (estate). **Navarro** Anderson Valley "Late Harvest" (estate).

Riesling (3 acres in Mendocino, 0 in Lake in 1970; 192 in Mendocino, 88 in Lake in 1990)

Like Gewürztraminer, appellation-specific Riesling is virtually exclusive to Anderson Valley in these counties. The regular contenders for Riesling Of The Year are Greenwood Ridge and Navarro. Both make the wine just off-dry, and should. Without a softening touch of residual sugar either might be too hard-edged for all but the most calvinist of Calvinists to enjoy. The flavors in both are Riesling's wonderful amalgam of grapefruit, tart berry, and a flower that resists precise identification.

Navarro has a monopoly on Late Harvest Riesling from the appellation, no surprise given the valley-bottom location of its vineyards. Like most Californians, Navarro Late Harvest and Cluster Selected Late Harvest taste riper and sunnier than their German counterparts, but less markedly so than rival wines from Napa and Sonoma. Even at their most concentrated, they manage to hold focus on the flavors of Riesling rather than botrytis and all its by-products.

Benchmarks:
Greenwood Ridge Anderson Valley (estate). **Navarro** Anderson Valley (estate). **Navarro** Anderson Valley "Late Harvest" (estate).

Sauvignon Blanc (34 acres in Mendocino, 14 in Lake in 1970; 863 in Mendocino, 517 in Lake in 1990)

Doubtless best adapted of all the white varieties to the wide range of climates and soils in these two counties, Sauvignon Blanc does notably well in every part of them, even cool, foggy Anderson Valley. As everywhere else in the North Coast, it sometimes expresses the melonlike side of its flavor range, sometimes the herbaceous one. But, to the distress of form players, it does not follow any transparent rule about where or why it does so.

Husch manages to coax melonlike flavors out of its La Ribera vineyard at Talmage in cool vintages as much as warm ones. Just downstream in the Sanel Valley, Jepson gets not only ripe flavors, but almost lush textures, not an everyday occurrence with Sauvignon Blanc. In the opposite direction, in Redwood Valley, Elizabeth Vineyards leans toward flavors of sweet grass, while near-neighbor Lolonis ranges from melony to a dusty floral note commoner in the Sierra Foothills. Obester, in its long experience with a vineyard in Potter Valley, has an unshakable record of flavors that range from fresh herbs to outright grass. Greenwood Ridge, amazingly, has coaxed a Sauvignon with some hints of melon in it from the Ferrington vineyard at the warmer, inner end of Anderson Valley, although sweet grasses come to mind faster.

Sauvignon Blanc perhaps hits its best stride of all in these two counties in the Clear Lake AVA, although in mysteriously differing ways. Buena Vista's Lake County bottlings have had dazzlingly rich flavors of melon in vintage after vintage. Konocti, meanwhile, catches more of herbs in a way both subtle and indelible.

Until 1989, the approach in almost every cellar had been to minimize oak or dispense with it altogether in favor of keeping vineyard flavors front and center. A few, most notably Buena Vista, used about half a percent of residual sugar to highlight the wine's fruit characteristics. Hidden Cellars was the loyal opposition, a reliable source of heartily oaked Mendocino Sauvignon Blanc from its first vintage on. Starting in 1989, more winemakers began using barrel fermentation and Sémillon to amplify the range of styles. The clearest example of what might happen began with two 1990s from Konocti: an oak-free Sauvignon Blanc and a barrel-fermented Grand Fumé.

Benchmarks:
Greenwood Ridge Anderson Valley "Ferrington." **Elizabeth Vineyards** (Redwood Valley, estate). **Husch** Mendocino "La Ribera" (Ukiah Valley, estate). **Parducci** Mendocino (Ukiah Valley). **Obester** Mendocino (Potter Valley). **Buena Vista** Lake County. **Konocti** Lake County (Clear Lake). **Konocti** Lake County "Grand Fumé" (Clear Lake).

Sémillon (0 acres in Mendocino, 0 in Lake in 1970; 32 in Mendocino, 24 in Lake in 1990)

Sémillon remained a rarity in both counties into the early 1990s, much of a small crop going into Sauvignon-Sémillon blends, especially at Hidden Cellars in Mendocino and Guenoc and Konocti in Lake. However, in the late 1980s, a sequence of richly figgy examples from Parducci suggested the variety might find a place of its own if ever the monomania for Chardonnay dies down.

Sparkling Wines

Trying to think about Mendocino classic-method sparkling wines is still like trying to handicap a long race in the mud using the results of two or three sprints on a dry track.

Roederer Estates uses a substantial amount of reserve wine in nonvintage blends clearly meant to echo the Pinot Noir-rich style of the parent in Champagne. Scharffenberger takes a leaner approach in general and sticks to vintages in particular. Handley holds the middle ground, perhaps leaning a little closer to Roederer.

Between the late 1980s and early 1990s, all three introduced *brut* rosés. Such wines can be, indeed have been, difficult to bring to heel, as it were. The desires in these early days were somewhat nobler than the deeds.

Differ although the three houses might in style, one clear upshot of their efforts is that Anderson Valley always gives a structure and depth of flavor not found in well-made fizz from the warmer side of the hills. Jepson is the case in point.

Benchmarks:
Roederer Estates Anderson Valley "Brut" (estate, from five properties). **Scharffenberger** Mendocino "Brut" (assembled, nearly all from Anderson Valley). **Scharffenberger** Mendocino "Blanc de Blancs" (assembled, nearly all from Anderson Valley). **Handley** Anderson Valley "Brut" (assembled).

The Anderson Valley's Deep End, a home for fine Gewürztraminer.

Red Wine Varieties

Barbera (0 acres in Mendocino, 0 in Lake in 1970; 15 in Mendocino, 5 in Lake in 1990)

Only Parducci Wine Cellars keeps the flame alight, but does it so well that the lack of more players in the game is to be lamented. As might be expected, the variety keeps a crisp acidity in Mendocino's interior valleys – in this case Redwood Valley – even while ripening fully.

Cabernet Sauvignon (110 acres in Mendocino, 45 in Lake in 1970; 1,108 in Mendocino, 954 in Lake in 1990)

The absolute prototype of a Mendocino Cabernet Sauvignon is a regular bottling from Parducci Wine Cellars. Name the vintage, and the wine will be supple enough to drink early, but balanced enough to last for several years – leaning more toward berry than herb in flavor, and not weighed down with a lot of oak. Husch Cabernets may be one shade darker and firmer, and oak may be a hint more prominent, but the wines will offer echoes more than contrasts. Both are based on Talmage grapes, but wines from other parts of Mendocino's interior valleys reinforce the picture again and again.

As more wineries get into the game, more vineyards establish individual identities, and more winemakers stretch the range of styles, the image may change at least somewhat, but the potential remains. Anyone who drank the Fetzer Cabernet

Sauvignon 1968 between 1978 and 1988 knows that the family's Home Vineyard in Redwood Valley can produce truly memorable mature Cabernet. Parducci Wine Cellar's 1975 Anniversary Bottling, from Talmage grapes, taught the same lesson between 1983 and 1988. Neither, incidentally, needed to push oak or tannin to achieve depth of flavor or longevity.

If much is yet to be learned about interior Mendocino, almost everything is still to be discovered about Clear Lake. To judge from Konocti's efforts with it, Cabernet from the Clear Lake AVA echoes the majority from the Russian River drainage basin in Mendocino in all but the finest details. A series of Lake County bottlings from Fetzer augmented the evidence between 1979 and 1986, but did not change it. Parducci sometimes makes a North Coast Cabernet using Mendocino and Clear Lake grapes. Blind tastings of this blend and appellation bottlings from each source show more clearly still how tiny the differences tend to be.

Based entirely on the wines of one winery, Guenoc, the Guenoc Valley AVA seems to give greater depth and intensity of color and flavor than Clear Lake. Unless Clear Lake changes, nothing will.

Benchmarks:

Husch Mendocino "North Field Selection" (estate, from La Ribera vineyard at Talmage). **Navarro** Mendocino (assembled). **Parducci** Mendocino (based on Parducci-owned vineyards at Talmage). **Guenoc** Lake (estate or anchored in it). **Konocti** Clear Lake (assembled from affiliated vineyards). **Parducci** North Coast (assembled from Mendocino and Lake).

Merlot (0 acres in Mendocino, 0 in Lake in 1970; 80 in Mendocino, 101 in Lake in 1990)

Plantings are so recent and scattered that little of use can be said as of 1992. Since starting with a prototypical 1987, Greenwood Ridge has made tiny annual lots of an Anderson Valley Merlot much in the vein of its Cabernet Sauvignon from the same vineyard. Konocti has, concurrently, seen several vintages of affable, indistinct red from young Clear Lake vines.

Much of the Merlot in Mendocino and Lake counties goes into Cabernet-based blends rather than varietal wines.

Petite Sirah (303 acres in Mendocino, 1 in Lake in 1970; 323 in Mendocino, 10 in Lake in 1990)

Some of the variety's best homes in all of California are in the warmer parts of Mendocino and Lake counties, but it is hard to learn many particulars for lack of wines to try.

In its "Cellarmaster" series, Parducci makes a more firmly tannic Petite Sirah than the rest of the winery's track record might promise, the sort of dark, solid wine one wants to drink with rich meat swimming in rich sauces. The regular bottling is much milder stuff, but still not to be wasted on bland dishes. Guenoc's estate Petite Sirah has a few more ounces of flesh on its bones than "Cellarmaster," and oak is a more prominent spice, but similarities outweigh differences in every aspect.

A great proportion of the Petite Sirah grown in Mendocino does honorable duty as the backbone for generic reds, in which its natural austerity can be tamed to suit fragile palates.

Benchmarks:

Parducci Mendocino "Cellarmaster" (Ukiah Valley). **Guenoc** Guenoc Valley (estate).

Pinot Noir (94 acres in Mendocino, 0 in Lake in 1970; 668 in Mendocino, 0 in Lake in 1990)

Although Roederer came to the Anderson Valley on the

grounds that its climate is every bit as bleak as Champagne's, there must be differences, or Anderson Valley Pinot Noir would be just another thin, sharp Bouzy Rouge. It is not: it is not grand stuff, at least has not been yet, but it has a depth of flavor and can have a balance that makes it a most agreeable young red, and a reasonably fetching middle-aged one. The trick, so far, is not to try too much, because mild regional flavors do not hold up against the sort of tannins that come from heavy pressing, or with long aging in new oak. Of a selection from the 1990 vintage, Greenwood Ridge Pinot Noirs had the lightest heart, Navarro's 'Methode à l'Ancienne' the most generous one.

The Anderson Valley still has much ground to be explored. Perhaps more years will give deeper, richer wines. Meanwhile, the ones it has give pleasure. Most of the crop goes into the sparklers of Roederer, Scharffenberger, and Handley, still more to others who reach in from outside.

Benchmarks:

Greenwood Ridge Anderson Valley. **Husch** Anderson Valley. **Navarro** Anderson Valley "Méthode à l'Ancienne" (estate).

Syrah (44 acres in Mendocino, 0 in Lake in 1970; 44 in Mendocino, 0 in Lake in 1990)

Through 1988, Syrah in Mendocino County was mostly what McDowell Valley Vineyards said it was. That winery's long-established plantings in McDowell Valley consistently produced, and still do, a wine of ample weight but curiously undefinable flavors. It appears under the subtitle of "Les Vieux Cépages." For a number of years, Frey Winery had been making the only alternative, an organic varietal wine from its vineyards in Redwood Valley; quantities, though, were too tiny and the wines too variable to teach many lessons. In 1989, Scharffenberger produced a broodingly dark, weighty, heady Syrah under the "Eaglepoint" label. The grapes came from Eaglepoint Ranch, well up in the hills east of Ukiah.

Zinfandel (632 acres in Mendocino, 108 in Lake in 1970; 1,643 in Mendocino, 251 in Lake in 1990)

On occasion Mendocino rivals Sonoma as the source of California's finest Zinfandel, most often from vineyards at Talmage and in Redwood Valley (when one wants ample scale), most beautifully of all from scattered plantings high on Greenwood Ridge, barely in or barely outside the western boundary of Anderson Valley AVA.

Lolonis and Whaler push their Zinfandels to full ripeness, give them a healthy dose of oak, and otherwise aim for wines with enough weight to do battle with a plate of ribs; they do not over-reach. Other wines from nearby vineyards have been less successful, being too much like dry port in style. In the Pacini vineyard, Hidden Cellars has found grapes that will take a healthy dollop of oak without caving in, and pursues that style accordingly. Parducci, characteristically, strikes the gentlest balance of the lot, and as a result its wines are sometimes some of the most age-worthy. Guenoc makes a Zinfandel much like its Cabernet: dark and firmly tannic, but not so ripe as the grapes might become in the warm, ever-sunny place where they grow.

Benchmarks:

Hidden Cellars Mendocino "Pacini." **Lolonis** Mendocino (estate from Redwood Valley). **Parducci** Mendocino (Ukiah Valley, anchored in winery-owned vineyards). **Whaler** Mendocino "Estate" (Ukiah Valley). **Guenoc** Lake (anchored in the estate).

Anderson Valley AVA

Established: September 19, 1983
Total area: 57,600 acres
Area in vineyard: 1,100 acres
Wineries: 10
Principal town: Boonville

For all its beauty – and this may be the most beautiful Californian wine valley of them all – the Anderson Valley was long isolated, and so insular that wary locals developed an argot called Boontling so that they, the Boonters, could talk over the heads of outsiders. The coming of State Highway 128 tied them a little closer to other parts of California, but not much. The coming of wine finally turned the valley into a destination for a broad and insistent world.

Grapes and wine echo the slow turn outward: viniculturally, Anderson Valley's debut came at the turn of the century when several farmers, mostly Italian, planted Zinfandel high on Greenwood and other ridges, making wine for the local cash-only, no-receipts economy. Its commercial beginning was in the early 1970s as a redoubt of urban dropouts who coincidentally shared a fancy for Gewürztraminer, Tony Husch of Husch Vineyards and Ted Bennett of Navarro Vineyards being leaders of that small group.

Their mistake, if they meant to remain isolated, was in making wine of real quality. Their other mistake, if they meant to create a mini-Alsace, was in planting Chardonnay too. Although Anderson Valley Gewürztraminer remained important to purists in the early 1990s, far more Chardonnay and Pinot Noir was sold, and classic-method sparkling wine dominated production to a striking degree.

By 1990, a pair of champagne houses owned the two largest firms, and almost half the vineyards. Roederer bought land west of Philo in 1983 on the grounds that the weather was every bit as bleak as Reims'. Pommery followed when it acquired Scharffenberger in 1989. Handley Cellars is a third classic-method sparkling-wine firm, also producing still wines, including a Gewürztraminer. Lazy Creek helps carry the flag for this last grape. Only Greenwood Ridge among the old guard eschews it, in favor of Riesling.

Nearly all the vines are on a succession of gently sloping terraces caused by the Navarro River cutting down into the base-rock in a battle against successive upward lurches of the North American plate. The alluvial soils on most of these benchlands are moderately to quite fertile. Soils higher up are leaner and more acidic.

Small as Anderson Valley is, it nevertheless has two further

The Anderson Valley is small enough to hide in its own shadows.

subdivisions. Boonter-drawn maps from various eras all have marked on them an unexplained line called the Mason-Dixon line, running on a northeast/southwest oblique through the village of Philo. While the original reasons for naming the line have been lost, the reasons for its existence are not imaginary. It runs along the top of a long, gentle slope to a point where hills crowd in from both sides until there is only a little more room than Highway 128 needs to sneak through the gap and onto a flat plain that reaches east past Boonville. It marks exactly the point at which the summer fogs stop, more days than not, and thin out on many others.

Out west, in what locals call Deep End, Pinot Noir thrives on the last west and southwest facing slopes before the short, swift Navarro River makes an abrupt turn toward the sea. Chardonnay can be difficult to ripen enough for well-balanced table wine, but never fails to be excellent for sparkling wine. Gewürztraminer is as good as California can grow it. Toward the interior, around Boonville, Pinot Noir can get too ripe, and, amazingly enough, Sauvignon Blanc can be splendid.

There are also a few patches of old-time, slow-ripening, above-the-fog, cool-country Zinfandel lingering around the appellation's western boundary. Would that there were more of them in a wider range of hands. At their best they are like none other from the variety: dark, lean, firm, balanced, and intensely berrylike in flavor.

Many young vineyards are on old farms throughout Mendocino.

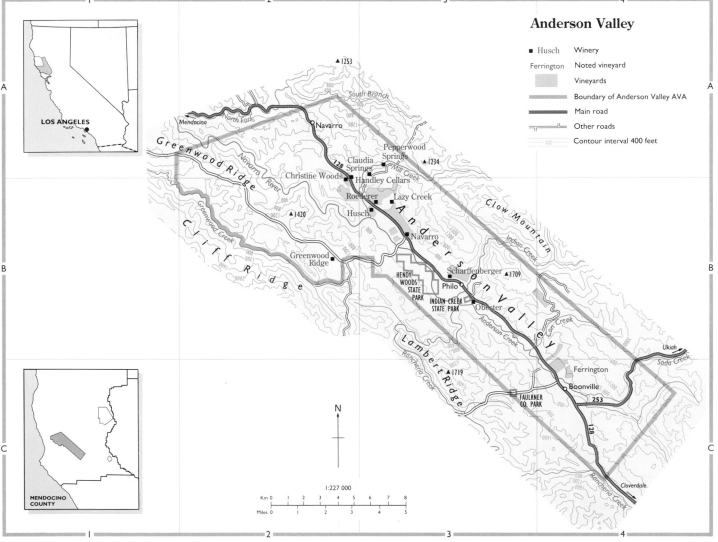

Anderson Valley

■ Husch   Winery
Ferrington   Noted vineyard
   Vineyards
   Boundary of Anderson Valley AVA
   Main road
   Other roads
   Contour interval 400 feet

LOS ANGELES

MENDOCINO COUNTY

N

1:227 000

Km 0 1 2 3 4 5 6 7 8
Miles 0 1 2 3 4 5

Ukiah-Hopland

This is the part of Mendocino that grew up making wines to be drunk without much fanfare, at no great cost. It is the only part of the North Coast where growers and winemakers still have soft spots in their hearts for Carignane and Colombard and other grapes that will put a sound bottle of wine on the dinner table for mere cents. Not surprisingly, quite a few of them take a relaxed view of appellations and other quibbles with nature.

Leaving aside the Mendocino AVA – a gigantic net cast over this area and the Anderson Valley – much of the county's major growing region was without appellation into 1993. While local vineyard and winery owners ponder the question or, in the case of several, ignore it, wine goes on. Two dips in the hills east of the Russian River's main course, Potter and McDowell Valleys, are official appellations with a greater air of being sub-appellations. Along the river itself, steep hills bow in and out to form three distinct valleys that look just as logical as sub-appellations, but have not yet been formally proposed as such. Redwood Valley is a steep-sided bowl, the northernmost of the three; Ukiah Valley, anchored on the town of Ukiah, is longer and more open; the Sanel Valley, surrounding Hopland, is shaped much like the Ukiah, but smaller.

The river runs quick and straight through a narrow, craggy, but not especially deep trough traversing the southernmost third of Mendocino County, always within a degree or two of true north-south. It has carved out a rock-solid boundary encompassing all five of the above areas. Homogeneous climate and soils would imply they are really pretty much all one district; however, no grower or winemaker would back this idea up either.

The short, fiery growing season will fully ripen almost any variety; old traditions of modest wines and newer habits of fancier ones ensure that it gets its chance. The details of what is planted are not such a muddle as one might expect, given a community where most people treat wine as a useful part of dinner rather than a refined art form. John Parducci keeps Zinfandel just north of Ukiah, Cabernet and Merlot at Talmage, and all white varieties at a third property near Hopland. Fetzer's Home Ranch in Redwood Valley concentrates on reds, especially Cabernet Sauvignon; its Chardonnay and Sauvignon Blanc cluster tightly around Hopland. Talmage is the transition zone, but even here Zinfandel and Cabernet are on the benchlands, Chardonnay and Sauvignon Blanc down on the river flats. Redwood Valley creates what muddle there is, largely because Chardonnay and Sauvignon Blanc have done well in among Zinfandel, Petite Sirah, Barbera, and Cabernet.

Greater precision comes hard as wineries have competed for limited resources for decades, making single-vineyard wines a luxury. It begins to look as if Cabernet does its best in the western hills, while Zinfandel grows well enough on the eastern bench-lands to rival Sonoma's best (Cabernet at Talmage is perhaps an exception). Barbera belongs exclusively to Redwood Valley and Petite Sirah defies categorization. Rare although they are, wines from single properties have made the most striking cases on behalf of these generalities. Particular examples include Fetzer Vineyard's Home Ranch Cabernet Sauvignon and Redwood Valley Pinot Blanc, a Simi Chardonnay from a Beckstoffer Vineyard at Talmage, and several Whaler Zinfandels from the east side near Talmage.

Parducci remains the beacon, the infallible source of wines that define their region, although Fetzer, given its size, has made a remarkable number equally regionally distinctive. Hidden Cellars, Lolonis and Whaler are more recent contributing names.

McDowell Valley AVA

Established: February 27, 1983
Total area: 2,300 acres
Area in vineyard: 540 acres
Wineries: 1
Principal town: None (Hopland nearby)

McDowell Valley is a one-winery, two-vineyard AVA situated toward the southern end of Mendocino's share of the Russian River drainage basin. In this small, tilted bowl in the first rank of hills east of Hopland, the Keehn family, owners of McDowell Vine-yards, is trying to establish a pocket-sized Rhône. Their rationale stems from Cabernet's tendency to overripen, while ancient plant-ings of true Syrah and Grenache mature in good order. They have bet much of the vineyard that they are right, planting substantial newer blocks of Syrah and Grenache, as well as Cinsaut and others better known at Châteauneuf-du-Pape than Hopland.

The proprietors have great hopes for Syrah as a varietal. Thus far a Syrah-Grenache blend called Le Tresor has appealed more. Zinfandel has had some good innings here too.

Potter Valley AVA

Established: November 14, 1983
Total area: 27,500 acres
Area in vineyard: 1,000 acres
Wineries: None
Principal town: None (Ukiah nearby)

The sparsely settled valley did not have its first winery as of 1992, but outsiders had already run up a promising track record with Sauvignon Blanc from its northern end. East and uphill from Redwood Valley, it is rather cooler than many suspect, so cool in fact that Scharffenberger and Shadow Creek both use Chardonnay from plantings here for classic-method sparkling wines. The sparkling-wine producers are attracted to the valley because it has the odd characteristic of being cooler than usual when the Anderson Valley and other shoreward areas are warmer than normal. The explanation is simple: in generally cool years, the interior does not heat up enough to pull sea-fogs from the Pacific into and through the Anderson Valley.

Outcrops of volcanic rock are common throughout the North Coast.

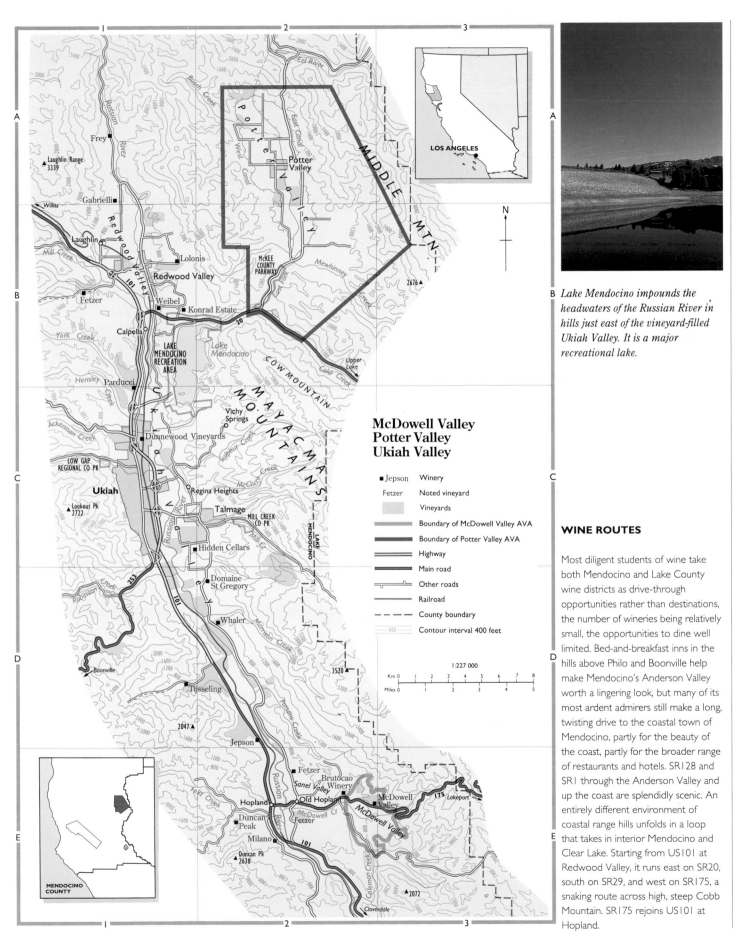

McDowell Valley
Potter Valley
Ukiah Valley

■ Jepson   Winery

Fetzer   Noted vineyard

    Vineyards

—————— Boundary of McDowell Valley AVA

—————— Boundary of Potter Valley AVA

—————— Highway

—————— Main road

——————— Other roads

⌐⌐⌐⌐⌐⌐ Railroad

– – – – County boundary

‒‒‒800‒‒‒ Contour interval 400 feet

1:227 000

Km 0   1   2   3   4   5   6   7   8

Miles 0   1   2   3   4   5

Lake Mendocino impounds the headwaters of the Russian River in hills just east of the vineyard-filled Ukiah Valley. It is a major recreational lake.

WINE ROUTES

Most diligent students of wine take both Mendocino and Lake County wine districts as drive-through opportunities rather than destinations, the number of wineries being relatively small, the opportunities to dine well limited. Bed-and-breakfast inns in the hills above Philo and Boonville help make Mendocino's Anderson Valley worth a lingering look, but many of its most ardent admirers still make a long, twisting drive to the coastal town of Mendocino, partly for the beauty of the coast, partly for the broader range of restaurants and hotels. SR128 and SR1 through the Anderson Valley and up the coast are splendidly scenic. An entirely different environment of coastal range hills unfolds in a loop that takes in interior Mendocino and Clear Lake. Starting from US101 at Redwood Valley, it runs east on SR20, south on SR29, and west on SR175, a snaking route across high, steep Cobb Mountain. SR175 rejoins US101 at Hopland.

103

Clear Lake AVA

Established: June 7, 1984
Total area: 168,900 acres
Area in vineyard: 3,200 acres
Wineries: 3
Principal towns: Lakeport, Kelseyville

If ever grapes were meant to dominate in the region, they lost their opportunity to pears during Prohibition. More recent times see only a handful of vineyards nestling among scores if not hundreds of pear orchards, almost all the vines out of sight from local roads.

Several substantial properties are on the Big Valley flats, between Lakeport and Kelseyville, but the major holdings (by size and number) lie in the rolling countryside west of State Highway 29, in the hills that form one side of Big Valley. Nearly all of Konocti Winery's growers are in one cluster or the other.

A handful of seasoned growers has opted to locate in the appellation, but farther from the tempering influence of the lake. Louis M. Martini is among them, on the grounds that Zinfandel grapes will ripen better without the lake's influence. Only three wineries were in business in the AVA in 1992: Kendall-Jackson, Konocti and Steele. Of these, only Konocti focuses on Clear Lake as the source

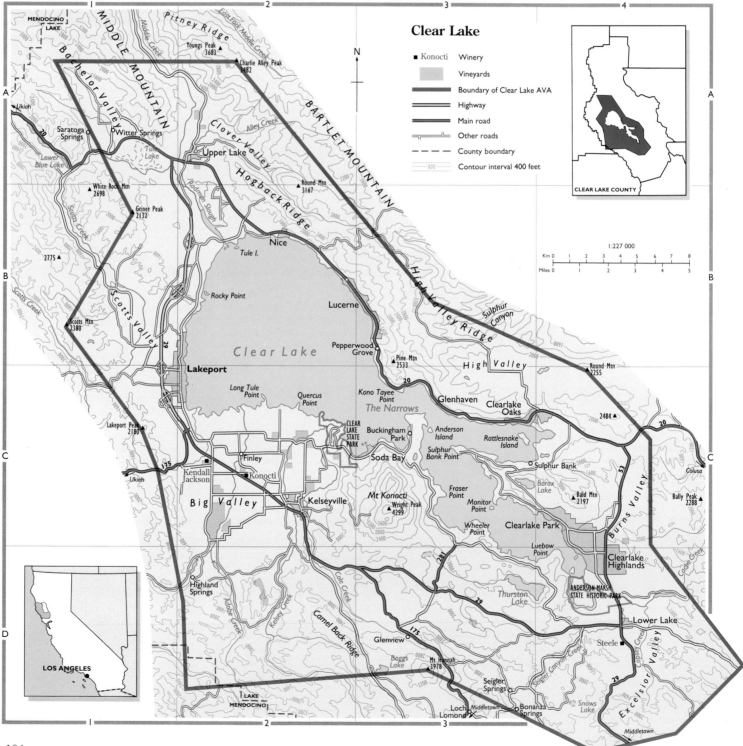

Clear Lake

- ■ Konocti Winery
- Vineyards
- Boundary of Clear Lake AVA
- Highway
- Main road
- Other roads
- County boundary
- Contour interval 400 feet

CLEAR LAKE COUNTY

1:227 000

of its grapes. This country is hot enough to deter growers from planting Pinot Noir, and few even think about Chardonnay. Sauvignon Blanc is the dominant and clearly best-adapted white tried to date. Cabernet Sauvignon and Zinfandel have been the leading reds, although some experimentally-minded souls have started looking into varieties from the Rhône.

Although pre-Prohibition history is meager, several old stories suggest that Zinfandel had pushed its way to the front rank well before the turn of the century.

The largest lake within California also tempers hot summers and cold springs for local grape growers.

Above: Clear Lake, cupped in a ring of steep hills, is one of California's most popular recreation spots for boaters.

Guenoc Valley AVA

Established: December 1981
Total area: 3,000 acres
Area in vineyard: 270 acres
Wineries: 1
Principal town: None (Middletown nearby)

William and Orville Magoon, major landowners in Hawaii, bought Lillie Langtry's old ranch in 1971, and immediately planted the first 20 of a current 270 acres of vineyard where Lillie had her vines in the late 1800s. The winery followed in 1981, and the appellation in time to cover the first crush. California has several one-winery AVAs, but only this one is owned entirely by the owners of the winery it serves. The situation is unlikely to change, for the Magoons own another 23,000 acres surrounding their appellation. The success of Zinfandel and Petite Sirah comes as no surprise, given a climate rather warmer and drier than the rest of Lake County, even a bit warmer than Pope Valley directly to the south across the Napa County line. The proprietors also have plantings of Chardonnay, Chenin Blanc, Cabernet Sauvignon, Merlot, and Cabernet Franc.

Benmore Valley

Established: Proposed
Total area: 1,000 acres
Area in vineyard: 170 acres
Wineries: None
Principal town: None

Sonoma's Geyser Peak winery not only owns this new appellation, but has also planted its first vines in a gamble that it will turn out to be a rewarding home for Chardonnay. A small experimental block of Syrah is the only hedge against that bet. The valley nestles just east of the highest ridge separating the Russian River drainage basin from that of Clear Lake's basin, barely inside the Lake County line.

Nearly all of the floor of McDowell Valley is planted with grapes, many of them traditional varieties of the Rhône. The Sanel Valley lies beyond the low hills in the middle distance.

MENDOCINO COUNTY PRODUCERS

Brutocao Winery (1986)
2300 Highway 175, Hopland, CA 95449. Tel (707) 744-1320. 10,000 cases. Producer of rustic wines from 200 acres: Cabernet Sauvignon, Merlot and Chardonnay east of Hopland.

Christine Woods (1983)
PO Box 312, Philo, CA 95466. Tel (707) 895-2115. 2,000 cases. Home-spun estate wines from 88 acres on 2 Anderson Valley properties west of Philo. Chardonnay is best known.

Claudia Springs Winery (1989)
PO Box 348, Philo, CA 95466. Tel (707) 895-3926. 1,500 cases. From bought-in Anderson Valley grapes: Chardonnay, Pinot Noir and Zinfandel.

Domaine St Gregory (1988)
4921 East Side Road, Ukiah, CA 95482. Tel (707) 463-1532. 3,000

cases. Solidly made Chardonnay and Pinot Noir are the familiar wines, Pinot Blanc and Pinot Gris the unusual ones, all from bought-in Mendocino County grapes. In 1991, owner-wine-maker Gregory Graziano set up "Monte Volpe" as a label for Barbera, Dolcetto, Nebbiolo, Sangiovese, and Tocai Friuliano from his 20-acre estate at the winery south of Talmage.

Duncan Peak (1986)
14500 Mountain House Road, Hopland, CA 95449. Tel (707) 744-1129. 500 cases. 4 hilly acres; estate Cabernet.

Dunnewood Vineyards (1946 as part of Guild, serially renamed) 2399 N State Street, Ukiah, CA 95482. Tel (707) 744-1728. 45,000 cases. Guild-owned (see p 189) producer of modest varietals, most designated as California or North Coast.

Elizabeth Vineyards (1987)
8591 Colony Drive, Redwood Valley, CA 95470. Tel (707) 463-2662. 1,500 cases. Grower label of a small ranch in Redwood Valley with estimable Sauvignon Blanc.

Fetzer Vineyards (1968)
PO Box 227, Redwood Valley, CA 95470. Tel (707) 485-7634. 2 million cases. Family-owned until acquired by Brown-Forman Distillers in 1992. Much-admired for broadly-sourced, moderate-priced Cabernet Sauvignon "Barrel Select," Chardonnay "Barrel Select" and Gamay Beaujolais – among others in a ranging, 3-tiered line-up (Reserve, Barrel Select and regular bottlings, sometimes called "Valley Oaks"). Second name is "Bel Arbors."

Frey Vineyards (1980)
14000 Tomki Road, Redwood Valley, CA 95470. Tel (707) 485-5177. 15,000 cases. Organic growers and producers drawing from 40 acres in Redwood Valley plus neighbors. Interesting Cabernet Sauvignon.

Gabrielli (1990)
10950 West Road, Redwood Valley, CA 95470. Tel (707) 485-1221. 1,000 cases. Chardonnay from bought-in grapes is the first wine. Sangiovese and Syrah planted in Redwood Valley.

Greenwood Ridge (1980)
24555 Greenwood Road, Philo, CA 95466. Tel (707) 877-3262. 5,000 cases. Built first reputation on charac-terful estate Riesling from 12 acres high in Anderson Valley's western hills. More recently has won critical acclaim for supple, herbaceous estate Merlot, melony Anderson Valley Sauvignon Blanc "Ferrington," and splendid Alexander Valley Zinfandel "Scherrer."

Varieties from the Rhône and Italy amplify recent Redwood Valley plantings.

Late starters Chardonnay and Pinot Noir were joining their siblings as critical favorites within 2 vintages.

Handley Cellars (1981)
3151 Highway 128, Philo, CA 95466. Tel (707) 895-3876. 15,000 cases. Launched to make classic-method Anderson Valley sparkling wines, partly from 25 owned acres. It has carried out its original aim while adding estimable Anderson Valley and Dry Creek Valley Chardonnays, and a superior Anderson Valley Gewürztraminer to its list.

Hidden Cellars (1981)
1500 Ruddick-Cunningham Road, Ukiah, CA 95482. Tel (707) 462-0301. 20,000 cases. The winery has never been shy about using oak in wines from its relentless explorations of inland Mendocino vineyards. Recent Chardonnays have finally begun to carry the lumber gracefully. The Zinfan-dels always did, especially the "Pacini."

Husch Vineyards (1971)
4400 Highway 128, Philo, CA 95466. Tel (707) 895-3216. 25,000 cases. Reliable family firm with 54 acres in Anderson Valley whence Gewürz-traminer and Pinot Noir; 110 acres in Talmage area for Sauvignon Blanc and often impressive Cabernet Sauvignon.

Chardonnay blends grapes from both regions to admirable effect.

Jepson Vineyards (1985)
10400 S Highway 101, Ukiah, CA 95482. Tel (707) 468-8936. 30,000 cases. Soft, round, easy Chardonnay, Sauvignon Blanc, and classic-method sparkling "Blanc de Blancs," all from 108 estate acres alongside the Russian River directly north of Hopland.

Konrad Vineyard (1980 as Olson, renamed in 1991)
3260 Road B, Redwood Valley, CA 95470. Tel (707) 485-0323. 10,000 cases. Organic Chardonnay and Zinfan-del from Ukiah and Redwood Valley are the mainstays for second owners. Working on estate Petite Sirah in 1992.

Lazy Creek Vineyards (1973)
4610 Highway 128, Philo, CA 95466. Tel (707) 895-3623. 4,000 cases. Regularly contends for top Gewürz-traminer, from 20 estate acres on upper slopes of west Anderson Valley. Good Pinot Noir from same source.

Lolonis Winery (1982)
2901 Road B, Redwood Valley, CA 95470. Tel (707) 485-8027. 8,000 cases. Family of long-time Redwood Valley growers rents space in a local

Above and left: Ted Bennett launched Navarro Vineyards especially to make Gewürztraminer, but he has succeeded with Chardonnay, Pinot Noir, and other types as well.

winery to make varietals from their 300 acres. Chardonnay and Zinfandel can be impressively ripe and rich.

McDowell Valley Vineyards (1979) 3811 Highway 175, Hopland, CA 95449. Tel (707) 744-1053. 100,000 cases. After years of fighting nature, the big effort is in Syrah, Grenache, and other Rhône varieties which had always performed best in their relentlessly sunny 300-acre pocket east of Hopland. Rhônish wines carry the "Les Vieux Cépages" label; an intensely fruity Syrah-Grenache blend called 'Le Tresor' has impressed the most.

Milano Winery (1977) 14594 S. Highway 101, Hopland, CA 95449. Tel (707) 744-1396. 3,000 cases. Family-owned winery and 60-acre vineyard near Hopland in the Sanel Valley has kept a blustery, oaky Chardonnay as its flagship while hearty to heady reds have come and gone and come back again.

Monte Volpe (See Dom St Gregory)

Navarro Vineyards (1974) 5601 Highway 128, Philo, CA 95466. Tel (707) 895-3686. 18,000 cases. One of California's best Gewürztraminers from 50 estate acres in western Anderson Valley, also firm, fine Chardonnay "Première Reserve" and Pinot Noir "Méthode à l'Ancienne." An intriguing source of local Late-Harvest Riesling and Gewürztraminer ranging up to *Trockenbeerenauslese* sugar levels.

Obester Winery (1977 San Francisco peninsula, to Mendocino in 1989) 9200 Highway 128, Philo, CA 95466. Tel (707) 895-3814. 10,000 cases.

The backbone is a fresh, melony Sauvignon Blanc from Potter Valley. The rest mostly from Anderson Valley.

Parducci Wine Cellars (1932) 501 Parducci Road, Ukiah, CA 95482. Tel (707) 462-9463. 400,000 cases. The family that kept Mendocino winegrowing alive after Prohibition until the 1970s wine boom continues to be a pillar of strength – not least because John Parducci knows well nearly every vineyard in the county. From its own 250 acres (in 3 ranches at Ukiah, Talmage and Hopland) and bought-in grapes, come polished, accessible, perfectly regional Zinfandel, Petite Sirah, Cabernet Sauvignon, Chardonnay, and Sauvignon Blanc. The "Cellarmaster" label is for bigger, firmer wines when a vintage goes just right.

Pepperwood Springs (1981) 1200 Holmes Ranch Road, Philo, CA 95466. Tel (707) 895-2920. 1,000 cases. A 1987 restart picked up with Chardonnay and Pinot Noir from 8 estate acres that had earned some praise for the original owner.

Roederer Estate (1983) 4501 Highway 128, Philo, CA 95466. Tel (707) 895-2288. 50,000 cases. From 528 acres in 4 major parcels scattered the full length of the Anderson Valley, Brut and rosé with evident, enticing, stylistic resemblances to the parent's Champagnes.

Scharffenberger Cellars (1983) 8501 Highway 128, Philo, CA 95466. Tel (707) 895-2957. 25,000 cases. After starting independently, buying grapes throughout Mendocino, the firm now focuses on Anderson Valley

as a subsidiary of Pommery. Estate plantings (120 acres) begin to dominate *cuvées* of understated non-vintage "Brut" and vintage "Blanc de Blancs", as well as curiously sturdy "Brut Rosé."

Tijsseling Vineyard (1981) 2150 McNab Ranch Road, Ukiah, CA 95482. Tel (707) 462-1034. 35,000 cases. Family winery making steady estate Chardonnay, Cabernet, and classic-method Brut from 300 acres in a box canyon running west from US101 north of Hopland.

Weibel (1945 in Alameda County; moving to Mendocino since 1962) 7051 State Street N, Redwood Valley, CA 95470. Tel (707) 485-0321. Originally focused almost entirely on modestly-priced sparkling wines, the firm has turned more toward similarly-priced table wines at the same pace it has turned toward Mendocino.

Whaler Vineyard (1981) 6200 East Side Road, Ukiah, CA 95482. Tel (707) 462-6355. 5,000 cases. At its best, estate Zinfandel from 35 acres just south of Talmage makes one wonder why anyone would grow anything else there.

LAKE COUNTY PRODUCERS

Guenoc Winery (1981) PO Box 1146, Middletown, CA 95461. Tel (707) 987-2385. 85,000 cases. 320 acres of vineyards in its own AVA at the county's south edge. Guenoc makes a dark, deep-flavored Zinfandel, a similar, daintier Cabernet, and, most impressively, a Petite Sirah with depths of flavor unexpected from this variety.

Horne Winery (1988) 22000 Highway 29, Middletown, CA 95461. Tel (707) 987-3743. 750 cases. Veteran grower making Cabernet, Petite Sirah, and Sauvignon Blanc from 17 estate acres near Middletown.

Kendall-Jackson Vineyards (1982) 600 Matthews Road, Lakeport, CA 95453. Tel (707) 263-9333. 400,000 cases. Draws from all California for a broad spectrum of wines. Major production is spritzy, butterscotchy, off-dry, soda-fountain Chardonnay. Most frequent home-county wine is Sauvignon Blanc, or Sauvignon-Sémillon blend.

Konocti Cellars (1975) PO Box 890, Kelseyville, CA 95451. Tel (707) 279-8861. 60,000 cases.

Small group of growers, most clustered along the lake shore between Kelseyville and Lakeport, provides the grapes for a crisp, thoroughly herbaceous Sauvignon Blanc, a well-wooded Grand Fumé from the same variety, and a typically accessible Cabernet.

Steele Wines (1991)
4793 Cole Creek Road, Kelseyville, CA 95451. Tel (707) 279-0213. 2,000 cases. Irrepressible Jedediah Tecumseh Steele, finally on his own after careers at wineries in both Mendocino and Lake counties, makes small lots of Chardonnay and Zinfandel from local vineyards prized since earlier days.

Roederer Estate in the Anderson Valley is owned by the famous producers of Cristal in Champagne.

Travel Information

PLACES OF INTEREST

Boonville The biggest town in the Anderson Valley is only a couple of blocks long, but that is enough to support one good restaurant, a county fairground (the sheepdog trials are memorable), a bar and a pretty good ice-cream parlor. Several bed-and-breakfast inns are in the hinterland.

Hopland A small commercial center straddling US101, lasting just long enough to include the tasting rooms of three wineries, one with a restaurant adjoining. The Fetzer Wine Center and Organic Gardens just east on SR 174 offers instructional tours.

Kelseyville Clear Lake's largest resort hotel sits well south of the small business district.

Lakeport Clear Lake's principal commercial center stretches languorously along the lake shore for well over a mile. The historic center is pleasing to the eye, with several pioneer stone buildings, and extends directly onto a shoreside promenade. The lake itself is a prime summer vacation destination for boaters and swimmers; as such, it can be especially attractive to families with children, whose tolerance of winery tours is limited.

Mendocino An old logging town turned tourist village, Mendocino sits as prettily as a town can on a wave-carved, flat-topped point that almost makes a sheltering cove at the mouth of the Little River. For decades it has been a refuge for artists and weary San Franciscans, but since the 1980s it has been discovered by a much broader audience. In the village, the

Mendocino Art Center is a community of artists' studios and performance venues. Numerous art and craft galleries, small inns and restaurants fill out a compact business district. The fine state camping parks of Van Damme and Russian Gulch flank the town.

Philo Philo's small size makes Boonville look pretty big, but it is still worth noting as the hub of a considerable number of small inns tucked away up in the hills.

Ukiah Mendocino's county seat and commercial center used to be exactly the right distance from San Francisco for road-weary travelers headed either toward the city or north into the redwood forests. Freeways have shortened the driving times on US101 so markedly that business travelers now outnumber tourists, but it remains a useful center for visitors to local wineries. Solid, comfortable motels are plentiful at the north end of town, and just to the south of it at Talmage. There is almost always one ambitious restaurant here, but it tends to be a different one each year, while a chain steak house goes on and on, to the satisfaction of most people.

HOTELS AND RESTAURANTS

Boonville Hotel Highway 128, Boonville, CA 95415. Tel (707) 895-2210. A scion of the owners of Napa Valley's famed French Laundry is the owner-chef. The menu has a few eclectic touches, but sticks close to the direct preparation and fresh foods usually called Californian cuisine. Good local wine list.

The bare brown hills that ring Clear Lake betray the region's hot, dry summer climate.

Café Beaujolais 961 Ukiah Street, Mendocino, CA 95460. Tel (707) 937-5614. Margaret Fox produces epic breakfasts and ever-imaginative lunches and dinners – based on fresh ingredients and borrowed from several cuisines, but especially American. There is an outdoor terrace for sunny weather.

Floodgate Store and Grill 1810 Highway 128, Philo, CA 95466. Tel (707) 895-3000. Several miles west at the dot-on-the-map of Navarro, the lone occupied commercial building offers hearty sandwiches and soups for lunch. An outdoor terrace is open in sunny weather.

Highland Ranch Philo, CA 95466. Tel (707) 895-3600. High above Hendy Woods State Park is an old ranch with horses, trail bikes, tennis courts, and a pool. The rooms are rustic but comfortable cottages surrounding the main house, where guests gather for breakfast and dinner.

Konocti Harbor Inn 8727 Soda Bay Road, Kelseyville, CA 95451. Tel (707) 279-4281. As golf, tennis, and boating resort hotels go, this is inexpensive and comfortable, although not luxurious.

Park Place 50 3rd Street, Lakeport, CA 95453. Tel (707) 263-0444. Fresh homemade pasta is the glory of a restaurant with few or no peers in close proximity.

Sundial Café 13500 S. Highway 101, Hopland, CA 95449. Tel (707) 744-1328. The Fetzer-owned restaurant shows off local produce, including a useful selection of Mendocino wines.

USEFUL ADDRESSES

Anderson Valley Chamber of Commerce PO Box 275, Boonville, CA 95415.

Lake County Chamber of Commerce 875 Lakeport Boulevard, Lakeport, CA 95453. Tel (707) 263-6131.

Mendocino County Convention & Visitors Bureau PO Box 244, Ukiah, CA 95482. Tel (707) 462-3091.

Mendocino County Vintners Association PO Box 1409, Ukiah, CA 95482. Tel (707) 468-1343.

Central Coast

Vineyards in the Central Coast follow the Mission Trail, the very heart of oldest California, yet are strangely divorced from it. From 1769 to 1835, Franciscan missionaries plodded northward from San Diego to San Francisco, using up saints' names at a pace much faster than their own, marking three of the 21 stages of an aching advance with Santa Barbara, San Luis Obispo, and Santa Clara. After California became a state, these became county names, to be joined by San Benito, Santa Cruz, and San Mateo. Among all the counties on the Franciscan path, only Monterey and Alameda have names inspired by other-than-holy thoughts.

And yet, in spite of a vineyard at every mission, vinicultural history in most of the region is in short supply. The Mission grape variety planted by the Franciscans proved to be unsuitable for most of their sites north of Santa Barbara, and they had no luck finding water in a land of rare rainfall. Only their luckiest efforts resulted in vineyards lasting longer than they did.

After the closure of the missions in the 1830s, the Gold Rush of 1849 produced a gigantic spasm in California's development. Bustling Los Angeles turned into an instant backwater, paltry San Francisco into an overnight metropolis, leaving the endless miles of grassy hills between them almost empty until long after both had become major cities. What history the Central Coast has reflects this early eminence of San Francisco. Winegrowing in both the Livermore Valley and Santa Cruz Mountains dates back to the 1870s, mostly because French emigrants fled chilly San Francisco in search of places warm enough for wine to grow. Both regions started small and have stayed small. Neither has a prospect now of expanding its vineyards to rival later comers because urban populations crowd in upon them. Indeed, it was the major growers in both who turned to Monterey in the 1960s for room to grow. Santa Barbara and San Luis Obispo followed a decade behind.

From a handful of tiny plots in small places then sprang huge ones in almost limitless terrain. Where grapes are so new in the landscape that history is measured in months and years rather than decades and centuries, dozens of plantings range between 1,000 and 3,000 acres, shocking figures to Bordelais,

The Golden Gate, with San Francisco in the background.

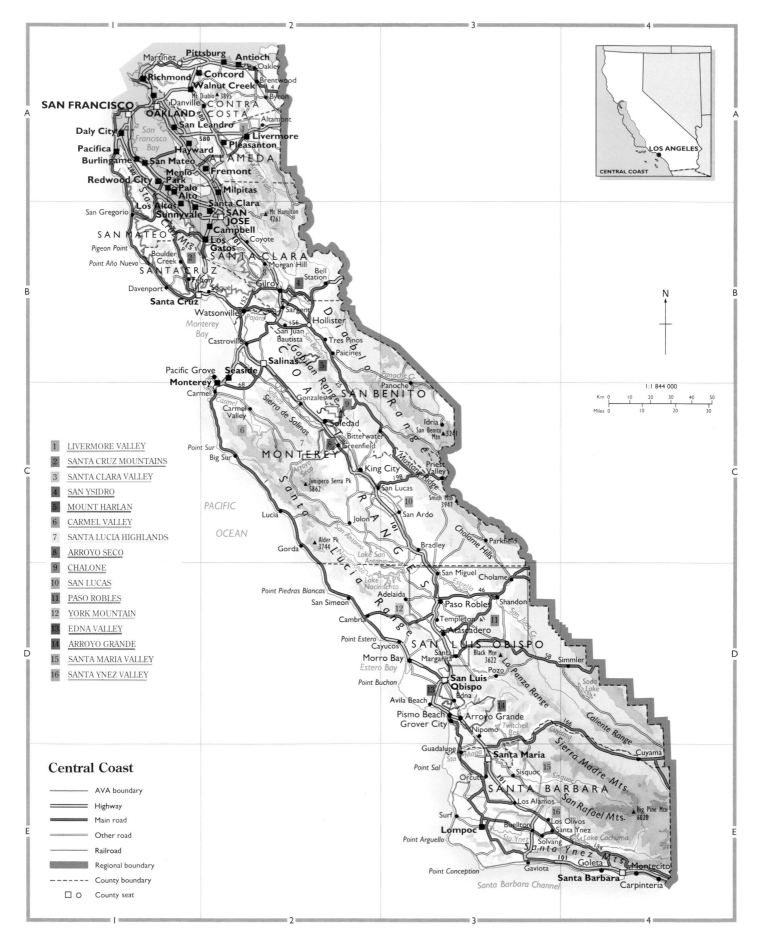

Pittsburg
Antioch
Martinez
Oakley
Richmond
Concord
Brentwood
Walnut Creek
CONTRA
SAN FRANCISCO
Danville
Mt Diablo 3895
COSTA
Byron
Daly City
OAKLAND
Altamont
San Leandro
Pacifica
580
Livermore
Hayward
Pleasanton
Burlingame
San Mateo
Menlo
ALAMEDA
Fremont
Redwood City
Park
Palo
Milpitas
Alto
San Gregorio
Santa Clara
Mt Hamilton
Los Altos
SAN
4261
SAN MATEO
Sunnyvale
JOSE
Pigeon Point
Campbell
Coyote
Los
Point Año Nuevo
Boulder
Gatos
SANTA CLARA
Creek
SANTA CRUZ
Felton
Morgan Hill
Bell
Davenport
Soquel
Gilroy
Station
Santa Cruz
157
Watsonville
Sargent
Monterey
Pajaro
Hollister
Bay
156
San Juan
Tres Pinos
Castroville
Bautista
Paicines
Pacific Grove
Seaside
Salinas
Monterey
68
Gonzales
SAN BENITO
Carmel
Panoche
Carmel
Sierra de Salinas
Soledad
Idria
Valley
Bitterwater
San Benito
Point Sur
Greenfield
Mtn 5241
Big Sur
MONTEREY
Junipero Serra Pk
King City
Priest
5862
198
Valley
Lucia
San Lucas
Smith Mtn
3947
PACIFIC
Jolon
San Ardo
OCEAN
Gorda
Alder Pk
Bradley
Parkfield
3744
Lake San
Cholame Hills
Antonio
Lake
San Miguel
Cholame
Nacimiento
46
Point Piedras Blancas
Adelaida
Estrella
Shandon
San Simeon
Paso Robles
Cambria
Templeton
Point Estero
Atascadero
Cayucos
SAN LUIS OBISPO
58
Morro Bay
Santa
Black Mtn
Simmler
Estero Bay
Margarita
3622
Pozo
La Panza Range
Soda
Point Buchon
San Luis
Lake
Obispo
Edna
Avila Beach
Pismo Beach
Arroyo Grande
Grover City
Nipomo
Twitchell
Guadalupe
Res
Cuyama
Santa Maria
166
Point Sal
Sierra Madre Mts.
Orcutt
Sisquoc
Caliente Range
SANTA BARBARA
Surf
Los Alamos
San Rafael Mts.
Big Pine Mtn
Lompoc
Los Olivos
6828
Buellton
Santa Ynez
Point Arguello
Solvang
Lake Cachuma
Santa Ynez Mts.
101
Goleta
Montecito
Point Conception
Gaviota
Santa Barbara
Carpinteria
Santa Barbara Channel

LOS ANGELES
CENTRAL COAST

1:1 844 000
Km 0   10   20   30   40   50
Miles 0   10   20   30

1   LIVERMORE VALLEY
2   SANTA CRUZ MOUNTAINS
3   SANTA CLARA VALLEY
4   SAN YSIDRO
5   MOUNT HARLAN
6   CARMEL VALLEY
7   SANTA LUCIA HIGHLANDS
8   ARROYO SECO
9   CHALONE
10 SAN LUCAS
11 PASO ROBLES
12 YORK MOUNTAIN
13 EDNA VALLEY
14 ARROYO GRANDE
15 SANTA MARIA VALLEY
16 SANTA YNEZ VALLEY

Central Coast

AVA boundary
Highway
Main road
Other road
Railroad
Regional boundary
County boundary
County seat

112

incomprehensible ones to Burgundians. There is no telling what a grower from Nuits-St-Georges would do with the 13,000 acre ranch in southern Monterey.

The simplest and strangest thing about the Central Coast is on a grander scale by far than a mere 13,000 acres. This immense geographic entity, towing Los Angeles behind it, will some day end up north of the North Coast if the earth's tectonic plates do not change course. This is nothing to wait for (a round of earthquakes in the deserts east of Los Angeles moved L.A. an inch and a half north in 1992, a huge leap by the reckoning of geologists), but it appears to be inexorable all the same.

Most of the Central Coast AVA is riding the Pacific Plate as it bumps and grinds north along the North American Plate, which holds all of the North Coast and is not going anywhere. Livermore and the east flank of the Santa Cruz Mountains are part of the North American Plate, or else are loose chips caught between the two.

In stretching almost 250 miles, from Woodside in San Mateo County to Santa Ynez in Santa Barbara County, but rarely spreading more than 25 miles from coast to eastern boundary, the region provides a more dramatic. demonstration than the boxy North Coast that horizontal distance is a minor factor, vertical measurement a major one, in determining local climate in California.

The nearly side-by-side San Lucas and Paso Robles AVAs are sheltered from the Pacific Ocean by the most formidable ramparts of the Santa Lucia Mountains. In direct consequence, they endure the hottest summers in all of coastal California. Both Santa Lucia Highlands to their north and Santa Maria Valley to their south are close to sea level and fully exposed to sea air from the Pacific Ocean. These, somewhat surprisingly given their latitude, have the two coolest growing seasons on the coast. More curious still, all four of them, and all but one of their peers, are pretty dusty between irrigations because rain is seldom plentiful south of the Santa Cruz Mountains.

Effects on choice of grape variety no doubt should be larger than they are. Livermore, the Santa Cruz Mountains and a fraction of Paso Robles aside, the entire Central Coast came into being after the oldest California districts had become market driven rather than tradition oriented, so it is full of Chardonnay and Cabernet, whether these varieties are suitable or not. The most glorious exception is Santa Barbara's coastal wedge, which has found its greatest moments in Pinot Noir. The most heartwarming exceptions are Paso Robles, which clings fiercely to its old patches of Zinfandel, and Livermore, which does the same with Sauvignon Blanc. Riesling and Gewürztraminer have their innings. So does sparkling wine.

Mission Santa Barbara, in the jewel-like city of that name.

Santa Barbara County

The history of Santa Barbara is rich, as Californian history goes. In glorious Santa Barbara city itself the shades of California's past are especially visible: the grandest of the 19 Franciscan missions, the Spanish-colonial city hall, the old beachfront Biltmore Hotel, and a dozen other places pay eloquent tribute to the opening up of California, from Spanish colonization to the Mexican era and on into modern times.

The visual record is sparser in the northern two-thirds of the county, where all the vineyards are, but Mission La Purissima Concepcion at Lompoc and Mission Santa Inez at Solvang offer concrete testimony to the early arrival of European settlers in these lands.

By contrast, the history of wine in Santa Barbara County before 1970 scarcely exists. To be sure there had been vinicultural stirrings at distant intervals. Mission vineyards started in the 1790s, peaked around 1810, and faded away soon after. Remnants still exist of a 600-acre vineyard and ambitious winery launched on Santa Cruz Island in 1885 and abandoned on the heels of Prohibition. Secondary sources say that a vineyard of 5,000 vines prospered in the Santa Ynez Valley at the turn of the century, but if it did exist, it disappeared as completely as the lost city of Atlantis. No winery buildings remain, no traces of ancient vines, no eulogies from vanished gourmets, no list of old labels.

All came to naught, in fact, until a Québecois architect named Pierre Lafond launched his Santa Barbara Winery a few blocks from Santa Barbara beach in 1962. It was not much more than a glorified retail store to start with, but for the next few years Lafond was the county's wine industry.

The real beginnings of Santa Barbara's winegrowing came in 1964, when a local farmer named Uriel Nielsen planted the first of 80 exploratory acres in the eastern Santa Maria Valley, and in 1975, when Firestone Vineyards fermented the first vintage from its vines in the Santa Ynez Valley. This opened the floodgates: the rest is current events.

Santa Barbara's two AVAs could not be more different. At the northern edge of the county, overlapping slightly into San

The Santa Ynez Valley demonstrates how a small river and geological uplift jointly create imposing benchlands.

Inside and out, La Purissima Concepcion is one of the richest restorations of an 18th-century Franciscan mission in the whole of California.

Luis Obispo County, the grittily agricultural Santa Maria Valley is short, broad, low-lying, fog-swept. Its only town, Santa Maria, is a no-nonsense commercial center for farmers and food processors. Agriculture rubs shoulders in the landscape with oil fields.

Most Santa Maria Valley grapes grow up on benchlands, the better to escape ever-present sea-fogs. All the vines are east of freeway US101 because the fogs cling so persistently to the sandy flats west of it that nothing sweeter than Brussels sprouts will ripen there.

The Santa Ynez Valley, on the other hand, is narrow at its seaward end, broad inland, gains steadily in elevation, and is home, part- or full-time, to a smart set of horse-breeders and Hollywood types, including Michael Jackson and Ronald Reagan. The Hollywood characters fit in well because the valley is close to being a stage set in the first place. In the 1940s Solvang began changing from a community of dairy farmers of Danish descent into a mildly loony caricature of a Hans Christian Andersen fairy-tale town for tourists, a process now advanced to the point that the T-shirt emporia and pizza parlors look just as Danish as the bakeries and hotels. Buellton is headed in the same direction. Los Olivos, on the other hand, has become a village of art galleries. Only Santa Ynez looks like towns in other parts of the Central Coast.

Vineyards are scattered all through the valley, most but not all of them beyond the ready reach of sea-fogs. Fittingly enough, motion picture and television producers and actors are among the owners, ex-cowboy actor Fess Parker the most visible among them.

At the outset especially, the regional approaches to grapes and wine differed as markedly as everything else. In the Santa Maria Valley, farm management companies tended large to huge holdings, selling most of their crops, sometimes all of them, to outsiders. In the Santa Ynez Valley, small wine estates are the norm.

As Santa Maria developed a reputation for Chardonnay and Pinot Noir, economically powerful wineries began to buy up lands originally farmed by management companies. Beringer Vineyards, Kendall-Jackson and Robert Mondavi were the first, outsiders all.

In between the Santa Ynez and Santa Maria valleys, and tucked in behind the rocket-launching facilities at Vandenberg Air Force Base, is the Los Alamos Valley. It falls between the other valleys not just by location, but in every sense. So hard to categorize that no one thought to make an AVA of it the first time round, it has proved to be so well adapted to grapes that it takes in a third of the county's vineyards without the benefits of formal boundaries or a name that can go on labels.

Already, the fogs that shroud some parts of Santa Barbara have many of the growers and winemakers there convinced that they drew the AVA lines all wrong in 1981 and 1984. As late as 1992, any changes had been in thought, not in deed. However, several growers were floating the idea of a Santa Barbara Coast appellation that would take in all of Santa Maria and Los Alamos, some of Santa Ynez and the San Luis Obispo County appellations of Arroyo Grande and Edna Valley. The burning question behind the proposal is where to draw a boundary between Pinot Noir on the one hand and the family of Cabernet Sauvignon on the other – this in a world already upside-down enough for the big vineyards to grow Pinot Noir while the little ones concentrate on Cabernet and kin.

Climate

In the process of dividing northern from southern California, the Transverse Range cradles Santa Barbara County's wine-growing districts among several of its many arms in such a way as to allow fog to roll in more freely than it does in the north-south valleys of the North Coast, or even the more northerly portions of the Central Coast. However, the fogbank is just a thin tail at this latitude, so cannot push hard or far inland. Resulting differences in climate are intense over short distances. Santa Maria is too chilly and foggy for grapes, as is Lompoc. Yet fewer than 20 miles away, the canyon leading from the village of Santa Ynez up to Lake Cachuma, at 750 feet elevation, has drier and hotter air than any grower has wished to combat. Hence all the vineyard climates are moderations of the extremes posed by the Santa Maria and Cachuma Lake weather stations. Temperatures over 100°F do occur at Solvang, but rarely. They are close to unheard-of at Santa Maria. Spring frosts are too rare to require the protective measures common in Napa and Sonoma.

Like the rest of the Central Coast, Santa Barbara County lies far enough south of the Aleutian storm track to receive scant rain, a fact visible in the lack of any kind of forest hereabouts. Santa Maria's average approaches 14 inches a year; the Santa Ynez Valley averages 16 inches.

* For the color code to the climate charts see pages 14–15.

Sanford & Benedict first made Santa Rita district famous for Pinot Noir.

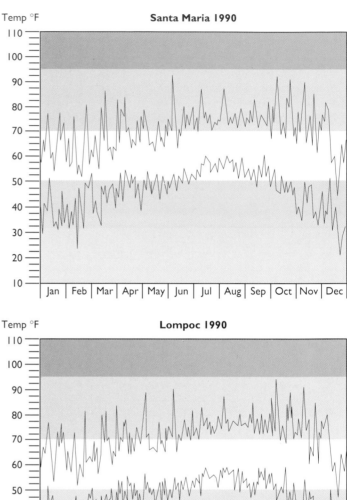

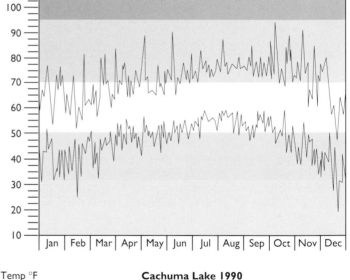

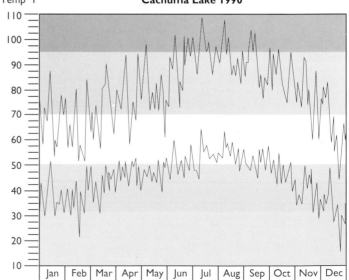

White Wine Varieties

Among white varieties Chardonnay has ruled in the county since the early days. Sauvignon Blanc, Riesling and Gewürztraminer challenge Chardonnay in quality from select spots, but not in acreage. Little else is planted, or has been, in a district too young to have needed Colombard or any of the other high-yielding varieties that carried older districts through the great depression of the 1930s and 1940s.

Chardonnay (9 acres in 1970, 3,585 in 1990)
Local winemakers generally operate on the theory that Chardonnay grapes from the coolest, foggiest locations will be tart, yet have nearly tropical flavors, while those from warmer spots will be softer in texture and closer to apples in taste. There is a certain truth in this contention, yet the core flavor of most Santa Barbara Chardonnays is a note that somehow suggests leafy herbs – a vegetal hint rather than a fruity or floral one.

Considering the youth of the region, there is a remarkable consensus of style, built around barrel fermentation, malolactic fermentation and lees contact. The hallmarks of that style are a leanness of texture that can verge on the austere, and definite but not overpowering toasty aromas.

Meridian Vineyards' Santa Barbara Chardonnay provides almost precisely the median experience of vineyard substance and winemaking style. Zaca Mesa has captured the high ground in recent vintages with wines of subtle but specific fruit flavors and a welcome silkiness on the palate. Much of the success is due to a vineyard in which clones, spacing, and other techniques are used with ever more attention to detail to broaden and deepen flavors before oak gets its say. Firestone, a near neighbor, shows how near siblings can come to being twins.

Santa Barbara Winery achieves an almost airy lack of weight, yet ample flavors that somehow dance a line between Chardonnay and toasty characteristics. Sanford Chardonnays shout out their ripe flavors and bold use of oak, and carry it all off with sheer power. Between them, they reveal the full range of styles.
Benchmarks:
Byron Vineyards (Santa Maria, estate). **Firestone Vineyards** Santa Ynez Valley (estate). **Zaca Mesa Winery** (Santa Ynez Valley, effectively estate). **Sanford** Santa Barbara (primarily Sanford & Benedict, but deliberately blended with Santa Maria grapes). **Meridian Vineyards** Santa Barbara (assembled from White Hills, Cat Canyon, Riverbench).

Gewürztraminer (0 in 1970, 209 acres in 1990)
The sparse and dwindling acreage – it peaked at 912 acres in 1985 – wrongly casts a shadow over Santa Barbara Gewürztraminers, for the variety comes to full flavor in much of the region, and, in the cooler parts, can often avoid being weighty, though not always. Only now and again does it achieve the complexity and depth common to Mendocino's Anderson Valley or Sonoma's Russian River Valley, but it has done. Curiously, the two superior examples not only grow in different climates but are also made in perfectly opposing styles: the lichee-like Firestone wine is given scant maturation time in wood, the spicier Babcock as much or more than it can stand.
Benchmarks:
Firestone Vineyards Santa Ynez Valley (estate). **Babcock Vineyards** Santa Ynez Valley (estate).

Oil wells pump right alongside vines throughout parts of both the Santa Maria and Santa Ynez valleys.

Riesling (34 acres in 1970, 722 in 1990)
Among the enigmas posed by young growing regions with disparate climates, Santa Barbara Riesling stands foremost in the early 1990s, having saved its best for vineyards otherwise suited more to Merlot than Pinot Noir.

Before the market slid, style was every bit as varied as a handful of producers could make it in response to dissimilar vineyards. A dwindling list of producers still manages to avoid any common theme, although dry was something of a watchword in the early 1990s. The Gainey Vineyard seeks and achieves dry understatement more successfully than several others. Firestone Vineyards, in its regular, off-dry bottling, aims for and achieves the note of apricots so common to California Riesling, but not all the weight that can come with that richness of flavor. Babcock Vineyards occasionally makes a barrel-fermented version, and that is exactly what it tastes like.
Benchmarks:
Firestone Vineyards Johannisberg Riesling (estate). **The Gainey Vineyard** (from Rancho Sisquoc).

Sauvignon Blanc (17 acres in 1970, 443 in 1990)
The conventional wisdom, accepted by a majority of the region's winemakers, would keep Sauvignon Blanc in the Santa Ynez Valley east of US 101 and not much farther north than Firestone. Even this group admits to a certain gray area extending through Rancho Sisquoc and on to the eastern end of Tepusquet Mesa.

Even in the warmest of Santa Barbara's zones, Sauvignon clings closer to sweet herbs than it does to the melonlike side of the variety, a fact that often brings the figgier, fuller Sémillon into blends. Oak aging is not uncommon, but several producers use no wood at all in their Sauvignons.

The Gainey Vineyard has a perfect model of what Sauvignon Blanc can be without oak. Byron Vineyard and Carey Cellars emphasize region and variety over oak or other winemaking flavors. All three value subtlety more than power, freshness more than age.

The Brander Vineyard, on the other hand, works hard to temper Sauvignon with both Sémillon and winemaking technique. The "Tête de Cuvée" bottlings, in particular, reveal barrel fermentation and oak aging, not as a flavor of wood but rather by tempering the taste of grapes. It is a style that cries out for well-sauced fish rather than the herb-basted, broiled chicken that pairs so well with Gainey et al.

Two iconoclasts favor Sauvignon from deepest, coolest Pinot Noir country: Sanford and Babcock Vineyards both use barrel fermentation, malolactic fermentation, and all the other tricks of Chardonnay to tame the herbaceous flavors that come with Sauvignon from cool vineyards, yet their results are very different. The juicy-rich, vibrantly tart Sanford trumpets herbaceous Sauvignon. The Babcock "Eleven Oaks" is riper, tastes more of oak and often is just a bit heady into the bargain. Babcock's success led the Gainey Vineyard to echo it with a "Reserve" that plays yin to the yang of that winery's regular bottling.

Benchmarks:

Byron Santa Barbara County (primarily Cramer, near Firestone). **Carey Cellars** Santa Ynez Valley (estate plus a neighbor's Sémillon). **Brander Vineyard** Santa Ynez Valley (estate, including Sémillon portion of blend). **The Gainey Vineyard** Santa Ynez Valley (since 1990 estate). **Sanford** Santa Barbara County (mostly or all Sierra Madre).

Other varieties

Chenin Blanc (503 acres in 1990) just shambles along; Muscat Blanc (22); Pinot Blanc (79); Sémillon (22), mostly blended with Sauvignon Blanc but occasionally surfaces as a varietal; Sylvaner (13), stoutly defended by Rancho Sisquoc, where it has produced consistently attractive wines.

Red Wine Varieties

Odd that Cabernet Sauvignon came before Pinot Noir when Santa Barbara was beginning its modern era of viticulture, but such is the case. Odder still that Cabernet should continue to have the greater acreage, now that Pinot Noir is king with the critics. The Cabernet family, meanwhile, still has loyal supporters, but more for Merlots and blends than for varietal Cabernet Sauvignon. Here, as with almost everywhere else in the state, Syrah is on trial, and Nebbiolo and Sangiovese are beginning to be.

Cabernet Sauvignon (37 acres in 1970, 825 in 1990)

Several local winemakers admit that the variety tends to yield less than lovable flavors, even in the most favored parts of the Santa Ynez Valley. If vegetal is not the word, pungently herbal does describe the typical flavor of pure Cabernet from the region. Cooked asparagus describes its least lovable qualities.

Alison Green at Firestone succeeded during the last half of the 1980s in finding the right sweetnesses in Merlot and French oak barrels to counter those flavors, to make something closer to berry out of the sum of the parts. Carey Cellars sticks a little closer to the herbaceous side of Cabernet without falling into the vegetable rack. Rancho Sisquoc does too in a wine that is noticeably leaner than most, from a region where all the Cabernet family tends to show soft tannins.

From a county where well over half the annual grape crop is exported to other regions, Cabernet is one of the leaders, for its intense character is exactly what is needed to spice up the bland product of vineyards in the hot San Joaquin Valley.

Benchmarks:

Firestone Vineyard Santa Ynez Valley (estate). **Carey Cellars** Santa Ynez Valley "La Cuesta" (estate). **Rancho Sisquoc** (estate).

Merlot (0 in 1970, 217 acres in 1990)

Merlot rather out-performs the more famous Cabernet Sauvignon in Santa Barbara County, particularly in the inner Santa Ynez Valley but also toward the eastern end of the Santa Maria Valley. Its flavors call fruit rather than vegetables to mind, and it fleshes itself out a bit more readily. Few winemakers use it alone. Most choose Cabernet Franc as a companion variety, and some use both that and Cabernet Sauvignon.

Merlot has been the red flagship for Firestone since 1984, if not earlier: a wine of immediate charm for its berrylike flavors and gentle balance, but with enough durability to acquire some of the more agreeable benefits of age. The Gainey Vineyard opts for a sterner, oakier style that wants a few years in bottle to throw off its adolescent sulks. Carey Cellars' Merlots offset more herblike flavors than these others with a bouncy freshness exactly right for early drinking. Buttonwood Vineyard and Rancho Sisquoc are other names to keep in mind.

Benchmarks:

Firestone Vineyard Santa Ynez Valley (estate). **Gainey Vineyard** Santa Barbara (assembled).

Cabernet family blends

In a search for ways to diminish the vegetal quality of many Cabernet Sauvignons, the Brander Vineyard and others began looking as early as the mid-1970s to blends with proportions of Cabernet Franc and Merlot exceeding the permitted 25 percent for varietal wine. Some of these suggest that Cabernet Franc bears watching in Santa Ynez even more than Merlot. Most suggest that a little Cabernet Sauvignon goes a long way.

Brander estate-bottled "Bouchet" had its finest hours when the proportion of Cabernet Sauvignon was lowest, although proprietor C. Frederic Brander remains convinced that only the latter variety has the depth of flavor he wants.

Pinot Noir (0 in 1970, 699 acres in 1990)

Pinot Noir appears to be Santa Barbara's red wine. Widely adapted in the county, especially in those shoreward regions where fog often appears, it grows well and has a particular flavor not entirely unique to the region, but nowhere better balanced than here.

That particular flavor sometimes brings to mind a leafy herb, maybe mint, maybe not. It lurks, like a seasoning, beneath more overt suggestions of strawberries. Perhaps it is just a bit of stem with the strawberry. In any case, the shadings are endless, and endlessly enticing, but the essence of the flavor makes Santa Barbara Pinots, tasted blind, easier than most to identify by region.

Corbett Canyon's silky Santa Barbara "Reserve" is as good a wine as any in which to go snuffling for the regional character in its purest form, but it is almost impossible to go wrong in choosing for the purpose.

Heavily toasted French oak barrels play a distinct role in most of the esteemed Santa Barbara Pinot Noirs, their sweetness of flavor complementing Pinot's strawberry tone while helping tame the regional mint, or whatever herb it is.

Given a noticeable dash of oak as an element of style, Byron and Zaca Mesa fight it out, year after year, for the honors of producing the most prototypical Santa Barbara Pinot Noir of the vintage. Santa Barbara Winery "Reserve" is another that gets very much to an oak-tinted heart of variety and region.

Sanford Pinot Noirs, always firm with tannins, moved farther in that direction when the winery recaptured Sanford &

Benedict Vineyard as its source of grapes, beginning with the 1990. As in all Richard Sanford's wines, the Pinot Noir almost distills varietal flavors to an essence. Oak is applied boldly on top of the original riches. Wild Horse Pinot Noirs show a similar richness of Pinot Noir flavors, but nudge both oak and tannins farther into the background. Au Bon Climat, on the other hand, pushes both oak and tannins more into the foreground than does Sanford.

There is much argument about where to draw the eastern boundary of perfect Pinot Noir country. Those who favor the westernmost vineyards say anything to the east gets too ripe. Those who favor the inner end of Santa Maria say that grapes farther west do not get ripe enough. Press for exact lines, and responses get fuzzy. The one point of agreement is that the Santa Ynez Valley east of US 101 at Buellton falls outside the boundary. Farther north, Firestone Vineyard trimmed its acreage of Pinot Noir sharply after the 1990 vintage. Even Zaca Mesa, at the northern tip of the appellation, no longer looks to its own vines for Pinot Noir.

Climate is only part of the equation. Lean, sandy soils that began as seabed are the other key. Here, again, the inner Santa Ynez is excluded.

To date, the great majority of Santa Barbara Pinot Noirs have peaked by six years, and declined markedly by ten, but the 1976 Sanford & Benedict and 1985 Sanford point toward greater possibilities as vines mature and site selection becomes more refined.

Experimental plantings hug the winery walls at The Gainey Vineyard in the Santa Ynez Valley.

Benchmarks:
Sanford (through 1989 mostly or all Sierra Madre, from 1990 all Sanford & Benedict). **Byron Vineyard** (through 1988 mostly or all Sierra Madre, since then increasingly estate). **Corbett Canyon** "Reserve" (estate from the Los Alamos district; *see* page 136). **Wild Horse** (primarily Sierra Madre; *see* page 136). **Zaca Mesa** (in recent vintages principally or all Sierra Madre). **Au Bon Climat** "Sanford & Benedict" and "Bien Nacido." **Santa Barbara Winery** "Reserve " (winery-owned LaFond).

Other varieties
Cabernet Franc (47 acres) all devoted to blending, at least through 1991; Syrah (20 acres), one promising planting in Bien Nacido grows the grapes for Qupé's oft-praised example, while another at Zaca Mesa shows as much promise; Zinfandel (24 acres) has not excited much interest from wineries or praise from bibbers.

Santa Maria Valley AVA

Established: September 4, 1981
Total area: 82,180 acres
Area in vineyard: 4,800 acres
Wineries: 4 (but 11 producers)
Principal town: Santa Maria

The oddest aspect of the Santa Maria River Valley is that it has so much of Santa Barbara's vineyard area and so few of its wineries. This is because its vineyards are huge, 400 acres being as close to paltry as it is to important.

More than half the district's vineyards are on what the locals call Santa Maria Mesa, in spite of its having slopes steep enough to ski on. A narrow, sharp-edged shelf squeezed

A vineyard of 400 acres is normal in size in the Santa Maria Valley. This is part of Byron Vineyards.

between the plummeting slopes of the San Rafael Mountains to the north and a sheer 20-foot drop to the river on the south, the Mesa is so long that it encompasses the extremes of weather in the valley.

Nearly 3,000 acres of the AVA's vineyards grow on this sometimes dizzying pitch, starting with Bien Nacido on the west and continuing with Cambria, then Robert Mondavi's Byron properties. Another 800 acres are directly below, down with the chickens and row crops on the valley floor, ranging eastward from the tatty village of Sisquoc, part of it Cambria, part Wine World's River Bench. Sisquoc's vines are the last. Farther inland all is cattle range on steepening hills.

Most of the remaining acreage is well to the west, in two vineyards that wander across ancient dunes that climb from the river south into the Solomon Hills. One of them, 660-acre Sierra Madre, is arguably the present-day jewel in the crown because of its Pinot Noirs. The other, Santa Maria Hills, chases it closely in size (530 acres) and reputation.

Uriel Nielsen began planting a modest 80 acres to get the region started in 1964; that property is now folded into the Mondavi ranches. James Flood followed with 211 acres next door at Rancho Sisquoc. Then, in 1972, Louis Lucas began

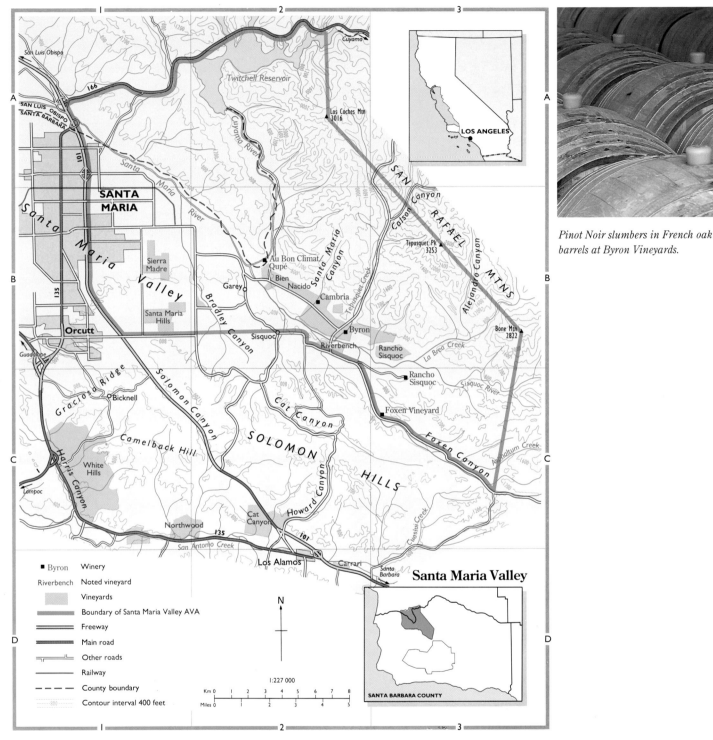

Pinot Noir slumbers in French oak barrels at Byron Vineyards.

Map legend:

■ Byron — Winery
Riverbench — Noted vineyard
Vineyards
Boundary of Santa Maria Valley AVA
Freeway
Main road
Other roads
Railway
County boundary
Contour interval 400 feet

1:227 000

Km 0 1 2 3 4 5 6 7 8
Miles 0 1 2 3 4 5

N

Santa Maria Valley

SANTA BARBARA COUNTY

covering most of Santa Maria Mesa with the 1,200 acres he called Tepusquet, now divided between Cambria and Mondavi. Large to huge properties have been the rule ever since, leaving winemakers to argue not about vineyards, but about particular blocks within them as the holiest grails.

As luck would have it, Nielsen's pioneering effort hit upon a transition point between the cooler, foggier areas to the west and the warmer, drier ones immediately to the east and south. His plantings at the inner end of the Santa Maria Mesa could have been (but weren't) misleading for early growers, who might well have thought that the district was more versatile in climate than it has proved to be. From the outset, Pinot Noir and Chardonnay have dominated the critical successes of this valley, Pinot Noir most especially from plantings in its cooler western half, Chardonnay more broadly. Only at the innermost end do the Bordeaux varieties Merlot, Cabernet Sauvignon, and Sauvignon Blanc perform well, leaving Rancho Sisquoc with, one could think, greater kinship to the Santa Ynez Valley than the rest of Santa Maria. Riesling is a most attractive orphan in most of the AVA.

Santa Ynez Valley AVA

Established: May 16, 1983
Total area: 154,000 acres
Area in vineyard: 1,200 acres
Wineries: 13
Principal towns: Solvang, Buellton, Lompoc, Los Olivos

Not as simple a matter as the Santa Maria Valley, Santa Ynez is where the argument between Pinot Noir and Cabernet/Merlot grows truly heated.

A narrow east-west watershed from its beginnings just upstream from Lompoc on up to Buellton, it widens quickly at Solvang, then becomes hydra-headed beyond Santa Ynez town. From there one part of the drainage reaches south up ever hotter San Marcos Canyon toward Lake Cachuma, while a larger, marginally cooler, one reaches north into Foxen Canyon until it touches the Santa Maria Valley's inner end.

US 101 at Buellton is everyone's dividing line between damply marine downstream and sun-dried inland. Pinot Noir is the grand grape downstream in what is called the Santa Rita district, above all at Sanford & Benedict vineyard, but in Lafond and perhaps Babcock as well. East of US 101, Sauvignon Blanc and Merlot reign in a long, narrow stretch along Alamo Pintado Road then Foxen Canyon Road from Solvang north through Los Olivos. The vines of Firestone, Carey, Buttonwood, and Brander compete for honors with the Bordeaux varieties. Gainey extends the district eastward along State Route 154.

The northern tip of the valley, around Zaca Mesa winery, is usually cooler than the eastern edge near Gainey because freer air circulation from the Santa Maria drainage basin rules Foxen Canyon.

Santa Ynez differs from its neighbor in another important way. It has a score of small wineries, and small vineyards to match. Firestone's 255 acres is the largest holding in a district where 20 acres is far more typical.

Los Alamos Valley

In the cup of the "U" formed by the two AVAs lies a considerable expanse of mostly rolling, lightly settled farm country. Within the short, narrow part called Los Alamos Valley are to be found slightly more than 3,000 acres of vines, rather prized for Chardonnay and Pinot Noir. Corbett Canyon (*see* page 136) produces highly regarded Pinot Noirs from its 330-acre ranch at the mid-section of the valley. Meridian (*see* page 135) anchors a highly creditable Chardonnay in the fierce hummocks and gullies of its 1,900-acre White Hills Vineyard at the northeastern corner of Vandenberg Air Force Base, and in the softer rolls of 390-acre Cat Canyon Vineyard, straddling US 101 at the innermost end of the valley.

The continued lack of official pedigree for this part of Santa Barbara is symptomatic of an unease about sensible boundaries for appellations that plagues growers and wineries alike.

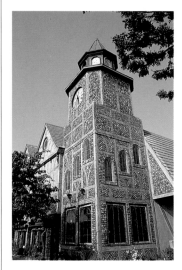

Mock Danish architecture and horse breeders share space with vineyards in the Santa Ynez Valley.

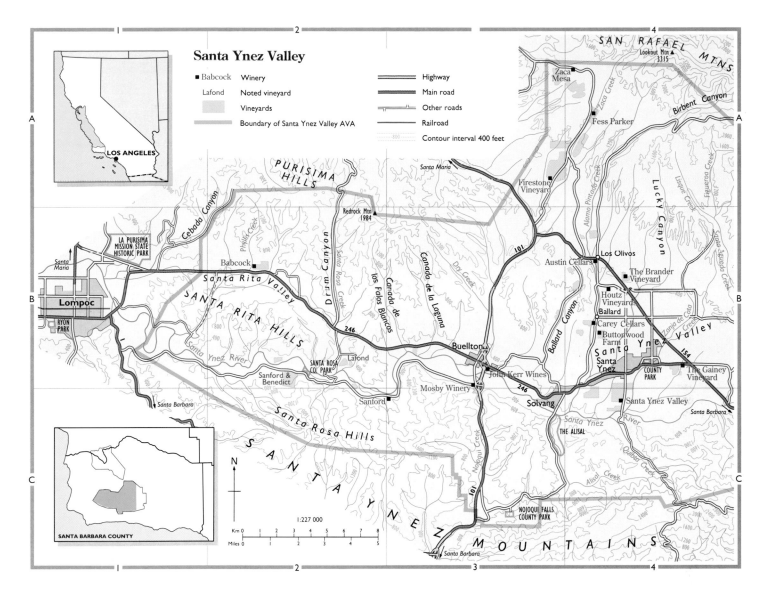

Santa Ynez Valley

- ■ Babcock — Winery
- Lafond — Noted vineyard
- Vineyards
- Boundary of Santa Ynez Valley AVA
- Highway
- Main road
- Other roads
- Railroad
- Contour interval 400 feet

LOS ANGELES

SANTA BARBARA COUNTY

1:227 000

PRODUCERS

Au Bon Climat (1982)
PO Box 113, Los Olivos, CA 93441.
Tel (805) 937-9801. 10,000 cases.
Specialist in ultratoasty, single-vineyard
Chardonnays (Bien Nacido) and Pinot
Noirs (Sanford & Benedict, Bien
Nacido). Other, equally singular, wine
types come from the same building on
Bien Nacido vineyard via affiliated or
interconnected labels: Qupé (Syrah),
Terra Vita Nova (Cabernet-based
blend), Il Podere dellos Olivos
(Nebbiolo).

Austin Cellars (1981)
PO Box 636, Los Olivos, CA 93441.
Tel (805) 688-9665. 2,400 cases. Pro-
ducer of 7 wines, mostly from bought-
in grapes. Erratic, often fascinating
Pinot Noir and late-harvest Sauvignon
Blancs arouse greatest interest.

Babcock Vineyard (1984)
5175 Highway 246, Lompoc, CA
93436. Tel (805) 736-1455. 8,800

cases. Experimentally minded Brian
Babcock makes intense, well-wooded,
sometimes heady Pinot Noir,
Chardonnay, Sauvignon Blanc, Riesling,
and Gewürztraminer from 50 acres
the family grows well west of Buellton.

The Brander Vineyard (1981)
PO Box 92, Los Olivos, CA 93441.
Tel (805) 688-2455. 7,000 cases.
C. Frederic Brander's lean, faintly
smoky Sauvignon Blanc and Bouchet
come from 37 estate acres at Los
Olivos, as does a steady Chardonnay.

Buttonwood Farm (1989)
PO Box 1007, Solvang, CA 93463. Tel
(805) 688-3032. 1,000 cases.
Sauvignon Blanc, Cabernet Franc, and
Merlot from a 75-acre planting north
of Solvang. The well-established vineyard has given impressive wines for
others.

Byron Vineyard (1984)
5230 Tepusquet Road, Santa Maria,
CA 93454. Tel (805) 937-7288.

Brian Babcock (left) and
C. Frederic Brander (right) take
dissimilar views of Sauvignon
Blanc in the wineries bearing
their names.

123

Byron Kenneth Brown, a driving force behind the emergence of Santa Barbara wine.

27,000 cases and growing. Velvety, rich Pinot Noir and deftly toasty Chardonnay are mainstays for founder-winemaker Byron Kenneth Brown, primarily from a section of what originally was the east end of Tepusquet, the pioneer Nielsen plantings, and another block at the winery – all owned since 1990 by Robert Mondavi, as are the cellars. Also: fine Sauvignon Blanc, and Cabernet from Santa Ynez Valley grapes.

Cambria Vineyards (1988)
5475 Chardonnay Lane, Santa Maria, CA 93454. Tel (805) 937-8091. 50,000 cases. The Santa Maria Valley arm of Kendall-Jackson owner's far-flung empire concentrates on Chardonnay and increasingly impressive Pinot Noir from more than 700 acres on Santa Maria Mesa. This is the larger part of the original Tepusquet Vineyard.

Carey Cellars (1978)
1711 Alamo Pintado Road, Solvang, CA 93463. Tel (805) 688-8554. 6,500 cases. Small cellar owned and directed since 1987 by Kate Firestone, producing mostly estate wines from 25 acres between Solvang and Los Olivos. Subtly herbaceous, juicy-rich Cabernet Sauvignon "La Cuesta" (from the hilliest of three blocks), Merlot, and Sauvignon Blanc are especially to be sought.

Chimere (1990)
1800 Sequoia Way, Santa Maria, CA 93454. Tel (805) 922-9097. 2,000 cases. Gary Mosby buys local grapes for winemaker label Chardonnay, Pinot Blanc, Gamay, and Pinot Noir.

Cottonwood Canyon (1990)
PO Box 3459, San Luis Obispo, CA 93403. Tel (805) 549-9463.

At its founding a grower label for Chardonnay and Pinot Noir from 60 acres adjoining Santa Maria Hills vineyard in the Santa Maria Valley.

Firestone Vineyard (1975)
PO Box 244, Los Olivos, CA 93441-0244. Tel (805) 688-3940. 80,000 cases. The major grower-producer of Santa Ynez Valley is most intriguing for supple Merlot, solid Gewürztraminer, and increasingly toasty Chardonnay. It has a particular reputation for Riesling. Cabernet Sauvignon is gaining. All come from a 255-acre, mostly mesa-top, vineyard in Santa Ynez Valley north of Los Olivos, or a neighbor.

Foxen Vineyard (1987)
Route 1, Box 144A, Santa Maria, CA 93454. Tel (805) 937-4251. 3,000 cases. 10 acres on inner Santa Maria Valley slopes yield Chardonnay, Chenin Blanc, and Cabernet Sauvignon; grapes for dark, intense, sometimes dazzling Pinot Noir are bought-in from vineyards in the Santa Maria Valley.

The Gainey Vineyard (1984)
PO Box 910, Santa Ynez, CA 93460. Tel (805) 688-0558. 15,000 cases. Long-time Santa Ynez winemaker Rick Longoria makes polished, thought-provoking Sauvignon Blanc (estate), Merlot (assembled), and Pinot Noir (Sanford & Benedict), plus well-regarded Chardonnay, Johannisberg Riesling, and Cabernet Sauvignon.

Houtz Vineyards (1984)
PO Box 897, Los Olivos, CA 93441. Tel (805) 688-8664. 2,100 cases. Chardonnay, Sauvignon Blanc, Chenin Blanc, Cabernet Sauvignon from the

owners' 16-acre Peace and Comfort Farm in Los Olivos, and the next-door neighbor.

Kalyra (1988)
PO Box 865, Buellton, CA 93427. Tel (805) 963-0274. 800 cases. Michael Brown's winemaker label for Chardonnay, Cabernet Sauvignon, and sparkling wines.

John Kerr Wines (1986)
PO Box 7539, Santa Maria, CA 93456. Tel (805) 688-5337. 800 cases. Busman's holiday cellar of winemaker John Kerr offers full-tilt Chardonnay, Syrah, and Pinot Noir.

Mosby Winery (1979)
PO Box 1849, Buellton, CA 93427. Tel (805) 688-2415. 7,000 cases. Sturdy to rustic Chardonnay, Gewürztraminer, Riesling, and Pinot Noir lead a list principally from the proprietor's 75 acres. An individualistic Sangiovese (called Brunello) comes from Carrari grapes.

Fess Parker Winery (1989)
PO Box 908, Los Olivos, CA 93441. Tel (805) 688-1545. 7,000 cases. Former baseball player and actor Fess Parker produces Johannisberg Riesling, Chardonnay, Merlot, and Pinot Noir, increasingly from his young vineyard north of Los Olivos.

Qupé (1982)
PO Box 440, Los Olivos, CA 93441. Tel (805) 688-2477. 8,000 cases. Ultratoasty Chardonnay battles for attention with a roster of hearty, well-wooded wines from Rhône-originated varieties: Marsanne, Viognier, Syrah, and Mourvèdre.

Rancho Sisquoc Winery (1977)
Route 1, Box 147, Santa Maria, CA 93454. Tel (805) 934-4332. 5,500 cases. From the easternmost vineyard in the Santa Maria Valley come ripe, juicy Chardonnay, leaner Sauvignon Blanc, subtly herbaceous Merlot, and what may be the last surviving Californian Sylvaner (called Franken Riesling).

Sanford Wines (1981)
7250 Santa Rosa Road, Buellton, CA 93427. Tel (805) 688-3300. 30,000 cases. In a district of individualists, Sanford stands out for the depth of his Pinot Noirs (long from Sierra Madre, since 1990 from the regained Sanford & Benedict), and the outright power of his Chardonnay (assembled from Sanford & Benedict, Sierra Madre, and others) and Sauvignon Blanc (Sierra Madre). A "Barrel Select" Chardonnay and "Reserve" Pinot Noir double the stakes in those grape varieties.

Santa Barbara Winery (1962)
202 Anacapa Street, Santa Barbara, CA 93101. Tel (805) 963-3633. The winery became serious in 1974 with the planting of Lafond Vineyard in the Santa Rita district, and became a factor in 1978 with the advent of Bruce McGuire as winemaker. Especially notable for polished, flavorful Pinot Noir "Reserve" and Chardonnay "Reserve" from Lafond vines.

Retired actor Fess Parker built his sleek winery in the upper Santa Ynez Valley.

Travel Information

Richard Sanford is synonymous with Santa Barbara Pinot Noir at its best.

Santa Ynez Valley Winery (1976) 343 N Refugio Road, Santa Ynez, CA 93460. Tel (805) 688-8381. 12,000 cases. Began as a grower-producer of a broad range from 110 owned acres touching the southeastern quarter of Solvang. The original vineyard with its original owner remains the source of a still-broad range under a new winery owner.

Lane Tanner (1986) Route 1, Box 144A, Santa Maria, CA 93454. Tel (805) 934-0230. 1,000 cases. Consulting winemaker Lane Tanner makes firm, flavorful Pinot Noir for her own label, principally from Sanford & Benedict vineyard.

Zaca Mesa Winery (1976) PO Box 899, Los Olivos, CA 93441. Tel (805) 688-3310. 35,000 cases. After widely exploring sources and varieties one of the Santa Ynez Valley pioneers homed in on Pinot Noir (subtle, polished from Sierra Madre), and Chardonnay (a paradigm, recently estate). The winery begins to be of further interest for Syrah from the original 230-acre vineyard.

PLACES OF INTEREST

Buellton is a classic "cloverleaf" town built at a freeway exit, full of motels and restaurants aimed at travelers between Los Angeles and San Francisco.

Lompoc sits quiet and remote amid sprawling fields of nursery flowers not far from the mouth of the Santa Ynez River. Partly a support town to Vandenberg Air Force Base, it has a good supply of modestly priced hotels which are less likely to be fully booked than ones nearer freeway US101. It is of particular interest for the nearby presence of Mission La Purissima Concepcion (1787), one of the two or three best-restored and most complete Franciscan missions from the earliest colonization of California in the mid- and late-18th century. It is a state park.

Los Olivos small and incomparably quieter than Lompoc, has somehow become an outpost of Los Angeles art, with galleries radiating in all directions from the towering flagpole marking its exact center.

Santa Maria bustles in its own way as the commercial center for miles of surrounding farmland and as a freeway stopover for commercial travelers and vacationers.

Solvang is crazedly but not altogether illogically Danish. A commmunity of Danish dairy farmers faced by hard times decided in the 1940s to turn their town into a tourist destination. Thousands of plywood storks and mock-straw roofs later, pizza parlors and tartan merchants share the fantasy with bakeries, smorgasbord restaurants, curio shops and what seems like an infinity of gingerbread motels. Incongruously the chapel of the Franciscan mission Santa Ines (1804) squats in a dusty park at the eastern edge of the main business district.

RESTAURANTS AND HOTELS

The Alisal Guest Ranch 1054 Alisal Road, Solvang 93463. Tel (805) 688-6411. Horses, tennis, golf with casual resort accommodation.

Ballard Inn 2436 Baseline Avenue, Solvang 93463. Tel (805) 688-7770. Informal luxury at a semirural crossroads between Solvang and Los Olivos. Friendly staff produce spectacular breakfasts and abundant afternoon hors d'ouevres with local wines as part of the hospitality.

Downey's 1305 State Street, Santa Barbara 93101. Tel (805) 966-5006. Small, comfortable. The menu changes daily to keep up with the freshest seasonal ingredients.

Hitching Post II 406 E Highway 246 , Buellton 93427. Tel (805) 688-0676. Owner-chef Frank Ostini continues to raise open-fire cookery to new levels. Knowledgeably chosen local wine list fits the menu to perfection. Relaxing, subdued surroundings.

Los Olivos Grand Hotel PO Box 526 Los Olivos 93441. Tel (805) 688-7788. Rather staid luxury on Los Olivos's main street.

Santa Maria Inn 801 S Broadway, Santa Maria 93454. Tel (805) 928-7777. Quaint rooms in the original building, comfortable ones in a new tower, but its fount-of-information wine bar is the real draw.

Steamers 214 State Street, Santa Barbara 93101. Tel (805) 966-0260. Near-the-pier source of the freshest seafood in town.

Wine Cask 813 Anacapa St, Santa Barbara 93101. Tel (805) 966-9463 Good food is incidental to a thriving wine bar/wine shop specializing in local rarities but in no way limited to them.

Once a Dane-dominated farm town, now a tourist attraction, Solvang looks like this even when selling pizza.

San Luis Obispo County

San Luis Obispo is not the only Californian county schizoid enough to make an unshakable case on behalf of American Viticultural Areas. It is, however, the textbook example. Its boundaries ignore a dizzying pitch that grinds up to or plummets down from 1,521-foot Cuesta Pass, separating San Luis Obispo town and a foggy coastal shelf from Paso Robles and a sun-dried upland valley in ways neither political boundaries nor a mere 25 crow-flight miles can begin to explain. The two can hardly be discussed in the same breath.

San Luis Obispo town is not quite urbane, but it is affected by citified ways. That is, it has plenty of cowboys, but also has restaurants that serve white wine and quiche to locals who visit Los Angeles regularly and have attended the Biennale in Venice on two or more occasions.

The first European settlement gathered around the skirts of the Franciscan Mission San Luis Obispo de Tolosa, founded on the site of what is now the heart of the city in 1797. The town was already thoroughly secularized before publishing tycoon William Randolph Hearst started rolling through in the 1920s on his way to and from his San Simeon castle, two stops up the railroad line, but Hearst's perambulations helped call attention to the beach resorts of Arroyo Grande and Pismo Beach. The Franciscans and Hearst have long since given way to the local campus of California Polytechnic University as shaper of downtown Higuera Street and the rest of San Luis Obispo proper. Bookstores, sports-shoe emporia and coffee houses line Higuera and its cross-streets, a lookalike to university avenues all over the United States, except for an architectural emphasis on Spanish Colonial not to be found where Anglo-Saxons did the pioneering.

Paso Robles, meanwhile, was and remains resolutely aloof from city ways. Throughout much of its 19th-century existence, Paso Robles had its greatest reputation as an out-of-the-way place where Black Bart and other, less celebrated, bank and stagecoach robbers could retreat from the stresses of their jobs, certain that no lawmen would come to disturb their peace, and no neighbors would be nosy about their habits. In spite of a sharply reduced population of stagecoach and bank robbers, something of the old ethos remains, especially in the miles of steep, sparsely settled hills west of the town, where sheer space guarantees solitude to anyone who wants it.

Wine in San Luis Obispo County echoes the rest of the social order. Down on the coastal shelf, it is all pretty much sparkling wines and Chardonnay, made by people new since 1975 and quite enamored of European models. Maison Deutz, the sparkling-wine specialist, understandably clings to the notions that have made the name a success in France. Most of the others have less direct connections but no less ardent desire to do what is done in Burgundy, or Alsace, or wherever.

Up in Paso Robles it is red, red, and more red, and has been since 1880. The pioneering contribution was rugged Zinfandel, the kind that will stand up to venison or, in milder modern times, barbecued beef. More recent arrivals focused their attentions upon accessible Cabernet Sauvignon right from the

The lighthouse at Point Piedras Blancas.

Wet winters permit dry-farmed vines to survive the hot, dry summers in Paso Robles' western hills.

start, but old-style Zinfandel can still be obtained from more than one cellar.

Ignace Paderewski played the gentleman vintner in Paso Robles from 1914, before making the career change from concert pianist to President of Poland. Something of a cultural anomaly, he was wise enough to let pioneer winemaker-grapegrower Andrew York do most of the real work behind his widely admired San Ignacio Zinfandel.

By 1960, nobody at York Mountain, Pesenti or Rotta gave a damn whether Paderewski had paused here or not. These last survivors of a more vigorous pre-Prohibition wine community were dug-in in the hills above Templeton, selling rustic wines to a local market and not looking to start a revolution. Reinforced by several dropouts from the 1960s, they remained set in their ways well after the first investors planted vineyards in the grasslands east of Paso Robles in the mid-1970s. When the new boys succeeded, a new air began to stir in the hills as well. Even diehard supporters of the old ways found themselves looking into Cabernet cuttings, stainless steel fermenting tanks and, perish the thought, filters. And people on both sides of the highway found themselves trading on the Paderewski legend.

Paso Robles Climate

High ridges of the Santa Lucias make for relentlessly sunny growing seasons. That fact, coupled with high elevation, produces the hottest days anywhere along the coast, but allows cool nights. 1990 was relatively mild by local standards.

The western hills are hotter than the valley floor behind the highest ridgetops of the Santa Lucias, cooler behind the lowest gaps. Similarly Templeton is substantially cooler than Paso Robles. Rainfall varies widely. Orographic effects produce averages as high as 45 inches a year at York Mountain. At Paso Robles airport the figure is a more typical 14 inches.

San Luis Obispo Climate

The Los Osos Valley threads between the Santa Lucias to the north and the Irish Hills to the south, providing a low-lying corridor for marine air to sweep across San Luis Obispo town and on into the marginally warmer Edna Valley. Fog from a nearly perpetual offshore bank further moderates both high and low temperatures. In the absence of high hills at Edna Valley's inland side, average rainfall is moderate at 22 inches a year. Arroyo Grande, even more open to the sea, has similar weather on the west, but is significantly warmer throughout the growing season near its hilly eastern boundary.

* For the color code to the climate charts see pages 14–15.

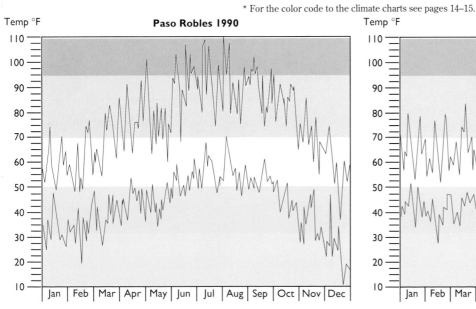

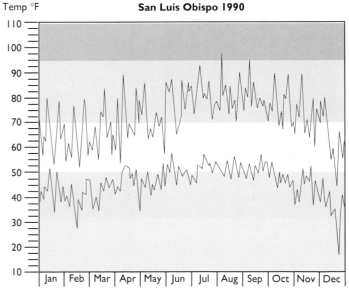

127

White Wine Varieties

White wine virtually did not exist in San Luis Obispo County in 1970, when Paso Robles had all the vineyards; records of the time show 10 acres, all Sylvaner. In the early 1990s white grapes have come close to equaling red acreage, primarily because tiny Edna Valley is given over almost entirely to Chardonnay.

Chardonnay (0 in 1970, 1,973 acres in 1990)
Usually Chardonnay insists on being itself across a wide range of growing conditions, but San Luis Obispo County forces it to show two markedly different faces. In Edna Valley, which has a startling 1,600 acres of the total, and Arroyo Grande the wines tend to be lean, a bit tart, and flavored subtly but certainly in the direction of pineapple. Most wines from Paso Robles emerge fat, and somewhat coarsely perfumed, especially those from the Estrella Prairie. If a handful of examples are right, some of the cooler canyons above Templeton strike the middle ground.
Benchmarks:
Meridian Vineyards Edna Valley (until recently from Paragon, now from the winery's own adjacent vineyard); **Edna Valley Vineyards** Edna Valley (essentially estate-bottled from affiliated Paragon).

Chenin Blanc (0 in 1970, 324 acres in 1990)
Although evidence is sparse, the variety appears to be serviceable in the Paso Robles AVA, where it can have more delicate flavors than might be expected.
Benchmark:
Martin Brothers Paso Robles (Originally from Tierra Rejada, since 1988 estate).

Gewürztraminer (0 in 1970, 22 acres in 1990)
A monopoly of Paragon Vineyards in the Edna Valley until it removed the plot after the 1990 harvest, leaving Claiborne & Churchill to find its grapes in Monterey. Paragon's grapes performed well over a span of several vintages.

Sauvignon Blanc (0 in 1970, 650 acres in 1990)
Although one of the most impressive examples comes from Edna Valley, much of the San Luis Obispo County Sauvignon Blanc that can be tracked to finished, bottled wine grows in the Paso Robles AVA. Domenic Martin of Martin Brothers proved that the varietal wine can be made tart and age-worthy there before abandoning the variety. However, prevailing local style results in soft, ripe, quick-to-fade wines. Sauvignon has fired and fallen back a bit from its 1986 peak of 929 acres, whether because of regional style, the fragile market for Sauvignon in general, or both.
Benchmark:
Carmenet Edna Valley (from Paragon; *see* page 88).

Muscat Blanc (0 in 1970, 163 acres in 1990)
This may well be the best adapted white variety in the Paso Robles AVA, most especially on Estrella Prairie, where nearly all the county's acreage is planted. Most wines from it are made as light, sweet Muscat, which is to say about 12 percent alcohol and 3 to 6 percent residual sugar. The finest of them begin with a greater delicacy of flavor and texture than typical whites from here, or typical Muscats from elsewhere. Nearly all wines bottled before 1990 went by the name Muscat Canelli, since

ruled off the course by the federal government in favor of Muscat Blanc.
Benchmark:
Eberle Winery Estate Paso Robles .

Other varieties
Pinot Blanc (57, mostly for sparklers); Sémillon (65, nearly all blended into Sauvignon); White Riesling (26).

Red Wine Varieties

By 1970 a small industry with 19th-century roots had dwindled to a tiny one, with three wineries drawing on a bare 400 acres of vineyards, nearly all in Zinfandel. Among four other varieties then growing, Carignane, with 17 acres, was the most important. On the heels of strong contemporary interest in Cabernet have come sparks of interest in Syrah, Nebbiolo, and Sangiovese.

The hills that ring Edna Valley's vineyards are typical of the Central Coast, and provide a ready explanation for California's nickname: the Golden State.

Cabernet Sauvignon (10 acres in 1970, 1,395 in 1990)
All but a handful of plantings are in the Paso Robles AVA, most on Estrella Prairie, where Cabernet ripens early and well, yielding softly approachable wines with little or none of the vegetal flavor so often dominant in Central Coast Cabernets. Almost all the local producers play down oak. Only Eberle seeks an extra tannic grip. Depth and age-worthiness are only beginning to be tested, but none can deny the immediate accessibility of typical Paso Robles Cabernet. Partly because of this easy charm no other AVA produces such a high proportion of winners in wine competitions. Small plantings of Cabernet in the west hills have not been around long enough or in adequate numbers to assess, but they promise to be firmer textured.
Benchmarks:
Eberle Winery Paso Robles (since 1985 estate-bottled from the Estrella Prairie vineyards of winery partners Gary Eberle and Howard Steinbeck).
Meridian Vineyards Paso Robles (estate-bottled from selected blocks originally planted in 1972 as Estrella River). **Castoro Cellars** Paso Robles "Hope Farms Reserve" (from the Hope ranch near Paso Robles Airport).

J. Lohr Paso Robles "Seven Oaks" (estate-bottled from steadily expanding acreage next door to the Hope Farms planting near the airport). **Adelaida Cellars** Paso Robles (assembled; in earlier vintages from ranches on Estrella Prairie, since 1988 mostly from the west hills).

Merlot (0 in 1970, 125 acres in 1990)
University of California studies in the 1880s vigorously discouraged planting of Merlot in Paso Robles because of its tendency to overripen there. Although modern growers have made strides, no Merlot vineyard or wine has yet emerged as distinguished as the best from elsewhere in California. Merlot wines of some promise have been produced from cool zones near Templeton by Wild Horse, JanKris (originally Farview Farms) and York, and more plantings are going into that area.

Petite Sirah (0 in 1970, 110 acres in 1990)
Although the acreage is substantial in Paso Robles, varietal wine bearing this appellation is so rare that no generalizations can be made about the grape's performance in the region.

129

Pinot Noir (5 acres in 1970, 169 in 1990)
Through the early 1990s, Pinot Noir does not appear to be San Luis Obispo's grape variety. Plantings are concentrated in the Edna Valley and Arroyo Grande AVAs. It has performed marginally in Edna Valley, wines from there having been much outshone by those from similar climates in Santa Barbara County. In its first two vintages the Talley vineyard in Arroyo Grande promised to measure up better. The odd patch in hilly country west of Paso Robles has done well in cool years, but usually will yield plummy to raisiny flavors. A few of the chilliest canyon bottoms west of Templeton are beginning to be explored with Pinot in mind.

Syrah (0 in 1970, 33 acres in 1990)
The one major planting is east of Paso Robles, in what began as Estrella River and is now Meridian. Estrella's wines were sound but ordinary. Starting with 1988, Meridian sharply reduced yields to produce dark-hued, firm examples with a boldness that will require time before preliminary evaluations begin.

In 1992 the proprietors of Beaucastel were bringing Syrah (and other Rhône varieties) from their Châteauneuf-du-Pape vineyard to the Adelaida area, where interest had already been stirred by a few rows belonging to Adelaida's John Munch. The first commercially available Syrahs from the west hills should come from vintages in the mid-1990s.
Benchmark:
Meridian Paso Robles (estate-bottled).

Zinfandel (402 acres in 1970, 1,260 in 1990)
Vintages in the 1970s, made from vines that were gnarled and old back then, tended to be strong in alcohol and strong in the plummy and raisiny flavors of fully to overripened Zinfandel. More recently, wilful modern winemakers have tempered both qualities, largely through vineyard management, partly in the cellar. Greater clonal selection and younger plantings add variety. Locals say Templeton Zinfandels tend to show a black peppery edge while those from Adelaida taste sweetly of strawberry. Limited plantings on Estrella Prairie echo those of Adelaida in flavor.

Mastantuono and Tobin James accept the inherent boldness of local Zinfandel, but achieve both polish and balance on that large scale. Adelaida manages considerable restraint. Ridge seeks and finds definite tannic austerity typical of its style.

One grower in the Arroyo Grande AVA, Saucelito Canyon, echoed the old pruney-ripe style of Paso Robles in vintages through 1990.
Benchmarks:
Ridge Paso Robles, Dante Dusi Vineyard (*see* Santa Cruz Mountains, page 158); **Adelaida** Paso Robles (assembled from varying sources); **Tobin James** Paso Robles (assembled with Dante Dusi vineyard as the base); **Mastantuono** Paso Robles (from mature vines in Peachy Canyon).

Other varieties
Gamay (63 acres); Gamay Beaujolais (22 acres); Nebbiolo and Sangiovese acreages remained minuscule in 1992.

Right: Topping-up is essential throughout the world of wine, in few places more so than hot, dry Paso Robles.

Paso Robles AVA

Established: November 3, 1983
Total area: 614,000 acres
Area in vineyard: 6,300 acres
Wineries: 23
Principal town: Paso Robles

As drawn, the Paso Robles AVA manages to take in miles of wasteland on the east, cut out some promising hill country on the west, and miss dividing lines that cleave the land within into halves at the least, more likely into quarters.

The linchpin in all of this is Templeton. From there north to Monterey County the Salinas River and US Highway 101 mark an obvious frontier between rumpled, grassy valley floor rolling eastwards, and steep, wooded hills rising as high as 2,850 feet to the west. Zinfandel in the wooded hills and Cabernet Sauvignon out on the grassy rolls have become the favorite weapons of those, currently a minority, who would carve one AVA into two.

As for the hills and Zinfandel, dozens of growers were dry-farming California's old warhorse red on the chalky slopes of the Santa Lucias before the turn of the century. Two acres here and five there, one still stumbles across gnarled, head-trained survivors that go back almost to the start. Although some credit clones more than climate, these graybeards offer wines of two such distinct flavors that several contemporary growers believe they can draw a climatic line dividing the west hills into two zones. To the north of Kiler Canyon, high hills screen out sufficient marine air to create a climate hot enough not just to ripen Zinfandel, but to have attracted the owners of Beaucastel for its kinships to the southern Rhône. To the south of that canyon, cooling ocean air streams through Templeton Gap, creating cool spots where Zinfandel can be so hard-put to ripen that some would substitute Chardonnay, even Pinot Noir. Terrain keeps holdings small in the hills. In 1992, about 60 growers had not quite 500 acres planted among them.

Cabernet Sauvignon has had barely more than a decade out on the grasslands, not enough to permit firm, final judgments about a wine that is only supposed to get going after it is 10 years old. None the less, the great grape of Bordeaux has begun to stake a heavy claim in some spots and no claim at all in others.

The ridge beneath Templeton deflects cool air from the gap upstream along the Salinas River, not down, creating effects so

specific that, cool year or hot, Ken Volk at Wild Horse could not ripen Cabernet Sauvignon beyond the green chilli/bell pepper flavors so common in Monterey and Santa Barbara.

On the other side of the ridge, Cabernet ripens easily everywhere, perhaps too easily in some quarters. In any case, it is both the dominant and the defining variety of the grasslands. Estrella Prairie is the coolest part of the grasslands, and the favored one for Cabernet. It is a triangle roughly defined by the Salinas River on the west, the Estrella River as it angles northwestwards toward its junction with the Salinas, and Union Road the southerly third leg. Soils weathered out of the Santa Lucias help define it, but the last sighs of Templeton Gap breezes

keep this rumpled landscape markedly cooler than the Adelaida hills just to the west, cooler still than the Cholame Hills well to the east.

Meridian, J. Lohr, and Arciero have plantings in the 500-acre range, Cabernet well represented in them all. Another 30 growers have smaller but not tiny properties. Shandon hugs the eastern boundary of the AVA out on the Cholame slopes. It is the orphan of these intellectual storms, largely because it has yet to declare itself specially adapted to any one variety. Three substantial and a couple of smaller vineyards fall within the warmer climates and less chalky soils that define the district. The Creston Vineyard is the best-known of them.

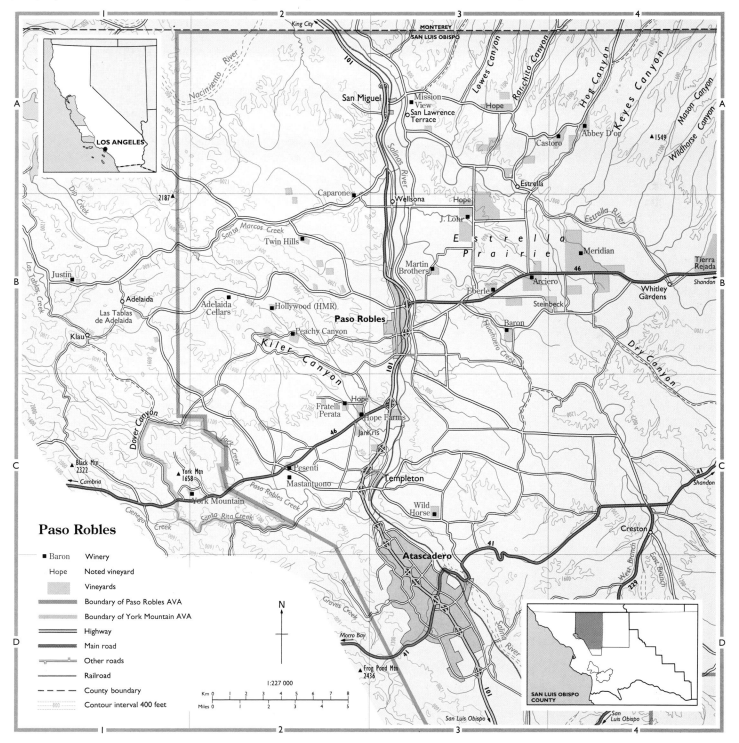

Paso Robles

- ■ Baron   Winery
- Hope   Noted vineyard
-     Vineyards
-     Boundary of Paso Robles AVA
-     Boundary of York Mountain AVA
-     Highway
-     Main road
-     Other roads
-     Railroad
-     County boundary
-     Contour interval 400 feet

1:227 000

York Mountain AVA

Established: September 23, 1983
Total area: 5,200 acres
Area in vineyard: 30 acres
Wineries: 1
Principal town: None (Templeton closest)

Because it sits right at the throat of Templeton Gap, York Mountain is far cooler than any other part of the Salinas River watershed in San Luis Obispo County. It is little planted because so much of it plunges from razorback ridgelines into V-bottomed canyons. Wines eligible to wear the AVA name are rare, but its mere existence has become a beacon for growers elsewhere in the west hills of the Paso Robles AVA.

One vineyard of Chardonnay, Macbride, has gone into wines that advertised the source on their labels. It is the major planting in the appellation.

Milk cartons around the bases of the young vines are California growers' first line of defense against hungry rabbits.

Edna Valley AVA

Established: June 11, 1982
Total area: 22,400 acres
Area in vineyard: 1,550 acres
Wineries: 4
Principal town: San Luis Obispo

As much shallow bowl as valley, one of California's smaller AVAs nestles between San Luis Obispo and the beach resort community of Pismo Beach.

Although the northerly boundary of Edna Valley AVA runs right through downtown San Luis Obispo as a sentimental gesture to the Franciscan priests who planted the first vines during the 1790s, viticulture here really dates from the 1970s, when the Jack Niven family began planting its Paragon Vineyard some miles south.

All existing plantings are in the chalky clay loams and clays of the valley floor, between the elevations of 100 and 300 feet, although slopes to a maximum 600 feet of elevation fall inside the AVA boundaries. Small as it is, the valley is not absolutely homogeneous. A cool-air sink and the heaviest clays come together near Corbett Canyon winery, where trial plantings

ripened so poorly that the firm abandoned thoughts of a local vineyard and bought 330 acres in Santa Barbara County's Alamos district.

Paragon dominates plantings with 700 acres, the first portion planted in 1974. Chamisal (57 acres) and MacGregor (100) are other names familiar from labels going back to the late 1970s. A recent spurt of new plantings includes 96 acres of Chardonnay by Meridian (*see* page 135). The remaining acreage is only beginning to bear crops. A small additional percentage of the AVA could be planted, although much of the arable land is already carved into smallholdings sought after by people who like to keep a horse or two.

Chardonnay has far the largest acreage at 1,300 and has enjoyed the greatest critical success. Gewürztraminer (now gone) and Sauvignon Blanc from Paragon have performed well. Once-great hopes for Pinot Noir faded after it yielded too many curiously vegetal, shortlived wines, but growers have not given up. Altered vineyard techniques lie behind a new generation of Pinots begun with 1990s from a sparse 65 acres.

Small though the AVA is, a substantial part of its crop goes elsewhere for lack of local wineries. Edna Valley Vineyards is the primary local producer.

Arroyo Grande AVA

Established: February 5, 1990
Total area: 42,880 acres
Area in vineyard: 420 acres
Wineries: 3
Principal town: Arroyo Grande

The newest, smallest, and southernmost of the three San Luis Obispo AVAs falls within much the same maritime climate as Edna Valley to the north, and Santa Maria Valley to the south in Santa Barbara. Part of a fairly uniform slope faces across built-up flatlands to the San Luis Bay/Pacific Ocean shore just four miles west; the rest of it is sheltered by only one low hill. Maison Deutz has by far the largest vineyard, the first of a current 300 acres planted in 1982 with sparkling wines in mind. In 1992 Chardonnay, Pinot Noir, and Pinot Blanc from these vines were only beginning to dominate *cuvées* based originally on bought-in Santa Maria Valley grapes. Saucelito Canyon and Talley Vineyard produce table wines from their vineyards in Arroyo Grande. Of these, Talley Pinot Noir has won the greatest praise to date. But almost every judgment on this fledgling district involves nine parts speculation to one of certainty.

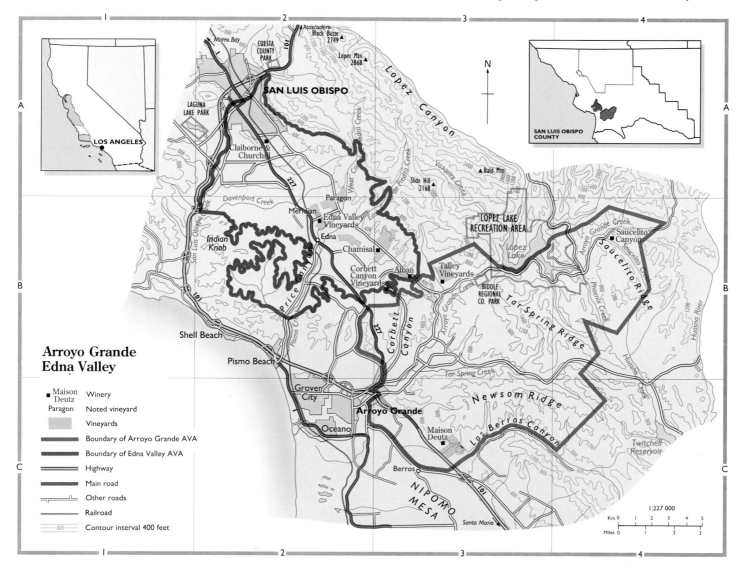

Arroyo Grande Edna Valley

- ■ Maison Deutz — Winery
- Paragon — Noted vineyard
- Vineyards
- Boundary of Arroyo Grande AVA
- Boundary of Edna Valley AVA
- Highway
- Main road
- Other roads
- Railroad
- ──800── Contour interval 400 feet

1:227 000

133

PASO ROBLES PRODUCERS

Abbey D'or (1987)
Star Route Box 4620, San Miguel, CA 93451 Tel (805) 467-3248.
3,000 cases. From 130 acres just north of Estrella Prairie come estate-grown Chardonnay, Chenin Blanc, Cabernet Sauvignon, Pinot Noir, and Zinfandel.

Adelaida Cellars (1981)
5805 Adelaida Road, Paso Robles, CA93446. Tel (805) 239-0190. 5,000 cases. From sources shifting ever westward toward the cellars comes consistently attractive Cabernet Sauvignon. Zinfandel, added in 1988, follows in its footsteps. New-in-1992 partners of founder John Munch began bringing substantial west hills vineyards into the fold.

Arciero Winery (1984)
PO Box 1287, Paso Robles, CA 93447. Tel (805) 239-2562. Capacity is 500,000 cases. Third-largest grower-producer in the region draws on 525 acres in 3 parcels, 2 in Estrella Prairie, 1 in Shandon. Chardonnay, Chenin Blanc, and Cabernet Sauvignon are anchors, Petite Sirah and Zinfandel specialty items. Wines appear under the Arciero and secondary Monteverde labels.

Baron Vineyard (1986 as Baron & Kolb, renamed in 1990)
1981 Penman Springs Road, Paso Robles, 93446. Tel (805) 239-3313. 7,000 cases. Ex-fire chief grows and produces Sauvignon Blanc, Muscat Canelli, and Cabernet Sauvignon from 30 estate acres in Estrella Prairie and Chardonnay from bought-in Creston grapes.

Caparone Vineyards (1979)
2280 San Marcos Road, Paso Robles, CA 93446. Tel (805) 467-3827. 4,000 cases. Grower-producer Dave Caparone has a passion for Sangioveto grosso, which he calls Brunello, and Nebbiolo from his 7 acres north of Paso Robles. Bought-in Cabernet, Merlot, and Zinfandel pay the bills.

Castoro Cellars (1979)
PO Box 954, Templeton, CA 93465. Tel (805) 467-2002. 10,000 cases and growing. In addition to flagship Cabernet (especially Hope Farms Reserves) and Zinfandel, the winery also produces Chardonnay, Fumé Blanc, and Pinot Noir. A negociant in its early years, Castoro acquired 250 plantable acres and a winery site in Hog Canyon in 1990.

Eberle Winery (1979; winery built in 1984)
PO Box 2459, Paso Robles, CA

Above: Gary Eberle, who led Paso Robles into the era of Cabernet. Right: The Eberle Winery.

93447. Tel (805) 238-9607. 9,500 cases. Consistent leader with sturdy Cabernet Sauvignon, pneumatically soft Muscat Canelli from his own 35 acres at the winery and partner Howard Steinbeck's nearby 80 acres, both on Estrella Prairie.

Fratelli Perata (1989)
1595 Arbor Road, Paso Robles, CA 93446. Tel (805) 238-2809. 1,000 cases. Estate Cabernet Sauvignon, Merlot, and Zinfandel from 25 acres west of Templeton.

HMR Estate Winery (1972)
5065 Adelaida Road, Paso Robles, CA 93446. Tel (805) 238-7143. Currently inactive, but hopes exist for revival of winery with 58 estate acres in Adelaida hills.

Hope Farms Winery (1990)
2175 Arbor Road, Paso Robles, CA 93446. Tel (805) 238-6979. 4,800 cases. Startup winery belongs to long-time growers farming 220 acres of vineyards in 3 parcels, 2 in Estrella Prairie, the other with the winery west of Templeton. Cabernet from well-established plantings near Paso Robles airport has earned awards for Hope's own label, Castoro and others. Other estate grapes: Chardonnay at the airport property, Sauvignon Blanc and Zinfandel on Cross Canyon, Cabernet, Merlot, and Chardonnay at the winery.

JanKris Vineyards (1990)
Route 2, Box 40, Bethel Road, Templeton, CA 93465. Tel (805) 434-0319. 4,500 cases. Current owners bought and renamed Farview Farms, best known for Merlot. Also planted

Pasquale (Pat) Mastan vigorously defends the Zinfandel tradition.

Chardonnay and Zinfandel in the 54 acres. The proprietors also acquired the Laura's Vineyard label and stocks in 1990, but not the vineyard.

Justin Winery (1987)
11680 Chimney Rock Road, Paso Robles, CA 93446. Tel (805) 238-6932. 4,000 cases. Grower-producer of Chardonnay and Cabernet Sauvignon/Cabernet Franc/Merlot blend, both from 65 estate acres in westernmost Adelaida hills.

J. Lohr (1974)
Far-flung empire now includes more than 700 acres of Paso Robles vineyard, mostly Cabernet, and a fermentation winery near Paso Robles airport. See also p 160.

Martin Brothers Winery (1981)
PO Box 2599, Paso Robles, CA 93447. Tel (805) 238-2520. 15,000 cases. Partner-winemaker Domenic Martin looks increasingly to his Italian roots with Nebbiolo, Aleatico, etc, from 70 estate acres on Estrella Prairie, but made his first mark with Chardonnay (bought-in), Chenin Blanc

(now estate) and a memorably tart, now discontinued Sauvignon Blanc from Tierra Rejada.

Mastantuono (1977)
100 Oak View Road, Templeton, CA 93465. Tel (805) 238-0676. 10,000 cases. City boy turned advocate of traditional, gutsy Paso Robles Zinfandel, Pasquale Mastan uses old vines from 15 acres in Peachy Canyon west of Templeton. He also makes Paso Robles Chardonnay, Sauvignon Blanc, Cabernet Sauvignon and Muscat Canelli from bought-in grapes.

Meridian Vineyards (1984, reorganized in 1989)
PO Box 3289, Paso Robles, CA 93447. Tel (805) 237-6000. 220,000 cases. One-time busman's holiday label of Chuck Ortman is now a well-financed (by same owners as Beringer in Napa and Château Souverain in Sonoma), well-run grower-producer with 550 acres in Paso Robles, 100 in Edna Valley, and free choice of the best from 2,900 divided among 3 ranches in Santa Barbara. Ortman is a proven adept with Chardonnay-Santa Barbara and Chardonnay-Edna Valley. Since 1989 has also been making gallop-sized strides with Cabernet Sauvignon and Syrah from Paso Robles and Pinot Noir from Santa Barbara.

Mission View Estate Vineyards & Winery (1984, reopened 1988)
PO Box 129, San Miguel, CA 93451. Tel (805) 467-3104. 6,000 cases. Based in 41 bluff-top acres at the southeast corner of San Miguel, whence barrel-fermented Chardonnay, Sauvignon Blanc, Cabernet Sauvignon and Zinfandel.

Peachy Canyon Winery (1989)
Route 1, Box 115C, Paso Robles, CA 93446. Tel (805) 238-7035. 800 cases. A specialist in well-made, traditional Templeton Zinfandel from the Benito Dusi vineyard.

Pesenti Winery (1933)
2900 Vineyard Drive, Templeton, CA 93465. Tel (805) 434-1030. 30,000 cases. Old-line family firm with 65 acres of vineyards at Templeton makes broad spectrum of mostly rustic wines typified by Zinfandel.

Tobin James (1985)
PO Box 2867, Paso Robles CA 93447. Tel (805) 239-2204. 4,000 cases. Ex-Eberle cellarman making consistently impressive Zinfandel: set up on his own once he discovered a talent for making it big, yet polished. It comes from bought-in west-side grapes. Also exploring Merlot (JanKris), Cabernet Sauvignon (Justin & Steinbeck), and others.

Twin Hills Ranch Winery (1981)
2025 Nacimiento Lake Drive, Templeton, CA 93465. Tel (805) 434-10030. 15,000-case capacity. Grower-producer with 40 acres of Chardonnay, Cabernet Sauvignon and Zinfandel northwest of Paso Robles.

Typical Paso Robles tasting room.

135

Ken Volk of Wild Horse Winery.

Wild Horse Winery (1983)
PO Box 910, Templeton, CA 93465. Tel (805) 434-2541. 25,000 cases. Owner-winemaker Ken Volk has shown an uncanny touch with Pinot Noir from varied sources, usually Santa Barbara (mostly Sierra Madre, some Santa Maria Hills, and Bien Nacido) but sometimes Paso Robles (HMR), and a sure hand across the rest of his range. Volk grows Chardonnay and is looking at Merlot and Pinot Noir on his 70 acres southeast of Templeton. Cabernet Sauvignon is mostly bought-in.

York Mountain Winery (1882)
Route 2, Box 191, Templeton, CA 93465. Tel (805) 238-3925. 5,000 cases. Pioneer family sold to Max Goldman in 1970. After marking time, the winery turned a corner in 1982 and 1983 under the direction of second-generation Steve Goldman; since then of particular interest for Merlot.

OTHER PRODUCERS
(not mapped)

Creston Vineyard (1982 as Creston Manor, renamed 1988)
17 Mile Post, Highway 58, Creston, CA 93432. Tel (805) 238-7398. 25,000 cases. Substantial producer of Cabernet, Sauvignon Blanc, Pinot Noir from its own 155 acres (100 in Shandon, 55 near Adelaida) plus purchased Paso Robles AVA grapes.

Harmony Cellars (1989)
PO Box 2502, Harmony, CA 93535; Tel (805) 927-1625. Outside the AVA in Cambria, it draws on a wide range of sources for a long list of varietals.

EDNA VALLEY AND ARROYO GRANDE PRODUCERS

Alban Vineyards (1990)
1115 Peach Street, San Luis Obispo, CA 93401; Tel (805) 546-0305. 500 cases. Amid all the Chardonnay, a Rhône specialist has planted 50 acres at the south tip of Edna Valley with Viognier, Roussane, Syrah, and small amounts of Mourvèdre and Grenache.

Chamisal (1979)
7525 Orcutt Road, San Luis Obispo, CA 93420; Tel (805) 544-3576. 3,000 cases. Grower-producer Norman Goss makes ultra-toasty Chardonnay from 57 estate acres in Edna Valley.

Claiborne & Churchill Vintners (1983)
860 E Capitolio Way, San Luis Obispo, CA 93420. 3,000 cases. Family-owned producer of worthy dry Gewürztraminer originally from Paragon, now from Monterey, and Riesling, still from Paragon Vineyard.

Corbett Canyon Vineyards (1983)
2195 Corbett Canyon Road, Arroyo Grande, CA 93420. Tel (805) 544-5800. 300,000 cases. Although in Edna Valley, the winery has no vines there, instead drawing on its 330 acres in the Los Alamos district of Santa Barbara County for consistently attractive Chardonnay and Pinot Noir, and buying other varieties as far afield as Napa Valley. Its signature Santa Barbara Pinot Noir "Reserve" reveals the very essence of its region.

Edna Valley Vineyards (1980)
2585 Biddle Ranch Road, San Luis Obispo, CA 93401. Tel (805) 544-9594. 50,000 cases. Joint venture of grower Paragon Vineyards and winemaker Chalone shows how refined toasty-school Chardonnay can be in both its regular and Reserve bottlings.

Maison Deutz (1983)
453 Deutz Drive, Arroyo Grande, CA 93420; Tel (805) 481-1763. 30,000 cases. A specialist in classic-method

Below: Claiborne Thompson and his wife Fredericka Churchill.

sparkling wines at Arroyo Grande. Owned by William Deutz of Ay in Champagne, its early *cuvées* came from grapes bought in Santa Maria Valley. Increasingly they come from 300 winery-owned acres of Chardonnay, Pinot Blanc, and Pinot Noir around the Arroyo Grande cellars.

Maison Deutz visitor center.

Saucelito Canyon Vineyard (1982)
1600 Saucelito Creek Road, Arroyo Grande, CA 93420; Tel (805) 489-8762. 1,500 cases. A specialist in estate Zinfandel from 15 acres anchored in a rehabilitated 19th-century vineyard in warm, fog-free hills at the eastern margin of the Arroyo Grande AVA.

Talley Vineyards (1986)
3031 Lopez Drive, Arroyo Grande, CA 93420. Tel (805) 489-0446 4,000 cases. The Oliver Talley family grows and produces Chardonnay, Riesling, and a promising Pinot Noir from 100 estate acres in Arroyo Grande, just where it touches Edna Valley.

Tiffany Hill (1987)
5880 Edna Road, San Luis Obispo, CA 93401. Tel (805) 544-9080. 1,300 cases. Essentially a grower-label for a small Edna Valley Chardonnay vineyard owned by the Jack Niven family, and kept apart from their Paragon property.

Travel Information

PLACES OF INTEREST

Avila Beach Sheltered, sun-warmed shoal waters along sandy beaches are just remote enough for a low-key village to be a useful all-family vacation spot within comfortable reach of all the San Luis Obispo and Santa Barbara wine districts.

Paso Robles A sturdy, no-nonsense commercial center for local agriculture and a freeway stopover point, it also has a colorful farmers' market along-side the town plaza on Wednesday evenings in summer. The few remaining structures of the Franciscan Mission San Miguel (1797) are in a village of the same name 9 miles north alongside US101.

Pismo Beach An oceanfront resort town in the midst of a slow evolution from outdated and inexpensive to chic and mid- to upmarket, offers wine-drinkers a handy location midway between San Luis Obispo and Santa Barbara wine regions as well as its basic reason for being.

San Luis Obispo The major town in San Luis Obispo County is also its historic center, largely because of the presence of Mission San Luis Obispo de Tolosa (1772), one of the most successful of the 19 Franciscan churches through which California was first colonized by Europeans. The campus of California Polytechnic University at

San Luis Obispo has packed down-town Higuera Street with student hangouts. These and other college town qualities rule, except Thursday evenings in summer, when this main thoroughfare is transformed into a colorful farmers' market and barbecue party. (Barbecue is to these central coast towns what coffee is to Seattle, a competitive mania.) A location astride US101 midway between San Francisco and Los Angeles makes this town a convenient stopover point for motorists: it has more than 1,200 guide-rated motel and hotel rooms.

RESTAURANTS AND HOTELS

Cafe Roma 1819 Osos Street, San Luis Obispo, CA 93401. Tel (805) 541-6800. Calls itself a Roman tratto-ria but has a more ambitious menu than that. Very much a local favorite for its cheerful atmosphere, skillful kitchen, and attentive serving staff.

Madonna Inn 100 Madonna Road, San Luis Obispo, CA 93401. Tel (805) 543-3000. Amid a score of comfort-able motels and motor hotels, enough of an unbridled fantasist's dream to have figured in Umberto Eco's "Travels in Hyperreality."

Main Street Grill 416 Main Street, Templeton, CA 93465. Tel (805) 434-0655. In a restored Victorian building on an old-time main street, it offers

views of a grain elevator and a well-executed menu using only the freshest ingredients. Thoughtful list of local wines.

Olde Port Inn Port San Luis Pier 3, Avila Beach, CA 93424. Tel (805) 595-2515. On a pier pointing into San Luis Bay; to be sought for the freshest fish of the day and a superior, wide-ranging wine list.

Paso Robles Inn 1103 Spring Street, Paso Robles, CA 93446. Tel (805) 238-2660. Once luxurious; now a quaint hotel. Garden cottages are quiet where road noises make quiet hard to find.

San Luis Bay Inn Avila Road, Avila Beach, CA 93424. Tel (805) 595-2333. Laid-back, away-from-it-all golf and tennis resort near sandy, safe beaches. The owner is an active sup-porter of Central Coast wines.

Spyglass Inn 2705 Spyglass Drive, Pismo Beach, CA 93449. Tel (805) 773-4855. One among many high-quality motels in the beach town.

Vineyard Inn 512–13th Street, Paso Robles. CA 93446; Tel (805) 238-7515. Restaurant in a deconsecrated church. Yankee main ingredients mixed with familiar Asian and mid-eastern sauces and seasonings. Wine list focuses on locals. Originally Joshua's.

WINE ROUTE

The cheerful college town of San Luis Obispo is a perfect headquarters for visiting not only the Edna Valley, but Paso Robles to the north and any district as far south as the Santa Ynez Valley in Santa Barbara County. The beach towns of Pismo Beach and Arroyo Grande are at least as good for those looking north, perhaps better for those focused southward.

US101 links all the districts. Wineries in them are near the high-way with rare exception. Driving thus becomes less important than climate (mild here) and a much broadened choice of accommodation and restaurants.

That said, the quirky old town of Paso Robles has a wayward charm of its own, especially for those who are used to soaking up heat in summer. It also has a great enough concentration of visitable cellars to merit a two-day stay.

Left: The Pacific Ocean shore is mostly rugged, but San Luis Bay (above) offers sheltered, sun-warmed waters to fishermen, even swimmers.

Monterey County

When winegrowers first started coming to Monterey's 85-mile-long, 12-mile-wide Salinas Valley in the 1960s they thought they had found paradise, and plunged in on a scale to match.

It was, and is, an odd-looking paradise. A handful of dusty, wind-whipped, utilitarian farm towns dot its length, sparse beads on the string of US Highway 101. Spanish is a more serviceable language than English in most of the stores in Gonzales and Soledad, and even, in spite of its name, in Greenfield. Any building taller than 26 feet is sure to be full of farm equipment, or wine. But University of California climate studies held it out as a new Elysium for grapes, where land cost mere cents compared to the North Coast – this when urban pressure was making Livermore and the Santa Clara Valley untenable for vineyards. It did not hurt that tiny Chalone, up in its eyrie east of Soledad, was already making waves in the community of wine collectors.

In 1962, Mirassou Vineyards began planting 1,200 acres for itself and the first 1,000 of Paul Masson's eventual 4,500. Wente Bros. followed modestly on their heels with 700 acres. Early wines from this trio promised enough to lure an even more ambitious second wave in the 1970s. A farm management company assembled squads of investors to buy 9,600 acres for the first incarnation of The Monterey Vineyard, while a Texas corporation bought and planted most of 13,000 acres for the now-defunct San Martin winery, leading locals to think of 150 or 200 acres as boutique-sized plantings. At its swiftly reached peak, Monterey had 37,000 acres under vine, an astonishing invasion of a region that, for years, had stuck to its role as America's salad bowl. Monterey, or rather the Salinas Valley, has been searching for its proper scale as a vineyard district ever since, and for many other truths as well.

In those heady first years people planted whatever varieties they wished wherever they wished, seduced by a growing season so long and so benign that grapes could hang on the vines until Christmas if need be. However much water a vine could use, that much it could have, and without risking mold or mildew, because water almost never falls from the summer sky yet can be drawn at will from the underground Salinas River. (There are few places in the world where a river looks more like a desert than the region it irrigates, but this is one: almost all its flow is well below the surface, in a deep, gravelly channel covered by a thick layer of silt.)

In some of the larger vineyards single rows equaled more than two acres because growers could see no reason to make them shorter. Mechanical harvesters picked faster, and seemingly surer, than human hands. There had been virtually no vineyards in the valley, hence no phylloxera, so every vine was planted on its own roots, just the way the French did back when clarets were really clarets.

Grievous mistakes, every one. Rolling terrain and variable soils caused the middle of some rows to ripen before the ends, so harvesters sometimes traveled miles to pick a few yards and needed as many as three weeks and four or five passes to pick a row clean. All-too-well-watered vines never stopped growing,

leading to wines with pungent flavors widely identified as the "Monterey veggies," and just as widely scorned. Phylloxera took 20 years to find the vineyards, but it did find them during the 1980s and has been a spreading plague ever since. The greatest of all the mistakes, however, was growers putting all their faith in air temperatures, regardless of the effects of wind, sun, and soil.

After the pioneers learned to stop irrigation earlier in the season, they discovered that the incessant, infernal winds can slow ripening as much or more than water, with much the same grim effect on flavor. They are just beginning to discover that the interplay of fog and exposure can make side-by-side

parcels of vines almost twins, or as different as Woody Allen and Arnold Schwarzenegger. Because people were making mistakes on the same heroic scale as their investments, the Salinas Valley lost ground to other wine regions by giant steps throughout the decade following 1973.

The believers in its vineyards, still believing, began a quiet revolution even as the worst was happening. They cut the long rows into manageable lengths, revamped irrigation programs to stop cane growth so that fruit could ripen to more agreeable flavors, reshuffled the grape varieties in thousands of acres, and returned almost 12,000 acres to the crops that first made the valley's fame: lettuce, strawberries, peppers, and the rest of the salad bowl.

In the process, vineyard owners began carving the huge expanse of the Salinas Valley into appellations. Arroyo Seco and Chalone came early, San Lucas later, and Santa Lucia Highlands only in 1992. More are in the works.

For all the change, the valley remains very much a vinicultural work in progress. Even its stoutest defenders speak more of potential than they do of achievement. What is missing, what has always been missing, is enough wineries, especially small ones with a sharp eye for detail. A much changed The Monterey Vineyard still operates. Paul Masson finally moved into the valley lock, stock and barrel. Jekel and Ventana are the pioneer small firms. Only with the 1980s did Boyer and Morgan appear. Lockwood, Paraiso Springs, and Robert Talbott date from the 1990s. The roster is not yet nearly long enough for such an ocean of vines. Its members will have to be followed by many more rivals if much sense is to be made of the differences between Arroyo Seco and Santa Lucia Highlands, let alone the fine shadings within each.

Two tiny districts, Chalone and Carmel Valley, share neither the scale nor the climate of the Salinas Valley. Chalone overlooks it from such heights that it has in common only a few characteristics of what the French call *terroir*. Carmel Valley sits alone on slopes looking out to the Pacific Ocean. Elevation further separates this valley's vineyards from most in the county.

Left: Smith & Hook looks from the Santa Lucia Highlands west across part of Arroyo Seco to Chalone and the basalt outcrop of the Pinnacles National Monument.
Above: Close-up view of the Pinnacles.

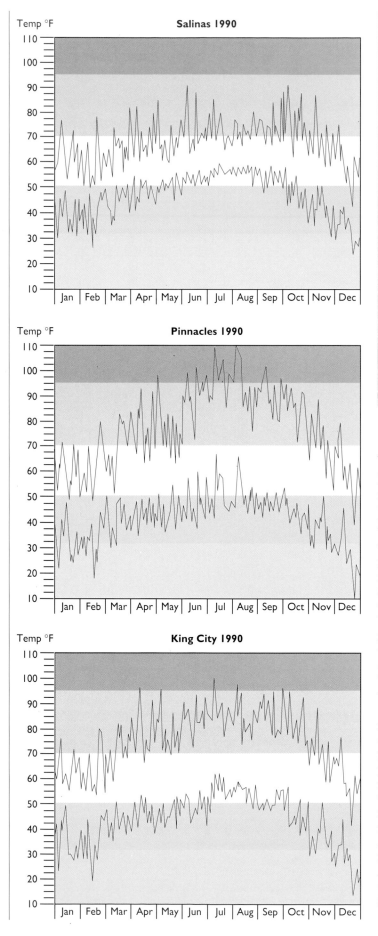

Temp °F — **Salinas 1990**

Temp °F — **Pinnacles 1990**

Temp °F — **King City 1990**

Climate

The vast Salinas Valley caricatures the typical climate of California's coastal winegrowing regions. Its north end, open to Monterey Bay, is too cool and foggy to grow grapes. From King City south to the San Luis Obispo County line, summer days are desert dry and not far from desert hot. The Napa Valley from Carneros to Calistoga is but a pale imitation of both the range and inexorable march of this progression. A wide mouth helps California's perpetual sea-fogs sweep into the northern end of the valley. The steadily rising height of the Santa Lucia Mountains and sheer vastness of the valley keep those fogs from reaching much farther south than Greenfield, but do less to temper the infernal winds generated by sea air rushing to feed the furnace farther south. Vineyards in otherwise bare hills on either side escape some or all of the fogs, depending on elevation. Those on the west, in particular, can be sheltered from winds so strong they will tear canes from their trellis wires on exposed sites.

Lack of rainfall separates the Salinas Valley even more from its neighbors. It sits far enough south for few storms coming down from the Aleutians to cross over it, and far enough north for tropical storms from Baja California to be rare. In the six years of drought, 1985–92, the valley averaged only 5 inches of rain annually. In the wettest times it gets 10 to 15 inches, less than its neighbors north and south. Only the Carmel Valley is a region climatically apart. The appellation drapes across slopes facing directly toward the Pacific. Although high enough to sit above the fog, they would logically seem to be cooler than similarly oriented slopes above the Salinas Valley. It may not be so. Although there is no weather station to measure the particulars, Cabernet Sauvignon ripens faster and fuller than it does farther inland, implying a warmer, drier region than Chalone.

* For the colour code to the climate charts see pages 14–15.

Chalone sits in bright sunshine while dense fog shrouds the Salinas Valley below. As so often in California, this is the key element in choosing which varieties to plant within short distances.

White Wine Varieties

Although white wines do not automatically escape the Monterey veggies, Chardonnay, Gewürztraminer, and Riesling have largely avoided that characteristic. Chardonnay, not unexpectedly, is the runaway leader in acreage.

Chardonnay (95 acres in 1970, 5,558 in 1990)
For all the diversity of sun and soil, Chardonnay nearly the whole length of the Salinas Valley has a charming, straightforward flavor of mild apples when it is made to keep fruit foremost. Lockwood was just beginning to make the case for the southerly third in 1990; Ventana's Gold Stripe bottling has done so for more northerly precincts for some years. They separate on texture: lean and firm in wines from the cooler climates, soft and round in those from warm vineyards at King City and south.

Despite the charms of the fruit-foremost style, a majority of producers aims instead for toasty, buttery notes from malolactic fermentation and prolonged aging in new oak barrels. Morgan, especially in the Reserve bottlings, is the prototype. Estancia struck a deft balance between the extremes in its first try, in 1990. Chalone, a quirky exception by origin, seems better able to withstand the heavyweight style than most, although its vineyard has disappeared beneath the weight of winemaking at times.

Chardonnay from Carmel Valley is too recent to categorize with any assurance, but two or three forthright butterscotchy ones have received praise in their first two or three vintages.
Benchmarks:
Ventana Vineyards Monterey "Gold Stripe" (estate). **Estancia** Monterey (estate, from the eastern bench at Soledad; *see* page 53). **Morgan** Monterey (assembled, primarily from Santa Lucia Highlands vineyards). **Boyer** Monterey (Ventana). **Chalone Vineyards** Chalone (estate).

Chenin Blanc (131 acres in 1970, 2,729 in 1990)
In much of Monterey, including the Carmel Valley, growers like the variety for its ability to make easy, affable, on-the-heels-of-the-harvest sippers. Chalone excepted, the prevailing style is off-dry, with little or no oak to complicate the issue. Chalone and Durney excepted, the scale of production is such that one has been much like another right across the board.

Gewürztraminer (68 acres in 1970, 732 in 1990)
Ventana Vineyard has had increasing success with this variety in recent vintages. Its vines give marked perfumes and a distinctive softness of texture both to Ventana's own wines and to all who buy grapes from its vineyards. Wente and Mirassou have had ups and downs, the ups suggesting that Gewürztraminer is at least as broadly adapted as Riesling.
Benchmarks:
Thomas Fogarty Monterey Gewürztraminer (Ventana Vineyard). **Claiborne & Churchill** Central Coast Gewürztraminer (Ventana).

Pinot Blanc (110 acres in 1970, 1,069 in 1990)
Not much Pinot Blanc from the valley floor is bottled as varietal wine under Monterey appellations. What there is, mostly from Mirassou and Jekel, has not met with overwhelming critical success due to lack of character, not faulty technique. Some is blended with other regions' in varietals and some goes into sparkling wines.

Chalone makes Pinot Blanc almost exactly as it makes Chardonnay: barrel and malolactic fermentations, the works. It stands apart from all others, a wine of dense flavors and solid structures. Whether it is a benchmark or uncopiable cannot yet be said.

Riesling *also* White Riesling, Johannisberg Riesling (49 acres in 1970, 2,624 in 1990)
Riesling was Monterey's first smashing success, unfortunately. The wines came just as the bloom of market acceptance began to fade from that particular rose, but not soon enough to keep the county's acreage from peaking at 3,844 in 1985. Vintages through the early 1990s won on rich flavors of apricot, almost always obtained at the sacrifice of the kind of light, crisp textures that make the variety noble in Germany. Some local growers, Ventana foremost, began in 1985 to experiment with close-spaced plantings in a hunt for flavor and ripeness at lower sugar levels; their hope is to drive alcohols from 12.5 down to 11 percent, bringing a greater lilt at no loss of flavor.

Botrytis is a regular visitor to the Arroyo Seco, sometimes with splendid results in the range of "Spätlesen." Wente's 1972 has yet to be equaled, but there have been several worthies.
Benchmarks:
Jekel Vineyards Arroyo Seco Dry Riesling. **Jekel Vineyards** Arroyo Seco Johannisberg Riesling. **Ventana Vineyards** Monterey Riesling.

Sauvignon Blanc (35 acres in 1970, 1,453 in 1990)
In the early stages, the Monterey veggies compounded Sauvignon's essentially herbaceous flavors to achieve hints of bell pepper at best, reeking tones of cooked asparagus at worst.

Not surprisingly, the variety lost favor and acreage in a long-running game of leapfrog. Although more plantings in warmer zones, new systems of vine training and more restrained irrigation schemes have begun to refine those flavors, Monterey's version is not yet Sauvignon for the timid. Producers more or less uniformly seek to keep Sauvignon flavors foremost, but it is not yet a universally good idea.

Ventana Vineyard's owner insists that he grows an entirely different, infinitely subtler clone than the grape commonly given the name of Sauvignon Blanc. Called "Musque," it may be easy to spot in the vineyard, but one is hard pressed to find unmistakable differences between this, and wines from vineyards chosen and managed to bring forth melon rather than herb from commoner clones.

Benchmarks:

Estancia Monterey Sauvignon Blanc. **Ventana** Arroyo Seco Sauvignon Blanc.

Other varieties

Colombard (494 acres); Gray Riesling (167 acres); Malvasia (227 acres); Muscat Blanc (172 acres); Sémillon (397 acres), and Sylvaner (138 acres).

In addition to fog, concentrations of quartz crystals separate Chalone from other vineyards nearby.

Red Wine Varieties

New districts always get off the mark faster with whites than reds. Even with that in mind, Monterey has advanced more slowly with reds than almost any other district in the United States, perhaps because neither Cabernet Sauvignon nor Pinot Noir has shown easy adaptability, perhaps because few other varieties have had serious trials, perhaps more for lack of small wineries to test the limits than any natural shortcomings.

Cabernet Sauvignon (156 acres in 1970, 2,741 in 1990)
Much of the blame for making Monterey veggies a derogatory description of wines from the region can be laid at the doorstep of Cabernet Sauvignon. In the early days at least two different producers were able to make wines that tasted exactly like the juice of bell peppers, or unable to make them taste otherwise. For years no vineyard from Greenfield north could improve upon canned asparagus as the dominant flavor in a varietal wine. The best one could hope for was a strong taste of dill to cover the other flavors.

The later emergence of San Lucas as a region gave Monterey the chance to make soft, approachable Cabernets much like those of Paso Robles, San Lucas's neighbor to the south. Still later, altered vine training, deeper roots, and more thoughtful cellar work began to diminish, although not extinguish, the vegetal tones in wines from Arroyo Seco and Santa Lucia Highlands. Healthy dollops of Merlot also seem to help. Growers there now believe they have slow-starting, long-aging wines that gain interest in the bottle. Perhaps they are right: proof awaits a broader, deeper range of samples than currently exists. For revelatory wines from the Salinas Valley, we may have to wait for sites still to be planted.

Durney Vineyards in the Carmel Valley produce a dark, firm Cabernet that, in most vintages, tastes herbaceous rather than vegetal, i.e., it bears a greater resemblance to North Coast Cabernets than its rivals in Monterey.

Benchmarks:

Smith & Hook Monterey (estate). **Durney Vineyards** (estate).

Merlot (1 acre in 1970, 412 in 1990)
Merlot has yet to make a real move in Monterey; few lots having been bottled as varietal wine to date, but it has seized the imagination of several growers and winemakers with its ability to mute the vegetal taste so often found in Monterey Cabernets. In the early 1990s Smith & Hook had slightly more than half of all plantings in its vineyards in the Santa Lucia Highlands. A few modest patches could be found in Arroyo Seco.

Cabernet-based blends

The first serious efforts to blend Cabernet and its Bordelais cousins are recent in Monterey. One, in particular, shows promise: Jekel's "Symmetry" from the Sanctuary Vineyard.

Petite Sirah (30 acres in 1970, 780 in 1990)
Just a trace of the Monterey veggies gives the wine depth rather than eccentricity. A second virtue is remarkably mild-mannered tannins. In spite of a rather handsome acreage, appellation-distinctive bottlings are rare. Mirassou Vineyards has been the steady hand with an estate bottling, but the single most memorable wine has been a 1990 in Benziger of Glen Ellen's "Imagery" series.

Smith & Hook's vines are on alluvial fans between deep creek courses. The property was once a horse ranch.

Pinot Noir (176 acres in 1970, 1,550 in 1990)
Because so much of the Salinas Valley north of Greenfield is cool and fog shaded, many early growers took great Pinot Noir as given. With the lonely exception of Chalone, results have consistently lacked in Pinot or any other distinctive flavor. The reverse of Cabernet Sauvignon, few have had enough of the Monterey veggies to give them that much identity. Mirassou has been a stop-and-start producer. Jekel gave up and called its results Gamay Beaujolais for the last years before grafting the variety out of its vineyards. A one-time winemaker at Ventana threw up his hands and moved to Oregon. The wavering faith is further reflected in an ebb and flow of plantings that went as high as 2,356 acres in 1977, and dropped to 1,125 in 1986 before starting back up again.

Some growers and winemakers, doubtless spurred by Chalone's example, still believe that all Monterey Pinot Noir needs is skillful specialists willing to isolate the right sites and fuss over the winemaking. Perhaps. Plantings have been broad enough to make observers wonder where the right site might lie. The leading hopes cluster in the Santa Lucia Highlands.

Although Chalone Pinot Noir is more oak and tannin than Pinot and velvet, it has had the only authentic varietal signature of any grown in Monterey County as late as 1991. However, its singular location does not offer the prospect of generating many imitators.

Zinfandel (20 acres in 1970, 1,868 in 1990)
Like Pinot Noir, Zinfandel seems to be looking for a place in Monterey. Few bottlings have carried any of the Monterey appellations, and of those that have, none has aroused unbridled admiration.

Nearly all the acreage runs from King City southward, the only part of the county reliably warm enough to ripen Zinfandel as fully as Sonoma, Paso Robles, the Sierra Foothills, or any other traditional source. Even here, the lack of distinctive flavor means most of the crop goes into commodity White Zinfandels.

For the valley from Greenfield northward, the whole story is wrapped up in Richard Peterson's dream of testing BATF's rule on vintage dating by harvesting some Zinfandel in January. (In the 1970s, a BATF rule required using the year in which the grapes were harvested, rather than grown, as the rule now reads.)

Then the founding winemaker at The Monterey Vineyard, Peterson never managed to wait until January, but he did wait well into December once. The result was more of a curiosity piece than something to emulate. Zinfandels produced in October and November also failed to raise the variety's stock at or north of Greenfield.

Other varieties
Cabernet Franc (67 acres, thus far mostly for blending); Early Burgundy (89 acres); Gamay Beaujolais (374 acres), and Grenache (113 acres).

143

Arroyo Seco AVA

Established: May 16, 1983
Total area: 18,240 acres
Area in vineyard: 2,200 acres
Wineries: 2
Principal towns: Greenfield, Soledad

That odd, outstretched little arm at the southwestern corner of the appellation is the key. In its fist are the parent soils of an arroyo that is also a benchland, limited on the east and north by the Salinas River, on the south by a long ridge.

The wry expression "Greenfield spuds" paints a fair picture of the shape and abundance of stones common to the soils of every vineyard in the AVA. The long, slow climb toward that defining southern ridge makes Arroyo Seco the signal transition point between coolly foggy and relentlessly sunny in the Salinas Valley.

One grower explains the shift within Arroyo Seco by the way it grows Chardonnay: four tons per acre of richly flavored grapes at Greenfield, three tons per acre of leaner, tarter ones at Soledad, barely two tons around Gonzales and Chualar. Rieslings, most especially botrytis-sweetened ones, have been the region's pinnacle of success. Much else about the picture remains cloudy, except for the fact that Cabernet Sauvignon will taste too much like bell peppers when planted where the afternoon winds can get at it.

Like the rest of the valley, Arroyo Seco has been hampered in finding its superior spots by an almost wholesale lack of wineries. Jekel Vineyards and Ventana Vineyards came in 1978. They remained the only two cellars in the region in 1992.

Ventana is by a wide margin the most celebrated vineyard in Arroyo Seco, first because proprietor Douglas Meador is a driven perfectionist, second because he has taken pains to sell grapes to outside wineries willing to put Ventana's name on

Salinas Valley is much the largest of California's coastal wine valleys.

their labels. For personal reasons, he eschews any identity with the AVA. The list of vineyard-designated wines from these 300 flattish, gravelly acres reaches into the dozens, most of them are Chardonnays, but there are also some most striking Gewürztraminers.

Jekel began to promote the distinctiveness of the property it calls Sanctuary in 1992. The vines reach into Arroyo Seco, sheltered by its steep walls in such a way that it shares more qualities with vineyards in the Santa Lucia Highlands than with properties out on the wind-exposed flats that make up most of its AVA. Cabernet Sauvignon and Merlot populate the most sheltered blocks. Chardonnay is out on more exposed terrain.

Other winery-owned vineyards produce wine eligible to use the appellation, but belong to firms that make their wine outside the region. They include J. Lohr (*see* page 160), Mirassou Vineyards (*see* page 160), and Wente Bros. (*see* page 154).

Santa Lucia Highlands AVA

Established: July 15, 1992
Total area: 22,000 acres
Area in vineyard: 1,850 acres
Wineries: 3
Principal town: None (Gonzales and Soledad nearby)

The Santa Lucia Highland's founders carved their AVA out of the western hills with the goal of establishing a red-wine district for the cooler reaches of the Salinas Valley. At the outset of the 1990s, Chardonnay and Pinot Blanc dominated the northerly two-thirds of the district, Cabernet Sauvignon and Merlot the southern third.

The owners of Smith & Hook, the major proponents of the appellation, believe they are onto something with Cabernet Sauvignon, and have begun to suspect that Merlot may yet be a better bet on exposed, east-facing slopes. Vintages after 1988 suggest they may indeed have found ways to overcome the extremes of regional flavor.

The appellation's vineyards are planted on a series of narrow, sharply tipped, recently quarried alluvial fans, the southernmost of them abutting Arroyo Seco near Greenfield, the northernmost opposite Gonzales. By their very nature these fans limit vineyard size to a mere 200 to 500 acres. They also provide a bewildering mosaic of elevations and exposures, and thus a bedeviling degree of differences in fog, sun, and, important here, wind effects. Just how far local growers are from knowing what their properties will do is revealed by the fellow who has unripenable Gewürztraminer on the sunny shoulder of a hill and early-maturing Cabernet Sauvignon in a foggy valley bottom, this in spite of the fact that most Highlands vineyards go back to the 1970s, survivors from original plantings for the Monterey Vineyard. Smith & Hook, Paraiso Springs, and Robert Talbott are all estate wineries in the appellation. Another seven properties sell all their grapes, sometimes to producers of single-vineyard wines. Modest plantings of Pinot Noir, Gewürztraminer, Riesling, and Sauvignon Blanc fill the niches left by Chardonnay, Cabernet, and Merlot.

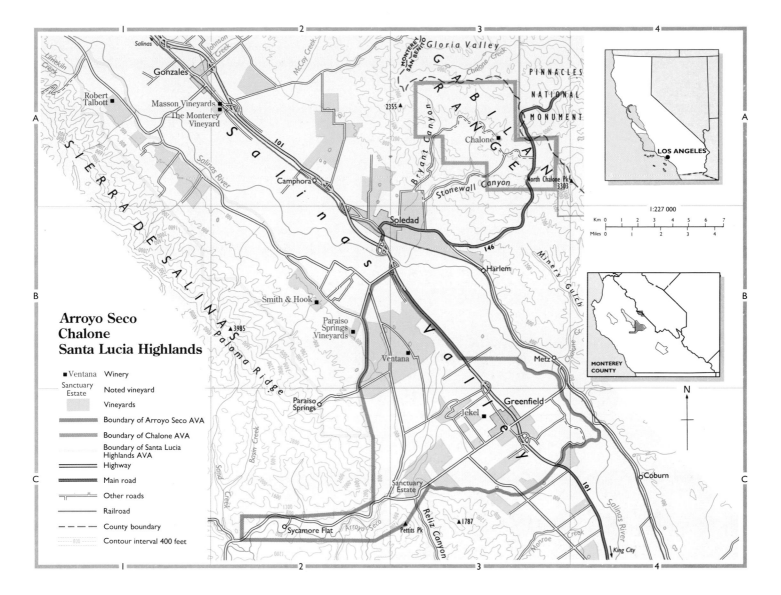

Chalone AVA

Established: July 14, 1982
Total area: 8,640 acres
Area in vineyard: 120 acres
Principal town: None (Soledad nearby)

This one-owner, one-winery appellation covers most of a small, quartz-rich shelf just below a monumental outcrop of black basalt called the Pinnacles and just above steep pitches leading down Stonewall Canyon into Soledad. The basalt is an aberration in the prevailing soils of the Gabilan Mountains. Although maps do not show it, the Gabilans are an extension of the Santa Cruz Mountains, their eastern edge framed by the San Andreas Fault. Because the AVA sits well above the morning fogs and tips toward the west, afternoon temperatures soar enough for Chenin Blanc to become ripe and rich, yet elevation makes the hot period brief enough for Chardonnay, Pinot Blanc, and Pinot Noir to have become Chalone's flagship wines. These varieties go back to the 1940s under a succession of owners. The site was first planted in 1911. Chalone's current proprietors added Cabernet Sauvignon in the mid-1980s.

San Lucas AVA

Established: March 2, 1987
Total area: 32,000 acres
Area in vineyard: 5,000 acres
Wineries: 1
Principal town: None (King City nearby)

At Monterey's southern boundary, the Salinas Valley is so broad and so far from the river mouth that it has more in common with nearby Paso Robles (*see* pages 130–1) than northern Monterey. Indeed, its summer temperatures are consistently warmer than those of King City just to the north. The San Lucas AVA has nothing but large-scale plantings draped across its rolling hills, and has never had anything else. Almaden Vineyards pushed the appellation into being on behalf of 1,300 acres it planted near San Ardo before Heublein bought and dismantled the company. Lockwood Vintners became its first winery in 1990. The region's active growers treasure it for large, reliably ripe crops rather than special ones, six tons to the acre being nothing to brag about here. Much of its fruit goes into "California" appellation wines of the Bel Arbors and

145

Glen Ellen Proprietor's Reserve stripe. Masson Vineyards blends its grapes with others from the north county to achieve agreeable Monterey AVA wines at modest prices. Lockwood bottles the pure item for similar purposes, although without "San Lucas" on its labels. Principal varieties are Chardonnay, Chenin Blanc, Sauvignon Blanc, and Cabernet Sauvignon.

Carmel Valley AVA

Established: January 13, 1983
Total area: 19,200 acres
Area in vineyards: 150 acres
Wineries: 4
Principal town: Carmel Valley

It is difficult to talk about Carmel Valley and the rest of Monterey in the same breath. The AVA sits alone on high, often vertiginous, slopes looking across Carmel and out to sea. Because of its elevation, its climate is sunnier than cool parts of the Salinas Valley and cooler than the sunny spots. It is rainier than either. The result: different wines, or so it would seem. There have been so few that bold characterizations do not come easily. Durney Vineyards is Carmel Valley's pioneer and, with more than half the total vineyard, its dominant force. Based on its example, Cabernet Sauvignon is not a bad bet. Chenin Blanc seems to have some substance, although America's chocolate-vanilla market has pushed it into the background. Younger, tiny wineries give hope for Chardonnay in the ripe, rich style.

Monterey AVA

A blanket Monterey appellation covers all the county's more defined regions, plus all gaps between. The most important plantings governed only by the blanket name stretch along the east side of the Salinas River from Soledad north to Chualar, and along the west edge of the valley from just south of Greenfield to and beyond King City. Among properties on the east side of the river the best-known are Mirassou Vineyards' Mission Ranch and Franciscan's Pinnacles Vineyard. Much of this area would fall within a proposed Pinnacles AVA. Between King City and the San Lucas AVA is the colossus vineyard, the 13,000-acre ranch owned by Delicato Vineyards (*see* page 190).

San Benito County

One pre-Prohibition vineyard, called Vaillant, led Almaden into the county in the 1960s, when the latter was still an independent winery. Within a decade Almaden had 3,500 acres of vines stretching south from Hollister to the hamlet of Paicines. In 1987, Heublein, Inc. bought the company and pulled out of San Benito County altogether, leaving most of the vineyards to whatever their fate. Two Almaden-invented AVAs, Paicines and Cienega, fell into limbo when the company moved away. Meanwhile, several tiny firms had puttered along at one side of the giant, each with a different goal. Of these, one came with much the loftiest ambitions: Calera owner Joshua Jensen saw in the chalky soils of the Gavilans hopes for Pinot Noir to rival good Burgundies, and the much closer-to-hand Chalone.

Mt Harlan AVA

Established: December 17, 1990
Total area: 7,440 acres
Area in vineyard: 47 acres
Wineries: 1
Principal town: None (Hollister is closest)

Joshua Jensen designed the AVA to identify his isolated vineyard by its 2,000-foot elevation, its lime-rich soils, and its eastward orientation; qualifications hardly shared by the rest of San Benito County's arable land. The theory was to make the slope synonymous with Pinot Noir, the proprietor's first love, and the source of nearly all of Calera's fame to date. However, even as the proposal was under government review, a little patch of Viognier was turning Jensen's head at least a tiny bit. Since the oldest blocks of Pinot Noir began to bear crops only in 1978, the Viognier in 1989, further evolutions are not out of the question from a property with another 100 plantable acres.

MONTEREY PRODUCERS

Boyer (1987)
PO Box 842, Soledad, CA 93960
Tel (408) 678-3404. 2,000 cases. The winemaker-owned label of Ventana's Richard Boyer goes on subtly toasty Chardonnays from his daytime boss's vineyard.

Chalone Vineyard (1960)
PO Box 855, Soledad, CA 93960.
Tel (408) 678-1717. 20,000 cases. Chardonnay, Chenin Blanc, Pinot Blanc, and Pinot Noir, all from the isolated 200-acre estate-cum-AVA, are highly stylized in imitation of Burgundies, yet distinctive by origin.

Jekel (1978)
PO Box 336, Greenfield, CA 93927.
Tel (408) 674-5522. 60,000 cases. Won its first fame for juicy, apricoty Riesling from 140 acres surrounding its red barn winery. This remains the most consistent of its wines in dry and off-dry bottlings. The big hope lies with Cabernet-based "Symmetry" from the 190-acre Sanctuary Estate.

Lockwood (1990)
Steinbeck Station, PO Box 1997, Salinas, CA 93902. Tel (408) 753-1424. 15,000 cases. The small production is meant to showcase a 1,800-acre vineyard in the San Lucas AVA. Estimable "Dry Refosco Rosé," agreeable Chardonnay the first successes.

Masson Vineyard (1852, revived 1940)
800 South Alta Street, Gonzales, CA 93926. Tel (408) 675-2481. 5 million cases. Vintners International corporation spun off Masson's 4,500-acre holdings after acquiring the firm from Seagrams in 1987, but has 1,200 affiliated acres providing the grapes for sound, conventional Monterey-appellation Cabernet Sauvignon, Chardonnay, Merlot, Riesling, and Sauvignon Blanc. Other labels for lower-priced wines: Paul Masson, Taylor California Cellars.

The Monterey Vineyard (1973)
PO Box 780, Gonzales, CA 93926.
Tel (408) 675-2316. 750,000 cases.

Seagrams-owned since 1983, it shares some production facilities with cheek-by-jowl neighbor Masson. The original vineyard network evaporated years ago; Seagram's 1,200-acre Paris Valley Ranch south of King City grows the grapes for run-of-the-mill "Limited Release" Cabernet Sauvignon, Chardonnay, and Pinot Noir.

Morgan (1982)
526 E Brunken Avenue, Salinas, CA 93901. Tel (408) 422-9855. 15,000 cases. The winemaker who made Jekel's reputation went independent to pursue his own dream of richly toasty Chardonnay. Also worth notice for Carmel Valley Cabernet Sauvignon, California Pinot Noir (half local, half Carneros grapes), and forceful Alexander Valley Sauvignon Blanc.

Paraiso Springs Vineyards (1987)
Drawer A, Soledad, CA 94960. Tel (408) 678-1592. 4,000 cases. From 200 acres in Santa Lucia Highlands come Chardonnay, Gewürztraminer, Riesling, and Pinot Noir.

La Reina (1984)
PO Box 1344, Carmel, CA 93921. Tel (408) 373-3292. 5,000 cases. Texas-owned label for ultratoasty, weighty Chardonnays, mostly from Santa Lucia Highlands grapes.

Smith & Hook (1980)
Drawer C, Soledad, CA 93960. Tel (408) 678-2132. 15,000 cases. In the Santa Lucia Highlands west of Gonzales, the 500-acre horse ranch turned wine estate specializes in dark, gutsy Cabernet Sauvignon with pronounced regional flavors and, more recently, Merlot of a subtler stripe. The vineyard name has appeared on Cabernets produced by others. Hahn Estate is a separate label for an estate-bottled Chardonnay.

Robert Talbott (1983 in Carmel Valley, to Santa Lucia Highlands in 1990)
Box 267, Carmel Valley, CA 93924. Tel (408) 675-3000. 7,000 cases. The winery is on a 60-acre vineyard near Gonzales, whence comes a toasty-school Robert Talbott Monterey Chardonnay. The original 32-acre parcel in Carmel Valley yields the still toastier Talbott Family Estates Carmel Valley Chardonnay.

Ventana Vineyards Winery (1978)
299 Monterey-Salinas Highway, Monterey, CA 93940. Tel (408) 372-7415. 50,000 cases. In his heart of hearts, owner Doug Meador is mostly interested in his 300-acre vineyard, but has always kept at least a showcase volume of wines going. In the

early 1990s production was more than that. Noteworthy: fruit-first Chardonnay "Gold Stripe," toastier Chardonnay "Crystal," Sauvignon Blanc.

CARMEL VALLEY PRODUCERS

Château Julien (1982)
8940 Carmel Valley Road, Carmel, CA 93922. Tel (408) 624-2600. 10,000 cases. Buys grapes throughout and beyond Monterey County; flag-bearer is Arroyo Seco Chardonnay "Cobblestone Vineyard." Second labels: "Emerald Bay," "Garland Ranch."

Durney Vineyard (1977)
PO Box 222016, Carmel, CA 93922. Tel (408) 625-5433. 15,000 cases. The pioneer estate in Carmel Valley best known for emphatic Cabernet Sauvignon; also grows and makes Chardonnay, Chenin Blanc, and Riesling from 140 mountainous acres.

Georis (1989)
PO Box 702, Carmel, CA 93921. Tel (408) 625-6731. 1,000 cases. From 15 acres near Durney come Merlot and a Merlot-based blend.

Jouillian (1987)
PO Box 1400, Carmel Valley, CA 93924. Tel (408) 659-2035. 2,500 cases. Cabernet Sauvignon, Sauvignon Blanc, and Chardonnay from 40 estate acres adjoining Durney.

OTHER PRODUCERS

Monterey Peninsula Winery (1974)
467 Shasta Avenue, Sand City, CA 93955. Tel (408) 394-2999. 10,000 cases. Originally eclectic to outright eccentric, Monterey Peninsula has settled in as an exhaustive explorer of Monterey Chardonnay, Cabernet Sauvignon, and Merlot, always powerful, frequently from named individual vineyards.

SAN BENITO PRODUCER

Calera (1975)
11300 Cienega Road, Hollister, CA 95023. Tel (408) 637-9170. 10,000 cases. Through the 1990s at least, the essence of both place and winery is damn-the-torpedoes Pinot Noir separately bottled from blocks called Reed, Mills, Selleck, and Jensen after friends and family. Calera also makes Viognier and Chardonnay from the vineyard on Mt Harlan.

A small, rebuilt chapel is all that remains of the Franciscan Mission Nuestra Señora de la Soledad.

Travel Information

PLACES OF INTEREST

Carmel (4,200), artist colony turned tourist village, still rejects street numbers and other modernisms. It has one of the most notable of the Franciscan missions in San Carlos de Borromeo de Carmel (1770). It also has several excellent inns and restaurants. The town flanks Del Monte Forest, site of Pebble Beach and four other awe-inspiring seaside golf courses. Several miles south of Carmel, Point Lobos State Nature Preserve has a savagely beautiful shoreline.

Carmel Valley (4,000) is a privileged enclave of golf, tennis, and good living well to the east of Carmel proper, not quite so far west of the several local vineyards.

King City (7,600) is well enough situated as a stopover point for a half dozen chain motels and fast-food restaurants to cluster around the exit from freeway US101. A couple of hole-in-the-wall Mexican restaurants make the old main street a more diverting place to find nourishment.

Monterey (32,000) is the commercial center for the Peninsula. Even more, as 50 major hotels attest, it is a capital of tourism. Its great attraction, the Monterey Bay Aquarium, is on Cannery Row, made famous by John Steinbeck in the novel of that name.

The Salinas Valley has not bent itself to tourism at all, but the Monterey Peninsula thrives on year-round throngs of visitors, who enjoy a beautiful shoreline and golf. Hotels in Monterey and Carmel must be booked far in advance.

Soledad (7,100) has on its western outskirts a few surviving walls of the Mission Nuestra Senora de la Soledad (1791), where the valley's first vineyard failed because local fogs were too cold for the Mission variety to ripen. Above Soledad to the east, Pinnacles National Monument has one of the west's most dramatic outcroppings of columnar basalt. The town has a comfortable motel.

RESTAURANTS AND HOTELS

l'Escargot Mission at 4th. Tel (408) 624-4914. Cheery, chummy atmosphere and sometimes quite refined French cookery.

Hyatt Regency 1 Old Golf Course Road, Monterey, CA 93940. Tel (408) 375-3960. A comfortable conference hotel on a golf course handy for the highway to Salinas and the vineyards.

Pine Inn PO Box 250, Carmel, CA 93921. Tel (408) 624-3851. A bit of the old, individualistic Carmel remains in a small, comfortable hotel going back to the turn of the century.

Rafaello Mission near 7th. Tel (408) 624-1541. Subtle northern Italian cuisine plus a good local wine list.

WINE ROUTE

Monterey's vast plantings of vines and most of its wineries are in the Salinas Valley, which has never even tried to be a tourist mecca. Because US101 runs the length of it, many travelers take advantage of one or another of its tasting rooms for a brief picnic lunch. It is also well located for day trips from the Monterey Peninsula. The romantic way is through Carmel Valley and across the bare hills to Greenfield on narrow, winding Jamestown-Arroyo Seco Road.

The Carmel Valley looks more promising than it in fact is. Only Chateau Julien is open to visitors; other cellars require appointments, because the firms are so small.

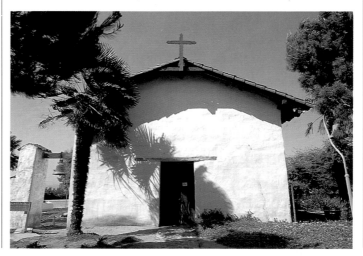

San Francisco Bay

In the wake of the Gold Rush of 1849 people fanned out from San Francisco in every available direction, to make wine, amongst other agricultural pursuits. The Napa Valley is their best-known destination, but there was also a vigorous push eastward to the Livermore Valley and south into the Santa Cruz Mountains.

Different sorts of people went in different directions. Sunbaked Livermore was hard-working farm country from the beginning, while the dramatically steep, fog-softened Santa Cruz Mountains almost instantly became a summer haunt for the socially prominent. Livermore is more industrial than agricultural as the 20th century winds to a close, and the barons of the Santa Cruz Mountains have many commoners for company nowadays. Still, important parts of the legacies remain.

Livermore Valley

Sauvignon Blanc and Sémillon are almost the only aspects of the contemporary Livermore Valley that might spark a poet. Out on their hot, flat, highway-scarred plain, the towns of Livermore and Pleasanton are two among scores of dormitory communities for commuters who work elsewhere in the San Francisco Bay area. Even where vineyards huddle closest together, houses, shopping malls and the looming presence of Lawrence Livermore Radiation Laboratories dominate the landscape more than vines and cellars do. However, Sauvignon Blanc and Sémillon from Livermore do rouse poetic thoughts, and the growers in this historic district are working hard to make themselves a more handsome and visible community.

In the beginning, during the 1880s, the winemaking part of Livermore was almost an outpost of Bordeaux, populated by Duvals, Mels, Bons, Chauches, and other French emigrants. The gravelly soils so resembled Graves', the story goes, that right-thinking Frenchmen could not resist. But they slipped away, one by one, as Prohibition approached, and when the national "dry" spell was over the dominant wine families were the German-descended Wentes, and the Italo-Irish Concannons.

Carl Wente and Joseph Concannon had set up cellars less than a year apart in 1883, and less than a mile apart on Tesla Road. Once Prohibition had done away with the competition, their families held sway from the 1930s until 1982, when circumstances forced the third and fourth generations of Concannons to sell their winery and vineyards to the first of several outsider corporations. By that time Wente Bros. had become much the larger firm.

By 1992 the Wentes were practically synonymous with wine in Livermore. They owned 1,300 of the valley's 1,600 acres of vines, the original family winery and a separate one for sparkling wine. Wentes also owned Concannon (rescued from outside owners) and a dormant Ruby Hill (rescued from developers), were a majority partner in Murrieta's Well, leased production facilities to Ivan Tamas Wines, and were selling grapes to several of the small-to-minuscule other wineries that round out the field.

Modest as this community of wineries might be, the current numbers represent a renaissance. At one point in the early 1970s, when Wente and Concannon had only two small cellars for company, the Livermore Valley was filling with houses at so swift a pace that Karl Wente planted vineyards in Monterey as a hedge against the extinction of vines on his home turf.

Even with the recent revitalization, from a casual glance it would seem impossible for Livermore to hold out long against the urban expansion pressing hard against the outer rows of vines where dry hills do not. In fact this valley could quadruple its vineyards. It is the enlightened view of the Wentes that they need more competitors, to which end they are leading a drive to establish another 3,000 acres of vines and a dozen new wineries in the valley by the new millennium.

The Pacific Ocean hides beneath its ever-present blanket of fog.

Santa Cruz Mountains

The Santa Cruz Mountains, meanwhile, has about 200 acres of vines scattered across one of the California coast's larger landscapes. Ridge, at 40,000 cases, is the unchallenged Titan among a score of wineries. It was not always so. From the 1880s until Prohibition, another community of French settlers had the hills above Los Gatos and Saratoga teetering on the verge of becoming a major wine district. Paul Masson called its most famous properties, including his own, La Chaine d'Or, a name which stuck. However, the French departed, and the spark dimmed. Now, its vineyards shrunken but its boundaries expanded, the appellation is in the hands of people pursuing intensely personal visions of what wine ought to be, many of them in part-time relief from the high-tech, high-pressure world of Silicon Valley, down on the flats below.

Eccentricity is every bit as much respected in these hills as on Hyde Park Corner, among winemakers as willingly as computer programmers. One who helped set the pattern, Martin Ray, used to strip to the waist and bang on a big gong to welcome guests. He also wrote open letters accusing his peers of making their wines out of dried apricots. Ray was quite level-headed compared to novelist Ken Kesey and some of the others then living in these mountains who did not make wine.

The Santa Cruz Mountains, one suspects, are a magnet for people who frown upon the conventional. Even on a warm, bright summer's day the woods up on these ridges can be spooky, as if all the different drummers to which the locals march had somehow pounded uneasy vibrations into the air. When the fog rolls in, or the rain beats down, spooky does not begin to describe it.

Maybe it is not different drummers at all, but earthquakes. In the Santa Cruz Mountains, alone among California's major districts, the San Andreas Fault runs straight through the AVA, north–south, with profound effects on soil and exposure and intermittent ones on the stirring of lees in barrels. In 1989 the Loma Prieta earthquake had barrels bouncing around cellars like the balls in lottery wheels. Tellingly, the winery owners got together, blended a wine from survivor barrels, called it Epicenter, labeled it with the tremor's seismographic footprint, and gave the proceeds of its sale to earthquake relief.

If the region is known for extreme styles, it also offers wines of classic measure, most often Pinot Noir and Chardonnay, sometimes Cabernet Sauvignon, occasionally Zinfandel.

Livermore Valley

Climate

Although high hills to the west screen Livermore from marine fogs throughout the summer, there is enough of a gap to allow the same sea wind that blows flyweight baseball pitchers off the mound at Candlestick Park to cool the valley by early evening, beginning on its west side and moving steadily eastward. It is an article of local faith that the daily high temperature peaks and begins to cool in Livermore five minutes later than it does at San Francisco International Airport. Encroaching urbanization has brought enough smog to lessen that cooling tendency by diminishing reradiation at night, but the effect remains important. Spring frost is barely a threat, winter cold not at all.

Like the rest of the Central Coast, Livermore lies to the south of the main winter storm track, thus sharing low rainfall totals with the rest of the Central Coast. The average declines sharply west to east, from 22 inches at Pleasanton to 14 at Livermore and 9 at Altamont. Before urbanization the water table allowed dry-farming of vineyards; since then, some irrigation has been required.

* For the color code to the climate charts see pages 14–15.

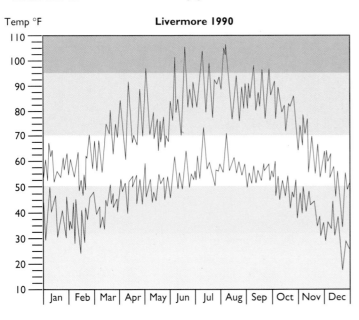

Bare, dry hills press in on the Livermore Valley's vines from one side, while population does from the other. The vineyard belongs to Wente Bros.

White Wine Varieties

Going back at least to the 1930s, probably to the beginning, Livermore's reputation has been far more for white than red wine. A whole generation of casual imbibers knew and loved it for Gray Riesling, while Sauvignon Blanc was and is the purist's choice. Market pressures and individual quirks have caused larger acreages to be devoted to less well adapted varieties. Chenin Blanc once led; currently the champion is Chardonnay.

Chardonnay (153 acres in 1970, 540 in 1990)
From the end of Prohibition until the 1960s Wente Bros. was California's dominant grower and producer of Chardonnay, but could not sustain its leadership once the variety began to proliferate elsewhere. High summer temperatures combined with lean soils appear to put Chardonnay at its margin here, the vines performing well only in Livermore's richest loams. Even in such soils their varietal character tends to be more modest than from a half dozen other districts north and south. Both the "Herman Wente" and Fenestra are generously oaked.
Benchmarks:
Wente Bros. "Herman Wente Vineyard." **Fenestra** "Toy Vineyard."

Gray Riesling (152 acres in 1970, 114 in 1990)
Once popular, Gray Riesling has lost favor swiftly in recent years, and in fact dipped to 30 acres between 1990 and 1992. Apparently it is a victim of the mysterious decline that has

affected everything called Riesling. In a way it is to be lamented, for the variety grew well in most of Livermore, yielding serviceable young quaffers of more intriguing flavors than many other varieties suited to the same purpose. The best of them do well with a year or two of bottle age.

Benchmarks:

Retzlaff (estate). **Wente Bros.** (estate).

Sauvignon Blanc (113 acres in 1970, 172 in 1990)
The early French, it turns out, were thinking straight when they saw Graves in the stony soils. Of all Livermore whites, Sauvignon has been the most memorable. Kept to poor, rocky ground it reliably gives distinctly herbaceous flavors to its wines, but none of the vegetal characteristics that come from farther south in the Central Coast. The greatest of Livermore Sauvignons have had enough power and depth to age on an upward curve for a decade and more. These have come from particularly rocky patches along Tesla Road, where the vine's vigor is most severely curbed.

Sauvignon arrived during the 1880s, probably from cuttings gathered at Château d'Yquem by Louis Mel for another pioneer Livermore grower, Charles Wetmore. It has never been absent since, replenished by succeeding generations raised from those original cuttings in Wente nursery blocks.

Benchmarks:

Concannon Vineyard (estate). **Wente Bros.** "Reserve" (from ground originally planted by Mel).

Sémillon (361 acres in 1970, 110 in 1990)
The same combination of warm summers and rocky soils that caused Mel and his pioneering colleagues to bring Sauvignon from Yquem also led them to put Sémillon into the basket with similar, perhaps even greater, success. It is not unreasonable to believe no other part of California grows an equal to the best Sémillon Livermore can offer. If its flavor closely approaches that of Livermore Sauvignon, a fuller body separates it from its cousin.

Benchmark:

Wente Bros "Louis Mel Vineyard" (estate).

Sauvignon-Sémillon blends
As tradition in Bordeaux points out, the two varieties mate well. Such efforts are recent in Livermore, but promising. No benchmark has yet emerged.

Other varieties
French Colombard (51 acres); St-Emilion (27).

Red Wine Varieties

Long eschewed, red wine has begun to have a presence in Livermore on the grounds that Cabernet Sauvignon should do well where Sauvignon Blanc and Sémillon do. Of scattered plantings given to other red varieties only Petite Sirah has established any reputation.

Cabernet Sauvignon (9 acres in 1970, 205 in 1990)
Cabernet Sauvignon has been a curious beast in Livermore to date, having little of the herb-and-cassis interplay of North Coast districts, and virtually none of the vegetal tones that dominate most of the Central Coast. Indeed, based on extremely limited bottled evidence, almost all from the Concannon vineyard, Cabernet's varietal character is understated to the point of extinction in wines otherwise reasonably well balanced, and stable over some years in bottle. Concannon Cabernets from 1970 and 1965, for example, remained sound in 1990, although no more highly distinctive in age than they were in youth. Perhaps in response, several winemakers have turned to Cabernet-based blends.

Petite Sirah (29 acres in 1970, 33 in 1990)
During the 1960s Concannon became one of the first in California to bottle Petite Sirah as a varietal, and so had the good fortune to help write the definition. The results from Livermore were and remain logical: understated flavors with some hints of dried fruit, and the softened textures typical of thoroughly ripened grapes.

Benchmark:

Concannon (estate).

Zinfandel (156 acres in 1970, 56 in 1990)
In spite of the acreage, a Livermore-appellation Zinfandel is a rare bird. In recent years Fenestra has had one from a tiny patch near Pleasanton, but finding a comparison bottle can be a difficult task.

Other varieties
Carignane (18 acres in 1990); Gamay Beaujolais (14); Mataro (14); Merlot (56); Pinot Noir (20).

Livermore Valley AVA

Established: October 1, 1982
Total area: 96,000 acres
Area in vineyard: 1,600 acres
Wineries: 11
Principal towns: Livermore, Pleasanton

In one sense, the Livermore Valley is just a wider spot in a long chain of identical valleys running north-south behind the East Bay Hills of San Francisco Bay. What sets it apart from all its neighbors in that chain are stones.

Livermore and stones are close to synonymous. In the most famous vineyards in the southeastern quarter of the valley, along Tesla Road, what Livermore growers call soil begins with egg-sized stones and works up by degrees to those that are melon- and even basketball-sized, deposited by rushing waters in what are now dry arroyos. These ancient stream beds can be as deep as 500 feet, including sandwiched layers of clay from periods of slow water. All Concannon's 180 acres are here, as well as the Wente blocks that have won individual names: Herman Wente for Chardonnay, Louis Mel for Sauvignon Blanc and the other Bordeaux varieties.

More conventional loams occur in islands among Tesla's stones, and prevail toward Pleasanton, where vineyards are

In owning the majority of Livermore Valley vineyards, Wente Bros. owns several of the region's historic 19th-century residential properties as well.

fewer and smaller; but even these richer patches have an abundance of gravel.

The AVA encompasses the entire valley floor, although no part of it north of freeway I580 has grown vines within living memory, and no one plans to change that. Its boundaries slip up into the surrounding hills, especially on the west and south, but vineyards are rare on the slopes for lack of soil and water.

Most of the increased acreage envisioned in the plan proposed by current growers lies east or south of existing vineyards along Tesla Road, or in a band linking Livermore and Pleasanton along the axis provided by State Route 84.

This is one of the warmest valleys from San Francisco down to southern Monterey County, sheltered from marine air not only by the high hills forming its west side but also by a second, much higher barrier, the Santa Cruz Mountains farther west beyond San Francisco Bay. It is kept from being downright hot by gaps to the west and the unbroken Altamont Ridge to the east, the latter high enough to block airflows back out of the San Joaquin Valley.

Enough marine air penetrates from the west to make Livermore marginally less hot than the northern end of the Napa Valley. The combination of temperature and lean soils makes it later to harvest than most of Napa. Chardonnay is seldom picked before the third week in September, while Cabernet can linger into mid-November.

If historically Sauvignon Blanc and Sémillon have won the valley its greatest fame, nowadays growers feel more and more that Cabernet Sauvignon and its cousins belong just as much, in spite of a modest track record.

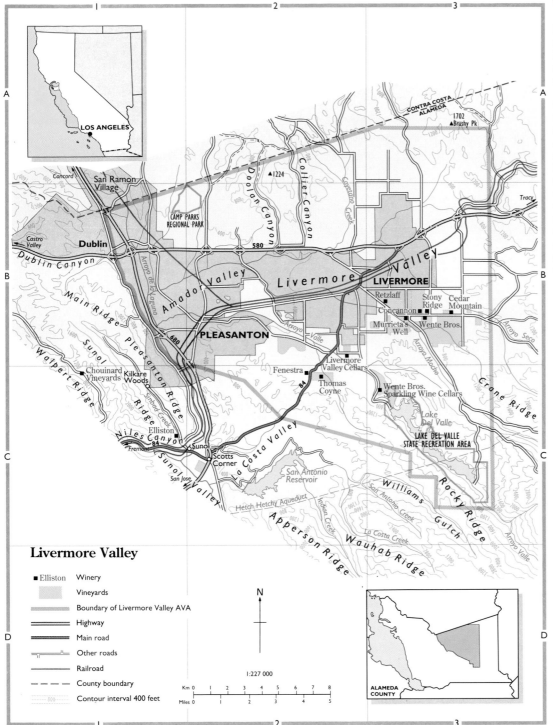

Livermore Valley

- ■ Elliston Winery
- ▨ Vineyards
- ▤ Boundary of Livermore Valley AVA
- ━━ Highway
- ━━ Main road
- ┬┬ Other roads
- ━━ Railroad
- ‐ ‐ ‐ County boundary
- ⠿800 Contour interval 400 feet

1:227 000

Km 0 1 2 3 4 5 6 7 8
Miles 0 1 2 3 4 5

ALAMEDA COUNTY

WINE ROUTE

Livermore, commuter town caught in a web of highways, is for devotees of its particular wineries, not for those in search of a day in the fresh air and countryside.

The Santa Cruz Mountains, contrarily, are surprisingly close to wilderness, especially in the higher reaches of SR 9 and along Bear Gulch Road. Accommodations can be found in the rough-hewn old resort towns of Boulder Creek and Felton. A broader set of options exists in Santa Cruz on the cool coast side, or Saratoga or Los Gatos on the sunnier inland side of the hills. One must plan ahead to visit wineries in this district. Far the greater number are open to visit only by appointment, many of them only at weekends.

LIVERMORE VALLEY PRODUCERS

Cedar Mountain Winery (1990)
7000 Tesla Road, Livermore, CA 94550. Tel (510) 373-3363. 1,500 cases. Chardonnay from an estate vineyard on Tesla Road was the planned centerpiece.

Chouinard Vineyards (1985)
33853 Palomares Canyon Road, Pleasanton, CA 94552. Tel (510) 582-9900. 4,500 cases. Cabernet,

Chardonnay from 3 owned acres at the winery in hills west of Pleasanton, plus bought-in grapes.

Concannon Vineyard (1883)
4590 Tesla Road, Livermore, CA 94550. Tel (510) 447-3760. 65,000 cases. Since 1991 owned by the Wente family, which is keeping the winery and 180 acres of rocky Tesla Road vineyard as a separate estate, focused on Cabernet Sauvignon, Sauvignon Blanc, and Sémillon produced as varietals, and Meritage-

type blends. Petite Sirah from 75-year-old vines stays in the roster.

Thomas Coyne Winery (1989)
2900 Main Street, Alameda, CA 94501. Tel (510) 373-6541. 2,000 cases. Currently in leased space in Alameda, Coyne makes a Livermore Cabernet Sauvignon from Kalthoff Vineyard, the planned site of an eventual winery. Merlots from several other regions are the other speciality.

Fenestra (1976 as Ventana, renamed 1980)
83 E Vallecitos Road, Livermore, CA 94550. Tel (510) 447-5246 weekends only. 4,000 cases. Chemistry professor Lanny Replogle makes tiny lots of many wines at weekends, all with bought-in grapes. Chardonnay and Zinfandel have had the most to say about Livermore vines.

Ivan Tamas (1985)
5565 Tesla Road, Livermore, CA 94550. Tel (510) 447-3603. 15,000

cases. Tamas and Steve Mirassou were looking in 1992 to build a winery after years as négociants in a leased corner at Wente Bros.

Livermore Valley Cellars (1978) 1508 Wetmore Road, Livermore, CA 94550. Tel (510) 447-1751. 475 cases. Old-line grower-turned-winemaker Chris Lagiss produces rustic whites from his property in Livermore's southwestern quarter and locally bought grapes.

Murrieta's Well (1990) 3005 Mines Road, Livermore, CA 94550. Tel (510) 449-9229. 2,400 cases. Phillip Wente and ex-Concannon partner Sergio Traverso are using the historic, Wente-owned Louis Mel vineyard and winery on Tesla Road to make Cabernet- and Sauvignon Blanc-based red and white blends.

Retzlaff Vineyards (1985) 1356 Tesla Road, Livermore, CA 94550. Tel (510) 447-8941. 3,000 cases. Lawrence Laboratories research chemist Robert Taylor makes wines at weekends from his family's 10 acres on Tesla Road and locally bought grapes. Along with a sentimental try to keep Gray Riesling going, Taylor produces Chardonnay and Cabernet Sauvignon.

Stony Ridge (1975, reborn 1985) 4948 Tesla Road, Livermore, CA 94550. Tel (510) 449-0458. 20,000 cases. One-time owners of defunct Villa Armando returned to the valley, bought an existing name, and are slowly transforming from négociant to producing cellar.

Wente Bros. (1883) 5565 Tesla Road, Livermore, CA

94550. Tel (510) 447-3603. 300,000 cases. The rock, the anchor, with 1,300 acres in vines and more than a century of history. Most intriguing for vineyard-named Sémillon "Louis Mel," Chardonnay "Herman Wente," &c.. The Wentes also own 700 acres in Monterey's Arroyo Seco AVA, from which they have made impressive Gewürztraminer and memorable late-harvest Riesling.

Wente Sparkling Wine Cellars (1980) 6,000 cases. In the restored Cresta Blanca property, using mostly Arroyo Seco-grown Chardonnay and Pinot Noir to make Brut and Grand Reserve.

All through the Livermore Valley, the residential streets of a fast-growing suburb flank vineyards that once sat remote from a sleepy farm town. When highways linked the area closely to major cities in the San Francisco Bay area, the old era ended.

Santa Cruz Mountains

Climate

The Santa Cruz Mountains are just high enough to allow sea-fogs to spill over their tops more often than not, guaranteeing moderately warm to outright cool days during the summer growing season, even on the inland slopes. They also are just high enough to squeeze more rain out of winter storms than any other district south of San Francisco.

The difficulty in generalizing beyond the foregoing comes from their San Andreas Fault-induced topographical tumult. Cataclysmic earthquakes buckled and twisted old seabed into a mountain range more complex in shape than most and lesser tremors continue to rearrange the smaller details at fairly frequent intervals. The two weather-reporting stations used for temperature graphs only hint at the irregularities of sun and

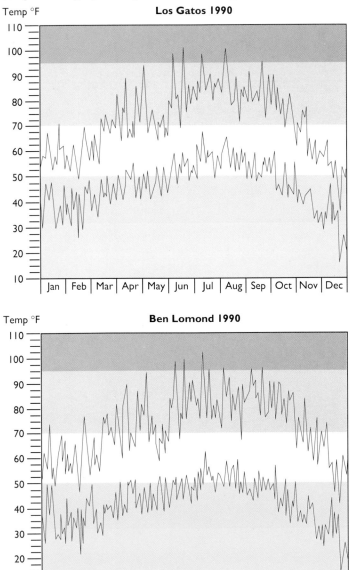

rain in these hills. Los Gatos, at low elevation on the inland side, gives a fairly accurate idea of the climate for the whole length of the AVA on that side. In much greater degree Boulder Creek can only speak for itself, although it gives a fair indication of how different the ridges can be from the lowlands. The coast side is cooler than either beneath its foggy blanket.

*For the color code to the climate charts see pages 14-15.

White Wine Varieties

Based on performance, Sémillon and Pinot Blanc should lead the list, but most if not all the old plantings of both expired when nothing could compete with Chardonnay in the marketplace. White Riesling, the other proven performer, remains in play in a very small way. Viognier, Marsanne, and Pinot Gris are new challengers, although from such limited acreage that their real virtues will be learned slowly.

Acreages noted here are rough estimates. This is because statistical reporting in California is by county, and the Santa Cruz Mountains encompass all the vineyards in San Mateo County, but only uncertain proportions of those in Santa Clara and Santa Cruz counties.

Chardonnay (10 acres in 1970, 120 in 1990)
Chardonnay grows well in much of the region, perhaps with greater versatility on east-facing slopes where there is more sun than on the ocean-facing side of the ridges. The prevailing style leans vertiginously to buttered toast and/or flamboyant oak, with Cronin the foremost proponent, Ridge and Mt Eden Vineyards only comparatively restrained.

Recent increases in acreage promise more Santa Cruz Mountain appellation Chardonnays than were common well into the 1980s, when most of the region's Chardonnay makers found themselves forced to reach out both north and south to find grapes. Many of those that exist come in such eyedropper volumes that only familiars of the wineries ever see them. Cronin, for example, makes other Chardonnays from Monterey and North Coast grapes to extend the barrel or two of home-grown stuff. Mt Eden Vineyards supplements its estate wine with a second, more voluminous, one from Monterey.
Benchmarks:
Ridge (estate). **Mt Eden Vineyards** (estate). **Cronin** Santa Cruz Mountains (estate).

White Riesling (15 acres in 1970, 10 in 1990)
In research reports published in the 1880s, scholars at the University of California had high praise for Riesling from the mid- and upper slopes of the Santa Cruz Mountains. In spite of this grape's commercial decline, the endorsement still rings true. As in other favored parts of California, the grapes achieve riper flavors and higher sugars than those of the Rheingau, let alone the Mosel, yet keep a firm, refreshing crispness best rewarded when the wines are dry enough to be versatile at table. Only Mendocino's Anderson Valley rivals their quality.

Storrs Winery has undertaken the obligations of nobility with consistent skill. The style is just off-dry, and hands Riesling the whole job of flavoring the wine.
Benchmark:
Storrs Santa Cruz Mountain (assembled from three or more small vineyard properties).

Red Wine Varieties

Randall Grahm of Bonny Doon had high hopes in the 1980s of pushing the Santa Cruz Mountains into the Syrah business, but the idea did not take, leaving the region to fall back on the grapes it has always stuck with: Cabernet Sauvignon, Pinot Noir, and some scraps and tatters of Zinfandel.

Cabernet Sauvignon (15 acres in 1970, 25 in 1990)
Cabernet producers in these rugged hills take with utmost seriousness their role as mountain winegrowers: they seek dark, emphatically tannic wines meant to keep long enough for the grandchildren to taste. Whatever the style, Santa Cruz Mountain Cabernets mostly tend toward the herbaceous, and can be almost as bell peppery as Montereyans in cool seasons. This characteristic has led to fairly widespread use of American rather than French oak, as it is more complementary in flavor.

Ridge's sometimes vertiginous Monte Bello Vineyard is the paragon by reputation and performance, reliably delivering big, rock-solid, slow-maturing wines. The Kathryn Kennedy vineyard, although down on the flats in Saratoga, produces exactly the same sort of Cabernet.
Benchmarks:
Ridge Montebello (estate). **Kathryn Kennedy** (estate).

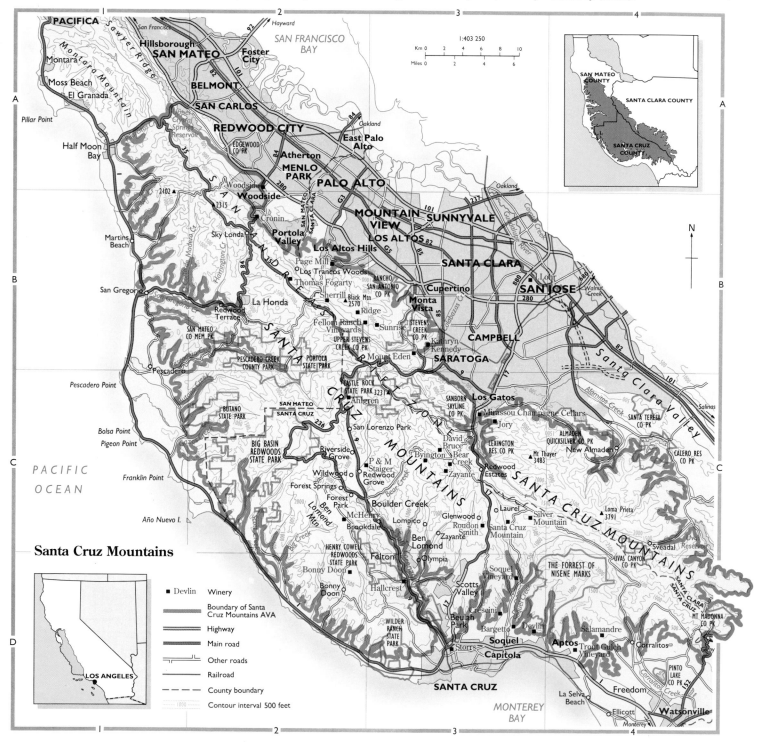

Santa Cruz Mountains

- ■ Devlin   Winery
- Boundary of Santa Cruz Mountains AVA
- Highway
- Main road
- Other roads
- Railroad
- County boundary
- Contour interval 500 feet

Pinot Noir (10 acres in 1970, 25 in 1990)
Dr David Bruce's estate vineyard has yielded two or three of California's most memorable, and in some ways most Burgundian, Pinot Noirs. However, the variables, which include the good doctor himself, are so many that the wines from his vineyard vary dramatically from year to year. Still, his noblest achievements say that a west-facing exposure at an elevation just above the mean fog-line would appear to be the best home this region has to offer Pinot Noir vines. The truth is probably more difficult to pin down than that. Just a few miles south of Bruce, the Santa Cruz Mountain Vineyard regularly overripens the variety. At an even shorter distance to the north, the McHenry Vineyard seems hard put to get it fully ripe.
Benchmark:
David Bruce (estate).

Zinfandel (10 acres in 1970, 10 in 1990)
Here, as almost everywhere else in California, exists a tradition of Italian family farmers who grew Zinfandel more for themselves than grand commercial purposes. After 1933 the woods were more or less full of Locatellis and Picchettis selling jugs of red at the cellar door. All the old-guard Italian proprietors are gone, and nearly all their vineyards as well. One, Sunrise – the old Picchetti place – lingers. Ironically, many producers offer Zinfandels from the Sierra Foothills, Sonoma, and elsewhere.
Benchmarks:
Ridge "Jimsomare" (from the neighbor). **Sunrise** (estate).

Long stretches of conifer forest still blanket the rugged, earthquake-racked Santa Cruz Mountains.

Santa Cruz Mountains AVA

Established: January 4, 1982
Total area: 112,000 acres (approx)
Area in vineyard: 200 acres
Wineries: 20
Principal towns: Los Gatos, Saratoga, Felton, Bonny Doon, Boulder Creek, Scotts Valley

The great temptation is to divide this long, sparsely planted region along the ridgeline of the low mountain range after which it is named, to slice it into a Pacific Ocean-facing western half and a San Francisco Bay-facing eastern half. To a degree, the east-west split would follow plantings of Pinot Noir (concentrated on the ocean side) and Cabernet Sauvignon (bay side).Those who drew the boundaries rather admitted to some differences when they set boundaries on the warmer, sunnier bay side at 600 feet elevation for most of the length, 800 feet near the southerly tip, while those on the often foggy ocean side hug the 400-foot level end to end. The weather reports from Los Gatos and Santa Cruz explain why.

No matter how defined, the division would fail in the details, for dips and draws turn one vineyard and its neighbor into small pockets that have little to do with each other or any other nearby property. The swiftness of change here makes the rest of California look orderly.

At this point the two star properties in a small cast are

Ridge's Montebello, because of its Cabernet Sauvignon, and Dr David Bruce's planting of Pinot Noir. They make the bay-side vs. ocean-side generalization particularly tempting, but no truer. The question of whether one or the other ought to dominate has been semi-mooted by Chardonnay, currently the dominant variety on both sides of the ridgepole. Whether it ought to dominate is a different question. Good as some of the Chardonnays are, the appellation's greater treasures are Pinot Blanc and Riesling, both lost or nearly so.

An old vineyard of Pinot Blanc farmed by Jesuit novitiates has gone, too steep to farm economically. However, this and a couple of other plots nearby yielded some of California's most memorable whites, especially at the hands of Daniel Gehrs when he made wine at the now defunct Congress Springs. Riesling had a reputation in the highest of these hills by the late 19th century. A couple of scraps linger, the quality of their wines crying out that there should be more.

Ben Lomond sub-AVA

Established: January 8, 1988
Total area: 38,500 acres
Area in vineyard: 100 acres (approx)
Wineries: 1

Ben Lomond is the first effort to isolate a particular zone within the vaster Santa Cruz Mountains AVA. Granitic parent soils are unique within the larger region; the prevailing 800-foot elevation, just above the upper edge of persistent summer fogs, makes that season sunny but cool; annual rainfall is 60 inches. Bonny Doon's vineyard is at its core. Identifiable wines from the sub-AVA remain too rare for useful comparisons.

SANTA CRUZ MOUNTAINS PRODUCERS

Ahlgren (1976)
PO Box M, Boulder Creek, CA 95006. Tel (408) 338-6071. 1500 cases. Husband-wife winery most instructive for single-vineyard Cabernet Sauvignon from Bates Ranch. Also buys Monterey Chardonnay.

The peaceful facade of Bonny Doon belies its restless nature.

Bargetto (1933)
3535 N Main Street, Soquel, CA 95073. Tel (408) 475-2258. 25,000 cases including fruit wines. Family firm makes a range of middle-of-the-road wines from Santa Cruz Mountains and other sources.

Bonny Doon Vineyard (1981)
PO Box 8381, Santa Cruz, CA 95061. Tel (408) 425-3625. 15,000 cases. Irrepressible Randall Grahm is trying to grow Marsanne and Viognier in a 25-acre ocean-facing vineyard near the winery. He also is developing a small vineyard near Soledad, planting varieties with origins in the Rhône and Italy. Meanwhile, Grahm buys widely for a long list of bold, biting Rhône- and Italy-inspired wines called by such whimsical names as Le Cigare Volant, Old Telegram, Le Sophiste, Ca' del Solo, &c.

David Bruce (1964)
21439 Bear Creek Road, Los Gatos, CA 95030. Tel (408) 354-4214. 30,000 cases. Owner-grower-wine-maker David Bruce is always on pins and needles to try something new, but his memorable wine in most vintages is an estate-grown Pinot Noir from 12 west-sloping acres above Bear Creek Road, 2,000 feet up.

Byington Winery and Vineyard (1989)
21850 Bear Creek Road, Los Gatos, CA 95030. Tel (408) 354-1111. 12,000 cases. At start-up Byington bought all of its grapes from points beyond the appellation, but began planting 82 estate acres in its first year, almost all to Chardonnay.

Cinnabar Vineyards & Winery (1986)
PO Box 245, Saratoga, CA 95071. Tel (408) 741-5858. 2,400 cases. From 24 acres looking down to Saratoga from 1,600 feet come estate Chardonnay and Cabernet Sauvignon.

Crescini (1980)
PO Box 216, Soquel, CA 95073. Tel (408) 462-1466. 1,500 cases. Cabernet Sauvignon, Cabernet Franc, and Petite Sirah.

Cronin Vineyards (1980)
11 Old La Honda Road, Woodside, CA 94062. Tel (415) 851-1452. 2,000 cases. Owner-winemaker Duane Cronin makes a powerhouse toasty Chardonnay from his one acre at Woodside, and others in a similar style from Napa, Sonoma, and Monterey.

Devlin Wine Cellars (1979)
PO Box 728, Soquel, CA 95073. Tel (408) 476-7288. 8,000 cases. Chardonnay, Cabernet Sauvignon, and Zinfandel from vineyards in the appellation.

Fellom Ranch Vineyards (1987)
17075 Monte Bello Road, Cupertino, CA 95014. Tel (408) 741-0307. 1,500 cases. A family-owned winery on Monte Bello Road produces estate Cabernet from 12 acres, and both Cabernet and Zinfandel from the Saratoga Vineyard.

Thomas Fogarty Winery (1981)
5937 Alpine Road, Portola Valley, CA 94028. Tel (408) 851-1946. 7,000 cases. Beautifully crafted Chardonnay and Pinot Noir from 24 estate acres are the heart of the winery, but it buys the same two varieties from vineyards in several regions, and also makes an impeccable Gewürztraminer from Monterey's Ventana Vineyard.

Hallcrest Vineyard (1941, revived 1989)
379 Felton-Empire Road, Felton, CA 95018. Tel (408) 335-4441. 1,500 cases. In its third incarnation Hallcrest has returned to its roots after a period as Felton-Empire Winery. The regional wines are an estate White Riesling from 4 acres, Cabernet Sauvignon from the adjacent Beauregard vineyard, and a Chardonnay from the Meylay Vineyard.

Kathryn Kennedy Winery (1979)
13180 Pierce Road, Saratoga, CA 95070. Tel (408) 867-4170. 600 cases. Estate Cabernet Sauvignon from 9 acres that just begin to slope up at one edge of Saratoga.

McHenry Vineyard (1977)
330 Eleventh Street, Davis, CA 95616. Tel (916) 756-3202. 200 cases. Estate Pinot Noir by a weekend winemaker from 4 acres near the hamlet of Bonny Doon.

Mount Eden Vineyards (1972)
22020 Mount Eden Road, Saratoga, CA 95070. Tel (408) 867-5832. 5,000 cases. On much of what was originally planted as the Martin Ray Estate, Mt Eden produces Cabernet, Pinot Noir, and Chardonnay from its 2,000-foot-elevation, steep-pitched, east-looking 40 acres. It also buys Chardonnay grapes from outside the appellation to boost volume.

Page Mill Winery (1976)
13686 Page Mill Road, Los Altos Hills, CA 94022. Tel (415) 948-0958. 2,400 cases. A husband-wife winery buying most of its grapes from Napa and elsewhere, but does have one home-grown, a Chardonnay from the Elizabeth Garbett vineyard.

Ridge Vineyards (1959)
17100 Monte Bello Road, Cupertino, CA 95014. Tel (408) 867-3233. 45,000 cases. At this point the grand oldster of Santa Cruz Mountain wineries and by a long chalk the largest of them, Ridge is a veritable experiment station for hearty Zinfandels and other reds from vineyards south to San Luis Obispo and

An old cellar carved into the bedrock holds aging reds of Ridge Vineyards.

Far left: The rolling hills are some of the gentler ones in Ridge's Monte Bello Vineyard. From here, winemaker Paul Draper (left) has made a long series of dark, emphatic, slow-to-age Cabernet Sauvignons.

north to Sonoma, but its flagship was, is, and shall remain the dark, emphatic estate Montebello Cabernet. Also from the AVA: estate Chardonnay and Zinfandel from a neighbor.

Roudon-Smith Vineyards (1972)
2346 Bean Creek Road, Santa Cruz, CA 95066. Tel (408) 438-1244. 8,000 cases. Owned by the two families named on the label, the winery grows Chardonnay, Cabernet Sauvignon, and Pinot Noir on 5 acres near Scotts Valley, and buys Chardonnay and Pinot Noir from local growers. Zinfandel and Petite Sirah come from other regions.

Salamandre Wine Cellars (1985)
108 Don Carlos Drive, Aptos, CA 95003. Tel (408) 688-0321. 500 cases. A physician and weekend winemaker produces two single-vineyard Chardonnays, one from the appellation, the other from Monterey. He also makes a Santa Cruz Mountains Gewürztraminer.

Santa Cruz Mountain Vineyard (1974)
2300 Jarvis Road, Santa Cruz, CA 95065. Tel (408) 426-6209. 4,000 cases. Ken Burnap dotes on power in heady, fully ripe Pinot Noir from 15 ridgetop acres first planted in 1883 as Jarvis Vineyards. A Santa Cruz Mountains Cabernet follows style.

Silver Mountain Vineyards (1979)
Box 1695, Los Gatos, CA 95031. Tel (408) 353-2278. 1,000 cases. The only California winery destroyed in the Loma Prieta earthquake of 1989 got itself back in the game quickly. It makes a Chardonnay from 10 estate acres near the winery, and a Zinfandel from purchased grapes.

P & M Staiger (1973)
1300 Hopkins Gulch Road, Boulder Creek, CA 95006. Tel (408) 338-4346. 400 cases. From 5 acres near

Boulder Creek a husband-wife team makes sturdy to rustic Chardonnay and a Cabernet-Merlot blend.

Storrs Winery (1988)
303 Potrero Street, Santa Cruz, CA 95060. Tel (408) 458-5030. 2,000 cases. Skilled husband-wife winemaking team reaches into the Santa Cruz Mountains from a base in Santa Cruz town for several individual-vineyard Chardonnays and a too little-noticed White Riesling.

Sunrise Winery (1984)
13100 Monte Bello Road, Cupertino, CA 95014. Tel (408) 741-1310. 2,000 cases. A husband-wife winery has its anchor in an estate Zinfandel from 90-year-old vines, originally the Pichetti ranch. The label also covers a Cabernet from the AVA.

Trout Gulch Vineyard (1990)
8035 Soquel Drive, Aptos, CA 95003. Tel (408) 662-9586. 1,000 cases. Chardonnay dominates, Pinot Noir is secondary in 15 estate acres above Aptos.

Woodside Vineyards (1963)
340 Kings Mountain Road, Woodside, CA 94062. Tel (415) 851-3144. 800 cases. From remnants of the pre-Prohibition La Questa vineyard of E.H. Rixford, one of the most prized in all California in its time, the winery makes Chardonnay and Pinot Noir, but above all Cabernet Sauvignon, its original source of fame.

Zayante Vineyards (1990)
420 Old Mount Road, Felton, CA 95018. Tel (408) 335-7992. The most ambitious undertaking of recent times was planned to result in 90 acres of vineyard nestled into a warm, sunny spot south of Felton. The first blocks of which were Zinfandel and Chardonnay.

Other AVAs

In a gesture as much nostalgic as practical, a hardy band of small wineries in southern Santa Clara County established Santa Clara Valley as an AVA in 1990. A huge proportion of the district (not mapped) is more familiar to the modern world as Silicon Valley than as a wine district. Industrial buildings and residential neighborhoods cover many an old vineyard. Surviving blocks of vines come few and far between. Still, vineyards do cling to existence and U.S. labeling regulations make an appellation nearly imperative for the wineries owning them.

About 200 acres of vineyards and eight wineries are caught between ever-expanding Gilroy and the steep slopes of the Santa Cruz Mountains, the undaunted remnants of a bygone time in more senses than one. The area, known informally as the Hecker Pass, has for years been the state's last bastion of old-fashioned generic jug wines sold at the cellar door for mere pennies. Colombard, Sauvignon Vert, and Grenache were the varieties of choice for the jug generics. Varietal wines, some from local grapes, have also figured in production in recent years, but much of the old ethic remains. All of the vineyards and wineries are on or near SR152, the Hecker Pass Highway linking Gilroy and Watsonville.

Two slightly larger wineries with broader marketing schemes are not far away in the town of Morgan Hill.

Within the generously drawn Santa Clara Valley AVA is a tiny sub-AVA called winery called San Ysidro. It sits in a low spot between two hills which channel cool sea air coming up the Pajaro River across two substantial vineyards devoted predominantly to Chardonnay. The vineyards' names are San Ysidro and Mistral. Both have appeared from time to time on bottled wines, most notably from the now-defunct Congress Springs, also from a tiny cellar called Jory.

Two major firms find themselves more or less accidentally caught within the Santa Clara Valley appellation, although their wines do not come from it. These are Mirassou Vineyards, which moved all of its vineyards south to Monterey County years ago in response to urban pressures, and J. Lohr, which never owned a vine in the territory.

PRODUCERS

A. Conrotto Winery (1926)
1690 Hecker Pass Highway, Gilroy, CA 95020. Tel (408) 942-3053. 5,000 cases. The founding family still owns a small cellar given mostly to generic reds from its own small vineyard.

Fortino Winery (1970)
4525 Hecker Pass Highway, Gilroy, CA 95020. Tel (408) 842-3305. 30,000 cases. An immigrant from southern Italy brought a taste for ripe, fleshy wines expressed everywhere in a long, long list of varietals.

Emilio Guglielmo Winery (1925)
1480 E Main Avenue, Morgan Hill, CA 95037. Tel (408) 779-2145. 65,000 cases. A rather sizable firm with more than 100 acres of vines near Morgan Hill makes steady jugs under the Guglielmo name, varietals under the Mt Madonna label.

Hecker Pass Winery (1972)
4605 Hecker Pass Highway, Gilroy 95020. Tel (408) 842-8755. 1,800 cases. The more reserved brother of the man who owns Fortino makes steady, sturdy red wines in his own image. Zinfandel especially is worth trying out.

Jory Winery (1986)
PO Box 1946, Los Gatos, CA 95031. Tel (408) 356-2228. 5,000 cases. The one Santa Clara Valley winery dedicated to making a mark near the top of the lists; specializes in heavily buttered toasty Chardonnay from San Ysidro.

Kirigin Cellars (1976)
11550 Watsonville Road, Gilroy, CA 95020. Tel (408) 847-8827. 3,000 cases. A Croat with long experience in California's Central Valley jug wine business never forgot his roots. When he retired, it was to make proprietary reds and whites modeled on the ones he knew in his native land, but with his own Gilroy grapes.

Thomas Kruse (1971)
4390 Hecker Pass Highway, Gilroy, CA 95020. Tel (408) 842-7016. 2,500 cases. Kruse abandoned the academic life in Chicago with designs on reforming the Hecker Pass as a producer of upscale varietals. He has stuck around as an upholder of local tradition.

J. Lohr Winery (1975)
1000 Lenzen Avenue, San Jose, CA 95126. Tel (408) 288-5057. 230,000

Echo of Mission San Jose, destroyed in a 1863 earthquake.

cases. The winery started in a one-time brewery in downtown San Jose as an expedient when it owned only the 200-acre Cobblestone Vineyard in Monterey. It now grows 700 acres of Cabernet Sauvignon in Paso Robles (where it has a supplementary cellar) and a similar acreage of white varieties near Clarksburg. The instantly approachable Paso Robles Cabernet Sauvignon "Seven Oaks" offers fine value, as does the Monterey Chardonnay "Cobblestone."

Mirassou Vineyards (1937)
300 Aborn Road, San Jose, CA 95135. Tel (408) 274-4000. 350,000 cases. A family with winemaking roots in the Santa Clara Valley of the 1850s still has its cellars in San Jose, but gets most of its grapes from 1,100 winery-owned acres in two properties near Soledad in Monterey's Salinas Valley. In recent years the winemaking has been steady, the wines agreeable across a broad range.

Mirassou Champagne Cellars
300 College Avenue, Los Gatos, CA 95031. Tel (408) 395-3790. The same family that owns Mirassou Vineyards

has established a separate cellar for classic-method sparkling wines from its Monterey grapes.

Pedrizzetti Winery (1945)
1645 San Pedro Avenue, Morgan Hill, CA 95037. Tel (408) 779-7389. Pride of place goes to an estate-grown Barbera made from one of the oldest importations of vine cuttings of this variety growing in California.

Solis Winery (1988)
3920 Hecker Pass Highway, Gilroy, CA 95020. Tel (408) 847-6306. The winery revives a long-idle name in the district, and also revives an old cellar and 15-acre vineyard originally known as Bertero. Otherwise it looks ahead. The new owners are replanting with Chardonnay, Cabernet Sauvignon, Merlot, and a trial block of Sangiovese.

Sycamore Creek Vineyards (1975)
12775 Uvas Road, Morgan Hill, CA 95037. Tel (408) 779-4738. 2,500 cases. A Japanese firm bought an old Hecker Pass winery with thoughts of turning it to Sake production, but has stuck with grape wine instead.

Travel Information

PLACES OF INTEREST

Berkeley
In addition to its history of radical politics and its huge university population, Berkeley has a well-earned reputation as a gourmet ghetto. Its location in the East Bay makes it as handy as San Francisco to wine districts both north and south.

Livermore is not vacation country, not least because it lies within easy reach as a day trip from San Francisco, San Jose, even Sacramento. In 1992 its wineries took the first steps toward building a museum and demonstration vineyard in one of the city's historic estates.

Pleasanton has an historic main street with several tourist-oriented businesses along it, and is also the site of the Alameda County Fairgrounds.

San Francisco
Everyone's choice as the most European of American cities. If it does nothing else to justify that claim, it is by far the most attuned to wine. Scores of its restaurants sport fine wine lists and there are at least a dozen wine merchants of substance within the city limits or nearby. It has one further virtue for those who like thoroughly urban diversions in between forays into the countryside:

proximity to several of the state's best-known wine districts. The Napa Valley is slightly more than an hour away; Sonoma, Livermore, and the Santa Cruz Mountains all are slightly less when traffic is moving well.

Santa Cruz
The colorful heart of this oceanside resort town was severely damaged by the Loma Prieta earthquake of 1989, but its inhabitants are bringing it back steadily. Its several motels and hotels are relatively convenient for wineries in the southern end of the Santa Cruz Mountains appellation. A few cellars are right in town.

Saratoga
Although now mostly a bedroom community to Silicon Valley, Saratoga has a long enough history to have a character of its own. Within its small historic center are some good restaurants.

HOTELS AND RESTAURANTS

Amelio's 1630 Powell Street, San Francisco. Tel (415) 397-4344. Intimate formal dining room; intimate formal French menu. Owner-chef Jacky Robert's lighter side is on display in the adjoining, less costly café.

Ashbury Market 205 Frederick Street, San Francisco. Tel (415) 566-3134. Crackerjack staff, intensively researched international selection of wines across a wide price range.

Balboa Café 3199 Fillmore St., San Francisco, CA Tel (415) 921-3944. Homemade soups, pastas, but really to be sought for epic burgers. Short, thoughtful wine list.

Bedford Hotel 761 Post Street, San Francisco. Tel (415) 673-6040. Sunny atmosphere, handy location, modest prices by San Francisco standards.

Bentleys 185 Sutter Street, San Francisco. Tel (415) 989-6895. Great oysters and an extensive wine list all the time; jazz at weekends.

Bistro Roti 155 Stewart Street, San Francisco. Tel (415) 495-6500. From the proprietors of Napa's Mustard's Grill and Tra Vigne, a first-rate casual menu with spit-roasted chicken, fresh fish and pasta in the forefront.

The Blue Fox 659 Merchant Alley, San Francisco. Tel (415) 981-1177. Elegant Italian *cucina moderna* at not-quite Florentine prices.

California Culinary Academy 625 Polk Street, San Francisco. Tel (415) 771-3500. Tomorrow's chefs have some downs but a lot of ups; modest prices make the gamble worthwhile. The Careme restaurant is the elegant one, Academy Grill the casual spot. Good wine list.

Campton Place 340 Stockton Street, San Francisco. Tel (415) 781-5155. Superior small, luxury hotel in the heart of downtown. A formal restaurant fits in nicely.

Chancellor Hotel 433 Powell, San Francisco. Tel (415) 362-2004. Recently refurbished small, moderately priced hotel in the heart of town.

Chez Panisse 1517 Shattuck Avenue, Berkeley. Tel (510) 548-5049. Here began the almost obsessive attention to fresh, locally grown ingredients and imaginative recombinations of diverse cuisines that came to be called California Cuisine. It remains peerless in its style. Downstairs is a tough ticket; the casual upstairs café is easier to get into. Cost-conscious wine list.

Clift Hotel 495 Geary Avenue, San Francisco. Tel (415) 775-4700. The longest-running satisfaction-guaranteed luxury hotel in the city. Its French restaurant has a superior wine list.

Coit Liquors 585 Columbus Avenue, San Francisco. Tel (415) 986-4036. Some rarities in a ranging California section; good international stocks as well.

Cost Plus Imports 2552 Taylor Street, San Francisco. The wine shop emphasizes California; bargain prices; best to know what one wants going in.

Cypress Club 500 Jackson Street, San Francisco. Tel (415) 296-8555. Eclectic design, thoroughly American but hardly a traditional menu; stunningly complete American wine list.

Dining Room at the Ritz Carlton Hotel 600 Stockton Street, San Francisco. Tel (415) 296-7465. Chef Gary Danko is an absolute original without trampling on a single classical notion of French or American cookery. The luxury hotel almost smothers guests with attention.

Draper & Esquin 655 Davis Street, San Francisco. Tel (415) 397-3797. Solid wine merchants with splendid import and good California stocks.

Etrusca Rincon Center, 101 Spear Street, San Francisco. Tel (415) 777-0330. Good enough Italian cuisine to attract Teresa Lungarotti when in town. Polished service and a fine wine list.

Fleur de Lys 777 Sutter Street, San Francisco. Tel (415) 673-7779. Jewel box restaurant. First-rate menu by the city's most-praised traditional French chef. Excellent wine list.

Il Fornaio 1265 Battery Street, San Francisco. Tel (415) 986-0100. Good Italian food amidst a happy hubbub. Semi-sheltered outdoor dining suited to San Francisco summers. Thoughtful wine list.

Fournou's Ovens in the Stanford Court Hotel 905 California Street, San Francisco. Tel (415) 673-1888. Seasonal, French-influenced American menu. Fine wine list. The hotel on Nob Hill is one of the most luxurious in town.

Green's Building A at Fort Mason Center, San Francisco. Tel (415) 771-6222. Vegetarian brought to rarefied heights. Thoughtful wine list. Great views of the Golden Gate are a bonus.

Harris's Steak House 2100 Van Ness Avenue, San Francisco. Tel (415) 673-1888. Steaks, steaks, steaks! Useful wine list.

Hayes Street Grill 320 Hayes Street, San Francisco. Tel (415) 863-5545. Near the Opera House; imaginative, respectful preparation of the freshest of fish. Extensive wine list.

Kuleto's 255 Powell Street, San Francisco. Tel (415) 397-7700. Happily raucous bar, jolly Italian restaurant; in the usefully located, moderately priced hotel Villa Florence.

The London Wine Bar 415 Sansome Street, San Francisco. Tel (415) 788-4811. Exactly what the name promises in every detail from selection to decor.

Marin Wine Cellar 2138 Fourth Street, San Rafael. Tel (415) 456-9463. It is well outside the city, but on the way to Sonoma. One of the grand collections of older wines in the state.

Masa's 648 Bush Street, San Francisco. Tel (415) 391-2233. Ever-changing menu with roots in classic French cookery and branches reaching everywhere fine food can be found. Extensive wine list, many by the glass. In the equally refined and expensive Hotel Vintage Court.

Le Mouton Noir 14560 Big Basin Way, Saratoga. Tel (405) 867-7017. A California menu, but heavily influenced by France. A Victorian dining room is supplemented in good weather by an outdoor terrace.

Mulhern & Schachern Pier 33, The Embarcadero, San Francisco. Tel (415) 788-3330. Noisy, vital atmosphere, well suited to vigorous new American menu. Short but thoughtful wine list.

Pacific Heights Bar & Grill 2001 Fillmore Street, San Francisco. Tel (415) 567-3337. Oysters and other fresh seafood in an atmosphere that approaches clubby. Well-chosen wine list.

Ridgetop windmills east of Livermore generate electric power.

Pacific Wine Company 124 Spear Street, San Francisco. Tel (415) 896-5200. Many small California producers on the list. Tasting bar.

Postrio 545 Post Street, San Francisco. Tel (415) 776-7825. Hard to get in except at breakfast, but worth real effort at lunch or dinner for innovative menu by Wolfgang Puck and on-the-spot chefs Anne and David Gingrass. Fine wine list.

Square One 190 Pacific Avenue, San Francisco. Tel (415) 788-1110. Wonderful pan-Mediterranean menu leans now this way, now that, but mostly toward Italy. Splendid wine list with skillful staff to advise.

Stars 150 Redwood Alley, San Francisco. Tel (415) 861-7827. Owner-chef Jeremiah Tower is never at a loss for a new idea about a menu dominated by fresh, local ingredients. Good wine list.

Tadich Grill 240 California Avenue, San Francisco. Tel (415) 391-2373. Impeccably traditional San Francisco seafood house is a perfect escape from trendiness of any sort.

The Waterfront Pier 7, The Embarcadero, San Francisco. Tel (415) 391-2696. A no fuss, no feathers seafood restaurant with a high regard for freshness in the fish. Good wine list.

Wente Restaurant 5050 Arroyo Road, Livermore. Tel (510) 447 3696. On the grounds of Wente Sparkling Wine cellars, an airy, pavilionlike building. Steadily evolving menu anchored in fresh regional produce. Ranging California wine list.

161

Temecula

One here, one there, the odd vineyard crops up all through Southern California, especially behind the first range of coastal hills in Ventura, Orange and San Diego counties, but only Temecula is a coherent district.

Situated at the southwestern tip of Riverside County where it abuts San Diego and Orange counties, Temecula took its first wobbly step toward becoming a winegrowing district in 1964, when the owners of a 90,000-acre land development called Rancho California planted a demonstration vineyard as part of an effort to create a mixed residential, industrial, and agricultural community on a dusty, erosion-scarred mesa blessed by well-developed water supplies in the hills to the east.

Four years later a couple named Vincent and Audrey Cilurzo planted the first commercial vineyard in Rancho California. The now-defunct Brookside Winery was Rancho California's first major taker, buying and planting 350 acres to supplant lackluster vineyards in nearby Cucamonga. The driving force, however, turned out to be an aggressive corporate manager-marketer named Ely Callaway, who acquired 105 acres in 1969 and soon thereafter launched the first and strongest of eight pioneering cellars in the region. Callaway brought not only money but determination to winegrowing in Temecula, and thus stability. Although he has long since sold to corporate owners, Callaway Vineyards & Winery remains the anchor in a district where the next largest cellar is less than a third its size, and all 12 others put together do not produce half as much.

What marketing-whiz Callaway understood early on was how ready the wine-obsessed Los Angelenos were to support a respectable wine district of their own. That was the good news.

Piconi (foreground) and Mount Palomar vines roll with Buck Mesa.

Climate

The closest station, Elsinore, is slightly warmer than Temecula, but still a useful indicator. The distinguishing quality of climate at Temecula is its narrow range between moderate daily highs and balmy overnight lows. Annual rainfall is modest in total, but sometimes comes in one or two torrents, especially in times of El Niño. (The El Niño effect follows incursions of warm, equatorial ocean waters into more northerly latitudes, causing torrential tropical storms to follow different tracks.)

* For the color code to the climate charts see pages 14–15.

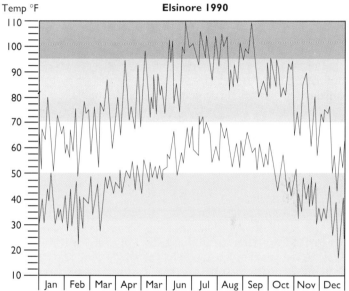

Temp °F   **Elsinore 1990**

The last rows of Temecula houses are just west of Callaway vines.

The bad news is that Temecula has not been able to escape the smothering attention of Los Angeles in another sense: the tide of population pushes ever eastward and Temecula increasingly becomes one more link in a taut chain of densely populated commuter towns.

When local vineyards were just beginning to send their roots deep, a motorist driving the four empty miles between Temecula village and Callaway could wait for a red racer to slither from one side of Rancho California Road to the other without holding up another car. By 1992, these impressive snakes had become scarce, the last rows of houses were flanking the first rows of vines, and traffic was no longer about to put up with stopped cars in the roadway.

However, there is a ray of hope. In 1989 local grape and citrus growers won a breathing space when Riverside County set aside 7,000 acres of Buck Mesa as a Citrus and Vineyard Rural Policy Area until 2025: a new vote then will kill or keep the vines. The race to see whether bedrooms or barrels will be more precious 25 years after the millennium has one forlorn, "what-if" aspect. Old records suggest that during the 1840s an expatriate Frenchman named Jean Louis Vignes foresaw prime grape country in what is now Temecula. However, he seems to have done little about it beyond planting a patch of Missions. Thereafter vineyards did not figure in the local landscape until the developers of Rancho California used them as a come-on for their larger purpose of selling sites for houses.

White Wine Varieties

Temecula's list of white grape varieties is as short as its list of black ones. Sauvignon Blanc is the ever-reliable, Chardonnay the ever-popular choice. Although the market will not help him prove his case, at least one winemaker suspects Chenin Blanc makes Temecula's most impressive white. Riesling and Gewürztraminer persist, but in minute quantities.

Chardonnay (0 in 1970, 1,052 acres in 1990)
Temecula may not have hit upon its signature variety, but it certainly has elected a dominant one. Oddly enough it came late to Temecula because available clones in the 1970s fared poorly in the region.

Soft textures and undemanding fruit flavors give the wines immediate appeal if they are allowed to be themselves. Temecula Chardonnays do not seem to take especially well to oak. Even small doses of it tend to obliterate the grape flavors and sharpen the textures. Callaway abandoned wood altogether several years ago in favor of aging Chardonnay on its lees in stainless steel tanks. Its most successful rivals have had their greatest success when they have used barrels sparingly if at all. Mt Palomar 1986, Maurice Car'rie 1989, and Hart 1990 come particularly to mind. Still, consistency in style remains rare enough to make benchmarks hard to find.
Benchmark:
Callaway "Callalees."

Chenin Blanc (30 acres in 1970, 111 in 1990)
A weak market for Chenin Blanc has not helped local wine-makers hold a focus on the variety which, much like Chardonnay, turns up soft-textured and mild-flavored given half a chance. When botrytis has appeared in Temecula, this variety has been the most susceptible to it. No recent example of a botrytized Chenin exists; early tries exaggerated a curiously vegetal flavour which lurks beneath the surface of dry wines.
Benchmark:
Callaway.

Sauvignon Blanc (0 in 1970, 258 acres in 1990)
Sauvignon hit a peak of 726 acres in 1986, then dropped much more sharply than the overall market for the varietal wine. At its best, it has been Temecula's most impressive white, and certainly its most ranging in character. Callaway achieves a sweetly floral aroma in its Sauvignon Blanc with some regularity, but has ranged back through melon to outright herbaceous-ness in cool years. Baily managed in its well-made 1991 to capture a *pipi du chat* worthy of Washington State. Callaway excepted, consumers cannot yet expect consistent style in this variety any more than the others.
Benchmark:
Callaway Sauvignon Blanc (a Fumé Blanc is oak-aged and tastes of that as much as Sauvignon).

White Riesling (4 acres in 1970, 133 in 1990)
The variety peaked at 584 acres in 1980, then began to erode as the market for this variety virtually collapsed in the United States. One cannot mourn much. The wines were and continue to be bland and varietally indistinct.

Other varieties
Gewürztraminer (16 acres at its peak, 4 now) yielded surpris-ingly flavorful wine from Filsinger vineyards at times; Muscat Blanc (12); Sémillon yielded two richly flavorful wines for Mount Palomar in 1986 and 1987, but was grafted out of that vineyard in 1990 in favor of the far more salable Chardonnay.

Red Wine Varieties

The roster of varieties is short, Temecula having emerged after other districts turned the market to a short list of varietals. Callaway battled with Cabernet Sauvignon, Petite Sirah, and Zinfandel for years before giving up red wine completely in 1982. As its proprietors were rethinking that decision in 1992, others were diminishing their plantings of those varieties in favor of experiments with Syrah, Mataro (Mourvèdre), Nebbiolo, and Sangiovese.

Cabernet Sauvignon (0 in 1970, 116 acres in 1990)
Like all red varieties in Temecula, Cabernet has dropped back from a peak, in this case 250 acres in 1979. In a rare few instances, its wines have come close in character to the norms of the North Coast, but for the most part they have been curiously soft, and rather dim in varietal flavors. Winemaker Joe Hart believes cooler, east-facing vineyards in the Santa Margaritas hold out the best hope. John Moramarco and Dwayne Hellmuth of Callaway are beginning to see promise in their oldest plantings, survivors from the start-up years.

Petite Sirah (1 acre in 1970, 0 in 1990)
The extreme case of peak and valley reached 218 acres in 1977 and immediately began to decline toward official but not factual zero. Maurice Car'rie continues to make Petite Sirah from a block first planted by Cilurzo in 1969. Temecula Petite Sirah may be as much a victim of a Cabernet-dominated market as any weaknesses of its own. Although many tended to taste of raisins and be disconcertingly soft, the finest have been Temecula's most pleasing reds to date.

Zinfandel (173 acres in Riverside County in 1970, 106 in 1990)
Nearly all the Zinfandel is north, in the century-old, almost extinct, district of Cucamonga. Only one certified Temecula Zinfandel exists currently, that made by Hart and sold under the Dos Sabas label of its grower.

Other varieties
Although acreages remain minuscule, several growers have experimental plantings of Nebbiolo, Sangiovese, Syrah, and Mataro/Mourvèdre. The first tiny lots of Syrah and Sangiovese came from 1990.

Below: Culbertson Winery faces the vineyards of Callaway.
Right: Grapes just at flowering time.

Temecula AVA

Established: November 23, 1984
Total area: 100,000 acres
Area in vineyard : 1,700 acres
Wineries: 14
Principal town: Temecula

Heated argument surrounded the drawing of Temecula's AVA boundaries in 1982. Callaway Vineyards & Winery sought a narrow definition taking in only 33,000-acre Buck Mesa due east of Temecula village. Others wanted a looser boundary reaching far enough west, north, and east to treble the area. Callaway lost the battle but won the war, for all but a few existing vines fall within the limits of its defeated proposal. The *de facto* (as opposed to official) Temecula AVA is California's most homogeneous by any measure.

Ely Callaway set much store by the climatic effects of Rainbow Gap, a narrow breach separating the Santa Rosa and Santa Margarita mountains, that exposes Temecula to cooling afternoon breezes from the Pacific Ocean 24 miles to the west. Callaway contended that this gap funneled sea air over his vision of Temecula, but not over adjacent zones immediately

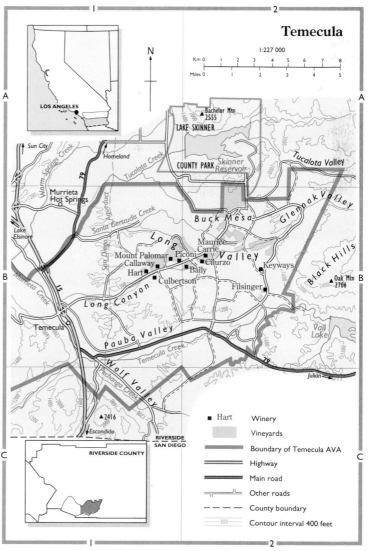

Maurice Car'rie has Temecula's most elaborate visitor center. The winery sits directly behind it.

north and south, and that wines would differ markedly as a result. Practical evidence lacked then, and will continue to do so, because Rainbow Gap breezes rustle the leaves of virtually every vine giving its fruit to wine entitled to the appellation.

Soils are even more consistent: coarse, fast-draining granitic sands washed down from the Magee Hills to the east make up all of Buck Mesa. Although flat enough to be called a mesa, this much of the Temecula AVA erodes so readily that almost every square foot slopes toward one gully or another, usually at a sharp pitch. Vineyards are mowed, not tilled, so that grassy thatches can keep the soil from eroding when rain comes. One sprinkler going full blast will start to carve a channel in bare earth in a matter of hours. A slight shower can make an unpaved road interesting to drive. Deluges alter whole landscapes.

Four small properties in the Santa Margaritas differ by exposure, soil, and elevation. Wines identifiably from them have been hard to come by, but the first few Cabernet Sauvignons have earned praise from local winemakers.

Callaway is by leagues the dominant grower, owning 710 acres. The independent Temecula Valley Vineyard comes second with 425. Mt Palomar and Maurice Car'rie have about 100 apiece. The remaining 500 come mainly in 8- to 20-acre parcels belonging to 50 growers.

PRODUCERS

Baily Winery (1986)
33833 Rancho California Road, Temecula, CA 92390. Tel (909) 676-9463. 2,500 cases. Young couple beginning to do well with Sauvignon, trying Carmine; mostly from 7 estate acres.

Callaway Vineyard & Winery (1969)
32720 Rancho California Road, Temecula, CA 92390. Tel (909) 676-4001. 250,000 cases. The first leader remains out front, especially for lees-aged Chardonnay and off-dry Sauvignon Blanc. Has made only white wines since 1982, but is reconsidering, especially on behalf of Cabernet Sauvignon.

Cilurzo Vineyard & Winery (1978)
41220 Calle Contento, Temecula, CA 92390. Tel (909) 676-5250. 10,000 cases. Pioneer growers and indefatigable supporters of the region, Audrey and Vincent Cilurzo planted 40 acres of Chenin Blanc and Petite

Sirah in 1968–69. They still have 8 acres of that property, but buy grapes for a long list. Style and technique have wobbled with the arrivals and departures of several winemakers.

Clos du Muriel (1989, 1984 as Britton)
40620 Calle Contento, Temecula, CA 92390. Tel (909) 676-2938. In suspended animation with money woes in spring, 1992.

Culbertson Winery (1981)
32575 Rancho California Road, Temecula, CA 92390. Tel (909) 699-0099. 80,000 cases. Specialist in sparkling wine buys nearly all of its grapes, mostly from Santa Barbara, but spices the product using local vineyards.

Filsinger Vineyards & Winery (1974)
39050 De Portola Road, Temecula, CA 92390. Tel (909) 676-4594. 7,000 cases. German-descended winemaking dentist has an affection for Riesling, some skill with Chardonnay. His wines come from his own 34 acres.

166

French Valley Vineyards (1984)
36515 Briggs Road, Murrieta, CA 92362. Tel (909) 926-2175. 2,500 cases. Owner Leon Borel helped establish experimental block in 1964, now contents himself with small lots of Chenin Blanc and Gamay.

Hart Winery (1980)
PO Box 956, Temecula, CA 92390. Tel (909) 676-6300. 5,000 cases. One of the steadiest winemakers in the region begins to be of interest for Cabernet from Hansen Vineyard at La Cresta. He has test patches of Syrah and Viognier in his 12-acre vineyard.

Keyways Vineyard & Winery (1990)
37338 De Portola Road, Temecula, CA 92390. Tel (909) 676-1451. Tiny newcomer with no track record.

Maurice Car'rie Winery (1986)
34225 Rancho California Road, Temecula, CA 92390. Tel (909) 676-1711. 10,000 cases. Aggressive newcomer has done well with local Chardonnay and Cabernet Sauvignon, mostly from its own 100 acres. The firm buys Merlot and Muscat Canelli from Santa Barbara County.

Mount Palomar Winery (1975)
33820 Rancho California Road, Temecula, CA 92390. Tel (909) 676-5047. 20,000 cases. Pioneer grower John Poole has offered one of the broadest ranges of Temecula wines, and continues to expand the horizons with test plots of Sangiovese, Syrah, and Merlot in a 105-acre vineyard now dominated by Chardonnay. A fine Sémillon sub-titled Paloverde is a thing of the past, alas, the vines replaced by still more Chardonnay. As do others, Mt Palomar buys elsewhere, especially Cabernet from Dry Creek Valley.

Piconi Vineyard & Winery (1981)
33410 Rancho California Road, Temecula, CA 92390. Tel (909) 676-5400. 8,000 cases. After purchasing the winery from founder John Piconi in 1991, Ben Drake and Bob Peterson planned to change the name and began experimenting with Sangiovese, Nebbiolo, Dolcetto, Mourvèdre, and Viognier. A Carmine stays in the line-up.

Santa Margarita Winery (1985)
33490 Madera de Playa, Temecula, CA 92592. Tel (909) 676-4431. Tiny cellar just beginning to sell its wines in 1992.

Travel Information

POINTS OF INTEREST

Temecula is rather a mixed-up town, the original center intent on drawing tourists with quaint shops, the fast-growing newer parts single-mindedly residential-commercial east of freeway 115 and light industrial west of it. Lake Skinner County Park offers modest but close-at-hand picnic grounds and water recreation in a region closely ringed by resort towns ranging up in stature to Palm Springs.

HOTELS AND RESTAURANTS

Café Champagne 32575 Rancho California Road, Temecula, CA 92591. Tel (909) 699-0088. At Culbertson Winery, locally popular indoor-outdoor restaurant designed by former owner Martha Culbertson still carries her imprint: brightly inventive salads and sandwiches at lunch; meatier menu at dinner. Local and other California wines.

Doubletree 29345 Rancho California Road, Temecula, CA 92591. Tel (909) 676-5656 Most luxurious of a dozen motels and motor hotels catering for business travelers.
Temecula Creek Inn 44501 Rainbow Canyon Road, Temecula, CA 92390. Tel (909) 676-5631. Flossy golf and tennis resort.

WINE ROUTE

Nearly all of Temecula's wineries flank Rancho California Road or sit just off it on spur roads. To avoid retracing that route while adding two wineries to the possibilities, loop south then west on Glen Oaks Road, De Portola Road, and State Route 79. The route is easily driven within a day-trip from either Los Angeles or San Diego as long as one limits winery visits to three or at most four.

San Diego is within easy reach of Temecula, or vice versa. The port city is a major tourist destination.

Interior

Californians call it the Big Valley, the Great Central Valley, or just the Valley. It is a colossus in sheer size, more than 36,500 square miles of relentlessly flat, sun-baked farmland stretching 465 miles from Redding down to Weed Patch, and sprawling as many as 70 miles wide. More than that, it is a colossus of agriculture, so productive that the near-infinitesimal fraction of it devoted to wine grapes makes it America's Midi – long the source of all the everyday table wine the nation wanted – and its Jerez, Douro, and Madeira as well.

A complete miracle of contradictions, the Central Valley also grows a quarter of the nation's rice, a tenth of its cotton, all of its raisins, olives, and almonds, and nearly all of its canning tomatoes, garlic, nectarines, walnuts, prunes, plums, and lemons. It leads the nation in production of another dozen crops too. And as well as all this, there is quite a lot of oil under Bakersfield.

This is not a homely, picturesque sort of place. Novelist John Steinbeck caught one aspect of it in *The Grapes of Wrath*. The film *American Graffiti* captured a different, more contemporary, side. But art has hardly begun to explain it. Although it has hundreds if not thousands of family farms, the essence of it is Agribusiness, with a capital letter. Big companies do big business to fit a big place. Farm management firms handle thousands of acres for corporate investors, plunging into crops that look promising and racing away from those that go soft in the marketplace.

Wineries keep to the scale. The intensely secretive E. & J. Gallo will not reveal production or sales figures, but its spokesmen do not deny estimates of 55 million cases a year. Its closest rival, Heublein Inc., produces Almaden, Blossom Hill, Inglenook Navalle, and other high-volume wines at Madera, not far from Gallo headquarters at Modesto.

Flat and unbroken as it is, the Central Valley is, technically, two valleys. The Sacramento River Valley stretches from Red Bluff in the north down to Sacramento, while the San Joaquin River Valley reaches north to this town from Bakersfield. From there the joined streams wander as the Sacramento River through a maze of channels and sloughs to San Francisco Bay.

The Merced River in Yosemite National Park, in the Sierra Nevadas.

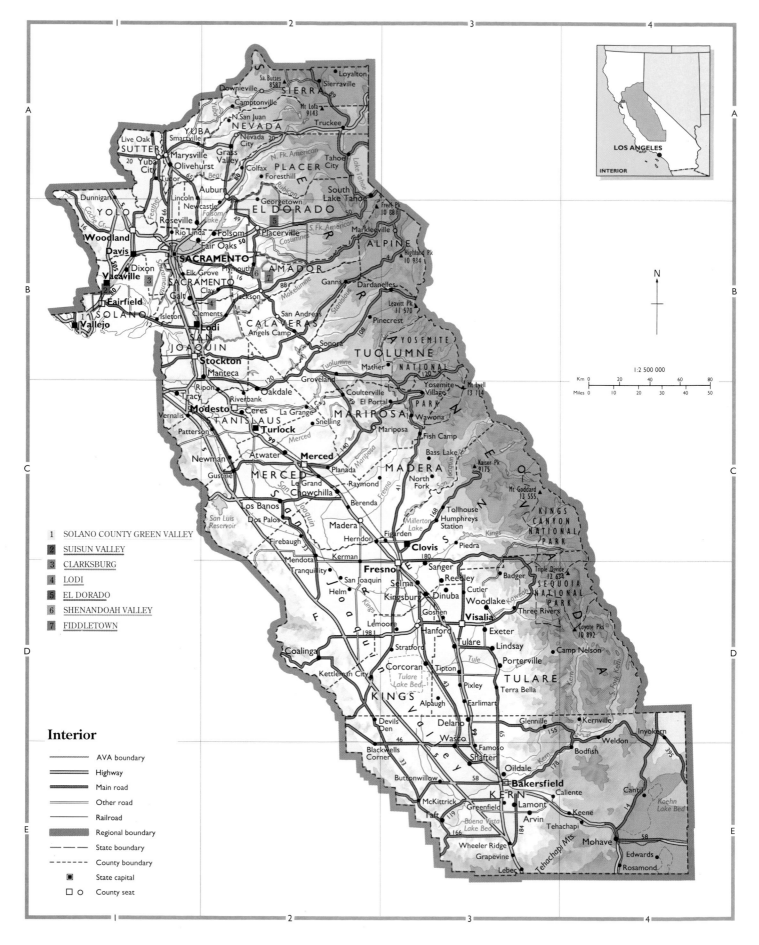

1 SOLANO COUNTY GREEN VALLEY
2 SUISUN VALLEY
3 CLARKSBURG
4 LODI
5 EL DORADO
6 SHENANDOAH VALLEY
7 FIDDLETOWN

Interior

———————	AVA boundary
═══════════	Highway
———————	Main road
———————	Other road
———————	Railroad
▓▓▓▓▓	Regional boundary
— — —	State boundary
- - - -	County boundary
■	State capital
□ ○	County seat

The two valleys mirror each other on a map, but not in some of the details most important to farmers. They share the high, unbroken wall of the Sierra Nevada Mountains as their eastern boundary, and the lower, less regular Coast Ranges delimit them to the west. As a result, in high summer both grow ever hotter and drier toward their upstream ends. They differ in that the Sacramento River Valley sees much more rain earlier in the season. The most dramatic practical effect is that the Sacramento Valley grows the rice, the San Joaquin the raisins.

As a direct consequence of raisins growing where they do, the San Joaquin Valley dominates wine-grape growing as well. The reasons are slightly complicated, but, at heart, all hinge on the grape variety called Thompson Seedless, useful in budget-conscious winemaking and indispensable for raisins.

Almost as soon as grapes came to the Central Valley, in the 1870s, scholars at the University of California partitioned the state's viticulture into two regions: coast and interior. That division, predicated on the nearly complete absence of marine air in the Central Valley, has stuck ever since. After Prohibition, it was reinforced by the coast turning ever more to Cabernet Sauvignon, Chardonnay, and other fine grape varieties while the interior opted for Chenin Blanc, Colombard, Carignane, and other vigorous yielders, and also kept Thompson Seedless foremost in the wineries.

Where marine air is completely absent, in most of the San Joaquin Valley, it is not a place for worrying about fine points of sun and soil because both are homogenous over huge expanses. Neither is irrigation in a rainless land a limitation because two enormous reservoir and canal systems, one state and one federal, capture water from the whole length of the Sierra and deliver it to farmers all along the valley at highly subsidized prices. And so growers put vineyards where they please, with the full expectation of a bumper crop year after year.

The one major exception to complete homogenization of sun and soil is where the Sacramento River has carved through the Coast Ranges, opening a path for sea air to push vigorously inland through the delta, rather less briskly into Lodi.

These roughly adjacent districts differ enough in climate, and perhaps in soil, to grow different grape varieties from hotter points both north and south, and somewhat different varieties from each other. Grapegrowers in them believe enough to have made AVAs of Clarksburg and Lodi. But they have not really distanced themselves from the rest of the valley by making wines that are regionally distinct – at least not enough of them to carve out reputations. Lodi could, with Zinfandel and perhaps with Ruby Cabernet. It might still if enough small growers and winemakers join the larger firms there. Clarksburg has a certain notoriety with its Chenin Blanc, principally because outsiders have pushed that variety forward; but their task is not made easy by a marketplace bent on Cabernet Sauvignon and Chardonnay and nothing else, and hang the provenance.

One completely divorced viticultural district is attached to the Central Valley more or less by default. It is the Sierra Foothills, the site of the Gold Rush of 1849, source of all the history, romance, and individualism missing down on the valley floor, and also a source of unflaggingly distinctive Zinfandels. Growing grapes in El Dorado and Fiddletown and other parts of the Sierra Foothills is as hard as it is easy in Fresno or Madera, sometimes because of terrain, sometimes because of mountain weather, sometimes because of both. Yet stubborn small farmers have persisted since the 1850s, often on the thinnest of hopes. In the 1960s, times were so grim that only

The Crystal Range of the Sierra Nevada Mountains looms above Sierra Vista vineyards in El Dorado County.

one winery survived and all the independent growers watched the grapes they had sold to valley floor wineries at rock-bottom prices disappear into fathomless vats of commodity wines called "Burgundy."

The demand for Sierra Foothills wine picked up markedly with the wine boom of the 1970s, but the rocks are as hard as ever, and the weather as treacherous. If it is tiny, hardly 2,000 acres of vines against 180,000 down on the valley floor, it is still where the thoughts of wine fanciers turn first when they look beyond the coastal counties. So it is with this book.

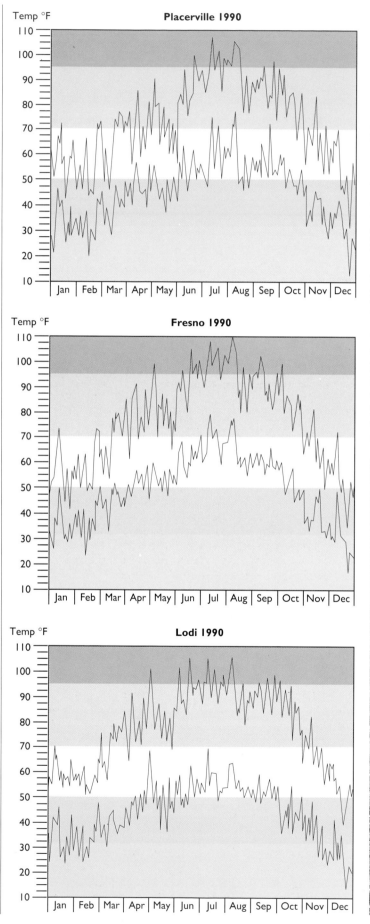

Temp °F — **Placerville 1990**

Temp °F — **Fresno 1990**

Temp °F — **Lodi 1990**

Interior Climate

Fog slips across San Francisco Bay and up the Sacramento River for a short way, weakening with each passing mile. It cools Clarksburg slightly, Lodi even less, and fails to reach to the Sierra Foothills in any consistent pattern or to veer north or south into the vastness of the Central Valley. Where the Coast Ranges at their maximum height and width finally remove fog from the weather pattern, California's two-season climate becomes a full-blown case of a long, relentlessly hot, dry season and a shorter, chilly wet season. To say wet season stretches a point: in many years, damp is more like it, as precipitation levels often dip to the 8-inch level and below. The great expanse of San Joaquin valley floor is nearly homogeneous in rainfall. In the Sacramento Valley it is greater in the north than the south, partly because of winter storm tracks, and partly because it narrows enough for mountains to squeeze rain onto it.

Growing season temperatures, meanwhile, warm from north to south in the San Joaquin Valley, and from south to north in the Sacramento Valley, the extremes of heat being at Bakersfield in the former, Redding in the latter.

While fog does not reach the Sierra Foothills regularly, elevation there produces an almost continental four-season climate. A comparison of the Placerville and Fresno graphs shows what 2,000 feet means over the course of year, especially in the spring and autumn. Frosty nights in winter are not unheard of on the valley floor, but are comparatively rare, and the deep cold of 1990 is a once-in-a-decade event, if that. In the highest Sierra Foothills vineyards, between 2,500 and 3,000 feet, winter snow is annual.

* For the color code to the climate charts see pages 14–15.

Sierra Foothills

California turned Yankee in these foothills after John Marshall discovered gold in Captain John Sutter's millrace on the American River in 1849. Until then it was part of Mexico.

Down in the Coast counties the red clay tile roofs, white stucco walls and rounded arches of Spanish colonial architecture are everywhere. Up in the foothills they hardly exist. Instead the forty-niners and their successors put up false-front wooden buildings and square brick ones that owe their design to Abilene (Kansas) and New Bedford (Massachussetts). Down in the Coast counties the towns are Santa Maria and Los Gatos, Gonzales and Sonoma. In the Gold Country they are Placerville and Fiddletown, Sutter Creek and Jackson. (County names in the foothills are, curiously, all Spanish.)

It is hard to tell whether this is the most Californian part of contemporary California, or the least, for the state has evolved so much and the Gold Country so little. In either case, these foothills are where the defining moment in California's history took place, a legacy to be seen everywhere: in rusting head-frames looming over old mines, in the bed-and-breakfast inn where the bedroom walls are still dented floor to ceiling by

Sierra Nevada run-off keeps ponds full throughout the gentle rolling landscape of Amador County's Shenandoah Valley.

long-gone stacks of gold, and in streets trodden by Mark Twain, Bret Harte, and Ambrose Bierce when they were chronicling the great Gold Rush.

California's state park system keeps a few ghost towns in what it calls "a state of arrested decay." In a way, the whole of the Foothills is in a state of arrested decay, or was until a few years ago when improved roads and an exploding population in Sacramento ended its isolation and started crowding in on its entrenched population.

Grass Valley and a few other towns close to the freeways now look like Anywhere City, but most of the old communities beaded along State Route 49 keep some of the old flavor, or a lot of it. It is no gastronomic capital, no place to go looking for country clubs or luxury hotels. But it is original and honest, and visitors remember it.

Wine in these parts holds up its end of the bargain. It arrived with the forty-niners, or hard on their heels. The old Fossati winery, now Boeger, firmly dates from 1860, when Placerville was known as "Hangtown" after the preferred mode of local justice. Swiss-born Adam Uhlinger started a cellar at about the same time in the Shenandoah Valley near Plymouth, with vines he planted in 1856. Three casks Uhlinger hewed from local oaks still exist in a small wine museum on his old property, now Sobon Estate. They held wine until a few years ago, although not advisedly.

By the 1870s the Foothills may have had as many as 100 wineries to slake the miners' gargantuan thirsts, many more than Sonoma or Napa had at the same time.

What the forty-niners drank was, surely, Zinfandel; ancient vineyards in Amador County are of that variety and almost no other. And to judge by Uhlinger's casks and other bits and pieces of evidence, it was the kind of wine that would light fires in the gullets of bone-weary miners in the chill of winter as readily as the heat of summer. The results of modern refinements are hearty enough to leave no doubts.

Among the modern refinements in Gold Country wine are distinctions between the vineyards. A blanket Sierra Foothills AVA takes in not only the core counties of Amador and El Dorado, but reaches south into Calaveras, Mariposa, and Tuolumne, and north into Nevada, Placer, and Yuba. Within that generous framework come the El Dorado, Fiddletown, California Shenandoah Valley, and North Yuba AVAs.

White Wine Varieties

Chardonnay (0 in Amador in 1970, 32 acres in 1990; 0 in El Dorado in 1970, 52 acres in 1990)

Chardonnay from the loftier vineyards in El Dorado County bears closer resemblance to that from the warmer parts of Napa and Sonoma than one might expect. It is ripe and round, with enough vineyard flavors to withstand some time in oak – as Sierra Vista and, especially, Lava Cap have shown over several recent vintages. Stevenot Chardonnays from estate grapes

173

This relic, one of the ways visitors know they are in a part of the Old West, crowns an endpost in an Amador vineyard.

have revealed much the same balance and character.

As their slight acreage indicates, the Sierra Foothills Chardonnays are relatively few. The range of styles makes generalizations even harder.

Chenin Blanc (0 in Amador in 1970, 6 acres in 1990; 2 acres in El Dorado in 1970, 25 in 1990)
A rarity in bottle under any Sierra Foothill appellation, it has shown best as a dry wine from Granite Springs.

Sauvignon Blanc (0 in Amador in 1970, 232 acres in 1990; 0 in El Dorado in 1970, 92 acres in 1990)
Shenandoah Valley Sauvignon Blancs lean toward the blowsy perfumes of sweet flowers, even sweet hay on the way to drying. The balance is big and soft, varying almost to weighty. Amador Foothill and Shenandoah Vineyard typify the style, which is near perfect for pepper-hot Mexican and Thai dishes. Every now and again someone will sacrifice the aromas for lighter, crisper wine.

In El Dorado the variety tends to be understated in flavor, and somewhat lighter in body than its counterparts from Amador, although not much. Boeger, which blends in a proportion of Sémillon, consistently produces an attractive, well-balanced Sauvignon.

Other varieties
Muscat Blanc (19 acres in Amador) rarely seen as a varietal; Riesling (12 acres in El Dorado) has been dry and firm to outright hard from Madrona; Sémillon (15 acres in Amador, 5 in El Dorado) is made only by Gerwer; Viognier (2 acres in El Dorado) is in its earliest try-out time.

Red Wine Varieties

Barbera (0 in Amador in 1970, 15 acres in 1990; 8 acres in El Dorado in 1970, 19 in 1990)
Piedmont's workhorse variety has been hugely planted in the San Joaquin Valley because it holds acidity so well in warm to hot growing conditions. That lesson has not been entirely lost on Foothills growers who find themselves with over-fat Cabernet Sauvignon.

Both Santino and Montevina have long histories of making full-bodied, well-ripened Barbera wines with light to vigorous touches of oak. Their examples have led to expanded interest in Amador. El Dorado and Calaveras both have growers with trial plantings in the ground.

Cabernet Sauvignon (0 in Amador in 1970, 46 acres in 1990; 1 acre in El Dorado in 1970, 57 in 1990)
With the United States market fixated on Cabernet Sauvignon, every winery in every climate hopes to do well with the variety.

The Foothills grow it well enough for the acreage to keep climbing; sales too are increasing. The pattern follows that of every other variety: wines from the higher, cooler vineyards in El Dorado can come very close in character and quality to those of Sonoma and Mendocino, especially in milder years. Sierra Vista shows this most often. The Stevenot Vineyard in Calaveras produces wines with even greater similarities to

coastal Cabernets. Lower down, in warmer zones, the Cabernets turn out fat and faintly port-like in flavor, not classic, perhaps, but not unpleasant company at the table. Shenandoah Vineyards exemplifies Amador.

Petite Sirah (0 in Amador in 1970, 2 acres in 1990; 0 in El Dorado in 1970, 10 acres in 1990)
It is difficult if not impossible to form a clear picture of Foothills Petite Sirahs because so few have been made. However, what evidence exists says the grape echoes Zinfandel more than it does not, producing bright, fresh wines in some of the higher reaches of El Dorado County (Granite Springs), bold to outright heady ones in the Shenandoah Valley (Karly).

Zinfandel (373 acres in Amador in 1970, 1,094 in 1990; 6 acres in El Dorado in 1970, 142 in 1990)
This, beyond all argument, is the great, proven grape variety of the Foothills, from end to end.

History and acreage give Amador County center stage, where it gladly plays. Shenandoah Valley and Fiddletown Zinfandels have sometimes astonishingly intense flavors of the ripest berries, most especially when the wines come from shy-bearing graybeard vineyards such as Grandpère, Eschen, Ferrero, and others at or near the century mark in age. Mere stripplings of 40 to 60 years, Baldinelli and Story prominent among them, tend to be slightly more modest in their dimensions, perhaps because the crops are at least marginally larger and the vines more vigorous.

The *cognoscenti* argue about whether to drink Amador Zinfandels young or keep them until they start to dodder just a bit. The debate will not be resolved. Some find greater pleasure in younger and fresher wines where Zinfandel's berrylike flavors stand foremost, most prominently from cool vintages. Others dote on the sun-dried flavors and softened tannins that emerge only with time, and most forcefully from warm seasons. One thing is certain: the alcohols are enough to keep any well-made example of these Zinfandels sound over a very long span of years.

If there is a problem with Shenandoah Valley and Fiddletown Zinfandels, in fact, it is in keeping alcohol from upstaging all the other players in the scene. Its prominence only afflicts city people and others of frail constitution; locals do not seem to want it any other way, especially when the chill and damp of winter set in.

Zinfandel vineyards in other counties, especially El Dorado, seem less inclined to produce such ultraripe, heady wines, higher elevations appearing to ripen Zinfandel fully with fewer raisined berries, hence less sugar. Even with this advantage, wines from cooler growing seasons show more deft balance and subtler flavors. Sierra Vista and Boeger show the way. As in most varieties, Calaveras Zinfandel almost mirrors El Dorado. Stevenot Vineyard's estate-bottled Reserves could hardly be improved either in the drinking or as models of their region.

Nevada City Winery's Nevada County Zinfandel appears to go one better than El Dorado County: in both flavor and balance recent vintages have more resembled Zinfandels from Sonoma's Russian River Valley and the ridges above Anderson Valley in Mendocino than other Foothills wines.

No Foothills winemaker is afraid of oak with Zinfandel. It takes an unbridled enthusiasm to obliterate its flavor. It has been done, but not often.

175

Side issue: there appeared, as of 1992, to be a trend away from White Zinfandel in favor of Zinfandel Nouveau. At least three wineries had made the switch, and two others were in the middle of changing over.

Benchmarks:

Stevenot Calaveras. **Boeger** El Dorado. **Granite Springs** El Dorado. **Nevada City** Nevada County. **Sutter Home** Amador County (*see* page 58). **Baldinelli** Shenandoah Valley. **Karly** Shenandoah Valley. **Santino** Shenandoah Valley.

Other varieties

Mission (20 acres in Amador) comes to a peak in a Harbor Winery dessert wine called "Mission del Sol;" Sangiovese (9 acres in Amador) has appeared under a grower label Noceto, and is in the trial stage at Montevina; Syrah (1 acre in El Dorado) has graduated from tryout to permanent status at Sierra Vista, although quantities will remain tiny for a few years.

The long rolls leading up to Lava Cap's winery buildings are indeed part of an outcrop of lava in El Dorado County, one of very few in a region where most soils are granitic.

El Dorado AVA

Established: November 14, 1983
Total area: 414,100 acres
Area in vineyard: 442 acres
Wineries: 11
Principal town: Placerville

El Dorado takes Sierra Foothill winegrowing to a different level. Vineyards range from 2,400 up to 3,000 feet, 1,000 feet higher than any of their neighbors, or more.

Although the appellation boundaries take in a huge territory north of Placerville all the way to the Nevada County border, the vineyards cling to a straight line from Placerville south to Amador County – where the El Dorado, Shenandoah Valley and Fiddletown AVAs meet along the Cosumnes River.

The relatively tight clustering of vines and wineries makes things look slightly more orderly than they are. El Dorado's highest vineyard, 3,000 feet up on Apple Hill, rises far enough above the valley's heat for Gewürztraminer to behave decently. Granite Springs and other vineyards near the opposite end of the chain sit at about 2,400 feet. These properties near Fair

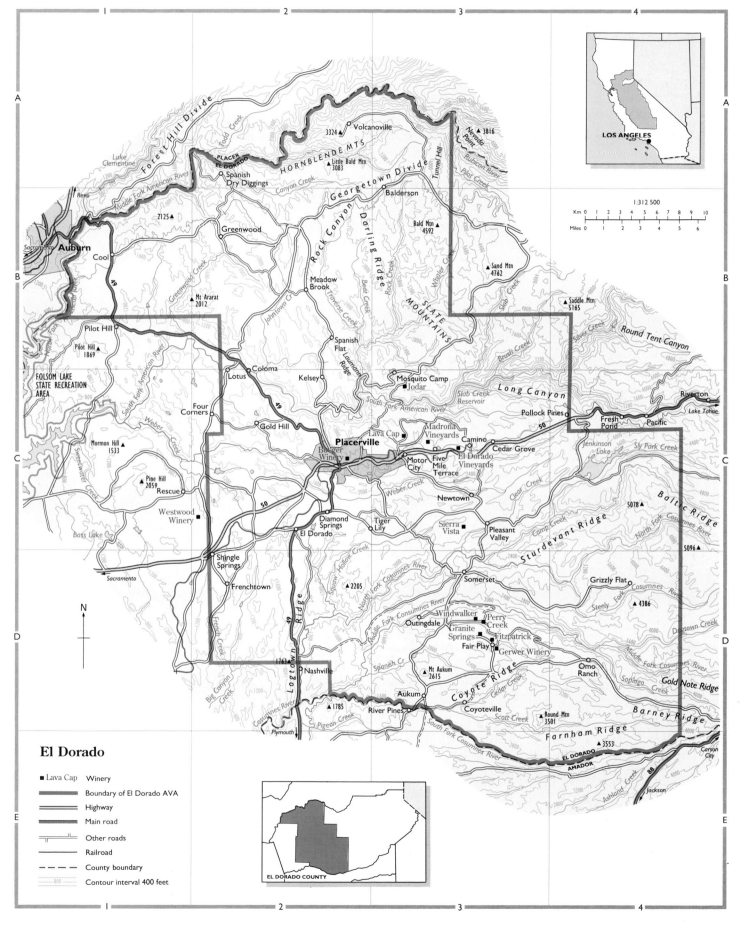

LOS ANGELES

1:312 500

Km 0 1 2 3 4 5 6 7 8 9 10
Miles 0 1 2 3 4 5 6

Forest Hill Divide

3324 ▲ Volcanoville

HORNBLENDE MTS

Nevada
Point ▲ 3816

PLACER
EL DORADO

Spanish
Dry Diggings

Little Bald Mtn
3083

Georgetown Divide

Tunnel Hill

Rubicon River

Pilot Creek

Lake
Clementine

Reno

Balderson

7125 ▲

Greenwood

Bald Mtn
4592

Auburn

Sacramento

Cool

49

SLATE

Sand Mtn
4762

Saddle Mtn
5165

Round Tent Canyon

Meadow
Brook

▲ Mt Ararat
2012

Pilot Hill

MOUNTAINS

Darling Ridge

Rock Canyon

Pilot Hill
1869

Spanish
Flat

Silver Creek

Long Canyon

Riverton

FOLSOM LAKE
STATE RECREATION
AREA

Lotus

Coloma

Kelsey

Laumann Ridge

Mosquito Camp
Jodar

Slab Creek
Reservoir

South Fork American River

Pollock Pines

Fresh
Pond

Pacific

Lake Tahoe

Jenkinson
Lake

Sly Park Creek

Four
Corners

Mormon Hill
1533

Gold Hill

49

Lava Cap

Madrona
Vineyards

Camino

Cedar Grove

El Dorado
Vineyards

Baltic Ridge

Placerville

Boeger
Winery

Motor
City

Five
Mile
Terrace

5078 ▲

Pine Hill
2059

Rescue

Weber Creek

Clear Creek

North Fork Cosumnes River

Newtown

Westwood
Winery

50

Sierra
Vista

Pleasant
Valley

Camp Creek

5096 ▲

Sturdevant Ridge

Bass Lake

Diamond
Springs

Tiger
Lily

Grizzly Flat

4386 ▲

El Dorado

Somerset

Steely

Cosumnes River

Shingle
Springs

▲ 2205

North Fork Cosumnes River

Sacramento

Frenchtown

Middle Fork Cosumnes River

Windwalker
Outingdale
Granite
Springs

Perry
Creek

Fitzpatrick

Gerwer Winery

Omo
Ranch

Dogtown Creek

Fair Play

Gold Note Ridge

N

49

Logtown Ridge

French Creek

1763 ▲

Nashville

Spanish Cr.

Mt Aukum
2615

Coyote Ridge

Cedar Creek

Middle Fork Cosumnes River

Big Canyon Creek

▲ 1785

Aukum

River Pines

Coyoteville

Scott Creek

Round Mtn
3501

Barney Ridge

Plymouth

Pigeon Creek

South Fork Cosumnes River

Farnham Ridge

Sopiago Creek

Carson
City

▲ 3553

EL DORADO
AMADOR

88

Ashland Creek

Jackson

El Dorado

■ Lava Cap Winery

━━━ Boundary of El Dorado AVA

═══ Highway

━━━ Main road

┴┬┴ Other roads

─── Railroad

- - - County boundary

〰️800 Contour interval 400 feet

EL DORADO COUNTY

Play appear to favor varieties from warmer origins, including the Rhône.

Apple Hill really is a hill full of apple orchards with vineyards tucked in here and there. If Gewürztraminer is possible, so is Zinfandel of a character not distant from that of the Russian River or Anderson Valley. These extremes leave most of the other varieties familiar in California as candidates for attention from growers and winemakers. Wineries on the hill have little history to go by. Boeger and Madrona are the old-timers, with founding dates in the mid-1970s.

Lower down and farther south, around Somerset and Fair Play, trial plantings spurred deepening interest in Syrah, Viognier, and other Rhône varieties as the 1990s were getting under way. Though most local growers and producers have succumbed to the twin temptations of Chardonnay and Cabernet Sauvignon, a handful of mavericks are sticking with Petite Sirah, Ruby Cabernet, and Chenin Blanc. Sierra Vista and Granite Springs have the longest, steadiest track records here. While Rhône types have been the object of intense interest in these areas for several years, Italian varieties are now almost as trendy, Sangiovese and Nebbiolo foremost among them. Little or no crossover exists; wineries choose one or the other.

To the east of the AVA, terrain immediately becomes too steep and rocky to cultivate, and too cold for grapes. West of the chain of vineyards, lower elevations absorb too much valley heat to produce distinctive wines. Lava Cap, as its name promises, sits on the cap of an old lava flow. However, nearly all of El Dorado's vineyards grow in decomposed or decomposing granite. Some of them, though, Granite Springs for one, thread their way between or around pond-sized outcrops of composed-looking granite.

California Shenandoah Valley AVA

Established: January 29, 1983
Total area: 10,000 acres
Area in vineyard: 1,200 acres
Wineries: 12
Principal town: None (Plymouth adjacent)

To satisfy the legalities of the AVA, this little valley must be called California Shenandoah Valley to make sure no consumer confuses it with the Shenandoah Valley in Virginia. Do not expect this mistake to happen. Until the earth swaps magnetic poles or leaves its orbit, Virginia will never grow the dark, assertively tannic, slightly sun-dried, mildly heady Zinfandel that is the history of this small fold in the Sierra Nevadas.

Esola and Grandpère, among other vineyards in the Shenandoah Valley, still have Zinfandel plantings from the 1860s and 1870s – as records reveal. When Amador hit bottom in the late 1950s and early 1960s, it had 370 acres of Zinfandel and very little else. In comparatively prosperous 1990, Zinfandel accounted for 1,100 out of 1,500 acres in the county. In short, Zinfandel has defined the valley as a winegrowing district from the Gold Rush days until now.

Zinfandelists could fear a weakening of its grip. Years ago

Now Sobon Estate, this old cellar-cum-museum began in the 1850s as Adam Uhlinger's winery, and later became d'Agostini.

Fiddletown AVA

Established: November 3, 1983
Total area: 11,500 acres
Area in vineyard: 310 acres
Wineries: None
Principal town: Fiddletown

This AVA finishes what the Shenandoah Valley starts, taking Zinfandel into higher, rougher country farther east until arable land runs out, or spring frosts make vines a practical impossibility. Growers estimate that no more than another 1,000 acres can be planted. Although this appellation pushes the climatic boundaries for Zinfandel harder than the Shenandoah Valley, somehow the wines come out in much the same vein: dark, port-ripe to faintly raisiny, firmly tannic, decidedly heady with alcohol. Because the appellation has no winery of its own, lovers of large-scale Zinfandels know the area first for the Eschen vineyard. From its ancient vines have come a number of stunning wines under the Amador Foothill, Santino, and other labels. Another baker's dozen of growers falls within the boundaries, all of them focused on Zinfandel, several of them still tilling very old fields, none of them regularly identified on labels.

Here and there the Sierra Foothills provide forceful reminders of their granite underpinnings.

Monteviña planted Barbera and Nebbiolo; since Sutter Home bought the winery in 1988, it has launched trials of Sangiovese and several other Italian varieties. Santino also has looked to Italy, mainly for Barbera. Karly has an affection for Petite Sirah. Sobon Estate is taking a hard look at Cabernet Franc. A couple of growers have small blocks of traditional port varieties. There has even been an interest in Sauvignon Blanc, which old-time residents look upon as something for the newcomers who commute to Sacramento, and who have not yet toughened up enough to handle a serious Foothills Zinfandel.

Bet on it: Zinfandel is the grape of the future here. The soils, homogeneous clay loams derived from Sierra granites, lend themselves to it. The climate is steady in a swathe that sticks very close to 1,100 feet elevation, high enough for cooler nights than Sacramento's but not cooler days, just the ticket for making it dark and juicy and fully ripe.

The very name Sierra Foothills paints a picture of tough, wiry vines clinging to rocky pitches. Shenandoah Valley, on the other hand, sounds soft and bucolic. Shenandoah Valley wins. No towns and few roads disturb the quiet. Sheep mow the grass between vine rows during the dormant season, and are retired to rolling meadows before the vine leaves begin to unfold. Woodpeckers drill holes in the fence posts all summer and squirrels stuff them full of acorns all autumn. The valley's dozen or so wineries welcome guests quietly.

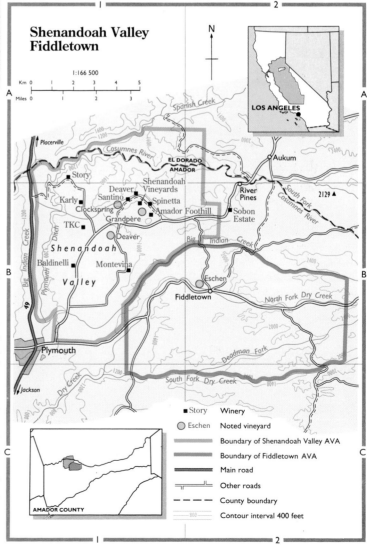

179

North Yuba AVA

Established: August 30, 1985
Total area: 17,500 acres
Area in vineyard: 365 acres
Wineries: 1
Principal town: None (Marysville nearby)

North Yuba is a one-vineyard, one-winery appellation developed by the Renaissance Winery. Its vineyards drape across soft hills on the first rise above the Sacramento Valley floor. The site is as beautiful as any in California, but warm temperatures in the region thus far have produced soft, plummy-to-pruney wines in every variety. Early vintages of Petite Sirah approached portstyle in flavor and weight; Sauvignon Blancs and Rieslings have been similarly weighty, somewhat raisiny, and quick to fade in vintages up to the end of 1989. Cabernet Sauvignon has come to dominate plantings, but as it was planted later, has yet to make its statement.

Calaveras County

Winegrowing has begun to thrive around the Calaveras County town of Murphys – otherwise distinguished mainly by an old hotel where Ulysses S. Grant and Mark Twain took rooms on their travels through.

Calaveras was a major vinegrowing region in Twain's day, but vineyards faded to extinction before Prohibition, not to be revived until Stevenot Winery launched a renaissance in 1978. Still much the largest producer in the county, it now has five cellars for company. Kautz Ironstone Vineyards is fair-sized, Indian Rock small, Black Sheep, Chatom, and Milliaire tiny.

In all, Calaveras vineyards totalled 190 acres in 1990. Zinfandel accounted for 49, Chardonnay for 42, Cabernet Sauvignon for 26. Virtually all the county's vineyards grow these three. Chatom Vineyards, with 65 acres, is also trying Sauvignon Blanc, Sémillon, Sangiovese, and several port varieties. The Kautz family is growing Bordeaux's whole starting five, Australian Shiraz, and Symphony in its 70 acres. Indian Creek is looking into Charbono. There is no track record for any of the newcomers yet.

Other Foothills counties

Vineyards and wineries are even sparser in other Foothills counties than they are in Calaveras. However, some of the adventuresome efforts in Nevada County's 127 acres (with 60 Chardonnay, 24 Cabernet Sauvignon, 10 Merlot) and Mariposa's 30 (12 of it Zinfandel in 1990) suggest that worthy wines can be made in them.

Nevada City Winery in Nevada County, Butterfly Creek in Mariposa, and Sonora Port Works in Sonora are the primary producers.

Shenandoah Vineyards winery and tasting room doubles as one of the Gold Rush country's busiest art galleries.

AMADOR COUNTY PRODUCERS

Amador Foothill Winery (1980) 12500 Steiner Road, Plymouth, CA 95669. Tel (209) 245-6307. 10,000 cases. Bold, firm Zinfandels, some vineyard designated, head the list. Sauvignon Blancs are ripe, fat, best young.

Argonaut Winery (1976) 13657 Mt Echo Drive, Ione, CA 95640. Tel (209) 274-4106. 1,500 cases. Sturdy to rustic Barbera and Zinfandel from local grapes.

Baldinelli Vineyards (1979) 10801 Dickson Road, Plymouth, CA 95669. Tel (209) 245-3398. 16,000 cases. Zinfandel and Cabernet Sauvignon from 70 estate acres are subtle by Foothills standards. The Sauvignon Blanc is regionally typical.

Deaver Vineyards (1990) 12455 Steiner Road, Plymouth, CA 95669. Tel (209) 245-6661. 500 cases.

A long-time grower focusing on Zinfandel from vineyard first planted in 1852.

Greenstone Winery (1981) Highway 88 at Jackson Valley Road, Ione, CA 95640. Tel (209) 274-2238. 10,000 cases. From 80 acres at the very first slopes of the foothills and bought-in grapes, Chenin Blanc, Colombard, Muscat Canelli, and the blended Zinfandel-Syrah.

Karly (1980) 11076 Bell Road, Plymouth, CA 95669. Tel (209) 245-3922. 11,000 cases. These old-vines Zinfandels are no shrinking violets, but they have balance and polish, as does an estate Petite Sirah. Sauvignon Blanc shows an occasional turn of speed.

Monteviña Winery (1973) 20680 Shenandoah School Road, Plymouth, CA 95669. Tel (209) 245-6942. 60,000 cases. Founded to explore the range of Zinfandel, it

Right: Boeger Winery uses the 1850s Fossati winery as its tasting room. The picnic tables overlook vineyards.

wandered aimlessly in the 1980s until Napa's Sutter Home Winery bought it in 1988, restored Zinfandel to eminence, and renewed vigorous attention to Italian varieties, especially Nebbiolo and Sangiovese.

Noceto (1990)
10901 Shenandoah Road, Plymouth, CA 95669. Tel (209) 245-6556. 250 cases. A grower-label is off to a pleasing start with Sangiovese.

Santino Winery (1979)
12225 Steiner Road, Plymouth, CA 95669. Tel (209) 245-6979. 35,000 cases. Vigorous, well-oaked Zinfandels, some blended, some from individual vineyards (especially century-old Grandpère), are foremost. A sturdy to heady Barbera and Rhône-inspired "Satyricon" amplify the red list. The White Zinfandel is a model.

Shenandoah Vineyards (1977)
12300 Steiner Road, Plymouth, CA 95669. Tel (209) 245-4455. 35,000 cases. From 167 acres in several Shenandoah Valley and Fiddletown parcels, Zinfandel, Sauvignon Blanc. More attention than most to port-style wines and Muscats.

Charles Spinetta Winery (1984)
12557 Steiner Road, Plymouth, CA 95669. Tel (209) 235-3384. 4,500 cases. Estate Chenin Blanc and Zinfandel from 30 acres' anchor production. Estate Barbera is in the works.

Sobon Estate (1989)
14430 Shenandoah Road, Plymouth, CA 95669. Tel (209) 245-6555. 3,000 cases. In the buildings of the pioneering d'Agostini winery, the owners of Shenandoah Vineyards have established a museum of local winemaking and a look-ahead label exploring Cabernet Franc, Syrah, and other varietals new to Amador.

Stoneridge Winery (1975)
13862 Ridge Road, Sutter Creek, CA 95685. Tel (209) 223-1761. 1,000 cases. Family owners have particular fondness for hearty, home-style Ruby Cabernet and Zinfandel from tiny local vineyards including their own 6 acres.

Story Vineyard (1973)
10525 Bell Road, Plymouth, CA 95669. Tel (209) 245-6208. 5,000 cases. A mature but not ancient Zinfandel vineyard has yielded attractively-balanced, flavorful wines, especially in cooler vintages.

T.K.C. Vineyards (1981)
11001 Valley Drive, Plymouth, CA 95669. Tel (209) 245-6428. 1,500 cases. Well-oaked Zinfandels by a weekend winemaker.

EL DORADO COUNTY PRODUCERS

Boeger Winery (1972)
1709 Carson Road, Placerville, CA 95667. Tel (916) 622-8094. 12,000 cases. From 60 acres of vines on Apple Hill come some of the Sierra Foothills' most polished, stylish wines. Merlot is the flagship; Cabernet Sauvignon and Zinfandel press it to head the list. Barbera, Sangiovese, Nebbiolo and Refosco are in the works. Also: Sauvignon Blanc, Chardonnay.

El Dorado Vineyards (1977)
3551 Carson Road, Camino, CA 95709. Tel (916) 622-7689. 800 cases.

Fitzpatrick Winery (1980)
7740 Fairplay Road, Somerset, CA 95684. Tel (209) 245-3248. 4,000 cases. The owners grow and buy grapes for a wide range of wines. Sturdy, steady Zinfandel, Cabernet Sauvignon (estate), and a Sauvignon Blanc "Eire Ban" are regionally typical.

Gerwer Winery (1980)
8221 Stoney Creek Road, Somerset, CA 95684. Tel (209) 245-3467. 5,000 cases. Rustic to outright homemade wines are of interest for including offbeat varietals: Ruby Cabernet, Sémillon, Petite Sirah, all anchored in 20 estate acres. There is also a Cabernet Sauvignon.

winery buys Foothills grapes to make Zinfandel, Cabernet Sauvignon, and Sauvignon Blanc.

Butterfly Creek (1986)
4063 Triangle Road, Mariposa, CA 95338. Tel (209) 966-2097. 2,500 cases. Pinot Blanc from 17 estate acres in Mariposa is the pride of this regional pioneer winery.

Chatom Vineyards (1991)
PO Box 2730, Murphys, CA 95247. Tel (209) 736-6500. 5,500 cases. The estate winery produces fully oaked Cabernet Sauvignon, Merlot, Zinfandel, Chardonnay, and Sauvignon Blanc from 65-acre vineyard 14 miles north of Murphys, Calaveras County.

Madrona Vineyards is the highest in Eldorado County at 3,000 feet.

Gold Hill (1986)
5660 Vineyard Lane, Placerville, CA 95667. Tel (916) 626-6522. 5,000 cases. Estate Cabernet Sauvignon, Merlot, and Chardonnay from 35 acres dominate production.

Granite Springs Winery (1981)
6060 Granite Springs Road, Somerset, CA 95684. Tel (209) 245-6395. 10,000 cases. Petite Sirah is the favorite in a rocky vineyard also planted with Cabernet Sauvignon, Sauvignon Blanc, and Zinfandel. Chenin Blanc comes from a neighbor. The winemaking is forthright.

Jodar (1990)
2393 Gravel Road, Placerville, CA 95667. Tel (916) 626-4582. 2,000 cases. The first 8 of a potential 30 estate acres push El Dorado plantings farther north than they have been, into an area called Swansboro Country. The debut wines are Chardonnay and Cabernet Sauvignon.

Lava Cap Winery (1986)
2221 Fruitridge Road, Placerville, CA 95667. Tel (916) 621-0175. 5,000 cases. One of the consistently stylish producers in the region draws on 23 estate acres of Chardonnay, Sauvignon Blanc, Cabernet Sauvignon, and Zinfandel that do indeed grow on a cap of lava, well up on Apple Hill.

Madrona Vineyards (1980)
PO Box 454, Camino, CA 95709. Tel (916) 644-5948. 10,000 cases. Sturdy more than refined White Riesling, Gewürztraminer, Chardonnay, Cabernet Sauvignon, Merlot, and Zinfandel come from an attention-grabbing vineyard reaching 3,000 feet.

Perry Creek Vineyards (1989)
7364 Perry Creek Road, Somerset, CA 95684. Tel (209) 245-5450. 4,000 cases. In 50 try-everything estate acres near Fairplay are planted Cabernet Sauvignon, Cabernet Franc, Merlot, Zinfandel, Syrah, Nebbiolo, Viognier, Sangiovese, and Muscat Canelli.

Sierra Vista Winery (1977)
4560 Cabernet Way, Placerville, CA 95667. Tel (916) 622-7221. 8,000 cases. The proprietors own 28 acres at the winery and lease another 13 nearby. Chardonnay, Cabernet Sauvignon, and Zinfandel dominate the plantings, but a range of Rhône varieties led by Syrah now command attention. The winemaking is consistent, the wines attractive.

Westwood Winery (1984)
3100 Ponderosa Road, Shingle Springs, CA 95682. Tel (916) 666-6079. 4,000 cases. Produces Reserve and regular Chardonnay and Pinot Noir from broad range of sources, but the focus increasingly is on Syrah and Italian varieties grown in El Dorado.

Windwalker (1990)
7360 Perry Creek Road, Somerset, CA 95684. Tel (209) 245-4054. 3,000 cases. 8 acres yield estate Cabernet Sauvignon, Chardonnay, and Chenin Blanc; Zinfandel from bought-in grapes.

OTHER PRODUCERS
(not mapped)

Black Sheep Vintners (1987)
PO Box 1851, Murphys, CA 95247. Tel (209) 728-2157. 1,000 cases. The

Below: John McCready, owner of well-named Sierra Vista (right).

Indian Rock Vineyard (1987) 1154 Pennsylvania Gulch Road, Murphys, CA 95247. Tel (209) 728-2266. 3,000 cases. The owners of 50 acres east of Murphys in Calaveras County were evolving from grower label to estate winery as their vines matured in the early 1990s. Chardonnay was joined by Cabernet Sauvignon, Merlot, and Charbono with the 1993s.

Kautz Ironstone Vineyards (1988) PO Box 2263, Murphys, CA 95247. Tel (209) 278-1251. 25,000 cases. Long-time major growers in Lodi built a winery next to 70 estate acres at Murphys, Calaveras County. They

released their first Calaveras Symphony in 1992.

Milliaire (1983) PO Box 1554, Murphys, CA 95247. Tel (209) 728-1658. 1,000 cases. The busman's holiday winery of Steve and Elizabeth Millier gives the long-time Foothills enologist a chance to make personally styled Cabernet Sauvignon, Zinfandel, and Chardonnay from selected Calaveras, Amador, and El Dorado vineyards.

Nevada City (1980) 321 Spring Street, Nevada City, CA 95959. Tel (916) 265-9463. 6,000 cases. The northernmost Foothills winery produces consistently attrac-

tive Zinfandel and sometimes intriguing Pinot Noir from local grapes.

Renaissance (1982) PO Box 1000, Renaissance, CA 95962. Tel (916) 692-2222. 12,000 cases. Communal society dedicated to collecting and producing fine and applied arts has planted almost 365 acres in Yuba County northeast of Marysville, especially Cabernet Sauvignon and Sauvignon Blanc, also Riesling and Petite Sirah.

Sonora Winery and Port Works (1986) PO Box 242, Sonora, CA 95370. Tel (209) 532-7678. 2,000 cases. The focal point is port-style wine from traditional varieties grown in Amador

and Calaveras. There are also heady, rustic Zinfandels, one from Foothills sources.

Stevenot (1978) PO Box 345, Murphys, CA 95247. Tel (209) 728-3436. 60,000 cases. The volume leader in Calaveras County buying grapes elsewhere for several wines, but Chardonnay, Cabernet Sauvignon, and Zinfandel labeled "Grand Reserve" come from 27 estate acres. All 3 speak particularly well of their region.

Travel Information

The Sierra Foothills, especially the areas where the wineries are, is lightly settled enough that bed and breakfast inns are much more common than major hostelries. Two wineries, Fitzpatrick and Perry Creek, have their own. (The chambers of commerce under Useful Addresses have long lists.)

Placerville started out as Hangtown, but renamed itself after a mining process as local society grew more refined. On freeway US 50, it is centrally located for El Dorado County's wineries.

Sacramento California's state capital has shed an old image of gray, faceless government town that tourists deliberately bypassed. Not only does it have fine restaurants and hotels, but also some striking museums of California history, most notably including the State Railroad Museum (in Old Town at 2d and I) which takes the age of steam from Tom Thumbs to behemoths. Sutter's Fort (2701 L Street) is a life-size pioneer community; on the same grounds is the revealing State Indian Museum. The Crocker Museum (216 O Street) is at its best for a small but intelligent collection of 18th- and 19th-century European painting. This urban oasis is an hour or less

Beatiful Emerald Bay lies off Lake Tahoe.

from the rustic charms of both El Dorado and Shenandoah Valley vineyard districts.

Sutter Creek A short main street keeps some of the frontier flavor in its architecture and above all its bars. This is in many ways the social headquarters for Amador County.

HOTELS AND RESTAURANTS

Biba 2801 Capitol Avenue, Sacramento. Tel (916) 455-2422. Splendid northern Italian cuisine in an airy, sunny room made more so by Biba Caggiano herself.

Chinois East/West 2232 Fair Oaks Boulevard, Sacramento. Tel (916) 648-1961. Just what the name implies, a cross-cultural melding of both ingredients and styles.

Zachary Jacques 1821 Pleasant Valley Road, Placerville. Tel (916) 626-8045. Country French, by a French family that knows what it is doing.

GOLD COUNTRY WINE ROUTE

State Route 49 neatly ties together most of the wineries in Amador and El Dorado counties, but the more enchanting route is the county road called Shenandoah Road in Amador, Mt Aukum Road, and then Snows Road

Above: The Gold Rush of '49 began a few hundred yards from here.

in El Dorado. The Shenandoah and Mt Aukum segments pass through sometimes bucolic, sometimes wooded countryside, and stick close to the wineries. The Snows Road portion offers some of the most dramatic scenery as it climbs to Camino at the top of Apple Hill.

USEFUL ADDRESSES

Amador County Chamber of Commerce
PO Box 596, Jackson, CA 95642. Tel (209) 223-0350.

Amador Vintners Association
c/o Amador County Chamber of Commerce (*see above*).

El Dorado County Chamber of Commerce
542 Main Street, Placerville, CA 95667. Tel (916) 621-5885.

El Dorado Winery Association
PO Box 1614, Placerville, CA 95667. Tel (916) 622-8094.

Sacramento Convention and Visitors Bureau
1421 K Street, Sacramento, CA 95814. Tel (916) 449-6711.

The Central Valley

The genius of the place as a producer of wines has been its willingness to expend prodigies of energy on making cheap red and white consistently sound and in a style the American drinking public finds agreeable.

Its size and essential homogeneity of sun and soil exactly suit it to the task. If a broad-scaled map suggests that the great Central Valley will not have many internal divisions, so will one far more intimate in scale, especially from Sacramento south. River-cooled, fog-cooled Lodi and Clarksburg have developed enough individual identity to be taken separately from the rest of the huge San Joaquin Valley that holds them, but only just.

The surest measure of Lodi's status is that several of the largest wineries from farther south in the San Joaquin Valley maintain memberships in its winery association, as do a couple of well-known names from Napa and Sonoma. The next surest measure is that none of them limits itself to grapes from the region, but rather blends Lodi with other regions closer to home.

Within the vastness of it all, a half dozen to a dozen large to huge wineries use much the most of 190,000 acres of wine grapes, and varying proportions of another 260,000 acres of Thompson Seedless. Several wineries of sizes that would be staggering, were it not for Gallo and Heublein, have no public face at all, but sell all of their wine in bulk to others with labels.

In addition to being prodigious farm land, the Central Valley is also populous enough to have three cities – Bakersfield, Modesto, and Stockton – of more than 100,000 population, and two, Fresno and Sacramento, with more than 250,000. The state's two great schools of viticulture and enology are in the valley, on the campuses of the University of California at Davis and Fresno State University.

Lodi excepted, sheer daunting size and the scarceness of wineries with visitor facilities makes the San Joaquin less than an enchanting place for enophiles to visit only to see wine, but if other reasons take one to it, a detour or two can be as illuminating as any look at smaller, more romantic districts.

White Wine Varieties

Although acreages devoted to Chardonnay and Sauvignon Blanc mount, identifiable bottlings from interior California remain difficult if not impossible to find. Only Chenin Blanc is around in revealing diversity.

Chenin Blanc

Clarksburg Chenin Blancs reveal themselves quickly to experienced tasters with flavors close to honeydew, or one of the other musky melons. Although they can have a relatively crisp acidity, they do not call for aging in bottle; their first, freshest hours best show off their fragrantly fruity charms. Chenin Blancs from the San Joaquin Valley tend to be softer in texture and blander in flavor to the point that varietal identity can be a difficult parlor trick for the most diligent blind tasters.
Benchmarks:
Hacienda Wine Cellars (*see* page 89). **Kenwood Vineyards** (*see* page 90). **Dry Creek Vineyards** (see page 88).

Red Wine Varieties

Reds are much the same story as whites. In spite of awesome acreage totals within the San Joaquin Valley, few varietal wines exist in enough numbers to allow instructive comparisons, Zinfandel excepted. In reds, even more than whites, coastal grapes come into wines in large enough proportion to cloud any regional character.

Zinfandel

Typical Lodi Zinfandel has some of the sunny, plummy to outright pruney character that marks Shenandoah Valley wines from the variety, but producers down on the valley floor look less to alcohol and tannin to reinforce the flavors, hence the wines tend to be a good deal milder.

Those who work at it can temper Lodi's baking sun quite well, as the now-vanished Barengo and Royal Host Zinfandels of the mid-1960s showed in vintage after vintage. Among contemporary producers, tiny Lucas Vineyard has reproduced these old results most faithfully.

Robert Mondavi-Woodbridge and Sebastiani do not limit themselves to Lodi grapes in their California-appellation Zinfandels, but the regional character tends to survive mainly intact; the Mondavi in particular is free of pruney notes. Most of the large-volume, low-price producers based in the San Joaquin Valley make their Zinfandels with a bold dash of sweetness.
Benchmark:
The Lucas Vineyard Lodi Zinfandel.

Port-types and other dessert wines

A few scattered producers attempt dessert-sweet wines modeled on ports, madeiras, brown sherries, and muscats. Their efforts are difficult to compare because the grapes are of differing varieties and sources. Still, they merit attention from the small audience of admirers of such wines.

Ficklin Vineyards, the old hand, has produced an impressively long string of richly flavorful, well-balanced, ageworthy wines under the general name of "Tinta Port." They are estate-bottled from the family vineyard at Madera, and entirely composed of traditional varieties of the Douro River Valley in Portugal. Ficklin winemaking is as traditional as the grape varieties. The vintage-dated special bottlings have been particularly memorable with age, but the nonvintage style endures to almost as great an effect.

Quady is another who has used traditional varieties in wines called Port or, wryly, Starboard. All the grapes in both come from Amador County, most of them from a planting called Frank's. The oldest vintages are just beginning to show that they, too, will develop complexities worth waiting to have. Quady is also making serious efforts with Black Muscat in a wine called Elysium and Orange Muscat in one called Essensia. Both of these come from grapes grown near Madera.

185

Lodi AVA

Established: March 17, 1986
Total area: 458,000 acres
Area in vineyard: 45,000 acres
Wineries: 11
Principal town: Lodi

Lodi is reluctantly but briskly turning its back on two long, honorable histories, one a table grape variety called Flame Tokay, the other grower-owned cooperative wineries. Tokay is giving way to Cabernet and Chardonnay at a pace that dropped it from first in acreage to fourth between 1985 and 1991. In almost exactly the same time, all but one of the coops were supplanted by family- or corporate-owned wineries. However, the baby has not gone out with the bathwater; Zinfandel is a more powerful factor than ever in a district where it has always held a place of honor.

Intensely flavorful Flame Tokay was, for decades, one of America's most popular table grapes. What was not sold as fresh fruit could be used in dessert wines and brandies. It was the advent of seedless varieties that finished its career as a table grape: Flame Tokay dropped from 21,000 acres to 13,000.

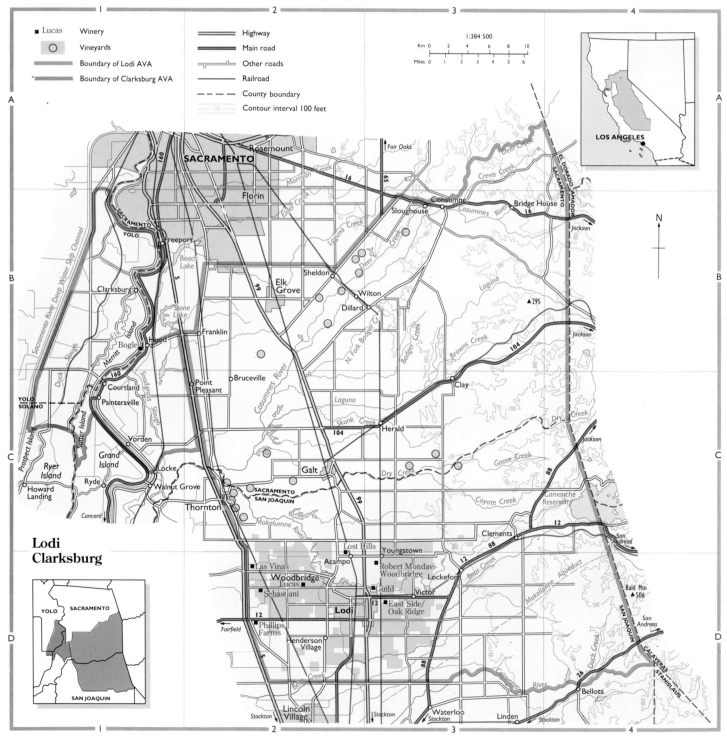

Man-high, head-trained Flame Tokay vines, once Lodi's lifeblood, are now swiftly disappearing from its landscape.

In percentages, the decline was from half of all acreage to 12 percent, and it is still declining. Meanwhile, wine varieties are climbing: Zinfandel has 33 percent of 45,000 acres, Chardonnay 17 percent and Cabernet 13 percent.

Grower-owned cooperative wineries date from early times in Lodi, introduced in the 1880s by a large population of farmers of German origin, to judge by all the Handlers and Haases and Mettlers on the boards of directors. In the 1950s, their last real heyday, a half dozen coops had most of Lodi's 650 growers as members. Then modern marketing techniques began to push both types and brands of wines in and out of fashion. The agility required to prosper in a fast-changing business climate did not come easily to companies run by large committees, the very definition of a coop. One by one they folded, until only East-Side remains.

The old Cherokee coop winery went through half a dozen owners before it became Robert Mondavi-Woodbridge. E. & J. Gallo bought the Liberty coop after buying all its wines for years. Sebastiani now owns the Woodbridge coop's winery, using it primarily for Vendange and August Sebastiani Country wines. Guild, which had several subunits, now belongs to Canandaigua Industries of New York. All these firms, like the coops before them, focus on high volume and low cost.

The democratic instincts that beget coops also balk at the competitive drive to single out one or two properties with special gifts. If Lodi has individual vineyards that tower above the others, the world has had little chance to learn which ones they are. The coops hid their grapes among all the others. Their successors are large-volume enterprises that stick to "California" as an appellation in order to keep their options open. Into the early 1990s, the Lodi appellation was appearing regularly only on the labels of the Lucas Vineyard, Las Vinas

and Phillips Farms, small, local firms every one. East-Side is beginning to use "Lodi" on its Oak Ridge varietal wines.

If particular vineyards are not known, the general outlines of planting in the district show exactly where Hanford Clay Loam has been laid down by the Mokelumne River. Grape vines and that soil are inseparable. Vineyards are dense right up to Interstate 5, but hardly exist west of it. To the east, vines crowd close to State Route 88, but do not go beyond it. To the south, Bear Creek is close to an absolute boundary. Only to the north are the shadings fuzzier, partly because the district extends into Sacramento County, where other fertile soils exist. That aside, a line running close to Peltier Road pretty well defines the northern boundary of Hanford soils.

Zinfandel came close to bringing Lodi a regional identity during the 1950s and early 1960s, when two winemakers got into the kind of "top-this" competition that makes winegrowing regions special. Dino Barengo in his own winery and Reg Gianelli at East-Side made a long string of balanced, flavorful Zinfandels that should have received more critical notice than they did. Their Ruby Cabernets, just as good, gained even less attention. They wearied of the game, retired, and the spark went out.

Still, Lodi has gained so much stature among Central Valley winemakers that several major ones (Bronco, Delicato, the Wine Group) have joined its winery association, although they are located outside the boundaries. Mondavi and Sebastiani also have membership. Lucas, Las Vinas, and Phillips Farms, meanwhile, have made wines that should rekindle the competitive fires.

Clarksburg AVA

Established: February 22, 1984
Total area: 64,640 acres
Area in vineyard: 5,500 acres
Wineries: 1
Principal town: Clarksburg

Clarksburg rivets the attention not because of viticultural history, which it completely lacks, but because it sits 10 to 20 feet below the river level in the intricate web of islands making up the Sacramento River delta. A great many pear orchards and a few vineyards crowd against the manmade riverbanks, permitting the giddying experience of watching sails float along on the tops of pear trees, or high above the ends of vine rows. No other appellation in California offers that opportunity.

Clarksburg's other and much more widely available gift to the senses is characterful Chenin Blanc. Sonoma wineries have defined this uncommon district for the outside world by making consistently distinctive Chenin Blanc and only Chenin Blanc from its vineyards. Hacienda, Grand Cru, Kenwood, and, later, Dry Creek Vineyard all have produced and promoted Clarksburg Chenin Blancs, the first of them in the mid-1970s, when the first plantings came into bearing. Clarksburg's own

Vines in the Clarksburg AVA sit behind 15- to 30-foot-high levees that keep the Sacramento River at bay.

wineries, Bogle Vineyards and the defunct R. & J. Cook, have not been able to bring such widespread attention to any other wine type from the region in their short histories.

The question may be mooted at least for a time. Chardonnay is shouldering Chenin Blanc and everything else aside. For the two dozen or so local growers, the big customers of the early 1990s are the likes of Fetzer Vineyards for its Bel Arbors label, Glen Ellen for its Proprietor's Reserve series, Robert Mondavi-Woodbridge and other producers of low-priced varietals, all hunting for Chardonnay wherever they can find it. While Chenin Blanc plantings dipped from 1,000 to 800 acres between 1990 and 1992, Chardonnay gained from 550 to 1,400, with more planned. Clarksburg has a substantial acreage devoted to red varieties, chief among them Merlot, Petite Sirah, and Cabernet Sauvignon.

Precise acreages are difficult to pin down because statistics are gathered by county while the AVA covers a paper-thin edge of San Joaquin County, a minor part of Sacramento County, and a more substantial part, but not all, of Yolo County.

By definition the AVA limits itself to some of the more solid terrain within the Sacramento's delta, in effect its northeastern quarter. Most delta islands south and west of the AVA boundaries are peat. Growers within Clarksburg describe the soils there as "poorly drained clay and clay loam." One wonders if the soils really drain poorly, or if they just never have a chance to show what they can do. Whatever else, they are fairly rich. Chardonnay routinely cranks out 5.6 tons an acre, Chenin Blanc 6.8 tons an acre

The San Joaquin Valley

This is America's Midi, its source of as much everyday wine as the country wants. It is also America's Douro and Madeira, source of its most intriguing port-type wines and muscats. If Lodi has not defined superior vineyards within its small ambit, the San Joaquin Valley south of there, in its Midi role, has not defined much of anything geographic within its awesome embrace. The valley has one appellation south of Lodi, the Madera AVA. However, it has been used little or not at all since the winery that petitioned for it went out of business.

At harvest time, convoys of trucks converge from all points of the compass on Gallo, Heublein's winery at Madera, Bronco at Ceres, and a few others. For any grapes destined to go into just plain red or white – mostly called Burgundy or Chablis – the first round of blending depends more on place in line than point of origin, as three, four, even a dozen truckloads mingle on their way to the fermenting tanks. This is but the beginning step in a process that will reach wider and wider until bottling. One way to think about it: the main blending tank at E. & J. Gallo's headquarters winery in Modesto can hold 1.1 million gallons, the wine from close to 7,000 tons of grapes, the crop from 800 to 1,000 acres of vineyard.

Such scale hardly tests the capacity of San Joaquin Valley vineyards. Barbera, scarce as a varietal, grew on 9,790 acres in Fresno, Kern, Kings, Madera, and Tulare counties as of 1990; the rest of the state added only 453 acres to the total. Grenache, the other major red, had 11,130 acres in the aforementioned counties. Among white varieties, Chenin Blanc covered 21,150 acres, Colombard a startling 48,874.

Barbera and Colombard are prized for their ability to retain acidity in the San Joaquin heat. Grenache wins on versatility as a source of red, rosé, and port-types. Chenin Blanc is prolific, mild in flavor, and salable as a varietal. Yields of all four varieties range between 7.5 and 9 tons an acre compared to 3 and 6 in the coast counties.

The x-factor is Thompson Seedless, classed economically as a raisin grape, but also widely used as both a wine and a table variety. With 260,900 acres in San Joaquin putting out 9 to 10 tons an acre, the raisin people hardly notice wineries siphoning off 240,000 tons in an average year. Much of it goes to brandy and flavored wines, but no small amount goes into cent-saver generic table wines.

In sheer totals, Fresno led all counties in grape acreage, 32,035 planted with wine varieties and 160,175 with raisin types (Thompson Seedless). Madera had 37,280 acres of wine grapes, 39,790 of raisin types. The other counties are Kern with 24,775 and 26,230; Merced with 13,190 and 1,800; Tulare with 9,090 and 30,890, and Stanislaus with 13,965 and 970.

San Joaquin Valley as Douro and Madeira could be quite a different matter from the San Joaquin as Midi. The market does not reward craftsmanly dessert wines enough to attract many serious producers, but the few who persist have some highly creditable products in their histories. Ficklin Vineyards and Quady Winery, both in Madera County, are the leaders.

"San Joaquin" causes some semantic confusion. San Joaquin County contains the Lodi AVA, which exists somewhat separately from the far larger San Joaquin Valley. However, vines in the southern half of the county are part and parcel of the larger valley.

The Sacramento Valley

Once the equal or superior of the San Joaquin Valley in vineyard acreage, the Sacramento has been a much shrunken shadow since Prohibition. A small comeback, begun during the 1980s, continues to gain momentum.

That comeback was fueled in large part by the fad for White Zinfandel, in smaller but perhaps more important part by the success of the R. H. Phillips vineyard and winery in the Dunnigan Hills northwest of the city of Sacramento, in northern Yolo County. Acreages are quite modest: 1,260 in Colusa, 1,475 in Glenn, 2,900 in Sacramento. Wineries are correspondingly scarce.

North of Clarksburg and east of Napa, in Solano County, two tiny appellations sit side by side between the main Sacramento Valley and the coast ranges. Each is dominated by a single winery. Solano-Green Valley AVA is the fiefdom of Chateau de Leu; Suisun Valley AVA is that of Wooden Valley winery. Although grapes have grown in the region for most of a century, both lack identity. The current powers are attempting to change that.

LODI AND CLARKSBURG PRODUCERS

Bogle Vineyards (1979)
Route 1, Box 276, Clarksburg, CA 95612. Tel (916) 744-1139. 40,000 cases. The Bogle family's 450-acre vineyard on Merritt Island produces grapes for Chardonnay, Merlot, and White Zinfandel.

East-Side Winery (1934)
6100 E Highway 12, Lodi, CA 95240. Tel (209) 369-4758. 175,000 cases. The last surviving grower coop in Lodi proper sells its varietal table wines under the Oak Ridge label, generics under the older Royal Host brand.

Guild Wineries & Distilleries (1934)
PO Box 55, Woodbridge, CA 95258. Tel (209) 368-5151. 39.8 million gallon capacity [volume not revealed]. Long the major coop in Lodi now belongs to New York's Canandaigua Industries (Richards Wild Irish Rose, etc). Labels include Cribari for everyday table wines, Dunnewood for varietal table wines, Cook's and Chase-Limogere for Charmat bubblies.

Lost Hills Winery (1988)
3125 E Orange Street, Acampo, CA 95220. Tel (209) 369-2746. 1.8 million gallon capacity [volume not revealed]. Housed in the old Dino Barengo winery, Lost Hills was idling along during the early 1990s.

The Lucas Winery and Vineyard (1978)
18196 Davis Road, Lodi, CA 95240.

Tel (209) 368-2006. 1,000 cases. A long-time local grower with 30 acres west of Lodi makes just enough Zinfandel to show what is possible with local grapes.

Robert Mondavi-Woodbridge (1979)
PO Box 1260, Woodbridge, CA 95258. Tel (209) 369-5861. 1.5 million cases. Lodi grapes are the anchors for reliable medium-priced Cabernet Sauvignon, Chardonnay, Sauvignon Blanc, and Zinfandel, but the winery draws from throughout the coast counties as well. See also p 29.

Phillips Farms Winery & Vineyards (1984)
4580 W Hwy 12, Lodi, CA 95242. Tel (209) 368-7384. 2,700 cases. A grower with 170 acres makes Merlot, Pinot Noir, Fumé Blanc, Cabernet Sauvignon, and Syrah, mostly as a showcase for the vineyards.

Sebastiani Vineyards (1988)
PO Box 1290, Woodbridge 95258. Tel (209) 938-5532. 2 million cases. The well-established Sebastiani winery of Sonoma Valley (see p 91) bought the old Woodbridge coop as a home for its broadly sourced, modestly priced, popularly styled, Vendange and August Sebastiani Country lines.

Las Vinas Winery (1986)
5573 W Woodbridge Road, Lodi, CA 95242. Tel (209) 334-0445. 15,000 cases. The home-grown is Cabernet Sauvignon "Peltier Vineyard," made in 300-case lots. The proprietors draw on their own 750 acres of vineyard but also reach outside for California

This riverside mansion in Clarksburg is one of many set between rich farmland and the Sacramento River.

appellation Cabernet Sauvignon, Chardonnay and Zinfandel. A Late-Harvest symphony is called "La Femme." The second brand, Quinta da Cotta, goes on Portuguese-style wines.

MAJOR SAN JOAQUIN VALLEY PRODUCERS (not mapped)

Bianchi Vineyards(1974)
5806 N Modoc Avenue, Kerman, CA 93630. Tel (209) 846-7356. 1.5 million gallon capacity; 200,000 cases. A 580-acre vineyard in Fresno County is supplemented by bought-in grapes from other districts for everyday-priced Cabernet Sauvignon, Chardonnay, White Zinfandel.

Bronco Wine Company (1973)
PO Box 789, Ceres, CA 95307. Tel (209) 538-3131. 43.8 million gallon capacity [volume not revealed]. C. C. Vineyard and J. F. J. Cellars are the

main labels for everyday generic and varietal wines. The company is also part-owner of the Montpellier label, and owns the Laurier and Grand Cru labels, all originally independent wineries in Sonoma.

Delicato (1935)
12001 S South Highway 99, Manteca, CA 95336. Tel (209) 239-1215. 35 million gallon capacity [volume not revealed]. Delicato is the main label, Settler's Creek a second one for generic and low-priced varietals. The main grape source is a winery-owned 13,000-acre ranch (8,000 planted with vines) in southern Monterey County, but much is also bought-in from the San Joaquin Valley.

Ficklin Vineyards (1948)
30246 Avenue 7½, Madera, CA 93637. Tel (209) 674-4598. 9,000 cases. The first serious producer of a post-Prohibition California port-type sticks to that last. Both the non-vintage and vintage (1983, 1986 most recently) bottlings are estate-bottled from the owning family's 40-acre vineyard of Tinta Cao, Tinta Madeira, Touriga, and Souzao. In 1993 a 10-

year-old Tawny joined the 2 ruby styles. The wines are stylish and almost immortal as agers.

E. & J. Gallo (1933)
PO Box 1130, Modesto, CA 95353. Tel (209) 579-3111. 300 million gallon capacity [volume not revealed]. The enormous power derived from making generic jug wines potable and reliable still rests with this family-owned firm; it is now embarked on a patient program of upgrading its lists for the varietal era. Its long list of labels include Reserve Cellars of E. & J. Gallo (for Sonoma Cabernet and Chardonnay), E. & J. Gallo (other varietals and generics based in Lodi and San Joaquin Valley grapes), William Wycliffe, and Carlo Rossi. Charmat sparkling wines sell under the names Tott's, Andre, Ballatore, and Eden Roc.

Gibson Winery (1939)
1720 Academy Avenue, Sanger, CA 93657. Tel (209) 875-2505. 11.4 million gallon capacity [volume not revealed]. Grower coop with one foot in Lodi district, the other in Fresno, makes low-priced everyday wines

under Gibson, Farley's, Ramano, Elk Ridge, Pheasant Hollow, and Silverstone Cellars labels.

Giumarra Vineyards (1946)
PO Bin 1969, Bakersfield, CA 93303. Tel (805) 395-7079. 16 million gallon capacity [volume not revealed]. A family with 10,000 acres of vineyard on gentle slopes southeast of Bakersfield uses those grapes for cent-saver generics labeled Giumarra, and blends Central Coast grapes into modestly priced varietals under the name Breckenridge Cellars.

Heublein, Inc. (1964)
PO Box 99, Madera, CA 93639. Tel (209) 673-7071. 112 million gallon capacity [volume not revealed]. A Madera winery is the central producing plant for everyday varietal wines under the names Almaden, Blossom Hill, Charles Le Franc, Inglenook Navalle, and other labels begun as individual wineries in the coastal counties. Le Domaine goes on the Charmat sparkling wines.

Montpellier Vineyards (1988)
PO Box 610, Ceres, CA 95307. Tel (209) 538-9083. 100,000 cases. A source of low-priced, fruit-first varietals from San Joaquin Valley grapes belongs to the owners of Bronco (the Franzia family) and members of the Robert Mondavi family. The long-range idea is to base the label in a 960-acre vineyard placed under development in 1988. Thus far the wines are being made in leased space.

Moresco Vineyards (1987)
16865 Gawne Road, Stockton, CA 95215. Tel (209) 467-3081.[Volume not revealed]. Zinfandel Petite Sirah, Cabernet Sauvignon, and White Zinfandel and generics are based in 158 acres of vines east of Stockton.

A. Nonini Winery (1936)
2640 N Dickenson Avenue, Fresno, CA 93722. Tel (209) 275-1936. 10,000 cases. Old-line family farmers with 200 acres of vineyards make throwback, everyday red and white table wine for a local clientele.

Quady Winery (1977)
13181 Road 24, Madera, CA 93637. Tel (209) 673-8068. 15,000 cases. Quady divides its attention between craftsmanly port-types and sweet muscats. The wryly named Starboard is all from traditional Portuguese varieties (Tinta Cão, Tinta Alvarelho, Rouriz) grown in Amador, as are vintage and nonvintage wines called Port. Deep red Elysium is from Black Muscat, pale Essencia from Orange Muscat. In counterpoint to 18 per cent alcohol Essencia is Electra, 6 per cent alcohol and slightly fizzy in the way of Moscato d'Astis.

Wine Group (1906)
PO Box 897, Ripon, CA 95366. Tel (209) 599-4111. 42.8 million gallons capacity [volume not revealed]. Franzia, Summit, Colony, Lejon and, it often seems, scores of other labels go on wines made in this winery on the southern edge of San Joaquin County. Most are generics, some are penny-saver varietals. The company also owns Corbett Canyon Vineyards in San Luis Obispo County (see p 136).

MAJOR SACRAMENTO VALLEY WINERIES (not mapped)

Chateau de Leu (1981)
1855 De Leu Drive, Suisun, CA 94585. Tel (707) 864-1517. 12,000 cases. The winery still buys grapes in Napa, but is making estate-bottled Chardonnay, Merlot and Syrah from 40 acres in Solano-Green Valley, and driving towards estate Sangiovese and Dolcetto.

Orleans Hill Vinicultural Society (1980)
PO Box 1254, Woodland, CA 95695. Tel (916) 661-6538. 10,000 cases. Produces a wide list of varietals from affiliated local vineyards, most of them offered under whimsical names slanted toward particular vacations.

R.H. Phillips Vineyard (1983)
26836 County Roads 12-A, Esparto, CA 95627. Tel (916) 662-3215. 200,000 cases. Varietals and blends from a going-on-500-acre vineyard in the Dunnigan Hills suggest that Sémillon, Sauvignon Blanc, and the red Rhône varieties may fare well in that region. Most of the wines are from broadly sourced bought-in grapes.

Wooden Valley Winery (1932)
4756 Suisun Valley Road, Suisun, CA 94585. Tel (707) 864-0730. 20,000 cases. The proprietors are growers first (300 acres) but make a wide range of Suisun Valley varietals and generics to satisfy a loyal following of cellar-door buyers.

TRAVEL NOTE

Because few of these wineries are open to visitors, and those that are open are too far scattered to form logical routes, recommendations for hotels etc are not given here.

California's State Capitol Building in downtown Sacramento.

Pacific Northwest

If ever an odd couple existed in the world of wine, Washington and Oregon is it. The two wine industries are a couple because their two states have been forever welded together as Siamese twins in the American mind, an outgrowth of the rest of the country leaving them to their own devices in the far northwest corner of the nation.

They are an odd couple because the two states were drawn all wrong from any sensible, geographical point of view. The Columbia River, although it is a boundary, unites Washington and Oregon over salmon fisheries and electric power generation. The Cascade Mountains, on the other hand, are not a boundary but ruthlessly divide both states into completely dissimilar halves. The western sides of both are rainy, forested, and maritime in outlook, while the eastern sides are harsh, desertlike and continental.

Washington's wines come from its eastern side, Oregon's from its western. And so, while the two often travel together, they almost always dine separately. Washington increasingly looks to Cabernet Sauvignon, Merlot, Sauvignon Blanc, and Sémillon, while Oregon has looked first, last and always to Pinot Noir, tossing a few crumbs to compatible whites. Exceptions exist: Washington has a smattering of vineyards west of the Cascades and Oregon has a similarly sparse number to the east of the mountains. Oregon also has a tiny enclave of Cabernet fanciers in its southwestern corner. However, the generalities are amazingly solid considering they arose within two decades of an absolute standing start.

Winery owners in both states long to have a history, a bit of tradition to follow. To that end they have ferreted out the existence of one or two 19th-century vineyards and cellars. But the fact is, contemporary growers and winemakers owe nothing to a past that left little or no record of which grape varieties grew, or how they were treated. Washington's first commercial wine of any quality was a Gewürztraminer from 1967. Oregon began with a trio of Pinot Noirs from 1972.

Every bit as striking as the swiftness of Washington's evolution into Cabernet and Merlot country, and Oregon's into a land for Pinot Noir, is the difference in character of the two

The Oregon coast near the resort town of Cannon Beach.

Pacific Northwest

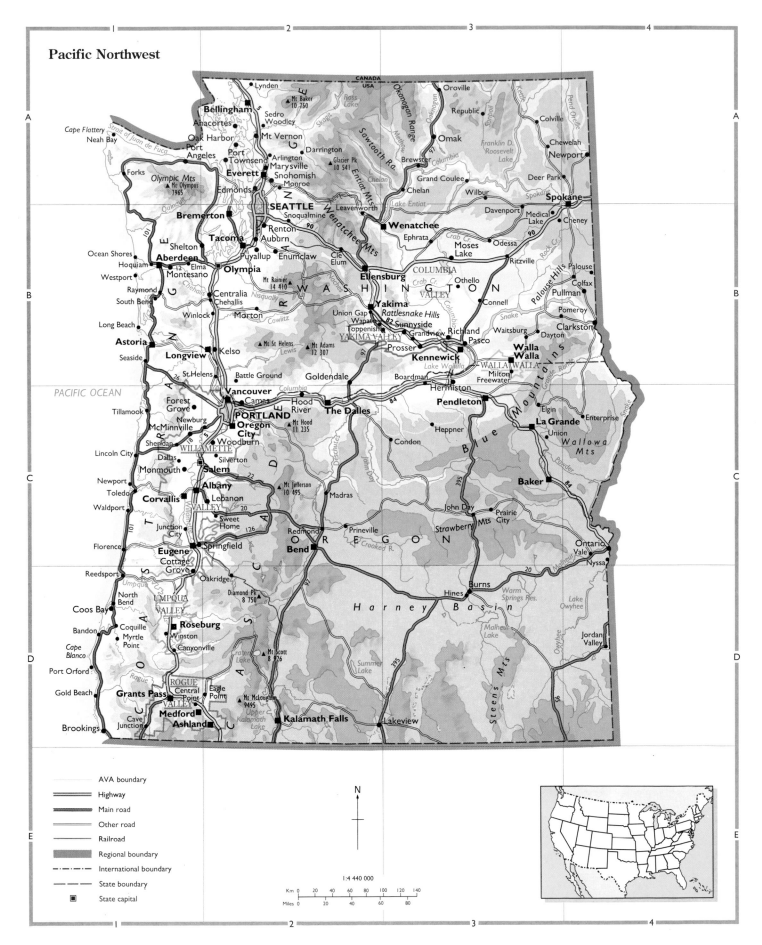

AVA boundary
Highway
Main road
Other road
Railroad
Regional boundary
International boundary
State boundary
State capital

N

1:4 440 000

Km 0   20   40   60   80   100 120 140
Miles 0   20   40   60   80

industries. Washington is almost entirely homegrown. If the traditional grape varieties of Europe came late to eastern Washington, farming did not. Irrigation began turning the Yakima Valley into one of the United States' richest and most versatile farmlands before the turn of the century. When wine grapes came along, established farmers planted them as one more cash crop among many on large general farms. A grower with 80 acres of grapes may be looking at less than 10 percent of his operations. Growers of exactly this stripe are still the backbone of the industry.

The producer of that revolutionary 1967 Gewürztraminer, Associated Vintners, started in a garage, the offshoot of a band of home winemakers. Its instant rival was Chateau Ste Michelle, the new name for an old company properly saddled with a reputation for making fairly awful to perfectly dreadful Concord-based wines called Nawico and Pommerelle. More important to the moment, it had a small vineyard of *vinifera* varieties and, by local standards, deep pockets. The evolution since 1967 has brought a number of well-financed, locally owned 25,000- to 150,000-case wineries along with dozens of small ones. Estate wines are a rarity even among the smallest.

Oregon, meanwhile, owes its beginnings to a small group of expatriate Californians who came to a Willamette Valley where farming had been economically marginalized. They brought huge ideals and tiny purses. David Lett wedged the winemaking for Eyrie Vineyards into an old turkey-.processing plant next to the railyards in McMinnville. Bill Fuller added a couple of walls to a strawberry-packing shed to house the cellars of Tualatin Vineyards. Their successors did not do much differently for several years. They all grew their own grapes in six-, eleven- and twenty-acre properties, supplementing, when they had to, with grapes from one-step-better-than-hobby growers with an acre or two at the back of the house.

A couple of substantial firms have emerged in recent years, but 25,000 cases is big in Oregon, and estate-grown is closer to the rule than the exception.

In all the critical kerfuffle over Northwest wines, one tends to forget that Washington's industry is tiny, and Oregon's minute. Washington's total acreage is slightly more than a third that of the Napa Valley Oregon's is not quite a sixth Napa's size.

Irrigation canal near Zillah in the Yakima Valley.

Washington State

The geography of wine in Washington is passing strange, as well it might be, considering its history. Nearly all the vineyards are east of the Cascade Mountains, as climate dictates, while most people live west of them, for reasons of comfort. Winery locations are divided about half and half, because the population needed all the education it could get in the early days.

At the start of the 1960s, Washington was what Americans call a Control State, one that monopolized the selling of beverages containing alcohol. Anyone who wanted a bottle for dinner had to overcome considerable psychological intimidation to choose from a short, obscure list at a state liquor store. Kafka could not have imagined some of the conversations that went on between customers and clerks about Pinot Noir, let alone Gewürztraminer. At the same time, the state levied punishing taxes on wines from elsewhere, in order to help local producers of wines made from Concord and other native grapes hang on to a bleak market.

As Control State legal barriers began to come down during the 1960s, a handful of locals began trying to grow *vinifera* varieties and make wine from them. Instantly, the potential of Washington wines became evident. Increased sales came harder though, consumers having learned to resist the local product.

Bustling Seattle is far from the vineyards, but home to many of Washington's most important wineries.

The pioneers knew from California's experience that the best means of educating would-be consumers was having wineries with tasting rooms right in the neighborhood, hence the early presence of Chateau Ste Michelle and Columbia Winery (originally as Associated Vintners), and the eventual arrival of Paul Thomas and other major players on the west side, a hundred miles or more from the vineyards that feed them.

As founding dates show, it was only in the 1980s that the tide of new wineries began to spread eastward. A still-growing number of producers on the eastern side now do a good job of luring west-siders across the mountains for tasting and a first-hand view of vineyards basking in the sun. But good as the wines are, much as critics praise them, recognition still outpaces growth, especially of vineyard acreage.

Considering that Washington's three appellations have only to encompass 12,000 acres of vines, their size staggers the imagination. The Yakima and Walla Walla Valley AVAs are big, maybe even huge. The Columbia Valley AVA swallows both of them and millions of acres more. Drawn with a first goal of including every known vineyard in eastern Washington, it loops boundaries around huge empty areas to take in some major plantings along the Columbia and minor ones near Moses Lake, some 100 miles to the north.

Total vineyard acreages from 1992 give an idea. The Columbia Valley, excluding Yakima and Walla Walla, has 6,375 acres, or 58 percent of all *Vitis vinifera* plantings in the state. Yakima has 4,308, or 40 percent. Walla Walla, just getting under way, has only 61 acres, less than 1 percent of the total. Everything west of the Cascade Mountains only adds another 158 acres. These figures do not include Concord and other native varieties, still heavily planted in the Yakima Valley but used almost exclusively for juice and jam now.

Climate

Eastern Washington weather trotted out all of its tricks in 1990, most particularly in showing off its capacities for summer heat and winter cold. Summer maximums will go higher and last longer, but 1990 provided a growing season slightly warmer than normal. Winter lows will plummet well below the –8°F of December 29, and stay near zero longer than the 13 days of this cold spell, but 1990's freeze damaged enough buds to reduce the succeeding harvest significantly. Spring and autumn, meanwhile, were close to prototypical. May warmed things up sooner and more than an absolutely average year, while September and October cooled down more than normal, but the variations from norms in both seasons were slight.

The mechanics of eastern Washington weather have their foundations in mountains to both east and west. To the west, the parallel Olympic and Cascade Mountains sit more or less directly beneath the Aleutian winter storm track, the great bringer of rain and moderate temperatures to the Pacific Northwest, or, rather, to a narrow coastal band of it. Rainfalls on the west side of the Olympics range upward of 100 inches per year while those on the west slopes of the Cascades exceed 50 inches. By the time air reaches the east side of the Cascades it is so dry that climatologists classify much of central Washington as semidesert, a few areas as true desert.

In the span of a few miles, thus, Washington's climate changes from classic west-coast maritime patterns to purely continental ones. Like other regions with continental climates, all of Washington east of the Cascades has four highly defined seasons. Also typical, the weather can change abruptly within a season. It is a curious contrast to coastal California, where the basic patterns are much more durable, but where the comings and goings of sea-fogs send temperatures soaring and plummeting from day to day rather than every few days.

To the east, the Rocky Mountains play a less immediate climatic role in all seasons except winter. True, they contribute much of the moisture that ends up as the Columbia River. However, their dramatic impact is not that. Rather it is that they and the Cascades can act as the two walls of a bobsled course that funnels Arctic winter air down across central and eastern Washington. The deep freeze of December 1990 was a perfect example of what happens when frigid air slips down between the two ranges instead of flowing down east of the Rockies. The prospects are that such a freeze will occur at least once in each decade, with one colder and longer-lasting than 1990 coming along every 20 or 30 years.

* For the color code to the climate charts see pages 14–15.

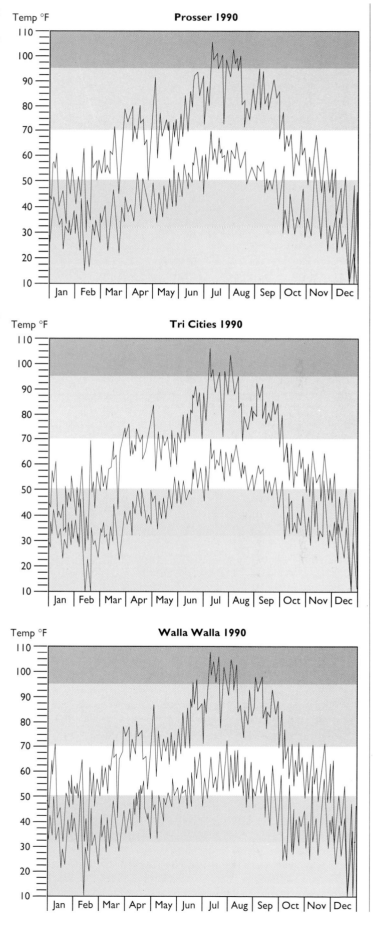

The Wines

A cautionary note: because so few vineyards cluster tightly together anywhere in Washington, and so many wines are assembled from vineyards scattered across the whole breadth of an awesomely large terrain, it is still impossible to paint regional distinctions with even the broadest strokes. At this point, Washington is Washington and that is that.

White Wine Varieties

The state's growers effectively limit themselves to six of the most familiar varieties in the world: Chardonnay, Chenin Blanc, Gewürztraminer, Riesling, Sauvignon Blanc, and Sémillon. Tiny acreages of rarer varieties exist: Aligoté is grown on the eastern side, while the western side has tiny plantings of Müller-Thurgau, Okanagan Riesling and Madeleine Angevine. All these rarities can be found bottled as varietal wines, although seldom from more than one or two producers, four at most.

Chardonnay (67 acres in 1970, 2,655 in 1990)

In depth, focus and sheer deliciousness, Washington Chardonnay ranks no better than third among the state's white wines behind Sémillon and Riesling, and may well be fourth after Sauvignon Blanc. If it can stand taller, no one has yet found the vineyards to raise its standing. Still, fourth best is a long way from out of the game.

In acreage the great white grape of Burgundy ranks first, partly because the audience seems to want no other white, partly because Washington's winemakers have finessed short-comings in the vineyards with barrel and malolactic fermentation, aging on the lees, and all the other ways of ornamenting a plain face.

The best wines do taste recognizably of Chardonnay, although not of any particular region. These benefit from oak for depth and complexity, but need a light hand to survive with any taste of grapes intact. A much greater number end up tasting mainly like oak, butter, or even butterscotch (and, it must be said, winning applause from the home audience for it). Stamina is suspect in all styles, but especially the butterscotchy one, although unpredictable exceptions exist.

A few small to tiny Chardonnay vineyards sit across the Columbia River from Portland, in Washington's southwest corner. The wines from Salishan and its neighbors are most usefully compared to those of the Willamette Valley.

Benchmarks:

The Hogue Cellars Washington State "Reserve" (assembled). **Paul Thomas** Washington (assembled). **Paul Thomas Winery** Washington "Reserve" (assembled). **Chateau Ste Michelle** Columbia Valley "Cold Creek" (estate). **Chateau Ste Michelle** Columbia Valley "River Ridge" (estate). **Gordon Brothers Cellars** Columbia Valley (estate). **Staton Hills Winery** Washington (assembled). **Stewart Vineyards** Columbia Valley (assembled).

Chenin Blanc (45 acres in 1970, 674 in 1990)

Chenin Blanc has been a reliable source of summer sippers from the earliest days of Washington *vinifera* winemaking. For a long time that was exactly what the home audience wanted. In recent years, however, the bloom has gone off. Chenin Blanc in 1992 had barely half the acreage it had as late as 1988.

Almost without exception the wines are fermented cold in stainless steel and kept cold in stainless steel until bottling. A

Kerosene heaters provide more psychological comfort than practical defense against frosts in the Columbia Valley.

little residual sugar is almost inevitable, a little spritz common. The resulting flavors are agreeable, but hard to pin down beyond the feeble generalization of "fruity." Often Washington Chenin Blanc and Riesling almost fade into each other as gently floral summer sippers. Chateau Ste Michelle, Columbia Crest, and Worden's typify the fresh style. One Chenin Blanc Ice Wine from Kiona became intensely floral in its perfumes, rousing hopes that more might be done with the variety as a late-harvest type.

Gewürztraminer (38 acres in 1970, 334 in 1990)

Gewürztraminer is dwindling away almost as fast as Chenin Blanc, its plantings having dipped from 532 acres in 1988. The fast fade is faintly ironic, inasmuch as the one wine that had most to do with launching *vinifera* winemaking in Washington State was Associated Vintners' memorable Yakima Valley 1967 Gewürztraminer. Further, the fade is unlikely to be complete because Biscuit Ridge and others remain devoted to its prospects as a direct challenger to the best Alsatian wines. If it is to do that, however, the road ahead is long. Although episodic bottlings have reached something like a spicy character, most are lucky to catch a hint of the muscatlike flavors Gewürztraminer can have. A majority have been just white table wine.

Riesling, *also* White Riesling, Johannisberg Riesling (110 acres in 1970, 2,118 in 1990)

It was Washington's bad luck that its first roaring success outside the home turf was Riesling, just when the variety was on its way to becoming the least wanted of all the orphans left behind in the United States by Chardonnay and Cabernet. However, a Chateau Ste Michelle 1972 came first in a huge blind tasting staged by the *Los Angeles Times*, and in one day set the state's then fledgling industry to chasing that star.

It was even worse luck for Washington that Riesling's star has ebbed so badly, because the vines grow well in every quarter, are frost hardy, and make some of the most distinctive wines anywhere in the world outside Germany. Preston Vineyards caught one of the most haunting scents imaginable in its Dry Riesling 1989, floral at heart and so distinctive that to taste it once was to know it anywhere for a long time after. The trouble is, no one knows how or why it arrived, or when to expect it again. The problem is not unique to Preston. The Hogue Cellars, Kiona, and Paul Thomas are much more typical, and quite consistent in character.

Riesling goes by a number of confusing aliases in Washington. Some call it simply Riesling. Others use Dry Riesling for dry and just Riesling for off-dry. Some identify their drier bottlings as Johannisberg Riesling, sweeter ones as White Riesling. All the variations on Late Harvest add mightily to the confusion.

Botrytis comes to Washington, often to memorable effect, but quite a few Rieslings are called Late Harvest simply because they are sweet. The latter can cloy for lack of concentrated flavor. Acreage devoted to Riesling has dwindled to second place behind Chardonnay, but Yakima Valley and other Washington wineries are still so oversupplied that they have tried Blush Riesling, sparkling Riesling, and every other trick to get rid of it.

Benchmarks:

The Hogue Cellars Yakima Valley Dry Johannisberg Riesling (assembled). **Kiona** Yakima Valley Dry Riesling (estate). **The Hogue Cellars** Yakima Valley Johannisberg Riesling. **Kiona** Columbia Valley White Riesling (assembled). **Covey Run** Yakima Valley Late Harvest White Riesling (assembled). **The Hogue Cellars** Yakima Valley Late Harvest White Riesling.

Sauvignon Blanc, *also* Fumé Blanc (14 acres in 1970, 807 in 1990)

Sauvignon Blanc, whether it ranks third or fourth, made tremendous strides during the last half of the 1980s while Chardonnay has marked time. Not long ago, to open a bottle of Yakima Valley Sauvignon was to invite suspicious glances at the family cat. Those days are nearly gone because vineyards have been rejigged to suppress musky smells in favor of melon-like ones, as Hogue demonstrates, vintage after vintage.

Being widely adapted to Columbia Valley growing conditions, Sauvignon Blanc manages to keep a lean, crisp, even hard edge about it if fermented and aged in stainless steel. For that reason many winemakers use a dash of Sémillon, a touch of oak (Covey Run most effectively), or both to round it out and add nuances to the flavors.

Washington winemakers show little tendency to look upon Sauvignon Blanc as an ager. Since locals dote on the freshest of them as a companion to fish and shellfish from Puget Sound and the Pacific, there is not much call to think otherwise.

Benchmarks:

Columbia Crest Columbia Valley Sauvignon Blanc (based in the Paterson vineyard). **The Hogue Cellars** Washington Fumé Blanc (assembled). **Covey Run** Washington Fumé Blanc (assembled). **Quarry Lake Winery** Columbia Valley (Pasco). **Chateau Ste Michelle** Columbia Valley Sauvignon Blanc (based in River Ridge at Paterson).

Left: Covey Run's handsome winery building sits on the first rise of the Rattlesnake Hills, which frame the Yakima Valley on its north side. Above: The ornamental gate belongs to Chateau Ste Michelle.

Sémillon (35 acres in 1970, 590 in 1990)

On its finest days, Sémillon from Washington competes with Australia's best, and handily surpasses everything from California. If any other part of the world marketed Sémillon as an unblended varietal, Washington would still stand in the front ranks because its kind of balanced, true-to-the-grape, true-to-the-vineyard wine cannot be pushed into the background.

The cliché is that Sauvignon Blanc ranges from grass to herb to melon, Sémillon from herb to melon to fig. Top-drawer Washington Sémillon catches some of all of those qualities and adds others. People have even mentioned potato and not been altogether wrong.

A second bit of conventional wisdom is that Sauvignon Blanc is lean and sharp, Sémillon fatter and fuller. This may be so. Certainly Washington Sémillon is fuller than its Sauvignon Blanc. However, it has the kind of straight spine and firm muscles that make collectors think of the long run, and eaters think of oysters.

Year in, year out, half a dozen or more wines run a bookmaker's nightmare of a race for top honors in the vintage. In the 1992 Western Washington Fair wine competition, five judges, looking at seven Sémillons, voted 35 medals without a word of discussion, a statistical near-impossibility. In such circumstances nominating bests and next-bests is foolhardy.

Most of Washington's producers make Sémillon for the sake of Sémillon, some with, some without a dash of wood. A few box it in oak.

In addition to its role in varietals, it has a vogue in blends with Sauvignon Blanc on the one hand (*see below*) and Chardonnay on the other.

Benchmarks:

Columbia Winery Columbia Valley Sémillon (based in Sagemoor). **Columbia Winery** Columbia Valley "Chevrier"–Sémillon Sur Lie. **Columbia Crest** Columbia Valley "Barrel Select" (assembled). **The Hogue Cellars** Washington (assembled). **Chateau Ste Michelle** Columbia Valley (assembled). Facelli Washington (assembled).

Sauvignon-Sémillon blends

The breed is still being formed, but the prospects are impressive, based especially on Covey Run's Yakima Valley La Caille de Fumé and Columbia Crest's Columbia Valley Sémillon-Sauvignon.

Typical, quarter-mile-long, self-powered irrigation machine.

Red Wine Varieties

Nearly all eyes are on Merlot and Cabernet Sauvignon, but Lemberger and Pinot Noir may have niches. A few other varieties still on a trial status bear watching, with Syrah and Nebbiolo leading the list.

Cabernet Sauvignon (144 acres in 1970, 1,419 in 1990)

Even at its most polite and polished best, Cabernet Sauvignon has not quite held even with Merlot, although the latter came to Washington later. In spite of Cabernet having had the head start, it has dropped behind its cousin in critical acclaim and in area planted. Perhaps it is not fated to do better. Its flavors are less bright and distinctive than those of counterpart Merlots. Most Cabernets lean more to herbaceous flavors than the berrylike Merlots, a trait shared with thousands of other New International Cabernets. The finest of them may have the greater depth of the two, but they seem more difficult to tame, less ready to find an equilibrium even when the winemaker is seeking balance, not power. If Washington Cabernets are to run off the pace set by Merlot, they will not lag disastrously, for the best of them are more than merely passable red wines.

Rather like Ridge in California, Columbia Winery has turned itself into a kind of experimental station, making single-vineyard wines from a range of vineyards to see what is out there. Its three single-vineyard Cabernets are a Cook's tour of established regions for the variety. Hard-edged, slow-aging "Red Willow" comes from the warm northern end of the Yakima Valley. Round, easy "Sagemoor" comes from still warmer Pasco. "Otis" is at Grandview, about halfway between the others. It is the coolest of the three properties.

Several other cellars let their vineyards say important things about Washington Cabernet Sauvignon. Covey Run has a Yakima Valley Cabernet that invites both comparison and contrast with Columbia's Otis Vineyard bottling: comparison because the vineyards are not far apart; contrast because the styles differ enough to invite a preference. For the same reasons Gordon Brothers' estate wine intrigues in comparison with Columbia's "Sagemoor."

Styles vary enormously, as they do in every young region. The Hogue Cellars shows off the virtues of skillful use of American oak. Leonetti pushes ripeness and long aging to the limits (almost always possible here) and comes off a favorite exactly because of all the flesh and spiciness that result. Rather too many pick earlier, press harder, and aim for more blatant oak with heavy, tannically austere results.

It is not yet clear what these or any of the other winemakers in Washington must do to produce Cabernet Sauvignons that age to greater glories. A few bottles of 1973 Chateau Ste Michelle linger in my cellar, tasting just about as much like slightly underripe blackberries as they did the day they were bottled. Many bottlings from the early 1980s, especially the overripe, overoaked ones, have gone from frisky youth to weary age without arriving at any of the storied improvements time is supposed to bring to classic reds.

Benchmarks:

The Hogue Cellars Washington (assembled). **Neuharth** Washington (assembled). **Chateau Ste Michell** Columbia Valley "River Ridge" (estate). **Stewart Vineyards** (anchored in a Wahluke Slope estate vineyard). **Covey Run** Yakima Valley (anchored in the estate). **Columbia Winery** Yakima Valley "Red Willow." **Columbia Winery** Columbia Valley "Sagemoor." **Staton Hills** Washington (assembled). **Kiona Vineyards** Yakima Valley (estate).

Lemberger (0 in 1970, less than 100 acres in 1990)
Although the wine trade roll their eyes and winemakers look bemused, growers in the Yakima Valley love Lemberger. Not long ago one of them told a visitor that he loved it because it could be grown more like Concord than any other red, and that it could get dark and ripe at 10 tons to the acre if one knew when to put the water on and when to take it off. He had a local winemaker in his sights when he said that, but the kernel of truth enriches his claim. Lemberger is hardier in Washington's cold winter than any other red variety, ripens full crops when others fail, and makes a properly dark red.

The only trouble with Lemberger is that it is called Lemberger. Washington's Wine Commission ought to send a delegation to Italy to find an ancestor called Destino or Rossini for the irrefutable fact is that this variety makes a splendid alternative to Dolcetto, one with nothing Lembergian about it when the winemaker keeps the oak down to a dull roar and does not press for tannins. Hoodsport is the unparalleled proof of the pudding. Covey Run and Hogue use a deft touch of oak to good effect.

Benchmarks:
Hoodsport Winery Washington (assembled). **Covey Run** Yakima Valley (assembled). **The Hogue Cellars** Washington (assembled).

Merlot (10 acres in 1970, 1,555 in 1990)
Curiously, for a variety that tends to reach its peak in very few sites elsewhere in the world, Merlot has shot to the forefront in Washington by delivering consistently appealing wines from almost every district in which it has been planted.

This swiftly claimed eminence is all the more unexpected because Washington Merlot is a high-roller's dream, an all or nothing play: all, because it has produced many of Washington's most memorable reds; nothing, because it shows signs of being too tender for winters that already have frozen hardier varieties to the ground three times in two decades. Still, because the all side of the equation offers so much hope, the state has more of Merlot than any other red now, almost every vine rooted in a south-facing slope with good air circulation and drainage, not only in the vineyard but farther down, on the grounds that each minute of winter sun gained, each degree below 0°F spared could mean the difference between a crop next vintage, or a year spent coaxing new life from below ground.

Merlot's current plantings more than double the acreage of 1988, a fact that gives pause to those winemakers with enough time on the track to remember eastern Washington's harshest winters. Until that bomb falls, if it is to fall, Washington Merlot is almost abundant.

Because of its late rise to prominence, Merlot has not gone through as much of the overripe, overextracted, overoaked phase as Washington Cabernet, though such can be found. The critical favorites press gently and go light on the oak, leaving flavors not unlike tartly refreshing berries to stand foremost. It can lean to the herbaceous side, and almost surely will from the coolest parts of the Yakima Valley around Prosser, but even there the note of fresh berries does not evaporate altogether.

Columbia's single-vineyard "Milestone," from Red Willow, and Columbia Crest's "Barrel Select" offer the two clearest expressions of the variety, even though Milestone has a healthy dollop of Cabernet Franc in it. Gordon Brothers Columbia Valley and the Hogue Cellars demonstrate perfectly how a little bit of American oak spices Merlot's own flavors with kindred ones.

With these in mind, the riper, heftier, more fully oaked style of Leonetti comes into clear focus. Nothing else stretches Washington's sunny summers any closer to their limit. The opposite end of the stylistic stick, occupied by Hoodsport, stays with tart fruit and no oak at all. Curious as it may seem, the latter wines seem farther from the middle of the road than the Leonettis by a long measure.

Benchmarks:
Columbia Winery Yakima Valley "Milestone" (Red Willow vineyard). **Columbia Winery** Columbia Valley. Columbia Crest Columbia Valley "Barrel Select" (based in Paterson grapes). **Gordon Brothers** Columbia Valley (estate). **The Hogue Cellars** Washington (assembled). **Chateau Ste Michelle** Columbia Valley (assembled).

Cabernet-Merlot blends
It just may be that blending Cabernet with Merlot will pay greater dividends here than California has found, primarily because Merlot brings greater delicacy of texture and intensity of flavor to the Pacific Northwest equation. Success will not be automatic. Several early tries have been as awkward as any fast-growing boy. But one or two hint at grander possibilities. A 1989 Hedges Cabernet-Merlot in particular, after showing early grace, began wafting up the sort of bouquets that get one to thinking of racks of lamb.

Pinot Noir (15 acres in 1970, 250 in 1990)
Pinot Noir appears to be hopeless in eastern Washington, except perhaps as a blending element with Pinot from the west side. In 1990 Columbia Winery put flesh on the bones of westside grapes in just that way. Pinot Noirs on their own from Washington's southwest corner are very much like those from Washington County across the Columbia River in Oregon, to judge from the Pinot Noirs produced by Salishan Vineyards.

Other varieties: (Total acreage, including Lemberger, 315 in 1990.)
Among pedigreed Italian hopes, the decision is not yet in on Nebbiolo, but one begins to hear positive murmurs through the jury-room door because Peter Dow's Cavatappi 1988 (Red Willow) is evolving better than seemed possible when it first appeared. Pale by Italian standards, and curiously velvety on the palate, its flavors are right on the mark.

Syrah has begun to quicken the heartbeat of growers and winemakers based on a single patch in Red Willow. David Lake at Columbia Winery has made dark, firm, deeply fruity wines from it since 1988.

Grenache is an aesthetic joy and a viticultural disaster. The best of its wines, red or rosé, will match up against any other country's top examples. However, Chateau Ste Michelle gave up on its old patch in Grandview years ago, and since has saved only the best 15 of 45 acres in its Cold Creek vineyard because the variety freezes to the ground in three years out of 10, and does little in five or six of the other seven. A few vines of Mourvèdre and Cinsaut also grow in the state; more are being bred.

A tiny bit of Gamay Beaujolais (from the Pinot Noir clone rather than Gamay Noir au Jus Blanc) was just beginning to appear with the 1990s.

Columbia Valley AVA

Established: December 13, 1984
Total area: 10,700,000 acres*
Area in vineyard: 6,375 acres*
Wineries: 11
Principal towns: Tri-Cities

Washington's great umbrella appellation makes California's broad Central and North Coast AVAs look toylike in comparison. The idea was to encompass all arable lands of the Columbia River drainage suspected of being suitable for vineyards. What came of it takes in a huge swathe of central Washington and a large piece of Oregon as well.

Its most settled, most intensively agricultural subregion is the Yakima Valley, a place where packing plants are big buildings and railroad tracks run right down the main streets of every town. Much of it is wilderness, about as pitiless as an environment for wine grapes can be: a place where neither desert-dry summer nor arctic-cold winter could be called a grower's best friend.

To see it is to believe its essential homogeneity, and be stunned by the unimaginable power behind the details. The entire region is a huge block of basalt, tipped slightly west to east by the upward thrust of the Cascade Mountains. Other tectonic forces pushing northward buckled its surface into a series of parallel east-west ridges. A succession of ice ages scoured parts of it, in the process causing the Columbia River to carve half a dozen different north-south channels through it, one still visible in the awesome cliffs of Dry Falls, the others mostly covered up by later erosion of the Cascades. In the end, everything is bare rock on exposed heights and mantles of soil in the sheltered spots. Most of the soil is basalt sand, some of it loess. Here and there ancient riverine gravels rise to the level of vine roots.

The towering wall of the Cascades screens out rain with almost alarming efficiency. Even so, water is abundant in the midst of a semidesert because both the Cascades to the west and the Rocky Mountains to the east funnel far-distant downpours into the Columbia River system, dammed into a long chain of reservoir lakes that permit prodigies of irrigation.

In addition to dwarfing California's most sweeping AVAs, the Columbia Valley differs further in that it covers millions of acres not defined more closely by smaller subunits. Exclude the Yakima and Walla Walla valleys, and its 6,375 acres of vineyard amount to 58 percent of all the plantings in Washington, and float in 10.7 million acres of land. With that as a starting point, the surprise is not how little is known about the details, but how much. All the plantings are on low ridgetops, on the south-facing slopes of higher hills, or else hug the river. In each case, warding off winter cold influences the choice more than avoiding summer heat.

From south to north, identifiable districts are the Horse Heaven Hills, Pasco, the Wahluke Slope, and, just beginning to emerge, the Royal Slope. The Horse Heavens, relatively low and flat-topped, separate the Yakima Valley from the Columbia River once the latter has turned west toward the sea. The owners of Chateau Ste Michelle and Columbia Crest have nearly 2,000 acres called River Ridge just above the Columbia at

*Excludes acreage in Yakima and Walla Walla sub-AVAs.

Paterson, and another 460 first planted in 1992 a few miles downstream on Canoe Ridge. California's Chalone Inc. is a neighbor on Canoe Ridge with 101 acres. Both of these look straight onto the broad waters. Well west is Mercer Ranch, like River Ridge away from line-of-sight exposure to the river, but close enough for the microclimate to be moderated by it.

The market has driven plantings so heavily to Cabernet Sauvignon, Merlot, and Chardonnay that few other varieties offer a track record to study. Mercer Ranch, oldest of the vineyards, has done wonders with Lemberger. Chateau Ste Michelle has high regard for the Sauvignon Blanc on its River Ridge vineyard.

Pasco fills in the space between the Yakima and Walla Walla valleys with a cluster of vineyards bearing some of the most familiar names to students of Washington wine labels. For most of the 1970s, Sagemoor Vineyard supported almost every

Left: Gordon Brothers vines slope down to the sustaining waters of the Snake River not far below Ice Harbor Dam, one of the many hydroelectric dams in a huge region of sparse population.
Above: A community hall in the Horse Heaven Hills.

winery in the state after Chateau Ste Michelle. In those years the late Alex Bayless, its original managing partner, would go home to his kitchen with newly printed awards lists from regional competitions and circle the medal winners made from Sagemoor grapes. As often as not his grapes produced roughly half of them, no matter the variety. Two of its finest blocks, Dionysus and Bacchus, are sometimes identified on wines in place of the more general name.

Sagemoor's first vines grow right on the east bank of the Columbia. Not far inland from the 300-acre property are the 190-acre Preston Vineyard and 181-acre Balcom & Moe. A few miles upstream on the Snake River are the 80-acre Gordon Brothers and same-sized Charbonneau vineyards. No other district has as compact a collection of familiar vineyard names, nor offers as many wines for direct comparisons. Some of the richest Sémillon in the state comes from these properties, and

much the ripest Chardonnay, twin reflections of Pasco's having one of the warmest climates among districts currently planted to vines. Faintly pruney Merlots sometimes tell the same story.

Farther north and still east of the Columbia River, the Wahluke Slope appears to be Pasco's nearest rival for top rung on the heat scale. Its long, consistent exposure to the south and superior air drainage make it one of Washington's least freeze-prone territories. State Route 24 cuts right through it from the town of Mattawa eastward. One of the more tantalizing aspects of it is that both Riesling and Sémillon grow well on much of its long face. The Stewart and Tagaris wineries both have Chardonnay, Cabernet Sauvignon, and Merlot planted here.

One range of hills to the north, and almost exactly parallel to the Wahluke, is the Royal Slope, only beginning to be tested in the early 1990s, but already tabbed as having one of the coolest growing seasons on the east side of the Cascades.

203

Yakima Valley AVA

Established: May 1983
Total area: 640,000 acres
Area in vineyard: 4,310 acres
Wineries: 22
Principal towns: Prosser, Sunnyside, Grandview

Reach the crest of Manashtash Ridge on Interstate 82 just east of Ellensburg, and a semidesert fills the windshield in the same instant that a lush farm valley disappears from the rearview mirror. That shock is nothing to the one two bony ridges later, when the Yakima River's main valley suddenly stretches wide to the eastern horizon, vital green where irrigation water has reached, wasted brown where it has not, a dividing line so abrupt it can only be explained by the laws of water rights, not those of nature.

Dozens of water district boundaries criss-cross the Yakima Valley, invisible to outsiders but deeply felt by farmers completely dependent on irrigation in a land where rain and reservoirs are rare and sandy soils are not. These districts have senior to junior water rights depending only upon their founding dates. When the Yakima River flow slows, junior water shuts off first. Thirsty vineyards must, thus, outperform cherries, hops, mint, asparagus, corn, and a dozen other crops to pay their way in the heart of the valley, where rights are senior. They may only have to resist drought on some thin-soiled outer slopes where water is almost as much a newcomer as they are.

Summer water is the easy half of the equation. The hard half comes when Yakima imports its winter weather from the Arctic and keeps it locked inside an almost unbroken ring of hills. Once in 20 years, on average, a mass of Alaskan air will sneak down behind the Cascades to settle over eastern Washington for a fortnight, a month, even longer if that is what it takes to kill vines right to the tips of their roots with night after night of sub-zero temperatures. Tender varieties freeze to the ground oftener than that. And still the farmers find the courage to retrain their vines in the difficult years, and replant them in the disastrous ones. Most of the vineyards, ranging from 80 acres downward, survive by being part of much larger general farming operations, or else by belonging to wineries.

Twenty-two wineries call the valley home, a somewhat misleading figure because a number of wineries reach into it from elsewhere for some or all of their grapes. There is a tit for tat on the point; most of Yakima's wineries reach out into the broader Columbia Valley for part of their supplies. The Hogue Cellars is

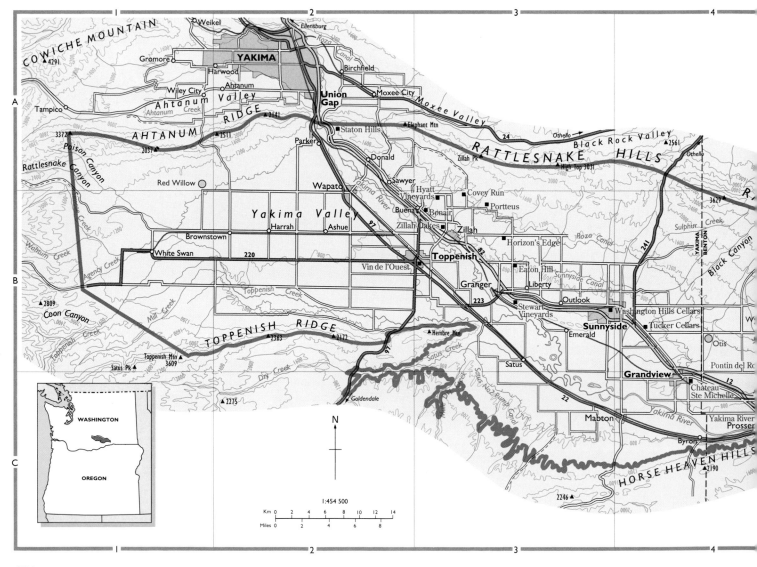

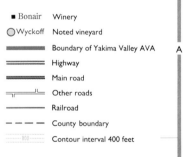

Yakima Valley

■ Bonair   Winery

⊙ Wyckoff   Noted vineyard

Boundary of Yakima Valley AVA

Highway

Main road

Other roads

Railroad

County boundary

800   Contour interval 400 feet

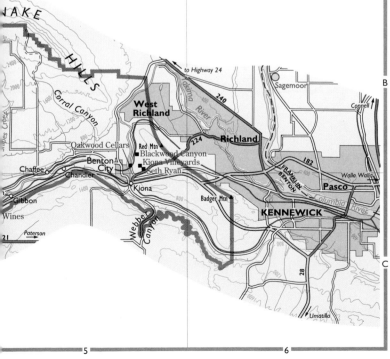

Top: An irrigation canal near Zillah brings lush green vegetation to a land that can otherwise only be barren. Bottom: The outcrops of basalt rock are typical of much of the region east of the Cascade Mountains.

the biggest and perhaps the most praised winery with all its production facilities in the Yakima Valley, although the far larger Chateau Ste Michelle has one of its producing wineries at Grandview. Covey Run, Kiona, Staton Hills, and Stewart Vineyards are other substantial firms with long histories, as history is measured hereabouts: they date from 1984.

The single best-known vineyard in the Yakima Valley at present is Red Willow, a lonely 80-acre parcel within the far larger farm of Mike Sauer and the northernmost *vinifera* vineyard in the valley. The most identifiable area within the appellation is Red Mountain, at the opposite end, not far from the Yakima's confluence with the Columbia. Red Willow, in one of the warmer parts of the valley, much of it carved into the gravels of one of the Columbia's ancient courses, first earned its great reputation with Merlot, especially in the "Milestone" bottlings of Columbia Winery. Cabernet Sauvignon from it is fine if tannically austere. Cabernet Franc, Syrah, and Nebbiolo are all coming along. Sauer is not sure that Chardonnay ripens well enough, and is dead sure that Pinot Noir ripens too much.

Red Mountain is notably warmer than Red Willow, and not at all gravelly. Most of it is sand with a fairly high calcium content. Growers on the south-facing slope have gravitated swiftly to Cabernet Sauvignon, Cabernet Franc and Merlot, but kept early plantings of Riesling because, unaccountably, they do well.

In between, the valley is cooler than either end, with low-lying spots around Prosser coolest of all. The trick for growers from Zillah down to Prosser is to find south-facing slopes, or, where the hills flatten into valley floor, to ferret out places with enough air circulation to minimize winter damage. On lower ground the difference between good Chardonnay conditions and good Cabernet conditions is often a matter of a few yards laterally and a foot or two vertically. One vineyard owner near Sunnyside can ripen nothing but Chardonnay in front of his house, while Cabernet and Merlot mature nicely at the back of it. It is not an unusual story.

Sauvignon Blanc and Cabernet Sauvignon are useful marker varieties. Both will ripen, or even overripen, in the warm spots, but fail to escape vegetal flavors in the coolest ones. Sémillon has been difficult everywhere in Yakima, except when it can be used as a lean, tart substitute for Sauvignon Blanc in a blend with riper Sémillon from Pasco or another hotter spot. Merlot, earlier than Cabernet Sauvignon, will ripen well in almost every situation, but has to be planted with much forethought about possible winter damage.

The mass of Mt Rainier looms above much of the Yakima Valley. Young, drip-irrigated vines in the foreground belong to Covey Run. The interplay of vineyard and orchard is a constant theme in this area.

Walla Walla AVA

Established: March 1984
Total area: 179,200
Area in vineyard: 61 acres
Wineries: 6

Because it laps so far up the the Blue Mountains, Walla Walla may turn out to be the Northwest's most diverse AVA east of the Cascades for sun, rain, and soils. However, any judgment is well in the future. No more than half a dozen vineyards planted with no more than half a dozen varieties have yielded no more than half a dozen wines eligible for the AVA: not enough to support a generalization. At the end of 1992 its most famous vineyard was Seven Hills, Oregon, source of Cabernet Sauvignon and Merlot under its own label, Merlot under the Leonetti marque. The most provocative was a small patch of Gewürztraminer belonging to Biscuit Ridge, whose owner believes his sloping location in the Blue Mountains is cool and rainy enough to approximate to Alsace. Waterbrook had slightly more than half the total acreage in the AVA in ·1992. Dominant varieties of course are Chardonnay, Cabernet Sauvignon, and Merlot.

COLUMBIA VALLEY AND YAKIMA VALLEY PRODUCERS

Badger Mountain Vineyards (1987)
110 Jurupa, Kennewick, WA 99337. Tel (509) 627-4986. 25,500 cases. An organic farmer with 80 acres of vineyards has elected to make his own Chardonnay, Chenin Blanc, Riesling, and Cabernet Sauvignon to show what they can do. Most is sold in bulk, only small lots bottled.

Barnard Griffin Winery (1983)
1707 W Eighth Place, Kennewick, WA 99336. Tel (509) 586-6987. 5,200 cases. The long-time winemaker at Hogue, Rob Griffin, has branched out on his own to make vigorously oaked, firmly built Chardonnay, Sémillon, Sauvignon Blanc (with considerable success), Cabernet Sauvignon, and Merlot.

Blackwood Canyon Vintners (1982)
Route 2, Box 2169-H, Benton City,
WA 99320. Tel (509) 588-6249. 4,400 cases. Thoroughly ripe, well-oaked Sémillon and Cabernet Sauvignon are both estate-grown on Red Mountain at Yakima's southern tip. Technical troubles sometimes peek through.

Bonair Winery (1985)
500 S Bonair Road. Zillah, WA 98953. Tel (509) 829-6027. 3,000 cases. Owner–winemaker Gail Puryear makes butterscotchy estate Chardonnay "Puryear Vineyard" and dark, weighty Cabernet Sauvignon "Morrison" among other single-vineyard wines.

Bookwalter Winery (1983)
2708 N Commercial Avenue, Pasco, WA 99301. Tel (509) 547-8571. 6,000 cases. Vineyard manager–grape broker Jerrold Bookwalter uses insider's insights to buy grapes for Chardonnay, Cabernet Sauvignon, and a deft Merlot.

Champs de Brionne Winery (1983)
Route 1, 98 Road "W" NW, Quincy, WA 98848. Tel (509) 785-6685. 2,000 cases. The business has had ups and downs in its brief career. Chardonnay, Sémillon and Cabernet-Merlot have been the mainstay types.

Chateau Gallant (1988)
1355 Gallant Road South, Pasco, WA 99301. Tel (509) 545-9570. 2,000 cases. The Gallant family makes Chardonnay, Gewürztraminer, Riesling, and others from 25 acres of vines on their multicrop farm near Pasco.

Chateau Ste Michelle (See p 210)

Chinook Wines (1983)
PO Box 387, Prosser, WA 99350. Tel (509) 786-2725. 2,000 cases. Owner–winemaker Kay Simon favors sturdy, plain-spoken, vineyard-first Chardonnay, Sauvignon Blanc, and Merlot, all from bought-in, mostly Yakima Valley, grapes.

Columbia Crest Winery (1984)
PO Box 231, Paterson, WA 99345. Tel (509) 875-2061. 475,000 cases. The lower-priced sibling of Chateau Ste Michelle turns out a steady flow of solidly made, attractive wines. Deft Sémillon "Barrel Select" and polished, distinctively flavorful Merlot "Barrel Select" show the way. Most of the grapes come from company-owned vineyards at Paterson and Cold Creek.

Covey Run Vintners (1982)
1500 Vintage Road, Zillah, WA 98953. Tel (509) 829-6235. 60,500 cases. One of the Yakima Valley's older firms has shown across-the-

Walla Walla Valley

1:454 500

board strength in recent vintages, but especially with Caille de Fumé (Sémillon-Sauvignon blend), Fumé Blanc, and Cabernet based on its 180-acre vineyard at the edge of the Rattlesnake Hills. Lemberger from bought-in grapes is one of the best.

Eaton Hill Winery (1988)
530 Gurley Road, Granger, WA 98932. Tel (509) 854-2220. 900 cases. Riesling and Sémillon from 7 acres is the start-up roster. The proprietors plan to broaden the list and enlarge production.

Gordon Brothers Cellars (1983)
531 Levey Road, Pasco, WA 99301. Tel (509) 547-6224. 1,700 cases. Washington's first, perhaps still only grower label covers refined, supple Merlot and Cabernet Sauvignon and a deftly oaked Chardonnay from an 80-acre vineyard next to the Snake River just below Ice Harbor Dam.

Hinzerling Winery (1976)
1520 Sheridan Avenue, Prosser, WA 99350. Tel (509) 786-2163. 1,000 cases. One of the early names has been the shuttlecock in a game of buy-and-sell in recent years. As of 1992 it was with original owner Mike Wallace, whose bent is toward Merlot and Cabernet Sauvignon.

The Hogue Cellars (1982)
PO Box 31, Prosser, WA 99350. Tel

Top: Columbia Crest's tasting room sits atop its winery.
Bottom: The Hogue Cellars' visitor center sits out front.

(509) 786-4557. 190,000 cases. Arguably Washington's best across-the-board winery, certainly one of its most reliable. It is based in 300 acres owned by the Hogue family, but buys widely in the Columbia Valley for refined but indelible Sémillon, polished Merlot, and Cabernet Sauvignon, fruitier than usual Chardonnay, and top-drawer Rieslings.

Horizon's Edge Winery (1983)
4530 E Zillah Drive, Zillah, WA 98953. Tel (509) 829-6401. 900 cases. Both the Chardonnays and Cabernet Sauvignons have tended to be for-

ward on release, and quick to age from there. The winery has 15 acres of vineyard.

Hunter Hill Vineyards (1984)
2752 W McMannaman Road, Othello, WA 99344. Tel (509) 346-2736. 1,200 cases. Chardonnay, Cabernet Sauvignon, Merlot, and Riesling in diverse styles come from the winery's own 28 acres.

Hyatt Vineyards (1987)
2020 Gilbert Road, Zillah, WA 98953. Tel (509) 829-6333. 4,500 cases. Chardonnay, Sauvignon Blanc, and

Merlot from a 73-acre estate vineyard dominate the list.

Kiona Vineyards (1980)
Route 2, Box 2169-E, Benton City, WA 99320. Tel (509) 588-6716. 10,000 cases. Chardonnay and all the reds see plenty of oak; delicately perfumed dry White Riesling and sweeter Johannisberg Riesling are left to shine on their own. A Chenin Blanc 1989 Ice Wine was a marvel. The winery's owning families grow 70 acres of grapes on Red Mountain.

Oakwood Cellars (1986)
Route 2, Box 2321, Benton City, WA 99320. Tel (509) 588-5332. 2,000 cases. The winery name fairly announces its style for Chardonnay, Sémillon, Cabernet Sauvignon, and Merlot. It has 40 acres of vines.

Pontin del Roza Winery (1984)
Route 4, Box 4735, Prosser, WA 99350. Tel (509) 786-4449. 10,000 cases. Fumé Blanc leads a list that also includes forthrightly oaky Chardonnay and Cabernet Sauvignon. The owners have 15 acres of vines.

Portteus Winery (1984)
5201 Highland Drive, Zillah, WA 98953. Tel (509) 829-6970. 1,200 cases. Cabernet Sauvignons have been the headliners. There are also a Chardonnay and a Sémillon that tries to be a Chardonnay. The wines are estate-bottled from 47 acres.

Preston Wine Cellars (1976)
502 E Vineyard Drive, Pasco, WA 99301. Tel (509) 545-1990. 46,000 cases. Irrepressible Bill Preston has never feared to go haring off after new approaches to style, with the result that every vintage provides one new adventure or another. The 190-acre vineyard just north of Pasco has yielded some notably flavorful Chardonnays and, more especially, Rieslings.

Quarry Lake Winery (1985)
2420 Commercial Avenue, Pasco, WA 99301. Tel (509) 547-7307. 12,000 cases. Maury Balcom has scored impressively with Sauvignon Blanc and Cabernet Sauvignon from the affiliated Balcom & Moe vineyard, 181 acres across Vineyard Drive from Preston.

Seth Ryan Winery (1985)
Route 2, Box 2168-D1, Benton City, WA 99320. Tel (509) 588-6780. 1,600 cases. Weekend winemakers are edging toward larger production of Chardonnay, Gewürtraminer, and Riesling from bought-in grapes.

Staton Hills Winery (1984)
71 Gangl Road, Wapato, WA 98951. Tel (509) 877-2112. 41,000 cases. One of the sturdiest winery operations in the Yakima Valley has 16 experimentally farmed acres of its own and more than 225 leased acres upon which to draw for a broad list headed by fine Sémillon, understated yet stylish Cabernet Sauvignon, and similar Merlot. The Chardonnay carries a deft touch of wood.

Stewart Vineyards (1983)
1711 Cherry Hill Road, Granger, WA 98944. Tel (509) 854-1882. 8,200 cases. Consistently attractive wines are based in 50 acres divided between a small vineyard near Toppenish, and a larger one on the Wahluke Slope. Both Sauvignon Blanc and Chardonnay showcase the vineyards. A Cabernet Sauvignon is subtly styled.

Tagaris Winery (1987)
PO Box 5433, Kennewick, WA 99336. Tel (509) 547-3590. 10,000 cases. Fumé Blanc and Cabernet Sauvignon are steady. A Chardonnay is not quite their equal. All come from a vineyard on the Wahluke Slope.

Tefft Cellars (1989)
2862 N Outlook Road, Outlook, WA 98938. [no tel]. The busman's holiday winery of a long-time cellar foreman in the Yakima Valley.

Thurston Wolfe Winery (1987)
PO Box 9068, Yakima, WA 98909. Tel (509) 452-0335. 1,500 cases.

Another busman's holiday winery; this one belongs to viticulturalist Wade Wolfe, who launched it with a well made Lemberger.

Tucker Cellars (1981)
70 Ray Road, Sunnyside, WA 98944. Tel (509) 837-8701. 10,500 cases. An old-line Yakima farm family favors both its Chardonnay and Cabernet Sauvignon fully ripe and well oaked. They grow 55 acres of vines within a far larger general farming operation.

Vin de l'Ouest (1990)
101 Toppenish Avenue, Toppenish, WA 98948. Tel (509) 453-9600. 1,000 cases.

Washington Hills Cellars (1988)
111 E Lincoln Avenue, Sunnyside, WA 98944. Tel (509) 839-9463. 175,000 cases. A major new player produces solid, attractive Sémillon, Fumé Blanc, and Cabernet Sauvignon at modest prices. The affiliated Apex label is reserved for superior lots of the same types.

White Heron Cellars (1986)
101 Washington Way N, George, WA 98824. Tel (509) 785-5521.

Yakima River Winery (1978)
Route 1, Box 1657, Prosser, WA 99350. Tel (509) 786-2805. 5,200 cases. Self-taught owner–winemaker John Rauner has kept to a sturdy, sometimes rustic style with Sauvignon Blanc, Cabernet Sauvignon, and Merlot among others.

Zillah Oakes Winery (1986)
PO Box 1729, Zillah, WA 98953 Tel (509) 829-6990. 5,200 cases. What began as a second label for Covey Run soon acquired a life of its own. The main wines are modestly priced Chardonnay and Riesling.

WALLA WALLA VALLEY PRODUCERS

Biscuit Ridge Winery (1987)
Route 1, Box 132, Waitsburg, WA 99361. Tel (509) 529-4986. 500 cases. The Blue Mountains foothills have convinced the proprietor that he has the perfect spot for Gewürztraminer and a good one for Pinot Noir.

l'Ecole #41 (1983)
PO Box 111, Lowden, WA 99360. Tel (509) 525-0940. 1,750 cases. Weighty, oaky Sémillon and curiously floral Merlot are the list. All the grapes are bought-in.

Leonetti Cellar (1978)
1321 School Avenue, Walla Walla, WA 99362. Tel (509) 525-1428. 3,100 cases. The original style was for

ultraripe, full-bodied Cabernet Sauvignon and Merlot. Recent vintages have pulled back to more classical balances, to fine effect. Most grapes are bought-in from the Columbia Valley; a single vineyard Merlot comes from Seven Hills, in the Oregon half of the Walla Walla Valley appellation.

Patrick M. Paul Vineyards (1988)
1554 School Avenue, Walla Walla, WA 99362. Tel (509) 522-1127. 1,200 cases. Concord wine from owner's 4 acres and purchased grapes.

Seven Hills (1988)
235 E Broadway, Milton-Freewater OR 97862. Tel (503) 938-7710. 1,200 cases. The first vineyard in the Walla Walla Valley to make a name for itself yields a gently flavored, quickly soft Cabernet Sauvignon for its own label and Leonetti's.

Waterbrook Winery (1984)
Route 1, Box 46, Lowden, WA 99360. Tel (509) 522-1918. 17,500 cases. Owner–winemaker Eric Rindal has hit a nice stride with supple, flavorful Merlot and Cabernet Sauvignon, also with an intensely herby Sauvignon Blanc. A Chardonnay is much in the toasty style. Some of the grapes come from 30 estate acres, the largest vineyard in the appellation.

Woodward Canyon Winery (1981)
Route 1, Box 387, Lowden, WA 99360. Tel (509) 525-4129. 2,600 cases. The big, ripe, well-oaked style rules in both an ultratoasty Chardonnay and a dark Cabernet Sauvignon primarily from bought-in Columbia Valley grapes, although owner Ric Small has 10 acres of vines in the appellation.

Other Wine Regions

SPOKANE PRODUCERS

Spokane is well beyond the last row of Columbia Valley vines, but has become a small center of winemaking because of its population. All the cellars noted – except Mountain Dome – welcome visitors with open arms.

Arbor Crest Wine Cellars (1982)
N 4705 Fruithill Road, Spokane, WA 99207. Tel (509) 927-9463. 39,000 cases. Pungent Sauvignon Blancs have been the pinnacle on a list that also includes well-wooded Chardonnay, Cabernet Sauvignon, and Merlot. All grapes are bought-in from Columbia Valley sources.

Latah Creek Wine Cellars (1983)
E 13030 Indiana Avenue, Spokane, WA 99216. Tel (509) 926-0164. 12,000 cases. Owner–winemaker Michael Conway has turned in recent years to reds bottled for freshness, whites made with ample oak. He buys Columbia Valley grapes.

Steven Thomas Livingstone Winery (1988)
5,200 cases. E 14 Mission Avenue, Spokane, WA 99202. Tel (509) 328-5069. Thoroughly oaked Sauvignon Blanc, Chardonnay, and Merlot from bought-in Columbia Valley grapes.

Mountain Dome Winery (1988)
16315 Temple Road, Spokane, WA 99207. Tel (509) 922-7408. 2,000 cases. Washington's first pure specialist in sparkling wines from home state grapes.

Worden's Washington Winery (1980)
7217 45th Avenue W, Spokane, WA 99204. Tel (509) 455-7835. 17,500 cases. Faintly spritzy, off-dry whites were the foundation stone. The focus has shifted to fully oaked Chardonnay and a dark, austere Cabernet-Merlot. A second label, Suncrest, is for organically grown Riesling, Gewürztraminer, and Chenin Blanc of airy charm.

PUGET SOUND PRODUCERS

Suburban Seattle is vigorously wine country without beginning to be grape country, for reasons noted in the introduction. In the further reaches of the Puget Sound basin, a few small vineyards feed wineries dedicated to Müller-Thurgau and other cool-climate grapes.

Andrew Will Cellars (1989)
8624 SW Soaper Road, Vashon, WA 98070. Tel (206) 463-3290. 700 cases.

Bainbridge Island Winery (1981)
682 Highway 305, Bainbridge Island, WA 98110. Tel (206) 842-9463. 2,000 cases. From its own small vineyard on an island in Puget Sound, an eclectic list best represented by Müller-Thurgau.

Cavatappi Winery (1985)
9702 NE 120th Pl, WA Kirkland 98033. Tel (206) 823-6533. 2,000 cases. A silky, delicately flavorful Nebbiolo under the name of Maddalena is the specialty. It comes

Chateau Ste Michelle's winery at Woodinville near Seattle.

from Red Willow vineyard at Wapato. Also: Sauvignon Blanc.

Chateau Ste Michelle (1967)
One Stimson Lane, Woodinville, WA 98072. Tel (206) 488-1133. 700,000 cases. With more than 3,000 acres of vines, most of them near Vantage (Cold Creek) and at Paterson (River Ridge, Canoe Ridge), the owning company behind Chateau Ste Michelle is the driving force behind Washington viticulture. With these vines, and important quantities of bought-in grapes, it anchors the winemaking. The Chateau Ste Michelle name is utterly reliable across a complete spectrum of varietals, and increasingly memorable for its vineyard-designated Chardonnays and Cabernet Sauvignons. The parent company, Stimson Lane, also owns Columbia Crest, a separate winery in the Columbia Valley, and the Snoqualmie, Farron Ridge, Allison Combs, and Saddle Mountain labels.

Columbia Winery (1967) PO Box 1248, Woodinville, WA 98072. Tel (206) 488-2776. 76,000 cases. If Chateau Ste Michelle drives Washington by sheer weight of numbers, Columbia Winery drives it with winemaker David Lake's relentless exploration of individual vineyards, especially in Yakima Valley. The finest results come from Merlot ("Milestone" from Red Willow as well as an assem-

Columbia's whimsical cupola.

bled regular bottling) and Sémillon, but the whole list is worthy.

Domaine Whittlesey-Mark (1984)
5318-22d Avenue NW, Seattle, WA 98107. Tel (206) 789-6543. 2,000 cases. Because proprietor Mark Newton has settled on Willamette Valley grapes as best suited to the purpose, but he does not wish to move, his winery is Washington's first specialist in Oregon sparkling wines.

Facelli Winery (1988)
16120 Woodinville-Redmond Road No1, Woodinville, WA 98072. Tel (206) 488-1020. 3,000 cases. Long-time winemaker Lou Facelli has settled in on his own, making attractive

Sémillon, Fumé Blanc, and Chardonnay, and promising Merlot.

E.B. Foote Winery (1978)
9354 Fourth Avenue S, Seattle, WA 98108. Tel (206) 763-9928. 3,400 cases. Insistently bone dry, austere, and flavored more by winemaking than grapes are Foote's Chardonnay, Cabernet Sauvignon, and even his Chenin Blanc and Riesling. All are from bought-in Columbia Valley grapes.

French Creek Cellars (1983)
17721-132d Avenue NE, Woodinville, WA 98072. Tel (206) 486-1900. 8,500 cases. Vigorous admiration for the taste of oak has informed French Creek wines, all from bought-in Columbia Valley grapes.

Hedges Cellars (1989)
1105-12th Avenue NW, Ste A-4, Issaquah, WA 98027. Tel (206) 391-4060. 30,000 cases. Washington's first really successful blender of Merlot and Cabernet Sauvignon began as a negociant label. It now has its own vineyard on Red Mountain to anchor its supple, stylish Cabernet-Merlot.

Hoodsport Winery (1980)
23501 Highway 101, Hoodsport, WA 98548. Tel (206) 877-9894. 17,500 cases. It started as a fruit winery, so came with a healthy respect for the flavors of grapes. Its Lemberger defines the variety; some others, such as Merlot, taste so unfamiliar without oak as to be distracting. An engaging curiosity: varietal "Island Belle" from 5 acres at the winery.

Johnson Creek Winery (1984)
19248 Johnson Creek Road SE, Tenino, WA 98589. Tel (206) 264-2100. 1,700 cases. Affiliated with a restaurant at the same address. The flagship is an estate Müller-Thurgau.

Lost Mountain Winery (1981)
3142 Lost Mountain Road, Sequim, WA 98382. Tel (206) 683-5229. 700 cases. The Washington wines (on a list that includes some from California grapes) are brash, heady Cabernet Sauvignon, Merlot, and a blended proprietary called "Poesia."

McCrea Cellars (1988)
12707-18th Street SE, Lake Stevens, WA 98258. Tel (206) 334-5248. 1,100 cases. A toasty Chardonnay is the mainstay, a Grenache-based blend from Columbia Gorge grapes the lodestar.

Mount Baker Vineyards (1982)
PO Box 626, Deming, WA 98244. Tel (206) 592-2300. 7,500 cases. A fascinating grower–producer of rare Madeleine Angevine (spicy-floral) and

Okanagan Riesling from 25 acres near the British Columbia border, not far inland from Puget Sound.

Neuharth Winery (1979)
148 Still Road, Sequim, WA 98382. Tel (206) 683-9652. 2,200 cases. One of Washington's steadiest producers of approachable, vineyard-first, but far from simple Merlot and Cabernet Sauvignon. They come from bought-in Columbia Valley grapes.

Quilceda Creek Vintners (1979)
5226 Machias Road, Snohomish, WA 98290. Tel (206) 568-2389. 1,000 cases. Specializes in an ultraripe, generously oaked, and otherwise stylized Cabernet Sauvignon from bought-in Columbia Valley grapes.

Silver Lake Winery (1988)
17616-15th Avenue SE, No106-B, Bothell, WA 98012. Tel (206) 485-2437. 15,000 cases. Early Chardonnays and Sauvignon Blancs won swift critical acclaim. Cabernet Sauvignon and Merlot were just coming onto the track in 1992. Bought-in Columbia Valley grapes are the source.

Snoqualmie Winery (1984)
1000 Winery Road, Snoqualmie, WA 98065. Tel (206) 888-4000. 15,000 cases. With Chateau Ste Michelle and others, a property of Stimson Lane Company, and a reliable producer of attractive whites.

Paul Thomas Winery (1979)
1717-136th Pl. NE, Bellevue, WA 98005. Tel (206) 747-1008. 26,000 cases. Like others that started as fruit wine wineries, Paul Thomas keeps the flavors of grapes foremost in all its *vinifera* wines. Unlike some others, it uses oak as a deft complication in the finished product. Especially to be sought for Chardonnay Reserve, Sauvignon Blanc, Cabernet Sauvignon – and "Crimson Rhubarb." The *vinifera* wines come from bought-in Columbia Valley grapes.

SOUTHWEST WASHINGTON PRODUCERS

A handful of small vineyards in the Columbia Gorge, and one small property across the Columbia River from Portland grow grapes and make wines quite unlike those from elsewhere in Washington.

Charles Hooper Family Winery (1985)
PO Box 215, Husum, WA 98623. Tel (509) 493-2324. 1,700 cases. The linchpin is Riesling, nearly all from the proprietors' own steep-pitched 6 acres in the Columbia Gorge.

Mont Elise Vineyards(1975) PO Box 28, Bingen, WA 98605. Tel (509) 493-3001. 4,400 cases. Gewürztraminer from 35 acres in the Columbia Gorge has been the signature; a Pinot Noir-based sparkling wine from the same vineyard is the new contender.

Salishan Vineyards (1975) 35011 North Fork Avenue, La Center, WA 98629. Tel (206) 263-2713. 2,000 cases. From a 12-acre vineyard across from Portland, steady Chardonnay and a Pinot Noir to rival many of the better examples from Oregon's Willamette Valley.

Travel Information

CENTRAL WASHINGTON PLACES OF INTEREST

Central Washington is very much close-to-the-earth, homespun farm country. With some exceptions in Yakima and the Tri-Cities, visitor facilities fit the style. Ask locals for a list of best restaurants, and at least three of the top five are likely to be "authenticmexican," pronounced all one word, a little like "damnyankees" in the south.

Tri-Cities The old farm towns of Kennewick and Pasco plus the World War II atomic energy boom-town of Hanford coexist, mostly in peace, as the Tri-Cities. The Hanford Science Center (George Washington Way at Newton Street, Hanford) is instructive about nuclear energy. Ice Harbor Dam (on the Snake River 12 miles east of Pasco) is equally informative about hydroelectric power. Sacajawea State Park, south of Pasco at the confluence of the Snake and Columbia rivers, has a museum of Indian artifacts along with lawns and beaches. The Columbia River runs through the towns, making them a boater's resort. They also sit exactly at the hub of Washington's vineyards.

Yakima Central Washington's largest, brightest, most bustling small city is to the west of the wineries and vineyards, but not so far that its other virtues do not outweigh the location. A local museum (1205 Tieton Drive) has well-mounted pioneer exhibits including one of horse-drawn vehicles.

HOTELS AND RESTAURANTS

Burchfield Manor, 2018 Burchfield Road, Yakima. Tel (509) 452-1960. Weekends only, no children, eclectic menu, good Northwest wine list, all in a stately pioneer house.
Chez Chaz, 5011 W Clearwater, Kennewick. Tel (509) 735-2138. Originally a dessert house, it has kept the sweet tooth but turned into a bistro. The most ambitious menus are Friday and Saturday evenings.
Clover Island Inn, 435 Clove Island, Kennewick, WA 99336. Tel (509) 586-0541. Comfortable inn on

the river next to a yacht basin.
Gasperetti's, 1013 N 1st Street, Yakima. Tel (509) 248-0628. Italian-continental; eternal favorite of all Yakima.
The Greystone, 5 N Front Street, Yakima. Tel (509) 248-9801. French-continental in handsome gray stone building. Excellent Northwest wines.
Red Lion, 2525 N 20th Avenue, Pasco, WA 99301. Tel (509) 946-7611. Sizable modern motor inn with a better-than-average restaurant.

PUGET SOUND PLACES OF INTEREST

Seattle Washington's largest city has acquired a considerable reputation in the larger world for a regional cuisine based on Pacific Northwest seafood. Others among its restaurants are every bit as good. It takes a guidebook to list all of its attractions: opera, symphony orchestra, art museums, science and industry museums, museum of flight and more.

HOTELS AND RESTAURANTS

Anthony's Homeport, Moss Bay Marina, Kirkland, Seattle. Tel (206) 822-0225. Casual, bustling. Huge portions of fresh fish and shellfish. Good northwest wine list.
Café Juanita, 9702 NE 120th Pl, Kirkland, Seattle. Tel (206) 823-1505. An Italophile does right by many traditional pasta and meat dishes. The Cavatappi Winery is belowstairs.
Campagne, 86 Pine Street, Seattle. Tel (206) 728-2800. In the famed Pike Place Market, a bistro with Provençal preparations of northwest seafood as the heart of its menu. Some northwest wines amid a host of Rhône and Midi bottlings.
The Hunt Club, 900 Madison Street, Seattle. Tel (206) 622-6400. Handsome dining room in handsomely refurbished Sorrento Hotel. The menu borrows styles from Seattle's ethnic rainbow for duck, seafood, and other northwest foods.
Inn at the Market, 86 Pine Street, Seattle. Tel (206) 443-3600. Elegant

small hotel on the doorstep of the historic Pike Place Market.
Kaspar's By the Bay, 2701 First Avenue, Seattle. Tel (206) 441-4805. Comfortable atmosphere and food from a Suisse Romande chef who chose Seattle for the quality of local ingredients.
McCarthy & Schiering Wine Merchants, 6500 Ravenna Avenue NE, Seattle. Tel (206) 282-8500. Fine universalists, selective on the northwest.
Metropolitan Grill, 820-2d Avenue, Seattle. Tel (206) 624-3287. Men's club decor, beef and seafood menu. Fine northwest wine list.
Pike & Western Company, 1934 Pike Pl, Seattle. Tel (206) 441-1307. The specialist merchant in northwest wines on the west side.
Place Pigalle, 81 Pike Street, Seattle. Tel (206) 624-1756. Mostly Mediterranean menu in a bistro-by-day, candlelight-by-night dining room in the old Pike Place Market. Long wine list includes older and rarer northwest ones.
Ray's Boathouse, 6049 Seaview

Avenue NW, Seattle. Tel (206) 789-3770. Spectacular views across Puget Sound to the snowy Olympic Mountains are the bonus at Seattle's premier seafood house. Splendid service. Spectacular northwest wine list.
Stouffer Madison Hotel, 515 Madison Street, Seattle, WA 98104. Tel (206) 583-0300. Executive hotel handy for downtown restaurants and freeways to everywhere.

USEFUL ADDRESSES

Washington Wine Commission, PO Box 61217, Seattle, WA 98121. Tel (206) 728-2252.
Yakima Valley Visitors & Convention Bureau, 10 North 8th Street, Yakima, WA 98901. Tel (509) 575-1300.
Tri-Cities Visitor & Convention Bureau, PO Box 2241, Tri-Cities, WA 99302. Tel (509) 735-8486.
Seattle Visitors & Convention Bureau, 800 Convention Place, Seattle, WA 98101. Tel (206) 461-5840.

Washington's huge fishing fleet supplies the complement to its white wines.

Oregon

Oregon winemaking began almost purely as the product of several personal revolts against California. Richard Sommer finished his studies at the University of California at Davis in 1961 and struck out immediately to plant his Hillcrest Vineyards in the Umpqua Valley. David Lett left the same training ground four years later and headed for the northern Willamette Valley to found the Eyrie Vineyard. Richard Erath of Knudsen Erath, Bill Fuller of Tualatin, and Richard Ponzi are other prominent pioneers who came north in the first wave.

Oregon's ranks of winery owners and winemakers continue to be fed by Californian transplants, a casual survey suggesting that at the outset of the 1990s, roughly half the state's wineries belong to one-time Californians.

Most if not all of these pioneers were discontented in California, some on social grounds, a majority because reliable sunshine did not give them the kind of wines they wanted to make. After as long as two decades, many of them still enjoy insulting almost everything Californian, and otherwise being testy. The fit between them and their new home seems perfect. Sunshine is anything but reliable and, socially, much of Oregon is a more convenient Alaska, a place where independent thinkers can put a lot of space between themselves and neighbors who might have different ideas.

Sommer arrived wishing to explore several grape varieties. Lett was bent on Pinot Noir. Fuller's first ambitions were Riesling and Gewürztraminer. Lett succeeded in pushing the Willamette Valley into the regional limelight with his first few Pinot Noirs. He, or they, or both, became the great magnet, leaving a handful of growers in the Umpqua and Rogue valleys to struggle along in the shadows while an ever-swelling army of converts hunted through Yamhill and Washington counties for vineyard land and winery sites. That trend has yet to let up. In 1992 the Willamette had 68 percent of the acreage, and a larger proportion of the wineries in the state. Both shares were growing.

Because Pinot Noir is king and a distaste for reliable sun lives on among the state's most influential winemakers, eastern Oregon has developed only a spare few vineyards, the reverse of the Washington experience. What few there are were scooped into Washington-born appellations, guaranteeing orphan status for a while, at least.

When the first wineries sprang up in the late 1960s and early 1970s, farming in most of western Oregon was on hard times, save for the pear orchards in the Rogue Valley. Willamette soils are not rich enough, and the climate is not warm enough for their cherries or apples to compete against other regions. Hazelnuts, although they grow surpassingly well, were being decimated by a blight. Farm land could be acquired at give-away prices, not unimportant to a first wave of wineries founded by idealists with little or no money in their pockets.

For its first ten years, Oregon's wine industry was fetchingly rustic, housed in reclaimed packing sheds and equipped with cast-offs from dairies and soft drinks bottling plants. Monied firms are in the industry now, and even the least wealthy of the first wave own first-rate equipment, but much of the architecture

harks back to the start. The early lack of funds did one other thing. It kept the vineyards small – Burgundy sized, their owners gladly think.

Only one trouble haunts this paradise. Where Washington found itself torn between grape-growing country on one side of the Cascade Mountains and population on the other, Oregon brings the two almost too close together. Already, conservative voices fret that a growing Portland is pushing hard against top-flight vineyard land in Washington and Yamhill counties, even harder than metropolitan San Francisco pushes against Napa and Sonoma in California. In a region where several famous vineyards are in the first ring of suburbs, the concern is real.

Above: Fat Burgundian barrels are the vessels of choice for aging Oregon Pinot Noirs. These are at Rex Hill winery.

Left: The end of a small storm drifts across Elk Cove's estate vineyard, leaving a late sun to promise a bright, sunny morrow. It is a promise not always kept, which is exactly what suits the Pinot Noir, Riesling, and other varieties planted in the Willamette Valley.

213

Climate

Western Oregon is the only Pacific State that has a reasonably predictable climatic pattern, warming steadily toward the equator. The lower Willamette Valley around Portland is cooler than the upper valley, which is cooler than Umpqua to the south, which in turn is cooler than Rogue Valley right on California's border. Rainfall dwindles from usual to infrequent in the same pattern, so swiftly that grape and orchard farmers in Rogue Valley routinely irrigate their properties in the summer. The Coast Ranges are the main engine of change. They begin low and broken by gaps at the Columbia River mouth, then build steadily until they become the Klamaths, a formidable barrier to sea air. The towering Cascade Mountains form the inland side of all three valleys, bringing rain from winter clouds and channeling cool air south in summer. Forest Grove's summer may have brief hot spells, as it did in 1990, but cool to moderate temperatures prevail throughout a long growing season that begins with an occasionally frosty, always showery, spring, and ends with heavy autumn rains more often than frosts. Eugene, 110 miles to the south, is marginally warmer and drier than Forest Grove throughout the growing season. Roseburg, in Umpqua Valley, is another 70 miles south, separated from Willamette's drainage basin by a substantial ridge. Its growing season is much warmer and drier than Eugene's. But the big shift in climate comes between the Umpqua and Rogue valleys. The Rogue, hemmed in on three sides by mountains, is an efficient heat trap like the southern San Joaquin Valley, the Siskyou Mountains to its south the equivalent of California's Transverse Range. Long heat spells are as common in Medford and Grants Pass as they are in Fresno and Madera. There are two differences between it and San Joaquin: the Klamaths are the only range between Rogue Valley and the sea, so some sea air finds its way up the Rogue and Illinois river courses; and its surrounding hills are much cooler than the valley floor, in fact closer to the conditions of El Dorado County in the Sierra Foothills than anywhere else. Damaging winter freezes are rare in western Oregon. The cold spell of December 1990, which saw temperatures as low as 3°F in Willamette, –4°F in Rogue, was a once-in-50-years event.

* For the color code to the climate charts see pages 14–15.

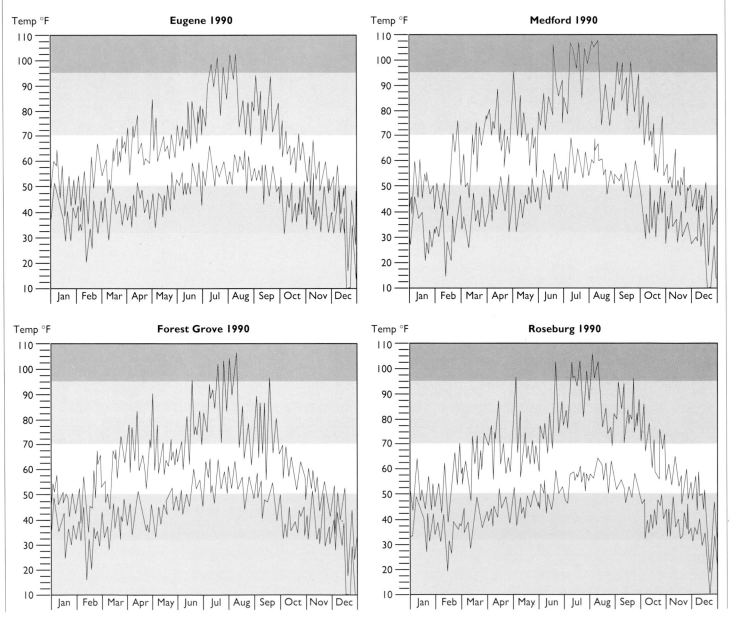

A casual picnic table symbolizes Oregon's folksy warmth. This one is at Bethel Heights.

White Wine Varieties

Chardonnay and Riesling have dominated plantings and wines since the 1970s. Gewürztraminer and Sauvignon Blanc have puttered along in niche roles throughout the formative era. Pinot Gris began mounting a real challenge to Chardonnay at the turn to the 1990s. Pinot Blanc, although still minimal in acreage, appeared poised to become important.

Chardonnay (20 acres in 1970, 978 in 1990)
The great white variety is even more prevalent than its position on the acreage charts would suggest. Until Laurel Ridge and Serendipity dared to open without Chardonnay on their lists, it might have been assumed that Oregon law required every winery to have one.

Logic dictates: if this be Pinot Noir country, how could it be other than Chardonnay country as well? The reasons are not yet clear, but experience drives one to go looking for a reason why. While Oregon's Pinot Noir can be intensely perfumed, its Chardonnay validates the great New York viticulturalist Philip Wagner's dictum: the flavors of wines from *Vitis vinifera* are mild tending towards neutral. Willamette Valley Chardonnay epitomizes Wagner's observation. Vineyards in both the Rogue and Umpqua valleys seem to show more fruit flavors than their rivals in the Willamette, but not by any great margin.

Sensibly, winemakers throughout the state use barrel and malolactic fermentation, aging on the lees, and all the other tricks Burgundians use in the Côte d'Or to build added flavors into their wines. Predictably, short experience in a marginal climate leaves lessons of proportion still to be learned by a considerable number of those winemakers. Even in the best vintages a great deal of Oregon Chardonnay remains awkward, tipped too far in one winemaking direction or another to be altogether agreeable company at dinner. Difficult vintages have overwhelmed the most skilled producers at one time or another.

Still, all hands push ahead and sparks of hope keep flying. Although the wines from existing vineyards seem forever fated to tend toward neutral when it comes to pure Chardonnay flavor, some of the most adroit winemakers in the state are finding ways to paint captivating miniatures rather than aiming for canvases of imposing sweep.

Over a short career, Tyee has captured the toasty notes of malolactic and aging in new oak barrels while still keeping clear notes of Chardonnay. Shafer Vineyards Cellar has managed to render some of the purest flavors of grapes. The others in the list of benchmarks lean, gracefully, on flavors from time in oak.
Benchmarks:
Bethel Heights Willamette Valley (estate). **Shafer Vineyards** Cellar Willamette Valley (estate). **Oak Knoll** Willamette Valley (assembled). **Tualatin** Willamette Valley (estate). **Tyee** Willamette Valley (assembled). **Bridgeview** Rogue Valley (estate).

Gewürztraminer (8 acres in 1970, 163 in 1990)
Way back in his first vintages Richard Sommers served notice that Gewürztraminer might have a place in Oregon. The variety has produced attractive wines ever since in both the Umpqua and Willamette valleys. In some vintages it comes right at the head of the list. The Rogue also has begun laying claim to it.

Illogical as it seems, most bottlings from the Willamette show Gewürztraminer in much the same light as eastern Washington does, tasting a little of mint and much of Muscat. The most impressive examples from the Rogue come closer to the licheelike flavors familiar from the cooler valleys of coastal California.

As in California, wineries have discovered that a place in the vineyard does not automatically mean a place in the market, and thus the roster of producers has trimmed down to those who care to do their best by the variety. A tendency for Gewürztraminer to yield poorly, often less than two tons per acre, has not helped its cause.
Benchmarks:
Amity Willamette Valley. **Knudsen Erath** Willamette Valley. **St Josef's Weinkeller** Willamette Valley. **Tualatin** Willamette Valley.

Müller-Thurgau (0 in 1970, 132 acres in 1990)
In Oregon, the best known of Germany's Riesling-based cross-breeds performs as well in the vineyard as the illustrious parent. Although no more than a dozen wineries produce it, the wines show well as light, off-dry, drink-quick varietals, exemplified by Tualatin and Chateau Benoit. A fair amount of the crop goes into everyday generic table wines.

215

Washington and Yamhill counties, at the Willamette's northern, downstream end, have nearly 100 acres of the total plantings, Polk County another 15. From those vineyards come most of the varietal bottlings. Columbia Gorge grows most of the rest.

Pinot Gris (0 in 1970, 150 acres in 1990)

Within a few vintages of its introduction, Pinot Gris has brought more rewards to winemakers and bibbers alike than has Chardonnay over a longer time. From the outset, Willamette Valley Pinot Gris has been characterful without being bold or simple. Better yet, it has sung sweet duets with Pacific salmon.

Its hallmark aroma somehow brings to mind delicate, dustily floral perfumes, much as the best Pinot Grigio from Trentino and the Veneto will do. It has its own depth and complexity without much if any oak aging, yet holds well through extended time in barrel. How it will last in bottle is still to be tested.

Producers and consumers alike have noticed its quality. Slight though the acreage remained in 1992, a survey in that year showed Oregon producing 22 of the United States' grand total of 35 Pinot Gris. The Eyrie Vineyard's David Lett should have much of the credit, not only for Pinot Gris' arrival in Oregon, but also for its swift emergence as the state's most intriguing dry white wine. He saw its possibilities as a companion to the Northwest's abundant seafood, and carved out a style to fit that niche. Most of the others follow his lead as best as their vineyards and knowledge allow.

Its star should continue to rise both for its quality and its comparatively generous yield in the vineyard.

Benchmarks:
Adelsheim Willamette Valley. **The Eyrie Vineyard** Willamette Valley (estate). **Rex Hill** Willamette Valley.

Sauvignon Blanc (0 in 1970, 103 acres in 1990)

There is little to know about Sauvignon Blanc in Oregon, except that the march appears to be ever southward, away from the Willamette and into the Rogue River Valley. Of a dozen producers in 1992, all but three were in the southern valleys, although bearing acreage is scattered evenly, if thinly, through all the state's vine-growing counties.

By all outward signs the climates of both the Rogue and the Umpqua should be better bets than the Willamette's. The Rogue, especially, appears to have ample sun and heat to ripen the variety fully. While firm evidence remains scant, no one in either valley has stepped forward to make an incontrovertible case.

Meanwhile, there is no sign that growers in the Willamette Valley despair of finding a congenial home for Sauvignon Blanc. It yields well, but even in warm years the wines insist on being austere to outright hard, and sharply vegetal.

Adelsheim Vineyards, in the very outskirts of Portland, grow a particularly firm, flavorful Pinot Noir bottled under the "Elizabeth's Reserve" label. Owner David Adelsheim is one of the region's more illustrious pioneers.

White Riesling (15 acres in 1970, 740 in 1990)

Year in, year out, White Riesling has given Oregon many of its most admirable white wines, not surprising, given a climate as cool and wet as Germany's own. Similar climate does not, however, mean identical wine. Riesling strikes a particular balance in Oregon, a little more alcoholic than the Rheingau but substantially less so than the coolest parts of California. With that the wines are less tart than the German ones, but crisper than the Californian. The sum of it all is that they refresh and still belong with food as well as any Riesling outside Australia. More important than balance, perhaps, is flavor. Oregon teeters closer to the grapefruity perfumes of Germany than the ripe berry notes of either California or Washington, but underplays them enough for the wine to suit cold cracked crab and even fried chicken. This affinity with food has led most producers toward the drier end of the scale, a few to bone dryness.

Oregon grows Late-Harvest Rieslings with much more caution than Washington. Only a few low spots near the Willamette River are visited by botrytis; only some years have the kind of Indian summer that allows it to develop cleanly. Some producers, notably Elk Cove, are beating the problem by harvesting grapes, then freezing them to enhance the concentrations.

Benchmarks:

Adelsheim Willamette Valley. **Chateau Benoit** Willamette Valley. **Elk Cove** Willamette Valley (estate). **Knudsen-Erath Vineyards** Willamette Valley (assembled). **Ponzi** Willamette Valley (estate). **Rex Hill** Willamette Valley (assembled). **Tualatin** Willamette Valley (estate).

Sparkling Wines

Logically, in a region where Chardonnay insists on understatement and Pinot Noir can bear a resemblance to Bouzy Rouge, classic-method sparkling wines have been a fascination from early days. A small company, Arterberry, originally set out to specialize in the bubbly when it opened in 1979. While it has turned increasingly to still wines, the field of hopefuls has grown steadily. Argyle is now the major specialist in a roster that includes seven other producers, at least three of them also intent on specializing in sparkling wine.

Through 1990, the results were ragged at best. As any *champenois* would be glad to explain, the learning curve for classic-method sparkling wines is even slower than it is for reds, not just because of the long aging period, but because the grapes must be harvested for entirely different qualities from still wines, and because the process involves so many steps having profound effects on final flavors.

Hopes should remain high in spite of the track record. Guy Devaux made trial lots of Willamette Valley sparkling wine for what eventually became Mumm Napa Valley. It was stunning.

Other varieties

Chenin Blanc (23 acres in 1990); Pinot Blanc (acreage still not reported in 1990) has kindled much hope with the importing of strains from Alsace; Sémillon (38 acres in 1990).

Willamette Valley vineyards cling to the slopes to avoid spring frosts.

Red Wine Varieties

In both acreage and number of producers, Oregon has had but two red wines, Cabernet Sauvignon and Pinot Noir. Of those, Pinot Noir is incontestably the dominating force. Merlot is beginning to have a presence. Other Bordeaux blending varieties and Nebbiolo were at the experimental stage in 1992.

Cabernet Sauvignon (10 acres in 1970, 202 in 1990)
The evidence is sparse, but Oregon Cabernet Sauvignons from sources as diverse as the Columbia Gorge, the southern Willamette and the Rogue persistently suggest Zinfandel's berries, not Cabernet's herbs. Only the Umpqua Valley has yielded wines tasting clearly of Cabernet as Bordeaux defines its flavors, and has done so since the earliest vintages at Hillcrest. Seven Hills, the pioneer in Oregon's portion of the Walla Walla AVA, showed early signs that that region is likely to produce Cabernets resembling those from the warmest parts of Washington.

The Umpqua in 1990 has Foris, Girardet, and Henry Estate producing Cabernet that reinforces the Hillcrest model.

Valley View dominates Cabernet production in the Rogue Valley, which has nearly half the state's plantings of the variety. In other districts both plantings and producers are so scattered that comparisons are hard to come by.
Benchmarks:
Girardet Umpqua Valley. **Henry Estate** Umpqua Valley. **Valley View** Rogue Valley. **Seven Hills** Walla Walla.

Pinot Noir (20 acres in 1970, 1,248 in 1990)
Almost from the beginning, and every day since, Oregon has put all but a few of its eggs in the basket of Pinot Noir, in acreage to be sure, still more in identity. Say "Oregon" to a wine collector and the Pavlovian response is "Pinot Noir" every time. The state does not have an Oregon wine festival, it has an International Pinot Noir Conference each July at McMinnville. And so on.

Within Oregon, Pinot Noir and Willamette Valley are synonymous, a geographical truth readily revealed by which wineries do not make it: Seven Hills in far eastern Oregon, Henry Estate and Serendipity in the Umpqua, and Valley View in the Rogue. In all the Willamette, only Dundee Wine Co. does not have a Pinot Noir on its list, because it puts all of its Pinot into its Argyle bubbly.

The first characteristic of Willamette Valley Pinot Noir is a bewitching intensity during its first flush of youth. Enough perfume for whole fields of berries will rise up out of almost every bottle that might come to hand, to be followed by flavors every bit as besotting. Critics, dazzled, rushed to anoint the region a new Côte d'Or, beginning around 1982.

In vintages from 1975 to 1985, the perfumes masked not only a lack of depth, but also a certain thin hardness. Someone rude once called young Oregon Pinot Noir of the era Beaujolais with balls. Even closer to the mark was a likening of it to Bouzy Rouge, the still red from Champagne.

When time began to chip away at the 1978s, the 1980s, the 1985s, and other much-praised vintages, most of them became less good to drink rather than more so. Critics revised their opinions downward. A number of hard-pressed souls in a small, undercapitalized industry took these changes of heart less than graciously. However, some producers in the Willamette have confessed, rather under their breaths, that as a group they were only just getting a handle on how to make wine from their grapes at the end of the 1980s.

The self-criticism dismissed wines from 1980 and earlier for taking too little from the grapes, leaving them without strength for the long haul. The subsequent overreaction took too much, leading to dark, dense, sometimes bitterly tannic giants. The insider theory is that by 1988, surely by 1989, the pendulum finally had narrowed its arc to a harmonious middle.

One can suspect, given far longer histories in far more tractable climates, that the learning curve is still leagues from its optimum end, and yet admire the distance traveled. In youth, quite a few 1988s and 1989s showed greater depth and richness than their predecessors. How they look after 10 years will tell how much more.

When David Lett first set about making Willamette Valley Pinot Noir at the Eyrie Vineyard, his idea was to tone down the perfumes, strip away the baby fat, and leave a firm core exposed. He has not wavered since the first vintage, 1970. Eyrie Pinot Noirs remain as stern as Oregon Pinot gets.

Most of his peers sought and seek more accessible textures. Among the most successful of them in recent vintages have been Adelsheim, Bethel Heights, and Elk Cove. They too calm the perfumes, mostly, it appears, by waiting for riper grapes.

It remained for Domaine Drouhin, the true Burgundian, to join Lett in eschewing silken riches in favor of a lean, firm wine. The two are not the same. Early vintages of the Drouhin were darker, more firmly tannic, and more heartily kissed by oak than typical Eyries.
Benchmarks:
Adelsheim Willamette Valley "Elizabeth's Reserve." **Adelsheim** Willamette Valley "Seven Springs." **Bethel Heights** Willamette Valley. **Bethel Heights** Willamette Valley "Reserve." **Domaine Drouhin** Willamette Valley (originally assembled, from 1991 estate). **Elk Cove** Willamette Valley "Estate." **Elk Cove** Willamette Valley "Wind Hills." **The Eyrie Vineyards** (estate). **Oak Knoll** Willamette Valley (assembled).

Other varieties

Merlot (35 acres in 1990) is produced by Adelsheim, Ashland and Valley View from Rogue vineyards, Foris and Hillcrest from Umpqua grapes, and Seven Hills from Walla Walla grapes. Zinfandel (15 acres in 1990) has a toehold in southern Oregon, where Hillcrest and Weisinger's of Ashland grow and make it. Callahan Ridge also has a Zinfandel. Oregon grows French-American hybrids in acreages too small to appear in statistical reports. Serendipity makes a varietal Marechal Foch. Others, notably Girardet, use their hybrids in generic or proprietary blends.

Willamette Valley AVA

Established: January 3, 1984
Total area: 3.3 million acres
Area in vineyard: 4,352 acres
Wineries: 51
Principal town: Portland

Because Pinot Noir so dominates public perception of Oregon winemaking, people think the Willamette Valley and Yamhill County are synonymous, but it is not so. Yamhill is indeed Pinot country. So is Polk, Yamhill's neighboring county to the south. However, to the north of Yamhill and west of Portland, Washington County has a penchant toward whites, especially the aromatic varieties. To the south and east of Polk, growers and winemakers in Benton, Lane, Linn, and Marion have made and continue to make efforts with Cabernet Sauvignon and half a dozen other varieties unrelated to Pinot Noir.

As the long list of county names implies, this is a huge valley, rivaling California's San Joaquin for sheer size, and not lagging too far behind it in population. Otherwise, it is not the same sort of valley at all. Old, uplifted seabed framed by upward pressures from colliding tectonic plates, some of it scoured by ice age glaciers, all of it constantly subject to eroding rains, it rolls restlessly rather than lying flat and placid the way the San Joaquin does. Especially at its downstream end the Willamette is a fine tumble of hills and hollows.

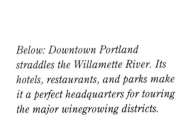

Left: The Dundee Hills vineyard's freshly turned earth explains why most of the long, gentle slope is called the Red Hills of Dundee. They are mainly given over to Pinot Noir, although Chardonnay and Pinot Gris are important as well.

Below: Downtown Portland straddles the Willamette River. Its hotels, restaurants, and parks make it a perfect headquarters for touring the major winegrowing districts.

Willamette Valley (North)

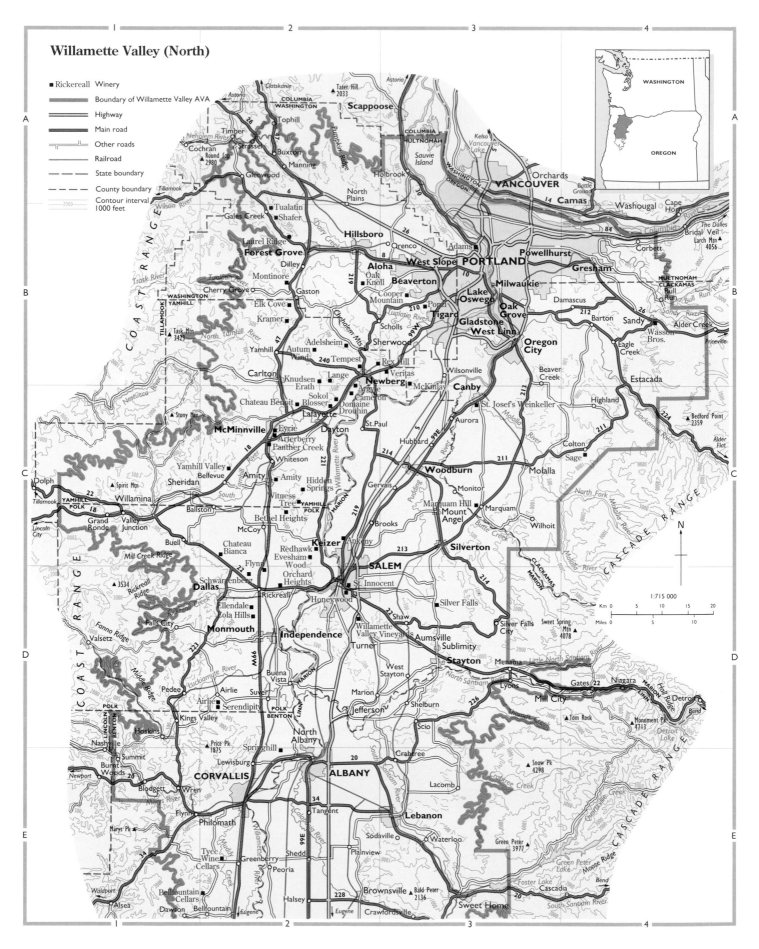

■ Rickereall Winery

▬▬▬ Boundary of Willamette Valley AVA

═══ Highway

━━━ Main road

Other roads

Railroad

State boundary

County boundary

Contour interval
1000 feet

1:715 000

Km 0   5   10   15   20

Miles 0   5   10

N

The estate vineyard of Elk Cove, not far north of The Red Hills of Dundee, has begun to emerge as one of the Willamette Valley's most impressive sources of Pinot Noir.

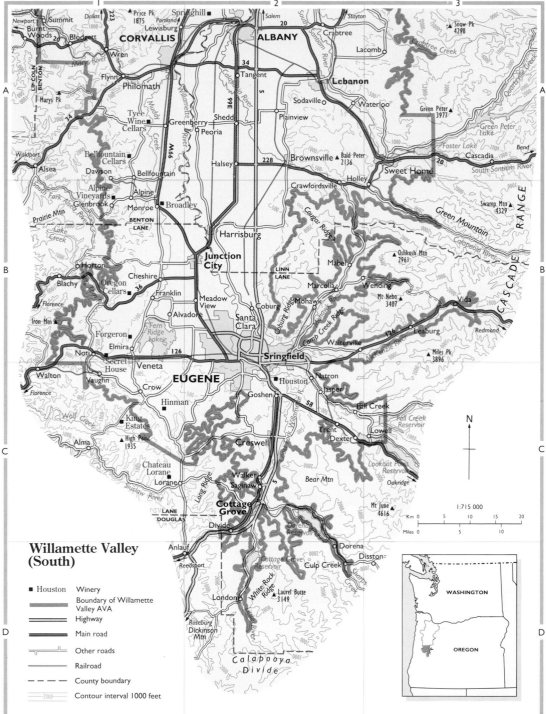

Willamette Valley (South)

- ■ Houston   Winery
- Boundary of Willamette Valley AVA
- Highway
- Main road
- Other roads
- Railroad
- County boundary
- ── 2000 ──   Contour interval 1000 feet

The scale of things – the height of hills and the intervals between them – is very much that of Tuscany or Umbria, but the resemblance stops there. Right through summer the cool, rainy Willamette is blanketed in fresh-washed greens, dark tones where firs still cluster, paler hues where loggers have done their work and passed the mantle to farmers. Every stick of architecture in the region has north European, mostly Anglo-Saxon, roots, except where shopping malls have brought the cookie-cutter buildings of chain stores and fast-food restaurants into the mix.

Thriving Portland, Salem, and Eugene have freed themselves from forestry and agriculture. In the long gaps between

them tiny farm and logging towns like Gaston and Amity look much as they did in 1884, except a little more frayed at the cuffs and collar. Wine grapes also persist in the long gaps, but rarely dominate the large landscape. They are always on the hillsides.

Suitable land for vineyards in this marginal growing region means south-facing slopes at elevations of 300 to 700 feet. More practically, it means elevations 125 to 300 feet above the valley floor, conditions almost identical to the ones eastern Washington imposes on its vine growers, but for almost precisely opposite reasons. Where Washingtonians choose their sites with bitter winters in mind, Oregonians in the Willamette select their exposures with a view toward tepid summers, their elevations with an outlook toward frosty springs.

Between the foothills, west and east, and the occasional upthrust out in the middle, the valley offers hundreds of square miles of south-facing slopes of 300- to 700-feet elevation from Portland southward beyond Eugene, where a single ridge separates the Willamette from the Umpqua drainage. With all of that to choose from, the Pinot Noirists huddled together in the northwest tip, starting in Portland's suburbs and reaching down into the northern outskirts of the state capital at Salem.

For richer or poorer, in sickness and in health, Yamhill County has pledged itself to Pinot Noir. This most heavily planted county in the state has 822 of its 1,670 acres in Pinot, totals that amount to 40 percent of all the Pinot Noir, 27 percent of all the grapes in Oregon. Chardonnay (400 acres), Riesling (173), Pinot Gris (156) and a handful of other varieties altogether equal Pinot Noir's plantings, but when winemakers and growers talk of suitable slopes for planting, they mean suitable for Pinot Noir.

Oregon Pinot Noir started in the Red Hills of Dundee with a 1970 from David Lett and his then new Eyrie Vineyards. Almost immediately Lett's critical successes became a magnet. Within two decades the Red Hills had more than 30 growers and eight wineries, among them many of Oregon's brightest lights. Knudsen Erath and Sokol Blosser joined in the early days. Cameron, Domaine Drouhin and the others arrived later.

As the name promises, Red Hills soils are rich in iron, of volcanic origin. Not all of the Dundee Hills are red. Their western fringe is pale, old seabed. Some draw a line just about where the soils change, partly because of that fact, more because cooler temperatures make grapes harder to ripen from that point west.

The Eola Hills – astride the Yamhill-Polk County line – share volcanic origins with the Red Hills of Dundee. Like the Dundee Hills, the Eolas are sufficiently warmer on their east side for it to be favored over the western slopes by Pinot growers. Bethel Heights more than any other vineyard has helped the area begin to rival Dundee, the way Burgundian communes compete among themselves.

The rest of Yamhill County is less tidily arranged, but has enough bright spots to command attention. Ridges of the Chehalem Mountains northeast of Dundee support Adelsheim, Rex Hill, and some of the latter's most prized independent growers, notably including Medici. Elk Cove sits alone on its hilltop north-northwest of Dundee.

Washington County, Yamhill's neighbor to the north, has impressive Pinot Noir in Wind Hills and other vineyards, but the variety dominates winemakers' thinking less, perhaps because Bill Fuller of Tualatin and other pioneers came intent

Dundee Hills vineyard stays with the high ground.

Exposure and elevation are utterly crucial to vinegrowing in the Willamette Valley. The Dundee Hills are among the most favored by nature, rising just enough to escape spring frosts, and tipped mostly to the south for heat and light.

upon Riesling and other whites. Plantings in 1992 hardly reflected that bent. Pinot Noir covered 354 of 935 acres, while Chardonnay had 205 acres, Riesling 130, and Pinot Gris 85. Tualatin, Shafer Vineyard & Winery, Ponzi, and Oak Knoll are familiar names with substantial track records. Montinore is, with 400 acres, the giant.

Parts of Washington County are among the warmest in the northern Willamette Valley because several of its hills trap and reflect sun heat.

On the south, the magic line for Pinot Noir runs cross-valley somewhere near the college town of Corvallis. Vineyards of Tyee Winery are on the Pinot side. From there to the southern boundary of the AVA, Pinot Noir is important (230 acres out of 525 total in Benton and Lane counties) but not close to the obsession it is farther north. Both vineyards and wineries in the southern zone are still comparatively sparse, still on the scout for a distinctive regional identity. With the exceptions of Alpine, Forgeron, and Hinman, they were all young at the beginning of the 1990s.

Gatherers of statistics separate vineyards from Clackamas, Linn, Marion, and Multnomah counties into the East Valley. It currently grows 340 acres of vineyard (119 acres of Pinot Noir, 70 of Chardonnay, 51 of White Riesling, 25 each of Gewürztraminer and Pinot Gris).

Rogue Valley AVA

Established: February 22, 1992
Total area: 975,000 acres (approx)
Area in vineyard: 433 acres
Wineries: 7
Principal town: Ashland

The Rogue Valley lacks focus, not for lack of will, but because of its abundance of confusions. Of Oregon's three west-side appellations, the Rogue is by far the most diverse, both terrain and climate ranging wide enough to encourage thoughts of grape varieties from a dozen parts of France.

The heights are cool enough to make some think of Gewürztraminer as the region's true calling, while the lowlands are toasty enough to have provoked at least one try at a port-type. Merlot will set and ripen only here in western Oregon, rousing still other hopes. Meanwhile, since the Rogue's revival began in the mid-1970s, most growers have fallen back on chocolate and vanilla. Cabernet Sauvignon had 97 acres in 1990, Chardonnay 123. Trailing these are Pinot Noir (73), Gewürztraminer (31), White Riesling (28), Pinot Gris (22), and Sauvignon Blanc (16).

The focus is improved from the 1880s, when this warmest and sunniest of western Oregon regions grew the Mission and Flame Tokay. Although these varieties remain only as memories, a tiny scrap of Zinfandel survives from that era.

The Rogue lies hard against the California border, hemmed on the east by the Cascades, on the south by the Siskiyous, and on the west by the Klamath Range. Ridges separating this from the Umpqua Valley to the north do not qualify as mountains by severe local standards, but they are the kind of hills that daunt bicyclists of Tour de France caliber. If the Rogue Valley has one major internal division, it separates the upper watershed of the Rogue River from its eventual tributary, the Illinois River.

Although the two streams converge several miles from the Pacific Ocean shore, they carve separate paths through the Klamaths, and thus get their marine influences in differing ways.

Bridgeview, Foris, and Siskiyou cluster around the village of Cave Junction in the Illinois watershed, well to the west. Indeed they crowd the western boundary of the AVA. Bridgeview's 74 acres made it the largest single vineyard in the Rogue in the 1990 census; Foris's 60 came next. Cave Junction, incidentally, marks the beginning of the road into Oregon Caves National Monument.

In numbers, most of the Rogue's existing vineyards cling to the hillsides of a broad bowl between Ashland on the east and Jacksonville on the west. The area, much of it, anyway, is sometimes called Applegate Valley after a more immediate tributary to the Rogue than the Illinois. Most of the vines here are in small to tiny parcels belonging to 30-odd independent growers. Valley View, the appellation's largest and oldest winery, has 26 acres near Jacksonville, a town born of a minor gold rush and now as much historic museum as municipality. Weisinger's of Ashland and Ashland Vineyards are near the town they name themselves after, a place widely known for one of the world's most-praised, longest-running Shakespeare festivals.

Rogue River Vineyards is away by itself near Grants Pass, the appellation's warmest area in summer, its rainiest in winter. Even here summers are dry enough to require irrigation.

Some locals hold high hopes for south-facing slopes on ridges separating Rogue from Umpqua drainages, but practical results had yet to be achieved in the early 1990s. Wherever in the Rogue, all vineyards range between 1,000 and 2,600 feet elevation, all of them above the maximum grapegrowing elevations of the Willamette and Umpqua valleys. It could not be otherwise; the lowest point, Grants Pass, is at 1,000 feet. The upper limit is almost as concrete, higher terrain being both too cold and too steep or rocky to plant.

Soils in the Rogue Valley are as confoundingly diverse as its climate, geologists having identified 87 series in Josephine County, 208 in Jackson. (The Napa Valley has but 82.) In broader terms, a large third of the appellation is of granitic origin.

Umpqua Valley AVA

Established: April 30, 1984
Total area: 768,000 acres
Area in vineyard: 384 acres
Wineries: 8
Principal town: Roseburg

The Umpqua Valley is where Oregon's rebirth as a winegrowing state began. Fate has not treated the first-born favourably, or at least has not caused it to grow.Tucked in between the Willamette and Rogue valleys, the Umpqua is warmer than the former, cooler than the latter. Its status as a transition zone is verified by the slow shift from fir to pine forests. As a milieu for grapes it is a little too versatile to be forced into accepting one dominant variety, not quite versatile enough to try everything. Acreage has puttered along in the 300s since the mid-1980s. The number of wineries has remained static as well, although the roster has turned over almost completely.

When Richard Sommers headed north from the University of California at Davis in 1962 to found Hillcrest Vineyards, in rolling country west of Roseburg, he was the first to plant wine grapes in the state of Oregon since Prohibition. A local schoolteacher named Paul Bjelland joined in immediately. A few others came during the late 1960s and early 1970s. They also departed again. Hillcrest aside, the founding dates of the Umpqua's working wineries are 1978 for Henry Estates, 1983 and later for the others.

While the region is markedly warmer than most of the Willamette Valley, its growers remain inclined to look to the north of Europe. Anchored on the long-time logging town of Roseburg and located entirely within Douglas County, in 1990 the appellation grew 82 acres of Pinot Noir, 70 of Chardonnay, 70 of White Riesling, 60 of Cabernet Sauvignon, 33 of Gewürztraminer, and 13 of Sauvignon Blanc.

One can wonder about the presence of Cabernet and Sauvignon Blanc only until a first-hand look demonstrates the range of elevations, exposures, and susceptibilities to sea air within the Umpqua's drainage. Sommers' first planting included Cabernet, Riesling, and Gewürztraminer within the scope of 23 acres. All three varieties have ripened handily in all but the most vexing seasons.

A couple of Willamette Valley wineries dip into the Umpqua for Pinot Noir, most gratefully when cool vintages force their own grapes to struggle for maturity. The same is true of Chardonnay.

The region's own wineries have managed to keep the state of confusion well advanced by suceeding sometimes with one variety, sometimes with another. They have never all managed to succeed with the same variety at the same time.

Columbia Gorge and Eastern Oregon

Grapegrowing and winemaking remained tenuous on the east side of the Cascade Mountains in the early 1990s.

Among them, six counties ranged along the Columbia River from Hood River to Umatilla were growing 850 acres of vineyard in 1990. After the hard freeze of that December killed 500 acres of young vines, the affected grower had no plans to replant.

Tiny vineyards on the Oregon side of the Columbia Gorge echo their counterparts across the river in Washington state, notably in leaning toward Gewürztraminer and Riesling as well-suited grape varieties. The area is sufficiently warmer than the Willamette to ripen Cabernet Sauvignon and Zinfandel. Finding a wine specific to the region demands diligence. Hood River, with 12 acres, sticks to local grapes. The only other winery in the region, Three Rivers, uses grapes from the Washington side.

One 30-acre vineyard in the Walla Walla AVA, Seven Hills, has the start of a reputation for Merlot and Cabernet Sauvignon under its own label and that of one of the best-known wineries on the Washington State side of the line, Leonetti (*see* page 209).

WILLAMETTE VALLEY PRODUCERS

Adams Vineyard Winery (1981)
1922 NW Pettygrove Street, Portland, OR 97209. Tel (503) 294-0606. 3,500 cases. A 25-acre vineyard in Yamhill County feeds a downtown winery mostly with Pinot Noir and Chardonnay; also a Sauvignon Blanc.

Adelsheim Vineyard (1978)
22150 NE Quarter Mile Lane, Newberg, OR 97132. Tel (503) 538-3652. 12,000 cases. At its best, one of the finest sources of Willamette Valley Pinot Noir, much of it from 43 estate acres near Portland. For immediate pleasure the silky "Oregon" sometimes surpasses "Seven Springs" (Eola Hills) and "Elizabeth's Reserve{ (estate) but the latter are better hopes for aging. Often among the best for estate Riesling and Pinot Gris. Also of interest: Rogue Valley Merlot.

Airlie Winery (1986)
15305 Dunn Forest Road, Monmouth, OR 97361. Tel (503) 838-6013. 5,300 cases. At the break point for Pinot Noir, 15 acres go to Chardonnay, Gewürztraminer, Müller-Thurgau, Riesling, and Pinot.

Alpine Vineyards (1976)
25904 Green Peak Road, Alpine, OR 97456. Tel (503) 424-5851. 3,500 cases. A 26-acre south Willamette vineyard is the source of unexceptional Pinot Noir, Chardonnay, Riesling, Gewürztraminer, and Cabernet Sauvignon.

Amity Vineyards (1976)
18150 Amity Vineyards Road SE, Amity, OR 97101. Tel (503) 835-2362. 8,750 cases. Gewürztraminers often show the way for all Oregon. Up and down but sometimes estimable Pinot Noir in several styles from several sources is the main event. The winery has 15 acres on hills above the town which shares its name and buys widely.

Argyle (1987)
PO Box 280, Dundee, OR 97115. Tel (503) 538-8520. 25,000 cases. A Franco-Australian partnership has set up classic-method Brut as the flagbearer. Still Chardonnay and Riesling round out the list.

Arterberry Winery (1979)
PO Box 772, McMinnville, OR 97128. Tel (503) 472-1587. 5,000 cases. The original notion was to specialize in classic method sparkling wine, but still wines from Pinot Noir and Chardonnay now dominate production.

Autumn Wind Vineyard (1987)
PO Box 666, Newberg, OR 97132. Tel (503) 538-6931. 1,500 cases. Pinot Noir, Chardonnay, Müller-Thurgau, and Pinot Noir-Blanc from 10 acres in the Red Hills of Dundee.

Bellfountain Cellars (1989)
25041 Llewllyn Rd, Corvallis, OR 97333. Tel (503) 929-3162. 1,000 cases. Pinot Noir, Chardonnay, Sauvignon Blanc, Riesling, and Gewürztraminer were the start-up list.

Bethel Heights Vineyard (1984)
6060 Bethel Heights Rd NW, Salem, OR 97304. Tel (503) 581-2262. 7,000 cases. Winemaking is steady across the board, but some of Oregon's most consistently velvety Pinot Noirs are the banner wines. A deftly oaked Chardonnay is equally to be sought. Also: Riesling, Gewürztraminer and,

surprise, Chenin Blanc. All of the wines are estate from 51 acres in the Eola Hills.

Broadley Vineyards (1986)
Box 168, Monroe, OR 97456. Tel (503) 847-5934. 2,200 cases. In the south Willamette, 15 acres of Pinot Noir and Chardonnay.

Cameron Winery (1984)
PO Box 27, Dundee, OR 97115. Tel (503) 538-0336. 3,500 cases. Has excited local critics, especially with Pinot Noir. Most of the grapes are bought-in. Also Chardonnay, Pinot Blanc.

Chateau Benoit Winery (1979)
6580 NE Mineral Springs Road, Carlton, OR 97111. Tel (503) 864-2991. 15,000 cases. The owners grow grapes on 22 acres at the west edge

Chateau Benoit sits above its vineyard.

of the Dundee Hills and also buy grapes for a broad range including classic-method sparkling.

Chateau Bianca Winery (1991)
17485 Highway 22, Dallas, OR 97338. Tel (503) 623-6181. West of Salem; focused on Pinot Noir.

Chateau Lorane (1992)
27415 Siuslaw River Road, Lorane, OR 97451. Tel (503) 942-5830. In the South Willamette near Eugene, a 30-acre vineyard is planted to Cabernet Sauvignon and Sauvignon Blanc as well as Pinot Noir, Chardonnay, White Riesling, and Gewürztraminer.

Cooper Mountain Vineyards (1987)
2,000 cases. Route 3, Box 1036, Beaverton, OR 97007. Tel (503) 649-0027. Pinot Noir, Chardonnay, and Pinot Gris dominate a 75-acre vineyard in Washington County.

Domaine Drouhin (1988)
PO Box 700, Dundee, OR 97115. Tel (503) 864-2700. 3,500 cases. One of the grand names in Burgundy epitomized the flavors of Oregon Pinot Noir in each of its first two vintages, in wines that also were boldly oaked and surprisingly firm with tannins. Grapes were bought-in while the first 35 estate acres matured.

Domaine Drouhin, the Burgundian vote of confidence.

Elk Cove Vineyards (1977)
27751 NW Olson Road, Gaston, OR
97119. Tel (503) 985-7760. 15,000
cases. Without much fanfare, a well-
established firm has crept near the
head of the class for velvety, well-fla-
vored single-vineyard Pinot Noirs
from its own 45 hilltop acres, the
nearby Dundee Hills Vineyard and
Wind Hills Vineyard in Washington
County. Assembled Pinots also worth
attention. Off-dry and late-harvest
Rieslings to watch from a list reliable
across the board.

Ellendale Winery (1981)
300 Reuben Boise Road, Dallas, OR
97338. Tel (503) 623-5617. 3,500
cases. Amidst all the seriousness a
winery offering Woolly Booger along
with the usual varietals. Some are from
13 estate acres southwest of Salem.

Eola Hills Wine Cellars (1986)
501 South Pacific Highway, Rickreall,
OR 97371. Tel (503) 623-2405. 8,500
cases. A winery south of Salem draws
on 107 affiliated acres in the Eola Hills
for Pinot Noir, Chardonnay,
Sauvignon Blanc, Cabernet Sauvignon,
and Chenin Blanc.

**Evesham Wood Vineyard &
Winery** (1986)
4035 Wallace Road Northwest,
Salem, OR 97304. Tel (503) 472-
6315. 1,800 cases. From 8 acres,
Oregon's Big Three: Chardonnay,
Pinot Gris, Pinot Noir.

The Eyrie Vineyards (1970)
PO Box 697, Dundee, OR 97115. Tel
(503) 472-6315. 5,200 cases. The Old
Master of Oregon Pinot Noirists is
most intent on lean, firm estate Pinot
Noir Reserve from 46 acres in the
Red Hills of Dundee and an assem-
bled Pinot Noir of similar style, but
pays close heed to Chardonnay, Pinot
Gris, and Pinot Meunier as well. The
anti-Riesling Lett also offers a Muscat
Ottonel of interest.

David Lett of Eyrie.

Flynn Vineyards (1990)
2200 W Pacific Highway, Rickreall, OR
97371. Tel (503) 623-8683. Intends to
specialize in classic-method sparkling
from 83 acres of vineyard.

Forgeron Vineyard (1978)
89697 Sheffler Road, Elmira, OR
97437. Tel (503) 935-1117. 8,000
cases. Typical of Eugene, a 20-acre
vineyard ranges from Müller-Thurgau
to Cabernet Sauvignon.

Hidden Springs Winery (1980)
4,000 cases. 9360 SE Eola Hills Rd,
Amity, OR 97101. Tel (503) 835-
2782. A 20-acre vineyard high on the
Eola Hills turns out thus far middle-of-
the-pack Pinot Noir and Chardonnay.
The winery also offers Riesling and
Cabernet Sauvignon.

Hinman Vineyards (1979)
35,000 cases. 27012 Briggs Hill Road,
Eugene, OR 97405. Tel (503) 345-
1945. Draws primarily on an affiliated
eastern Oregon vineyard for Riesling,
Gewürztraminer, Chardonnay, Pinot
Noir, and Cabernet Sauvignon. The
effort is for accessibility.

Honeywood Winery (1934)
1350 Hines Street SE, Salem, OR
97302. Tel (503) 362-4111. 5,000
cases. Originally a fruit winery, it has
dipped into *viniferas*, most successfully
with Riesling and Chardonnay.

Houston Vineyards (1983)
86187 Hoya Lane, Eugene, OR 97405.
Tel (503) 747-4681. 800 cases.
Produces only Chardonnay, and sells
largely in the local market.

King Estate Winery (1992)
80854 Territorial Road, Eugene, OR
97405. Tel (503) 942-9874. 20,000
cases. Ambitious first vintage produced Pinot Noir, Pinot Gris, and
Chardonnay from bought-in grapes,
while first blocks of proposed 350-
acre vineyard matured.

Dick Erath of Knudsen Erath.

Knudsen Erath Winery (1972)
PO Box 667, Dundee, OR 97115. Tel
(503) 538-3318. 32,000 cases. Burly,
gregarious Dick Erath has always made,
by Oregon standards at least, similarly
assertive Pinot Noir and Chardonnay
from 45 acres at the winery plus
bought-in grapes. Riesling, if not a
mainstay, is always worth a look.

Kramer Vineyards (1989)
26830 NW Olson Road, Gaston, OR
97119. Tel (503) 662-4545. 500 cases.
Near neighbors to Elk Cove make
Pinot Noir, Chardonnay, Pinot Gris,
Riesling, and Gewürztraminer from 12
acres.

Lange Winery (1987)
PO Box 8, Dundee, OR 97115. Tel
(503) 538-6476. 2,500 cases. Pinot
Noir, Chardonnay, and Pinot Gris
grow in 6 acres on a 27-acre property
at the heart of the Red Hills of
Dundee.

Laurel Ridge Winery (1986)
PO Box 456, Forest Grove, OR
97116. Tel (503) 359-5436. 10,000
cases. A long-established 74-acre vineyard in Washington County has come
back to life under its third label (originally Coury, later Reuter's Hill). The
emphasis is to be on classic-method
sparkling wines. From here came

*The homely atmosphere of Laurel
Ridge is typical of Oregon's
wineries.*

Oregon's one pre-Prohibition Riesling
good enough to claim a medal at a
world fair.

Marquam Hill Vineyards (1988)
35803 S Highway 213, Molalla, OR
97038. Tel (503) 829-6677. 2,000
cases. The pioneer east-side estate
winery makes Riesling,
Gewürztraminer, Müller-Thurgau,
Chardonnay and Pinot Noir from 23
acres northeast of Salem.

McKinlay Vineyard (1987)
10610 NW St Helens Road, Portland,
OR 97231. Tel (503) 285-3896. 2,800
cases. From the first 6 of 32 possible
acres near Newberg come the main
wines, Chardonnay and Pinot Noir.

Montinore Vineyards (1987)
PO Box 560, Forest Grove, OR
97116. Tel (503) 359-5012. 56,000
cases. The Goliath of all Oregon
grows 440 acres of vineyard on a 711-
acre estate in Washington County. A
long list includes Pinot Noir,
Chardonnay, Riesling, Dry Riesling,
Late Harvest Riesling, Müller-Thurgau,
Pinot Gris, Gewürztraminer, Chenin
Blanc, Sauvignon Blanc, and classic-

method sparkling wine. The melodious name contracts Montana-in-Oregon.

Oak Knoll Winery (1970)
29700 SW Burkhalter Rd, Hillsboro, OR 97123. Tel (503) 648-8198. 30,000 cases. Quietly goes along making reliably agreeable to outright fine Pinot Noir and similar Chardonnay. These, Riesling and Gewürztraminer all are from bought-in grapes.

Oregon Cellars Winery (1988)
92989 Templeton Road, Cheshire, OR 97419. Tel (503) 998-1786. 1,000 cases. Pinot Noir, Chardonnay, and sparkling wines were the start-up list.

Panther Creek Cellars (1986)
455 N Irvine, McMinnville, OR 97128. Tel (503) 472-8080. 3,500 cases. Another refugee from California called north by Pinot Noir. While all others make a to-do about the true Pinot Blanc of Alsace, the owner-winemaker stubbornly pursues Melon as a white.

Ponzi Vineyards (1970)
14665 SW Winery Lane, Beaverton, OR 97007. Tel (503) 628-1227. 6,500 cases. Pinot Noir is the great hope, Pinot Gris the great success. The winery supplements its 12 acres with grapes bough- in from Medici and other highly regarded vineyards in Yamhill and Washington counties.

Redhawk Vineyard (1987)
2995 Michigan City NW, Salem, OR 97304. Tel (503) 362-1596. 7,000 cases. Estate Pinot Noir and Chardonnay from 10 acres are joined by Merlot, Cabernet Sauvignon, Sémillon, Sauvignon Blanc, and Gewürztraminer from bought-in grapes. Estate Pinot Gris and Pinot Blanc were in the works in 1992.

Rex Hill Vineyards (1983)
30835 N Hwy 99 W, Newberg, OR 97132. Tel (503) 538-0666. 15,000 cases. Oregon's first really well-capitalized winery has spared no expense, but still has had a couple of rough patches. The finest of the ups are single-vineyard Pinot Noirs of depth and character, some from 22 acres at the winery, most from contracted vineyards. Pinot Gris has been a model. The winemaker is exploring Symphony.

Saga Vineyards (1989)
30815 South Wall Street, Colton, OR 97017. Tel (5030) 824-4600. 1,000 cases. Austrian owners are trying Pinot Noir, Chardonnay and Riesling from the most northeastern vineyard in the valley.

St Innocent (1988)
2701 - 22d St SE, Salem, OR 97302. Tel (503) 378-1526. 2,000 cases. The main aim is classic-method sparkling wine; meanwhile, silky, flavorful Pinot Noir caught critical eyes in the first vintages.

St Josef's Weinkeller (1983)
28836 S Barlow Road, Canby, OR 97013. Tel (503) 651-3190. 6,500 cases. One of the east-side wineries, it regularly does well with Gewürztraminer and Riesling, is spottier with Chardonnay and Pinot Noir.

Schwarzenberg Vineyards (198711975 Smithfield Road, Dallas, OR 97338. Tel (503) 623-6420. 10,000 cases. A Salem-area vineyard has 40 acres of Chardonnay, 15 of Pinot Noir.

Secret House Vineyards Winery (1989)
88324 Vineyard Lane, Veneta, OR 97487. Tel (503) 935-3774.

Serendipity Cellars Winery (1981)
15275 Dunn Forest Road, Monmouth, OR 97361. Tel (503) 838-4284. 2,000 cases. The focus is on Marechal Foch and Müller-Thurgau, on the grounds thatOregon needs no more Pinot Noir or Chardonnay. Also Chenin Blanc, Cabernet Sauvignon, and Zinfandel. Grapes are mostly bought-in.

Shafer Vineyard Cellars (1981)
Star Route Box 269, Forest Grove, OR 97116. Tel (503) 357-6604. 10,000 cases. At their lightly-oaked best, Shafer's are some of Oregon's finest Chardonnays. Riesling and Gewürztraminer are worth a look. Pinot Noirs are erratic but sometimes toward the head of the class.

Silver Falls Winery (1983)
4972 Cascade Highway SE, Sublimity, OR 97385. Tel (503) 769-9463. 2,500 cases. One of a handful of wineries using east-side grapes; Pinot Noir, Chardonnay, Pinot Gris, and Riesling are the list.

Sokol Blosser Winery (1977)
PO Box 399, Dundee, OR 97115. Tel (503) 864-2282. 25,000 cases. One of Oregon's more vigorously commercial wineries draws on 135 owned and affiliated acres in the Dundee Hills. Pinot Noir Yamhill, Pinot Noir Redland, and Pinot Noir Redland Reserve indicate not vineyards but style (and ascending price). Also: Chardonnay, Riesling, Müller-Thurgau, and, contrarians, a Sauvignon Blanc.

Montinore receives visitors in a stately mansion that predates the winery.

Right: Fermenting tanks at Rex Hill.

Springhill Cellars (1988)
2920 NW Scenic Drive, Albany, OR
97321. Tel (503) 928-1009. 1,800
cases. Pinot Noir, Chardonnay, and
Riesling are grown on an estate
isolated from concentrations both
north at Salem and south near Eugene.

Tempest Vineyards (1988)
9342 NE Hancock Drive, Portland,
OR 97220. Tel (503) 538-2733. 1,800
cases. Pinot Noir, Chardonnay, Pinot
Gris, and Gamay Noir from bought-in
grapes, until 1992 in Newberg, then in
permanent cellars in Amity.

Tualatin Vineyards (1973)
Route 1, Box 339, Forest Grove, OR
97116. Tel (503) 357-5005. 22,000
cases. All of the wines are estate-
bottled from 90 acres west of Forest
Grove. Owner-winemaker Bill Fuller
came from California with Riesling and
Gewürztraminer in mind, and regularly
makes some of Oregon's best. The
Chardonnay and Pinot Noir always of
interest but not always conventional.

Tyee Wine Cellars (1985)
26335 Greenberry Road, Corvallis,
OR 97333. Tel (503) 753-8754. 2,400
cases. Grapes from 6 affiliated acres
south of Corvallis plus bought-ins go
into consistently well-made, attractive
Pinot Noir, Chardonnay, Pinot Gris,
and Gewürztraminer.

Veritas Vineyard (1983)
31190 NE Veritas Lane, Newberg, OR
97132. Tel (503) 538-1470. 5,000
cases. Chardonnay is the flagship from
26 acres east of Dundee.

Wasson Brothers Winery (1981)
41901 Highway 26, Sandy, OR 97055.
Tel (503) 668-3124. A 14-acre 1,000-
cases estate vineyard gives one of the
best looks at east-side wines. The
roster includes Chardonnay, Pinot
Noir, Riesling, and Gewürztraminer.

Willamette Valley Vineyards
(1989)
8800 Enchanted Way, Turner, OR
97392. Tel (503) 588-9463. 18,000
cases. Bought-in grapes and 25 winery-owned acres go into middle-of-
the-road Pinot Noir, Chardonnay, and
Riesling.

Witness Tree Vineyards (1987)
7111 Spring Valley Rd NW, Salem,
OR 97304. Tel (503) 585-7874. 1,800
cases. Critics have taken notice of
Chardonnay and especially Pinot Noir
chosen from favored blocks of a 100-
acre vineyard west of Salem.

Yamhill Valley Vineyards (1983)
16250 Oldsville Road, McMinnville,
OR 97128. Tel (503) 843-3100.
15,000 cases. The 100-acre vineyard
west of McMinnville is a picture. Pinot
Noir, Chardonnay, Pinot Gris, and
Riesling mostly run with the pack.

UMPQUA PRODUCERS

Callahan Ridge Winery (1987)
340 Busenbark Lane, Roseburg, OR
97470. Tel (503) 673-7901. 7,500
cases. Riesling and Gewürztraminer
from dry to Late Harvest dominate
production by a German-schooled
owner-winemaker.

Girardet Wine Cellars (1983)
895 Reston Road, Roseburg, OR
97470. Tel (503) 679-7252. 8,000
cases. Pinot Noir and Chardonnay
from 18 estate acres are the flagships.
Generics with a proportion of French-
American hybrids are of interest.

Henry Estate Winery (1978)
687 Hubbard Creek Road, Umpqua,
OR 97486. Tel (503) 459-5120.
14,000 cases. A low-lying 31-acre
vineyard grows the grapes, but
American oak does noticeable proportions of the flavoring in Pinot Noir
and Chardonnay. A Gewürztraminer
speaks strongly of its variety in favorable vintages.

Hillcrest Vineyard (1963)
240 Vineyard Lane, Roseburg, OR
97470. Tel (503) 673-3709. 8,000
cases. Although the list of wines is
long, Riesling occupies two-thirds of a
rolling 35-acre vineyard, and is made
just off-dry and as a late harvest. The
Zinfandel is one of few in Oregon.

Lookingglass Winery (1988)
6561 Lookingglass Road, Roseburg,
OR 97470. Tel (503) 679-8198. 1,000
cases. The label, Rizza Cellars, goes on
Pinot Noir and Cabernet Sauvignon.

ROGUE VALLEY PRODUCERS
(not mapped)

Ashland Vineyards (1988)
2775 E. Main Street, Ashland, OR
97520. Tel (503) 488-0088. 4,000
cases. A family-owned 12-acre vineyard and winery. The owners are trying Müller-Thurgau, Chardonnay and
Pinot Noir from the cool end of the
spectrum, Cabernet Sauvignon and
Merlot from the warm end.

Bridgeview Vineyards (1986)
4210 Holland Loop Road, Cave
Junction, OR 97523. Tel (503) 592-
4688. 12,000 cases. Densely planted
74-acre vineyard is cooled enough by
coastal weather to produce sometimes memorable Gewürztraminer as
well as consistent Chardonnay and
Pinot Noir.

Foris Vineyards Winery (1986)
654 Kendall Road, Cave Junction, OR
97523. Tel (503) 592-3752. 8,000
cases. One vineyard in a warm area
yields Cabernet Sauvignon and Merlot,
a second in a cooler spot grows the
Pinot Noir and Gewürztraminer.

Rogue River Vineyards (1983)
3145 Helms Road, Grants Pass, OR
97527. Tel (503) 476-1051. 2,000
cases. Blush wines and even wine cool-
ers fill a list aimed at casual consumers.

Siskiyou Vineyards (1978)
6220 Oregon Caves Highway, Cave
Junction, OR 97523. Tel (503) 592-
3727. 7,000 cases. The vineyard is
warm enough for the owner to be
gravitating toward Cabernet Sauvignon
and Sémillon as the flagships.

Valley View (1976)
1000 Applegate Road, Jacksonville,
OR 97530. Tel (503) 899-8468.
10,000 cases. The dominant winery in
the Rogue Valley has done particularly
well with toasty, almost California-
style Chardonnays, and not badly with
round, well-wooded reds from the
Bordeaux varieties. The Barrel Select
label goes on premier lots, the Jazz
label goes on a lower-priced line.

Weisinger's of Ashland (1988)
3150 Siskiyou Boulevard, Ashland, OR
97520. Tel (503) 488-5989. 2,000
cases. Gewürztraminer dominated
early, but the Italophile owners are
looking into Nebbiolo and Sangiovese
for their warmest-in-western-Oregon
vineyard site in Bear Creek Valley.

COLUMBIA GORGE
(not mapped)

Edgefield Winery (1990)
2126 SW Halsey Street, Troutdale,
OR 97060. Tel (503) 669-8610.
Three acres of Pinot Gris are local, the
grapes for other wines bought-in.

Hood River Vineyards (1981)
4693 Westwood Drive, Hood River,
OR 97301. Tel (503) 386-3772. 2,500
cases. Begun as a fruit winery and still
active as such, it also produces several
vinifera wines from largely local grapes.

Three Rivers Winery (1986)
275 Country Club Road, Hood River,
OR 97031. Tel (503) 386-5453. 2,500
cases. Flagships are Riesling and
Gewürztraminer from the owner's
vineyard on the Washington side of
the Gorge.

Travel Information

WILLAMETTE VALLEY PLACES OF INTEREST

Eugene Though not quite at the center of things for winery touring, Eugene is close enough to a dozen wineries of its own and another dozen close to Salem to be an attractive headquarters. Further, its being home to the University of Oregon has led to a solid supply of agreeable motels and restaurants.

McMinnville A small commercial center and college town sits almost exactly at the center of all the Willamette Valley's wineries, and within striking distance of all but the most remote of them. In July each year it hosts the International Pinot Noir conference on the Linfield college campus. McMinnville has a handful of serviceable motels and one restaurant worth a detour.

Portland Oregon's largest city is, foremost, a deepwater port with access to the Pacific via the Columbia River. However coincidentally, it is also a perfect headquarters for all who like some urbanity along with their winery touring, the nearest cellars being about 20 minutes from the city center. The city has an abundance of hotels in all price ranges, and a steadily growing list of worthy restaurants.

HOTELS AND RESTAURANTS

Ambrosia Restaurant & Bar 174 East Broadway, Eugene. Tel (503) 343-4141. The brick, oak, and mahogany of an historic building provide the backdrop for a north Italian menu built around local ingredients. Ranging Oregon and Italian wine lists supplemented with choices from other regions.

Atwater's Restaurant 111 Southwest 5th Avenue, Portland. Tel (503) 275-3600. A top-of-a-sky-scraper expensive restaurant with a good feel for fresh Northwest ingredients.

Café Central 382 West 13th Avenue, Eugene. Tel (503) 343-9510.

Mostly seafood but quail, beef, and pasta add to the menu. The wine list is strong on Oregon.

The Heathman 1009 Southwest Broadway, Portland. Tel (503) 241-4100. A refurbished old hotel is the quintessence of solid, settled Oregon. It is handy for downtown restaurants (notably including its own) and for highways toward the Washington and Yamhill county wine districts.

Jake's Famous Crawfish Restaurant 401 Southwest 12th Avenue, Portland. Tel (503) 226-1419. Rollicking atmosphere in a place with some history behind it, a fine menu based in regional seafood, and a first-rate Oregon wine list.

McCormick & Schmick's Seafood 235 Southwest 1st Avenue, Portland. Tel (503) 224-7522. A newer seafood specialist manages to capture old Portland in the decor.

Nick's Italian Café 521 Third Street, McMinnville. Tel (503) 434-4471. Homemade pasta tells half the story. A long enough Oregon wine list to make this the winemakers' clubhouse tells the rest.

Perlina Restaurant & Bar 1425 NW Glisan, Portland. Tel (503) 221-1150. The cooking is by Giuliano, son of Italy's celebrated Marcella and Victor Hazan. The menu is Tuscan, the wine list international, the atmosphere upmarket.

ROGUE VALLEY PLACES OF INTEREST

The Rogue River Valley lies 250 to 300 miles south of Portland. Its economy is built on lumbering and fruit orchards, but it is best known to the outside world for its literary role.

Ashland Shakespeare, strange as it may seem, lifted a sleepy, ordinary town out of its rut and into international prominence. As by-products, the long-running Ashland Shakespeare Festival spawned good hotels and restaurants on and near a main thoroughfare of distinctive character.

HOTELS AND RESTAURANTS

Ashland Wine Cellar 38 Lithia Way, Ashland. Tel (503) 488-2111. Ranging stocks.

La Monet 36 South 2nd Street, Ashland. Tel (503) 482-1339. Rhone-influenced yet light handed kitchen right up to the cheese course.

Sammy's Cowboy Bistro 2210 South Pacific Highway, Tallent. Tel (503) 535-2778. Fresh regional ingredients used with striking imagination.

Left: Rugged Pacific Ocean shoreline at Cascade Head.

Above: Nick's Italian Café in McMinnville provides travelers with homemade pasta: a welcome relief from a diet of steaks.

Stratford Inn 555 Siskiyou Boulevard, Ashland, OR 97520. Tel (503) 488-2151. Comfortable rooms in the center of town, within walking distance of the theaters.

USEFUL ADDRESSES

Ashland Visitors Convention Bureau PO Box 1360, Ashland, OR 97520. Tel (503) 482-3486.

Oregon Winegrowers Association 1200 NW Front Avenue, Suite 400, Portland, OR 97209. Tel (503) 228-8403.

Portland Oregon Visitors Association 26 SW Salmon Street, Portland, OR 97204. Tel (503) 222-2223.

Roseburg Visitor & Convention Bureau PO Box 1262, Roseburg, OR 97470. Tel (800) 444-9584.

Index and Gazetteer

Map and grid references are given with the page number of the main textual references. Page numbers in italic refer to photographs.

Acknowledgments

ACKNOWLEDGMENTS

Thanks to all of the winery owners and winemakers of the three Pacific Coast states of the United States for providing information at every request. For particular help and for teaching longer and more difficult lessons, special thanks to:
David Adelsheim, Julianne Allen, Dr. Maynard A. Amerine, Charlene Guymon Ayers, David Beaudry, Ted Bennett, Mike Benziger, Dan Berger, Bob Betz, A.D. Blue, Greg Boeger, Ken Brown, Vernon Brown, Patrick Campbell, Tucker Catlin, Mark Chandler, Stan Clarke, Eileen Crane, Jill Davis, Cecil De Loach, Mike Dunne, Dawnine Dyer, William Dyer, Greg Fowler, David Graves, Gregory Graziano, Alison Green, Allan Green, Randy Green, Gene Guglielmo, David Hansmith, Joe Hart, Scott Harvey, Robert Iacopi, Barry Jackson, Hugh Johnson, Linda Johnson, Nancy Johnston, Kate Jones, Tor Kenward, Diane Kenworthy, Dan Lee, Mike Lee, David Lake, Tom Liden, Mark Lockhart, Zelma Long, Rick Longoria, Creighton MacDonald, Patricia McKelvey, Bob McRitchie, Frank Mahoney, Pamela Ostendorf Maines, Dennis Martin, Louis P. Martini, Michael Martini, Jay Milligan, Robert Mondavi, Tim Mondavi, John Moramarco, John Munch, Rebecca Murphy, Richard Nagaoka, Charles Ortman, John Parducci, Bernard Portet, Lou Preston, Michaela Rodeno, Mike Rubin, Russ St. Jean, Richard Sanford, Mike.Sauer, John Scharffenberger, Linda Seldon, Simon Siegl, Dr.Vernon Singleton, Robert Sobon, Tony Soter, Dr. Sara Spayd, Robert Steinhauer, Steve Storrs, Rodney Strong, John Stuart, George Taylor, Rick Theis, Rich Thomas, Bill Traverso, C. Gerald Warren, Barney Watson, Jack Weiner, Philip Wente, Rich Wheeler, Warren Winiarski, Wade Wolfe and Wilfred Wong.

Picture Credits
The photographs reproduced in this book were specially taken by Alan Williams except for the following:
Tony Stone Worldwide: 113(Larry Ulrich); 168/169(Sean Arbabi) 196(Cliff Hollenbeck); 219(Barbara Filet)
Harolyn Thompson: 162; 163; 164; 165; 166; 187
Zefa Picture Library: 167; 184b(K.L. Benser); 191
Faith Echtermeyer: 15

240